REORGANISATION AND RESISTANCE: LEGAL PROFESSIONS CONFRONT A CHANGING WORLD

Edited by

William LF Felstiner

·HART·
PUBLISHING

OXFORD AND PORTLAND, OREGON
2005

Published in North America (US and Canada) by
Hart Publishing
c/o International Specialised Book Services
5804 NE Hassalo Street
Portland, Oregon
97213–3644
USA

The editor and contributors have asserted their right under the Copyright,
Designs and Patents Act 1988, to be identified as the authors of this work.
Hart Publishing is a specialist legal publisher based in Oxford, England.
To order further copies of this book or to request a list of other
publications please write to:

Hart Publishing, Salters Boatyard, Folly Bridge, Abingdon Rd, Oxford, OX1 4LB
Telephone: +44 (0) 1865 245533 Fax: +44 (0) 1865 794882
email: mail@hartpub.co.uk
WEBSITE: http//:www.hartpub.co.uk

British Library Cataloguing in Publication Data
Data Available

ISBN 13: 978–1–84113–246–4 (paperback)
ISBN 10: 1–84113–246–2 (paperback)

Typeset by Avocet Typeset, Chilton, Aylesbury, Bucks
Printed and bound in Great Britain by
Biddles Ltd, King's Lynn, Norfolk

REORGANISATION AND RESISTANCE

List of Contributors

Richard L Abel is Connell Professor of Law at the University of California, Los Angeles and has taught at LaTrobe University, New York University, University of Southern California, Victoria University, and Yale University. abel@law.ucla.edu

Anne Boigeol is a sociologist at the Institut d'histoire du temps present of the CNRS (National Center of Scientific Research) in Paris, after working for some years in a research department of the Ministry of Justice. She is a member of the governing board of the Oñati International Institute for the Sociology of Law. boigeol@ihtp.cnrs.fr

Fred J Bruinsma holds a chair in Law and Society at Utrecht University in the Netherlands. He is a member of the selection committee for the judiciary and editor of the Dutch Journal for Law and Society (Recht der Werkelijkheid). f.bruinsma@law.uu.nl

Dai-kwon Choi is Professor Emeritus at Seoul National University and Chair Professor at Handong University, Pohang, Korea. He teaches constitutional law and the sociology of law at both universities. He was Head of the Legal Education Reform of the Presidential Advisory Commission for a New Education Community. He also was a member of the Presidential Advisory Commission for Judicial Reform. choidk@plaza.snu.ac.kr

William LF Felstiner is Honorary Professor of Law, Cardiff University. He was Associate Dean of the Yale Law School, Director of the American Bar Foundation, Scientific Director of the Oñati International Institute for the Sociology of Law and taught at the University of California, Los Angeles and the University of California, Santa Barbara. felstiner@cox.net

Héctor Fix-Fierro has been a full-time researcher at the Instituto de Investigaciones Jurdicas of Mexico's National University (UNAM) in Mexico City since 1991. fix@servidor.unam.mx

John Hagan is John D MacArthur Professor of Sociology and Law at Northwestern University, Senior Research Fellow at the American Bar Foundation, and University Professor of Law and Sociology at the University of Toronto. His previous faculty appointments were at Indiana University-Bloomington, University of Wisconsin-Madison and University of North Carolina-Chapel Hill. j-hagan@nwu.edu

John P Heinz is a Senior Research Fellow and former director at the American Bar Foundation and Owen L Coon Professor of Law at Northwestern University. jheinz@abfn.org

Fiona M Kay is Associate Professor of Sociology, Queen's University at Kingston. She was previously on faculty at the University of British Columbia and visiting scholar at Le centre de recherche en droit public, Facult de droit, Universit de Montreal. kayf@post.queensu.ca

Edward O Laumann is Professor of Sociology at the University of Chicago. ob01@midway.uchicago.edu

Sergio López-Ayllón, a full-time researcher at the Instituto de Investigaciones Juridicas of Mexico's National University (UNAM) in Mexico City until 2000, is Deputy Director of the Federal Regulatory Improvement Commission of the Ministry of Economy in Mexico. slayllon@prodigy.net.mx

Robert L Nelson is the Director of the American Bar Foundation and holds its MacCrate Research Chair in the Legal Profession and Professor of Sociology and Law at Northwestern University, where he also directs the Center for Legal Studies. r-nelson@nwu.edu

Rogelio Pérez-Perdomo is Dean of Universidad Metropolitana Law School (Caracas). He was Academic Director of the Stanford Program for International Legal Studies, Scientific Director of the Oñati International Institute for the Sociology of Law and President of the Research Committee on Sociology of Law of the International Sociological Association. rperez@unimet.edu.ve

Rebecca L Sandefur is Assistant Professor of Sociology at Stanford University. sandefur@stanford.edu

Ulrike Schultz is chair of the Didactics Department of the Law Faculty at Fern Universitat in Hagen and of the University Women's Council. She specialises in media work, project management, and practical skills training for lawyers. She has taught courses on women and law at the Universities of Essen and Bochum and is head of an international group focusing on women in the legal profession. ulrike.schultz@fernuni-hagen.de

Margaret Thornton is Professor of Law and Legal Studies at La Trobe University, Melbourne, Australia. m.thornton@latrobe.edu.au

Laurent Willemez is Assistant Professor of Sociology at the University of Poitiers, France. He is also a researcher at CURAPP (University of Amiens) and has taught political science at the University of Tours. laurent.willlemez@univ-poitiers.fr

Contents

LATIN AMERICA

NORTH AMERICA

1

Reorganisation and Resistance

WILLIAM LF FELSTINER

Introduction

In the beginning was the International Sociological Association. It works through research committees. There is a Research Committee on the Sociology of Law. It was founded during the cold war by Adam Podgorecki and William Evan to bring the sociology of law to the heathen, that is to countries in which it did not exist, and to support the sociology of law in states in which it was threatened by government, predominately the countries of eastern Europe. Though it had limited success in those endeavors, the Research Committee has acted in Europe, Latin America and Japan as an antidote to the threat, real or imagined, of the cultural imperialism of the American Law and Society Association. Politics aside, the Research Committee is actualised intellectually through working groups. One of these, in fact the largest and most productive, is the Working Group on the Comparative Study of Legal Professions. This book is a work product of that group.

The Working Group was the brainchild of Philip Lewis of Oxford. His efforts to organise comparative research on legal professions beginning in 1977 at a Research Committee meeting in Saarbrucken were substantially augmented when he was joined by Rick Abel after the 1979 meeting in Cagliari, Sicily. Disappointed with the manner in which earlier instances of large-scale comparative research on legal institutions seemed unable to deal effectively with linguistic and cultural differences, Lewis and Abel were wedded to what Lewis has called 'federated' research, the notion that, instead of a centralised project, comparative work should consist of research separately conducted in different countries, but taking into account common concerns and following common guidelines. The eventual result was the path breaking three volumes of *Lawyers in Society*.[1] Abel,

---

[1] *Lawyers in Society* covered seven countries or jurisdictions not included in this book

then in the course of writing his monumental studies of the British and American professions, had adapted to lawyers Magali Sarfatti Larson's model of the professional project, the idea that the work of professions was more devoted to market, income and prestige enhancement than quality and ethical control. Though there are different views of the extent to which Abel's perspective became a template for the country reports in *Lawyers in Society*, there is no doubt that it functioned as a sort of checklist of basic information that contributors were asked to provide while talking about variation.[2]

A major contribution of *Lawyers in Society* was the way that it highlighted the differences between the civil and common law worlds, right down to the basic building blocks of what constitutes a legal profession. Even then, the impact of these books may be more from what they did than what they said. They spawned research on legal professions where there was little so that now it is virtually a field by itself. In addition, the Working Group, as much a product of the Abel and Lewis effort as the books, has been extremely productive. In the ensuing years, under the leadership first of Terry Halliday and later of Benoit Bastard, it has nurtured a large number of subgroups dealing, among other subjects, with women and the profession, judges, legal aid, cause lawyering, large law firms, lawyers and clients, legal ethics, legal education, cultural histories, regulatory reform, mediation and transnational lawyering. Most of these subgroups have published one or more books and/or special journal issues.

Lawyers in Society was produced in what I think of as the grand manner. It was discussed at a series of Research Committee, Law and Society and Working Group[3] meetings over a period of years, many at attractive locations such as Oxford, Mexico City, Antwerp, New Delhi, Aix-en-Provence, Bologna, Vail, Chicago, Washington and (even) Madison, Wisconsin.[4] Subsidised by the Research Committee, the American Bar Foundation, the Nuffield Foundation and the Ford Foundation, it was able to put on an elaborate organising event in 1984 at Bellagio, the Rockefeller

---

(Scotland, New Zealand, Italy, Japan, Norway, Switzerland and Spain) while we have included chapters on two countries (Korea and Mexico), and parts of South America, not captured by Abel and Lewis.

[2] At an early stage a checklist prepared by Ben Sloot and edited by Abel and Lewis was used as a basis by the authors of the first four national reports, those on Scotland, Italy, Japan and Venezuela. At a later date Abel's draft report on the US was circulated as a model that all the contributors might follow. Lewis later noted that without some form of pre-determination of the questions being asked and some form of comparability, the results are likely to be chaotic or vacuous (1989, 3, 47). This book might be considered to be a test of that view.

[3] The Working Group was formally constituted in 1980.

[4] The gestation period for *Lawyers in Society* was lengthy, but hardly record breaking, and it was in actuality three different books. From Lewis' first explorations to publication in 1988–89 was an 11 year span.

Foundation retreat on Lake Como in Italy. I raise this brief history both because in some sense this book is a small sequel to *Lawyers in Society* and because our organisational history and theory of comparison are so different.

As the organiser of the Working Group meeting in Peyresq, France[5] in 2000 I put together a little panel on recent developments in legal professions in several countries. Harry Arthurs of Canada, Ulrike Schultz of Germany, Fred Bruinsma of the Netherlands, Hazel Genn and Rick Abel talking about the UK and Bob Nelson of the US were the participants. It was good stuff, so we decided on the spot to pull it together as a book, aided by some additional contributions from people who had not participated in the panel or were not present. That was it. There were no further meetings. There were no grants sought or provided. Though all but two of the original panel participants are represented in this book, in two instances putative contributors, forever unnamed, withdrew so we had to find latter day substitutes, for whose last ditch efforts the rest of us are extraordinarily grateful.

We also decided to abjure any explicit comparisons, in fact any plan whatsoever about the concomitants of any country analysis, in favor of a regime where each of the authors would describe whatever s/he thought were the important developments and issues in their country or region. In an ideal world, this approach would provide interesting insights into the parallels and divergences of what was thought to be salient and important across our nine countries and one continent. But in this world we must recognise that frequently scholars confuse what is important with what they know something about. So let us be content to put it this way. Each of the authors was asked to write about the important developments and issues in their domain.[6] Colleagues sometimes, in fact often, responded in terms of the gravitational pull of their own research. That research is frequently focused on rather important developments and problems, but the fit may be far from exact. With that warning, readers are asked to use their own judgment in weighing the valence of the remarks I am about to make.

We knew that our book would appear about 20 years after the Bellagio conference so we took that as the rough period to be covered. Even in this respect we had a loose approach since we recognised that our authors had worked, had data, or had an interest in periods that were both shorter and

[5] Though it has few French participants, the Working Group has with one exception met in France for the past 16 years, most frequently in Aix en Provence, Rouen and Peyresq. I understood this commitment to French venues to be a solemn obligation when I took over as President in 1994.

[6] This book has ten chapters about nine countries (two on the UK) and one chapter on a continent (South America). Thus, when talking about these different units of analysis comparatively or collectively I am going to use the term *domain(s)*.

longer than the model and would, in good academic fashion, write about whatever period in which they were invested, whatever guidance they might be given.

Sources of Change

One would not expect large, powerful professions heavily involved in the changing political, economic, and social environment of the modern world to stand still or be permitted to exist oblivious to or outside of the great flux of contemporary world life. And, of course, they have not. The changes in legal professions have taken many forms and courses, but we can characterise the sources of change along a very few axes. One is that between institutional change and demographic or evolutionary influence. Institutional change would be those alterations formally adopted, frequently abetted, if not forced in fact, by sources of power outside the profession. Examples would be the unification of the French legal profession by statute where avocats and conseil juridiques now constitute a new French bar (see Boigeol and Willemez), the abolition by the state of strictures that prevented German lawyers from organising their practices in economically competitive forms and the frontal assault by government on legal aid in the UK with the institutionalisation of budget caps, centralisation, salaried lawyers, conditional fee arrangements, new income thresholds and preference for forms of ADR (see Abel).[7]

Change by demography or evolution means that some alterations in the makeup of factors that constitute the profession such as in the labor force are so large that the result is structural change, frequently even more consequential than those produced by state intervention. In this respect, the entry of women into legal professions is the most dramatic and important change in the past 20 years. The ramifications of this demographic shift have yet to play out in full. But one important consequence in those countries where large commercial law firms are common (US, UK, Canada, Australia, the Netherlands) has been the creation of a work force of highly educated and talented women who, though frequently not given the opportunity to compete on equal terms with men, constitutes the backbone of labor at sub-partnership levels in that practice setting. Another example of significant evolutionary change is the growth of private (non-state) legal education in Mexico where the ascendancy of UNAM, the traditional

---

[7] Structural reform does not always prevail. Two attempts in Korea to reform university law education and legal training have been beaten back by the opposition of established lawyers and conservative law professors, for the most part trained in Germany (for the full story see Choi).

training ground of the political and bureaucratic elite, has been overcome by private law schools, new in origin, oriented toward the commercial sector, producing personnel for the elite business law firms and now considered to have among their ranks the top 5 law schools in the country.

A second axis of change is that between developments that originate in the environment of law practice and those that are indigenous to it. We chart in the book many instances of interaction between the social, economic and cultural context and legal professions. In the UK, the constriction and reorientation of the welfare state has led to the increasing costs of securing a legal education (preference in limited resources being channelled to the National Health Service and primary and secondary education) while the increasing multi-culturalism of Britain has led to a new importance accorded to representativeness in various dimensions of the profession (see Abel). In Australia, we see that a neo-liberal regime dedicated to the market, privatisation and globalisation has jettisoned a regulated economy, a strong public sphere, and attention to social justice, a trend that has increased the work available to legal practitioners (see Thornton where the trade-offs are seen to be more complex). In the US the declining salience of anti-Semitism in American society has dramatically improved the opportunities for Jewish lawyers, particularly in the corporate hemisphere of the profession where gender inequality and minority status play more important roles in professional stratification than ethno-religious characteristics (see Nelson).[8] In Latin American countries, human rights movements and international trade agreements like NAFTA have led to the development of an elite tier of lawyers accustomed to deal in a globalised market (see Pérez-Perdomo and Fix-Fierro and López). At the same time, national development efforts and privatisation and decentralisation in Latin American countries have created important roles for house counsel and government lawyers (see Pérez-Perdomo) while the radical politicisation of many universities has led to the growth of private legal education (see Pérez-Perdomo). In France, the consolidation of legal professions into a much more unified bar is understood to be a response to the challenge from the internationalisation of the economy, the construction of Europe as an economic and political reality and competition from international law firms (see Boigeol and Willemez). In the US, it is the cultural norms of the corporate world that has led to the rise in confrontation and litigation that has altered the centres of gravity in the organisation of large firms toward trial lawyers (see Nelson). Everywhere it is the changing nature of gender identities and of the organisation of families that has led to the substantial,

---

[8] It has been noted that dropping a quota limitation on Jewish High Court judges in the UK in 1950 was vital to transforming the English judiciary into a more creative and cosmopolitan body. No one has thought to suggest the same result for large American law firms.

sometimes incredible, increase in the numbers of women law students and lawyers. Finally, in most rich countries except Germany strained public purses, and frequently ideological imperatives, have led to constrictions in legal aid (see Abel; Nelson; Bruinsma; Thornton; Schultz).

Nevertheless, some important changes seem to be wholly or largely internally generated. The organisation of large law firms in many countries have been altered in various respects without much by way of external pressure—mid-level permanent arrangements have replaced up or out regimes, pro bono efforts have declined and business goals have overtaken a service emphasis, lawyers work longer hours and take fewer vacations, and have become more closely aligned with the political views of their clients (see Kay and Hagan, Nelson, Thornton). To some extent, legal education has become commodified by emphasising business courses over those involving individual rights (see Thornton). Conseil juridique augmented their bargaining power vis-a-vis avocats by developing in house training unknown to the bar, promoting client loyalty through offering varied services, increasing the talent pool by welcoming people not born into the bourgeoisie and lacking the social capital to become avocats, and coming more easily to terms with foreign lawyers and the major accounting firms (see Boigeol and Willemez).[9] In Korea, an increase in bar pass rates coupled to the disconnection between law practice and academic studies has seen cram courses virtually replace university training (see Choi). In the last analysis, however, most important changes seem to originate from the environment in which lawyers operate rather than within the professions.

Finally, from a progressive perspective, there are domains in which the legal profession seems to be going backward. In many countries, legal aid is on a terrible downward trajectory,[10] the introduction of large numbers of women into the profession has had a negative impact on the democratisation of the social origins of lawyers and judges (that is, women law students, young lawyers and, in some domains, judges come from higher class strata than men), and the increasing costs of legal education and training disproportionately affects students from poor backgrounds (see Nelson, Abel, Bruinsma, Thornton).

---

[9] The importance of class in France may partially explain why Bourdieu's ideas about social capital are so important to the sociology of law in France while in the US the corresponding social divider would have been ethno-religious affiliation, and now is gender and minority status, rather than class. In fact, women lawyers in the US face an uneven playing field despite generally having higher class affiliations than men.

[10] Korea is a delightful exception. In that country public interest (pro bono) service is mandatory while working for the national legal services corporation fulfils the obligation of compulsory military service (see Choi).

Women and the Professions

The most important change, virtually worldwide, in the nature of legal professions is the large increase in the number of women law students and lawyers. And the single most important dimension of that change is that women lawyers have a more difficult time achieving career goals than men. The numbers vary considerably. In Australia, Canada, Germany, Mexico and the US the proportion of women lawyers is slightly more than ¼. The highest proportion of women lawyers is in France, nearly ½, and in some Latin American countries where women lawyers are more numerous than men. The lowest proportion is in Korea, under ⅒.

In this book, the most intense focus on women lawyers is contained in the chapter on Canada by Kay and Hagan. They report that women work disproportionately by themselves and in large firms, they become partners at lower rates than men, particularly in small firms, they are disadvantaged in income and in access to positions of power and authority regardless of experience, fields of law, partnership status, size of organisation or sector of practice. They also find that high commitment to practice pays off for men, but not for women. These findings are echoed in the chapters on Australia, France, Germany, the Netherlands and the US where the authors are pessimistic that women will ever become partners in major firms at the same rate as their male counterparts.

Since the question of the income gap between men and women lawyers is ubiquitous, I will devote a few words to it. Broadly speaking, there are three theoretical approaches to gender and differential income. One, frequently called human capital theory and with relish attributed by its proponents to Nobel prize-winning economist Gary Becker, puts the onus on women themselves. The notion is that early in their professional lives women invest less in career and more in family life than men, and that these differential investments are translated over time into significant income differences. Why then do women who have made no less first order investments in career than men not earn as much? One answer is that these women are lumped, particularly by law firms, with other women who have married, had children, had interrupted careers, want to engage in part-time work, etc, so that there is something like an irrefutable presumption that women cannot be as committed to a legal career as men whatever their behaviour at the moment. This perspective, reflecting the triumph of myth over reality, is more prevalent in the UK than in North America where the view is more likely to be that the human capital theory is hogwash.

The second approach, frequently called gender stratification theory, adopted by most American researchers focusing on the income gap, attributes the differences to external forces rather than to choices made by women lawyers. Most of the research in this line is based on the supposed operations of law firms, most frequently large law firms. Thus the culprits lie among factors such as gendered discrepancies in work assignments, mentoring, forms of rainmaking or rainmaking potential, perceived commitment, interrupted careers, and responses to an on-demand culture.

The third perspective, derived originally from Bourdieu and proposed most vigorously by Hagan and Kay, is called social capital theory. Although initially rooted in advantages derived from family and education, in Hagan and Kay's formulation social capital is more or less equated to networking performance. Women become partners in law firms less often and make less money than men in part because they are less involved in professional activities and associations outside of 'regular hours' and because they spend less time representing institutional clients. However, women do less well even when these networking factors are equal. Thus either Hagan and Kay's surrogates for networking do not capture the full effect of social capital or the full picture reflects some combination of social capital, gender stratification and as yet unidentified factors. In the last analysis, it is possible that research has not yet unravelled all the strands that produce income differences because there are so many of them operating with different salience in different work sites.

Resistance to Change

Change and resistance are inextricably tied together in an oppositional tension where the greater weight shifts gradually from one to the other, even shifts backwards at times, but in the long view runs in the direction of change. The most obvious instance almost everywhere is the struggle of women in legal professions where improvement is undeniable even as resistance is varied and stiff. This tug of war in other arenas appears to be at different points, or proceeding at different speeds, in our domains. The most dramatic change seems to be in France where the resistance of the bar to a reorganisation of the several legal professions has been dramatically swept aside. This is in contrast to the lengthy and wearying war between barristers and solicitors and between each of them and the government in the UK which appears as if it will go on for another decade or two, if not forever. The most striking example of resistance appears to be in Korea where relatively straightforward reform of legal education has proved to be impossible, even though the Korean groundwork in favor of reform was quite influential in Japan. Legal education is resistant to change in countries other than Korea. In Mexico, for instance, the traditional law schools are thought to be too theoretical and insufficiently problem oriented though the response there, and in other Latin American countries, has been the growth of new schools with a heavy business emphasis. Finally, we can see, in Australia for instance, that change is not unidirectional, but may act in opposition to itself. As Thornton describes it, the fixed identity of Australian lawyers is elusive as they are pushed together by federalising pressures at the same time as they are pushed apart by specialisation, competition for business and competing ways of organising practice.

Similarities and Dissimilarities

If we put the details aside, we can see that the important developments in the last 20 years as reported in this book fall into three patterns and an outlier. One pattern is where the changes are demographic, where the crucial factors are the way the work of lawyers has changed, the way that the revenue from law practice has been re-distributed, the extent to which ascriptive barriers have been diminished or shifted, and the way that the profession has reacted to the large number of women entering its ranks. In this array of issues, the state is irrelevant and legal education is not of great moment. This pattern is predominantly North American, particularly in Canada and the US, but is also true of the Netherlands. A second pattern, reflected in the situation of Germany, the UK and Australia, combines the effect of demographic changes with a reorganisation of the profession, forced strongly by government in Germany and the UK and more by way of a limited form of co-regulation with government in Australia. In these countries changes in legal education play a peripheral role. When we move to Mexico, South America and Korea, transformations in the professions have not kept pace with transformations in the economy; changes and challenges to legal education take center stage while demographic shifts and institutional reorganisation are of much less importance. The outlier is France where, though there are demographic changes, their importance is swamped by the state-sanctioned unification of its several legal professions.

Convergence

One notion much discussed in the sociology of the professions is convergence, the prediction that as the economic and political arrangements of states become more alike, their legal systems, including their legal professions, will also come more to resemble one another. There is some evidence in this book to support the inevitability of convergence, but rather more that would call it into question. International trade and investment is a factor in the economic life of all our domains and the legal dimensions of such activity are generally managed by large international law firms, a form of practice that did not exist anywhere 40 years ago. However, the firms themselves originate for the most part in English-speaking countries, and then push their operations to wherever the multinational corporations who are their clients operate. Moreover, large law firms employ a growing share of lawyers, dominate the supply of experts in important fields of law and command an ever larger share of the income from law practice in many, but not all, rich and technologically sophisticated countries (France and Germany are exceptions). In like manner, one consequence of competition for corporate business in many countries is the arrival and legitimation of multi-disciplinary partnerships, but this is a development that has not happened outside the District of Columbia in the US, the world's biggest legal market. Where local legal business is concerned, the practices of lawyers do not appear to have shifted in significant ways toward any common mode. Two countries do not even restrict legal advice to lawyers (the Netherlands and Mexico), formalised alternative dispute resolution is noted to thrive in some countries, but not in others, countries with split professions continue to operate in that manner, though in somewhat attenuated form, and legal education and training seem to continue very much in localised ways that reflect more by way of historic continuity than common functional needs. Aspects of the economic and professional organisation of practice which are crucial in one country, such as the state examinations, certification of specialties and legal insurance in Germany, hardly exist in many others. In some countries such as Korea and parts of South America academic training is not even organised to produce the specialists needed in complex law such as banking, securities, corporate reorganisation, insolvency, acquisitions and mergers, anti-trust, patent, intellectual property and patents, while those subjects are considered to be overemphasised in another (Australia). All in all, it does not appear that legal professions can be considered to be some sort of franchised operations designed according to an American model, those of former imperial powers or any supranational convergent developments.

Acknowledgements

We have three debts to acknowledge. First and foremost to the Fondation Nicolas-Fabri de Peiresc, the keeper of the treasure that is the village of Peyresq, and to its President, Mme Mady Smets-Hennekinne, for her gracious hospitality, incredible energy, high spirits and unexpected, probably undeserved, but welcome, support. Second, we thank our colleagues in the Working Group, companions over the years in a terrific mélange of intellectual and gastronomic adventure. As partial payment, the royalties from this book will be turned over to its treasury. Third, the procrastinators among us appreciate the patience of those stalwart colleagues who met every deadline and suffered the frailties of the rest of us in silence.

Reference

RICHARD L Abel and Philip SC Lewis, *Lawyers in Society*, 1988–89, 3 vol., (University of California Press, Berkeley 1989).

2

The Professional as Political: English Lawyers from the 1989 Green Papers Through the Access to Justice Act 1999

RICHARD L ABEL

In the summer of 1988 English lawyers (especially barristers) might have been forgiven for breathing a collective sigh of relief. More than two decades of mounting criticism by scholars,[1] practitioners,[2] journalists,[3] politicians,[4] reformist organisations,[5] and government commissions[6] had achieved little or nothing. The Marre Committee, intended as a last effort to break the stalemate between the branches, had just endorsed the status quo.[7] The English animus against 'change for change's sake' appeared to have prevailed.

Such complacency, however, would not have taken adequate account of the Iron Lady. Having despatched the trade unions, defanged (Labour-dom-

---

[1] Johnstone and Hopson (Indianapolis, Indiana, Bobbs-Merrill, 1967); Abel-Smith and Stevens (London, Heinemann, 1967; London, Allen Lane, 1968; Zander (London, Weidenfeld & Nicholson, 1968; London, IB Tauris and Co Ltd 1988); Cain (Keele, *Sociological Review Monographs*, 1976); Griffith (London, Fontana, 1977); Thomas (Oxford, Martin Robertson, 1982); Podmore and Spencer (1982a; 1982b); Flood (Manchester, Manchester University Press, 1983); Abel (1986); Abel (Oxford, Basil Blackwell, 1988).
[2] Joseph (London, Michael Joseph, 1976); Joseph (London, Michael Joseph, 1984); Hazell (London, Quartet Books, 1978); Gifford (Harmondsworth, Penguin, 1986); Reeves (London, Waterlow Publishing Ltd, 1986).
[3] Berlins and Dyer (Harmonsworth, Penguin, 1982).
[4] Austin Mitchell.
[5] Justice, the Haldane Society, the Society of Labour Lawyers, the Consumers' Association, and the Legal Action Group.
[6] Monopolies Commission (1970); Committee on Legal Education (1971); Monopolies and Mergers Commission (1976a; 1976b); Royal Commission on Legal Services (1979); Lord Chancellor's Department (1983).
[7] Committee on the Future of the Legal Profession (1988).

inated) local government, and defied the universities and the media, Mrs Thatcher turned her gimlet eye on the professions—not least her own (she had qualified as a barrister). It was unclear whether this was ideology trumping natural party affinities or a politically savvy appeal to populist resentment. After the retirement of Lord Hailsham, the longest-serving Lord Chancellor in the 20th century and the Bar's loyal ally, and a brief interim with an ailing Lord Havers, she appointed James Mackay, a former mathematician, Wee Free (strict Presbyterian), and Scots advocate—and hence the ultimate outsider. Whatever political beliefs he brought to the office, he soon became more laissez-faire than the Prime Minister. A few months after the Marre Committee reported he hinted at proposals for major changes. At the beginning of 1989 he published three Green Papers proposing to end the two monopolies that defined the divided profession (barristers' higher court advocacy and solicitors' conveyancing), allow both branches to enter partnerships and employment with each other and other professions, and shift the cost of personal injury litigation from the state (legal aid) to the parties (conditional or contingent fees and legal expenses insurance). Lawyers and judges resisted vigorously, but by the end of the 20th century the British legal profession had been stripped of most of its 19th century rules (if not its 17th century customs, like horsehair wigs, winged collars, and gowns). This chapter tells the story of that transformation from the 1989 Green Papers through the 1999 Access to Justice Act.[8]

What Kind of Revolution?

The Green Papers initially did more to change the discourse about the legal profession than its actual practices. Before Mackay professional rules and customs enjoyed the presumptive legitimacy of tradition; after him they were suspect as 'shameless' restrictive practices, 'Spanish customs' raising costs and compounding delays. While conservatives continued to invoke beloved icons like Lord Brougham defending Queen Caroline, critics caricatured the Bar's anachronistic dress, speech, and habitat. Prominent judges damaged the cause of the Bar they championed by transparent partisanship, including a threat to close the courts to discuss the response to the Green Papers. Where the Law Society (LS), Bar Council (BC), and Inns of Court had long portrayed themselves as selfless protectors of professional integrity, critics now denounced them as trade unions defending

---

[8] For a full discussion of this decade, with citations, see my recent book, *English Lawyers between Market and State: The Politics of the Modern Professionalism* (Oxford, Oxford University Press, 2003).

closed shops. Grossly exaggerated comparisons of Mackay's modest proposals to Nazi Germany seriously discredited more measured reservations
and led to media glorification of the Lord Chancellor as a Scottish lion sav-
aging the Bar (a metaphor owing more to heraldry than geography). Hiring
Saatchi and Saatchi for a £750,000 public relations campaign was seen as
weakness. The press (including former allies like the *Times*, *Financial
Times*, and *Economist*) fuelled public resentment of barristers as 'fat cats'
with insufferable social pretensions, sustained by Old Boy networks. Lord
Mackay cleverly enlisted both the status resentments and economic ambitions of solicitors and employed barristers in his assault on the Bar.

It responded by attacking the market as a dogma advanced by
Department of Trade and Industry ideologues, sneering at the Grantham
grocer's daughter who saw everything in terms of tinned peas and canned
beans, and condescending to penny-pinching consumers who sought the
'best buy' at Marks and Spencer. (Adding a sexual insult, one opponent
said the reforms were by the Department of Trade and Industry [DTI] out
of the Lord Chancellor's Department [LCD].) Critics responded by
extolling Mackay as a British Gorbachev seeking to reform a sclerotic
economy, while the Bar erected a Berlin wall to stop leading barristers from
defecting to City of London firms. The Bar also felt obliged to engage
reformers on their own terrain, boasting (with some justice) of vigorous
competition *among* barristers; but this just let Mackay ask why they feared
external competitors. Both branches warned (correctly) that competition
fostered concentration and (more dubiously) that this reduced consumer
choice. City mega-firms would snap up the best barristers; the already concentrated mortgage lenders and home insurers would vertically integrate
with estate agents and conveyancers. Lawyers endlessly invoked 'independence': the Bar to resist partnerships and audience rights for solicitors
or employed barristers; solicitors to oppose corporate conveyancing.

If hyperbole debased the debate, myths distracted attention. Bar and
bench irresponsibly misrepresented the Advisory Committee on Legal
Education and Conduct (ACLEC) as empowered to withhold 'dog licenses'
from defiant advocates, hoping to inflame popular mistrust of quangos.
They elevated the Bar's easily evaded cab rank rule (acceptance of any
client willing to pay the barrister's fees) into a constitutional principle.
They constantly conjured up the spectre of Americanization: the invasion
of US megafirms (though their City rivals were just as large and imperial-
ist); unscrupulous district attorneys (although state officials prosecuted
everywhere but the UK); and litigiousness (although British tort victims
claimed at the same rate as American).

Although Labour seemed unable to turn Mackay's proposals to its political advantage, the Bar's allies on the bench and in the House of Lords (the

'Bar in Ermine') forced the Government to retreat significantly. The Courts and Legal Services Act 1990 abandoned proposals that all lawyers begin as solicitors (before qualifying as advocates) and be able to enter partnerships with each other, foreign lawyers, and other professions (although it let both branches permit this). It dropped contingent fees. It complicated and delayed corporate conveyancing. It relinquished power to draft regulations for entry and conduct. And it gave each of the four senior judges a veto over changes, most importantly rights of audience.

Can the Profession Still Halt the Tide?

English lawyers confronted challenges other than those generated by government reforms. Cumulative increases in the number of university law graduates and changes in their gender composition coincided with rapid fluctuations in legal work to produce sharp imbalances between supply and demand. First the extraordinary rise in housing prices and sales in the 1980s and the departure of many women (now half of new solicitors) to raise children created a labour shortage, leading firms to encourage part-time work. Then the collapse of the housing market during the recession of the early 1990s created a glut of lawyers, provoking leaders and mavericks in national and local professional associations to demand cuts in entry in order to sustain the incomes of existing practitioners. Lord Mackay, ACLEC, and the Director-General of Fair Trading (DGFT) resisted, reaffirming the government's commitment to laissez-faire.

Each constituency pursued its self-interest. Solicitors favoured common training, followed by specialisation (in advocacy, among other things). The Bar preferred to facilitate transfer, which it still controlled. Employed barristers wanted to offer pupillage (the mandatory apprenticeship). Those seeking entry tried to maximise their own chances of success while raising barriers to later cohorts.

The hurdles fared differently. Dinners at the Inns, already anachronistic warrants of character rather than expertise and tainted by male hazing, became optional when provincial students rebelled at commuting thousands of miles to participate in a meaningless ritual. Apprenticeship was increasingly hard to reconcile with academic education (now universal), and vocational courses were an uncomfortable hybrid between the two. Both branches lost their monopolies over those courses and hence control of the number of places.

All efforts to repair the dikes failed. Ridiculously redundant applications—for trainee and assistant solicitorships, pupillages and tenancies—

wasted enormous resources. Efforts to rationalise the process (through the Pupillage Application Clearing House, for instance) rewarded a few winners with multiple offers at a high emotional cost to the many losers. Both branches flirted with a numerus clausus on vocational course places but could offer no justification. Proposals to condition entry to these courses on apprenticeship either exposed the arbitrariness of the latter hurdle or postponed the bottleneck to entry-level positions. All selection procedures were increasingly suspected of gender, race, and class bias. Envying the Bar's safety-valve of employed barristers, the Law Society considered formalising paralegals as a subordinate status for qualified solicitors. Supply control opposed the profession to educators. The universities (whose numbers were doubled by the former polytechnics) found law departments a cheap and prestigious way to grow. Having attained competence as legal educators, they successfully demanded the right to compete with the Inns of Court School of Law (ICSL) and the Law Society College of Law (LSCL) in offering vocational courses. Existing course providers objected to the entry or expansion of others. The ICSL and LSCL competed by offering courses to the other branch. It was 'the same old story', complained the Law Society's vice-president, Robert Sayer, 'bums on seats, money, money, money.'

The one entry barrier that continued to rise during this decade was the market's own rationing device, cost: tuition for university degrees, the Common Professional Examination course (for non-law graduates), and the vocational course; and subsistence during the (five to seven) years of preparation. Government support declined, precipitately for the vocational course. Many students assumed substantial debt, which increasingly influenced career choice. Minimum salaries for apprentices and starting positions lowered class barriers to entry but also tended to reduce the number of places. In the end, lawyers' futile efforts to control the ebb and flow of supply further exposed their selfishness thinly veiled by professional pretensions to disinterest.

Reflecting Society

Recent acceptance of the view that privileged roles should reflect the ascriptive demographics of class, gender, ethnicity, sexual orientation, and physical difference should not blind us to the fact that the traditional goal of professions was exclusivity, as a means of and justification for limiting numbers and elevating status. The rhetorical transformation is virtually complete: Lord Chancellors, Lord Chief Justices, and the profession's leaders apologise for its unrepresentativeness and promise reform. Pressure for a representative judiciary increased when the Human Rights Act made it impossible to keep denying the political content of judging. The creation of the welfare state after World War Two gradually made class privilege a source of embarrassment rather than pride, but the profession felt obligated only to make the playing field a little less uneven, not to ensure success. The profession unreservedly condemned sexual discrimination and harassment (while covering up the latter or treating it leniently) and celebrated successful women (one of four senior judges, a Bar Council chair, a prominent silk who happened to be the Prime Minister's wife). By arranging part-time work for mothers but not fathers, however, it relegated the former to less remunerative and prestigious careers. Although discomforted by the under-representation and segregation of ethnic minorities, lawyers continued to oppose 'American' 'reverse discrimination'. A few leaders strongly condemned discrimination against gays and lesbians, but others sought to incite a backlash against 'political correctness' or invoked religious justifications elsewhere discredited by association with racism and patriarchy.

The excluded documented their absence, campaigned for anti-discrimination rules, enforcement, and resources, and even resorted to lawsuits against the Council for Legal Education (CLE) over examination pass rates and private and public employers over jobs. But most decisions were exempt from judicial review: chambers about tenancies, firms about partnerships, the Lord Chancellor about silk and the bench. Frustration at such impotence was one reason the Law Society boycotted the Lord Chancellor's 'secret soundings' for the selection of QCs and judges.

The problem of representativeness arises from the fact that the same academic institutions and meritocratic processes that make the profession more inclusive simultaneously reproduce and legitimate internal differentiation, moving unrepresentativeness downstream. Just as the traditional ethos within professions (or their formal strata) was equality, so the modern ethos is hierarchy. The central dilemma, therefore, is reconciling meritocratic warrants with representative outcomes. If the problem is intentional discrimination, the wrongdoer should be punished; but an inquiry into lower ethnic minority pass rates at CLE found no such evidence. It is easier to criticise and pressure individual decisionmakers (the Lord Chancellor granting silk or appointing judges) than collectivities (law firms selecting partners) and both of those secretive, subjective processes than more open, impersonal ones (examinations, markets). It is hardest to argue that unequal outcomes alone constitute a problem. Meritocracy's defenders respond that these reflect aspirant choices. Kamlesh Bahl, a tireless champion of women and minorities, endorsed part-time work for mothers as late as 1997, oblivious to the way this entrenches gender hier-archy. Lord Irvine, by contrast, sought to change 'preferences', hectoring ethnic minorities 'don't be shy, apply' for judgeships and accusing reticent women of 'robbing' him of appointments.

The dilemma of all other corrective measures is that they question the meritocratic legitimacy of either the process or the outcome. Lord Mackay's grant of silk to more women than Lord Hailsham and Lord Irvine's to more ethnic minorities than Lord Mackay suggest that at least one of each pair was betraying meritocracy. At the same time, Lord Mackay declined to 'lower the standards for appointment ... simply to ensure a different racial or sexual mix.' Compensatory education can stig-matise its beneficiaries; pairing 'ghetto' and white chambers patronised the former. All institutions find it easier to accommodate outsiders when demand exceeds supply. The 'recruitment crisis' of the late 1980s boom induced solicitors firms to allow mothers to work part time; the early 1990s recession led some professional leaders to defend nepotism as natu-ral, not biased. Tokenism is a convenient compromise: women managing partners at City firms, the first black woman silk, the first woman on the Court of Appeal; the first woman BC chair and soon (after an embarrass-ing failure) the first woman LS president.

Efforts to increase representativeness inevitably provoked backlash. Three of the four Inns of Court, still governed by old white men, refused to embrace the Bar Council's equality code. A solicitor who captured the Law Society presidency on a populist platform waged a virulent campaign against the 'discrimination industry', deploring the power of feminists and fomenting hatred against 'sado-masochistic [homosexual] proselytisers' who 'strut down Picadilly with banners, clad in leather and chains.' But he lost two re-election bids to champions of equality. Instead, the inevitable outcome of struggles over representativeness was the classic political com-promise of symbolic action: education, not regulation. Both branches announced targets for minority apprentices and first positions but explic-itly refused to monitor, much less enforce, them. Yet even exhortation establishes an aspiration that is difficult to repudiate and can be a source of leverage.

Defending the Temple

The Courts and Legal Services Act did not resolve the turf battles ignited or intensified by the Green Papers. Barristers continued to resist any intru-sion into the higher courts and respond to such threats by expanding direct access to clients and expressing interest in litigation. The few solicitors who gained and exercised audience rights were subject to petty humiliations by barristers and judges: forbidden to wear wigs, addressed as inferiors, or simply ignored. Solicitors and employed barristers smarted under repeated accusations of incompetence, insufficient independence, and unethical behaviour. The Bar aggravated these insults by seeking to exclude them from silk and judicial appointments. Just as the Conservative Government had pitted the branches against each other in 1989, so the Labour Government exploited divisions within the Bar in 1998. Because a third of all barristers are employed, advocacy by a significant proportion would seriously affect private practitioners. But employed barristers had little political power within the Bar Council (one fifth the representation in proportion to their numbers of private practitioners) and were divided between those in the private and public sectors (as well as those not practising).

If the Bar's ultimate defeat was attributable partly to the government's interest in reducing advocacy costs for prosecution, defence, and civil legal aid (and the lopsided parliamentary majority of both Conservative and Labour administrations), it also reflected changes in rhetorical strategy and effect. Reformers could invoke irrefutable logic: solicitors appeared in magistrates' courts (which could hear the vast bulk of criminal cases); jurisdictional changes constantly expanded solicitors' audience rights; barristers instantly lost and gained audience rights as they moved in and out of employment; restrictive practices did not apply to foreign clients. More important than logic (since restrictive practices are always illogical) was the emerging hegemony of laissez-faire. Both the Law Society and the government could invoke the powerful trope of consumer choice and make the common sense (if not always empirically valid) claim that one lawyer had to be cheaper than two. The Bar's market arguments were weak: it was intensely competitive (but only internally); silk offered the best information about quality (then why not make the selection process public and eliminate the 10 per cent quota). The Bar, therefore, tried other tacks. The state performed an essential role in levelling the playing field; in order to maximise consumer autonomy it should make solicitor litigators offer clients a choice of advocate and perhaps even refrain from advocacy in such cases. Specialisation was essential to competent advocacy. But the frequent medical analogies were inapposite: all doctors train together before acquiring formal specialist credentials. Furthermore, this argument could not be used against the Crown Prosecution Service (CPS) (or the proposed Criminal Defence Service (CDS)), whose lawyers specialised too much. The Bar could, and did, point to the chronic CPS problems of understaffing, high caseloads, and poor quality; but these were attributable to the government's very reason for wanting to employ more lawyers—cost cutting.

The Bar sought rhetorical trump cards outside market discourse. Even barristers now conceded that the cab rank rule, which had helped delay audience rights after the Green Papers, was easily evaded and that private practitioners (e.g., Treasury Counsel) could be just as partisan as employed. The Bar's ultimate defence was 'independence', advanced as a prerequisite for advocacy and an insurmountable objection to partnership and employment. The argument (never clearly formulated) apparently was that advocates must preserve distance from their clients in order to fulfil competing obligations to adversaries and the legal system. House counsel and Crown Prosecutors were too close to their private and public employers (although this objection was inconsistent with *any* CPS audience rights). Public defenders, however, suffered the reverse criticis—insufficient loyalty to clients. This exposed the fundamental ambiguity of the proper degree of independence. Furthermore, the Bar offered no evidence that employment fatally compromised independence. Job security might actually enhance it; and many private practitioners were at least as economically dependent on solicitors firms or the CPS. The notorious miscarriages of justice in the IRA bombing cases (prosecuted by private practitioners) hardly inspired confidence.

The buzz words suffusing this confrontation illuminate the dramatic and rapid shift in British values at the end of the 20th century. Competition, the market, choice, consumers, efficiency, and value for money were good; the closed shop, restrictive practices, monopoly, the monolithic state, strangleholds, entry barriers, curbs, double manning, and market rigging were bad. Reform (especially radical), change (even at breakneck speed), shake-ups, relevance, and modern were good, as were taking a battering ram to the Temple and a broom to the stables, hammering a nail in the coffin, opening the door to a long overdue breath of fresh air. Tradition, conservatism, delay, complacency, pomposity, snobbery, a sheltered world, the status quo, relics, and inertia were bad, as were anything anachronistic, antiquated, archaic, outdated, crusty, or irrelevant.

The Bar appeared to lose every battle. Solicitors and employed barristers gained plenary rights of audience. Although privately practising barristers could not enter partnership, employed barristers could serve their employers' clients and retain audience rights. Barristers could offer direct access to more clients. Although procedures for selecting silk and judges remained virtually unchanged (because the Lord Chancellor would not relinquish his patronage powers), political pressures and silks' reluctance to forego their fees for the bench ensured that the number of solicitor judges would grow. But history reminds us how slowly institutions and habits change. Barristers threatened to refuse briefs from solicitors who engaged in advocacy; solicitors threatened not to brief barristers who offered direct access. Judges openly favoured barristers over solicitor advocates. The Bar chose not to apply to conduct litigation. It allowed direct access cautiously, and few barristers took advantage (for fear of endangering their superior status and having to restructure their practices). Equally few solicitors engaged in advocacy: other work paid better; and they feared judicial prejudice and barrister condescension as well as client resentment of their inaccessibility.

Repelling the Barbarians

Although often couched in economic terms, the Bar Wars discussed in the previous section were more about status than market share. Aside from realistic fears that the CPS would bring virtually all prosecutions in-house, the most highly charged confrontations concerned the superiority associated with audience rights, dress and address in the higher courts, and appointments to that bench. The far larger solicitors' market, by contrast, tempted serious competitors: lenders, insurers, and estate agents for conveyancing; accountants for corporate work; foreign lawyers for global commerce; specialist solicitors; and laypersons. Although solicitors carefully cultivated an image of sweet reasonableness in contrast to the Bar's rigid traditionalism, their own response to competition was a protectionism that sometimes crossed over into illegality. The Law Society sought to agree an 'indicative' range of fees with the Council of Mortgage Lenders, only to be reprimanded by the Office of Fair Trading (OFT). Local law societies openly engaged in price fixing nearly 30 years after the abolition of scale fees. Law Society Council members seriously proposed defying the OFT in order to gain a few years before the Monopolies and Mergers Commission ruled against them. The Society advised local solicitors to 'discuss' prices and considered having the Solicitors Indemnity Fund (SIF) discriminate in premiums against solicitor price cutters. To increase revenues the Society sought to require separate representation for lenders and borrowers. To discourage multinational partnerships (MNPs) it proposed to require SIF membership by every partner of a foreign lawyer. It delayed approval of multidisciplinary partnerships (MDPs) for years. It waged all-out war against will writers and claims agents. The Solicitors Property Group threatened to withdraw client accounts from lenders who dared to engage in conveyancing. But cartels are always difficult to enforce: while some solicitors joined property centres (to compete with estate agents in getting to clients first), others refrained (to continue getting referrals from agents).

Nevertheless the genie of competition, like democracy, is not easily forced back into the bottle. Once the property market began to recover in the early 1990s, lenders and estate agents became interested in acquiring the right to convey, promised by the Courts and Legal Services Act. Foreign law firms and accountants were unconstrained by solicitors' restrictive practices. Claims agents could openly solicit clients and accept contingent fees. Solicitors' only hope was to get to the client first and subordinate other service providers. Solicitors could hardly offer a principled objection to tying-in when they sought to combine litigation with advocacy. They wanted to sell property, loans, and insurance rather than allow estate agents, lenders, and insurance companies to capture conveyancing. City firms wanted to dominate foreign lawyers within MNPs rather than be subordinated to Americans. Solicitors wanted to offer financial services rather than let accounting firms (especially the Big Five) control MDPs. Solicitors could not object to laypersons delivering legal services when for centuries they had relied on managing clerks (since updated to legal executives) and now were employing more paralegals. But they wanted to sell the labour of subordinates (at a profit) rather than be hired by laypersons to handle personal injury litigation.

Subordinated occupations responded by seeking to professionalise. Estate agents sought state licensure; will writers invited regulation; even some claims agents differentiated themselves from the 'cowboys.' Legal executives sought to expand their paraprofessional jurisdiction. But such efforts were stymied by the entrenched position of solicitors and the government's determination to control costs.

While external threats generally strengthened professional solidarity, internal competition increased divisions between generalists and specialists, large firms and small, entrepreneurial and traditional solicitors, younger and older. Solicitors accused price cutting conveyancers of charging too little and American firms of stealing the best law graduates by paying too much. Specialisation (and kitemarks) challenged the profession's basic precept of equality by formalising what everyone knew: lawyers differ greatly in quality. Just as professions suppress price competition, so specialisation seeks to avoid it by claiming superior quality. Generalists resent that and adamantly oppose jurisdictional exclusivity. Specialties seek authority to define standards and engage in self-regulation and governance, fragmenting professions by the same process that created them. MNPs and MDPs also eroded professional autonomy by subordinating solicitors to the regulatory authorities of other disciplines or countries.

The hegemony of laissez-faire was visible, once again, in the consensus between the (left-wing) Consumers' Association and the (right-wing) Adam Smith Institute that house sales had to be simplified. Government courted voter resentment of the high cost, and the media (too facilely) applauded lay competitors and DIY. Even solicitors admitted that secretaries learned conveyancing in 15 hours. Like barristers, solicitors resorted to anti-market arguments. The loan market was 'a vicious, highly competitive, plundering jungle' where 'the borrower is the prey.' One Law Society president warned against a 'free for all in dealing with the winding up of estates.' Another called MDPs 'an even more serious danger to the network of small firms of solicitors than conveyancing by institutions' and deplored that 'the rule of money would overwhelm the rule of law.' Solicitor critics accused cut-price conveyancing of incompetence and ethical defaults (the same charges the Bar levelled against employed barristers). Like the Bar Council, Law Society officials prophesied apocalypse. A vice-president did not 'think we will see High Street firms survive.' The Solicitors Property Group accused the Society of 'killing the goose that lays the golden egg' (an unfortunate metaphor) and cut-price conveyancers of 'killing their brethren.'

And like the Bar, the Law Society invoked 'independence' against the imperative of 'efficiency.' Solicitors employed by lenders, estate agents, or insurers or subordinated to accountants in MDPs would lack that essential virtue. A deputy vice president raised 'ethical objections when legal functions are carried out by organisations concerned to develop commercial profits' (unlike his own leading City firm, presumably). But clients rarely sought the financial advice 'independent' solicitors claimed to offer. Solicitors who enjoyed a 'natural' monopoly in small towns were unenthusiastic about a rule forbidding them from representing both buyer and seller. A LS vice-president dismissed conflicts of interest as 'complete nonsense.' And solicitors had no difficulty reconciling selling property and insurance themselves with doing the conveyance. While inveighing against corporate mass conveyancing they sought their own economies of scale, delegating extensively to the very paraprofessionals they reviled.

Although barristers are likely to retain much of their advocacy market without legal protections, solicitors are far more vulnerable. House selling will be vertically integrated and mass produced, and solicitors property centres are unlikely to be big winners. MNPs will capture much global commercial practice, though some City firms will dominate, rather than being subordinated, to foreign lawyers. MDPs will find ways to offer corporate clients one-stop shopping despite regulatory constraints. And the very division of labour that spawned the legal profession will foster specialisation. The market is truly inexorable.

Controlling Costs

Although governments had long complained about the cost of legal aid, the combination of fiscal pressure, ideological aversion, and political expediency produced a frontal assault on this welfare state relic in the 1990s. Following a strikingly influential Social Market Foundation paper, the government sought to cap a budget that had been demand-led for half a century, set priorities rather than let them reflect client preferences, and subordinate producers to 'market forces' (obscuring its monopsonistic power as both sole and third-party consumer). Remuneration rates once linked to private fees were cut to what the hungriest lawyer would accept. Government also sought to reduce the number of legal aid providers, accelerating the concentration already produced by subject and client specialisation and the need for economies of scale in order to eke out profits under falling remuneration rates. Seeking to portray cost cutting as quality control, the government explicitly questioned the competence of most lawyers, first by offering better terms to those it franchised and then through exclusive contracts. This violated the basic precepts of professions that they alone can evaluate expertise and all members are competent (hence their monopoly) and equal (hence the ban on self-promotion, especially quality comparisons, and the practice of random referral through the duty solicitor scheme).

The debate over cost cutting displayed numerous contradictions. If most solicitors were unqualified to represent legally aided clients, why allow them to practise on the privately paying? Government sought to mobilise popular resentment of lawyers by attacking the very concentration it was fostering, denouncing firms that mass processed clients and 'naming and shaming' the highest earners. Both government and the media played on popular ambivalence toward litigation (especially in contrast to social services like health, education, food, and shelter) by exposing fraudulent claims and caricaturing a complaint culture they imputed to America. Warning against the moral hazard of frivolous litigation, Lord Mackay wanted more clients to make larger contributions, maintaining (against all the evidence) that this would make them monitor lawyers more effectively. Government publicised losing claims (as though they were unique to legal aid litigation, or the ideal win rate was 100 per cent). The media compounded the unpopularity of criminal accused by publicising stories of apparently wealthy (often foreign) defendants running up huge legal aid bills. By not indexing means tests for inflation, government allowed eligibility to contract from 80 per cent to 50 per cent; the LCD Parliamentary secretary said this was 'not bad for a poor man's lawyer', confirming that charity to the neediest had replaced security for all. The contraction of eligibility and concentration of providers facilitated further cuts by shrinking the size and political clout of both legal aid constituencies.

If the public had little enthusiasm for the activities and beneficiaries of legal aid, they positively reviled the providers. Once the Social Market Foundation endorsed the ostensibly scientific concept of 'supplier-induced demand', both government and media redefined the problem from unmet legal need to unscrupulous practitioners, rejecting the possibility that exogenous social change fuelled rising demand (eg, crime and divorce rates) and legal complexity explained greater expenditure per case. Nevertheless, some lawyers acknowledged that they responded to standard fees by redirecting their energies to work that generated higher bills. Litigation was promoted both by individual lawyers (housing repairs, mass torts) and professional associations (the Law Society's Accident Legal Advice Scheme). Yet most lawyers, like the public, were uncomfortable about television advertising, leafleting, cold calling, door knocking, and the sale of lists of potential clients.

The profession defended legal aid in the name of its core value. Criticising limitations on access, the Vice Chancellor called civil justice 'the bulwark of a civilised state.' Highlighting notorious miscarriages of justice, the profession warned that government could not be entrusted with rationing because its abuses of power were one of the greatest threats. The profession preferred to defend eligibility (which also benefited clients) rather than its own remuneration rates. It sought alliances with groups representing clients—the poor, children, the mentally ill, medical negligence victims—and tried (unsuccessfully) to emulate the sacrosanct National Health Service. But some solicitors wanted the Law Society to jettison professional pretensions and adopt trade unionist attitudes and strategies. Instead, lawyers invoked their favourite trope—choice—insisting that franchising and exclusive contracts violated ethical rules. The Legal Action Group (LAG) equated government efforts to establish legal aid priorities with the 'Soviet command economy'; a silk associated them with Lenin, the Politburo, and Brezhnev.

Government responded with market rhetoric: franchising enhanced choice by improving information about quality; salaried lawyers increased the range of providers and services. Speaking as a former 'businessman', the Legal Aid Board chair demanded greater 'productivity', warning that 'justice is pricing itself out of the market.' The profession rejoined that cutting costs endangered quality. Since every profession's basic rationale is consumer inability to assess quality (because of information asymmetries), clients (and their government surrogate) should not be encouraged to trade off quality for price. The government retorted that if lawyers were true professionals, they would never betray clients by compromising quality.

Government sought to contain costs in many ways. It replaced hourly rates with standard fees, capped the budget, explored conditional fees, and displayed growing enthusiasm for salaried lawyers (contemplated by the 1948 Legal Aid Act but never funded). Salaried advice services were surprisingly wary. The United Kingdom Immigrant Advisory Service refused to accept responsibility for all immigration advice and representation; the Advice Services Alliance did not want to replace all private practitioners operating under the Green Form scheme. The latter naturally took umbrage at aspersions against the quality of their work (as when Labour MP Austin Mitchell said they gave legal aid matters the 'shoddy end of the stick—the service and attention that falls off the back of the practice'). Finally, government sought to reallocate resources from expensive lawyers to cheaper laypeople, disregarding numerous studies exposing the latter's shortcomings. It extolled the virtues of alternative dispute resolution without offering any evidence of superior quality. It promoted self-help despite the demonstrated difficulty of enforcing small claims judgments.

The profession's rebuttals carried little weight. When lawyers documented their costs to justify higher remuneration the government produced its own figures or simply ignored the evidence. Some 2000 furious lawyers confronted Lord Mackay at a public meeting—with no effect. When the profession mobilised only 300 a year later he did not even bother attending. The leading professional associations sought judicial review, lost, appealed, lost again, and yet continued to threaten litigation and invoke the European Convention on Human Rights. The failure of lawyers' apocalyptic visions to transpire further undermined their credibility. They could not translate widespread support for legal aid into effective political pressure despite spending millions of pounds on public relations. When professional associations conducted unprecedented boycotts of the duty solicitor scheme the public barely noticed, and government just waited until they collapsed. Lawyers threatened to strike, and the government confidently called their bluff. The profession was acutely uncomfortable claiming to champion client interests while employing trade union tactics that could seriously hurt them.

The media gleefully led populist attacks. The legal aid system was 'rotten, from top to bottom', a source of 'ignominy' and 'scandal', an opportunity for 'plunder' and 'fraud.' Lawyers were 'rich' 'bigwigs', guilty of 'chronic wastage', operating a 'sausage factory' for guilty pleas. Newspapers called for an end to the 'golden age' of 'blank cheques' and 'outdated privileges' for lawyers with a 'vested interest' in the legal aid 'pork barrel.' 'Loony' legal aid encouraged 'bizarre' lawsuits and served foreigners, crooks, and millionaires.

One reason for the profession's defeat was its disunity. Reinforcing the Bar Wars' bitter residue, government fostered inter-branch competition for legal aid advocacy. Barristers offered to work without solicitors, and solicitors sought to keep advocacy in-house. The Bar embraced standard fees before the Law Society did, hoping to capture more work. The 'naming and shaming' exercises of government and the media encouraged solicitors to denounce QCs' fees and barristers to accuse solicitors of frivolous litigation. Franchising divided those with and without the qualification. Concentration deepened differences between the few mass processors (increasingly represented by specialist associations) and the bulk of the profession (who did little legal aid and cared less about it).

 If government took satisfaction in overcoming opposition to its legal aid cuts, it still must have been appalled by the fury they provoked throughout the profession. The Lord Chief Justice and the Master of the Rolls sharply criticised the Lord Chancellor. Lawyers shouted 'rubbish' at him in public meetings and hissed the Attorney General (the Bar's titular leader). The British Legal Association called Mackay 'one of the worst Lord Chancellors in history and certainly one who is the worst enemy our profession ever had.' A Law Society president denounced him as 'an old style trade union negotiator' who had 'put his belief in Conservatism ahead of his belief in justice' and 'destroyed the legal aid scheme.' The next president told Mackay to 'put up or shut up' and stop crashing around in 'big boots.' When the Lord Chancellor accused lawyers of suffering withdrawal symptoms from their legal aid addiction, they called him a liar. The LS President dismissed the Legal Aid Board as 'the Government's poodle', to which 'the Lord Chancellor is not beyond giving ... a kick when it suits him' to 'satisfy the Treasury that he is as ready as the next minister to make people bid for their jobs.'

 By the end of Lord Mackay's nearly nine years the legal aid budget was still growing, the profession deeply alienated and even less effective politically, and access to legal services more limited than ever.

Ending Legal Aid as We Know It

If the paradox of Mackay's Lord Chancellorship was Conservatives betraying their natural allies in the legal profession in the name of laissez-faire, the paradox of Irvine's Lord Chancellorship (beginning in May 1997) was Labour drastically contracting the welfare state it had so proudly established after World War Two and made the centrepiece of its electoral strategy for half a century. In opposition, Labour had bitterly attacked Mackay's legal aid policies, blaming sinister 'Treasury influence.' It promised to restore eligibility and extend representation to tribunals, opposed budget caps, warned that fixed fees compromised quality and inadequate remuneration led to second-class service, and worried that family mediation would be insufficiently voluntary. It dismissed conditional fee agreements (CFAs) as 'little more than a gimmick', which offered no 'significant improvement in access to justice'; and it insisted the uplift be 'very much lower than 100 per cent.' But once in power Labour abandoned all these positions—while accusing Conservatives of attacking it for the very policies they had pursued in office. (Indeed, the Conservative-dominated House of Lords twice eliminated the CDS from the Access to Justice Bill.)

The Bar had high hopes for Irvine, who had achieved eminence as an English silk (although born and educated in Scotland). Within weeks, however, the new Lord Chancellor attacked fat cat barristers (one of which he had been), and the Prime Minister (his former pupil) denounced rising legal aid budgets, hinting at a preference for salaried lawyers. Irvine imputed professional self-interest to all opposition to his policies (even by lawyer MPs), declaring that 'the squealing of lawyers' would show his reforms were working. Home Secretary Jack Straw impugned vigorous criminal defence as financially inspired and hypocritical. Irvine carefully orchestrated 'naming and blaming' exercises and cynically capitalised on a ruling drastically cutting silks' fees in a highly publicised case.

In this increasingly bitter confrontation the media generally cheered the state, assailing 'clogged courts', 'archaic' 'restrictive practices', 'slow' and 'expensive' procedures, 'waste' and 'excessive fees' paid to 'fat cat' lawyers on behalf of 'drug traffickers and fraudsters' and plaintiffs in 'no-hope cases.' The *Times* reported 'huge' 'public anger' at the 'bloated' legal aid budget, which had become a 'grotesque drain on taxpayers.' Even papers generally supportive of legal aid, like the *Guardian* and *Independent*, attacked the taint of luxury, almost scandal, associated with incomes unimaginable to their readers. It was hard to explain why a few lawyers earned so much more than doctors or judges. That most of the profession lived modestly, and those doing significant amounts of legal aid work barely scraped by, was not news.

Labour stressed the moral ambiguity of legalism. Tony Blair blamed the high cost of legal aid on frivolous lawsuits and undeserving wealthy defendants. Irvine declared that no one should litigate with less than 75 per cent likelihood of success (never explaining why less winnable cases should not be brought). His Parliamentary Secretary, Geoff Hoon, complained about the expense of long, complex cases. Asked by Government to find ways to cut costs, Sir John Middleton wanted lawyers and clients to share the risk of loss. Commentators blamed an 'American-style compensation culture' for creating a 'Sue Nation' of 'grasping whingers and self-pitying milksops.' Immigration appeals offered an ideal target: aggressive solicitation of business, allegations of fraud, and clients (and many of their lawyers) vulnerable to deep-rooted British xenophobia.

Government sought to reduce legal aid expenditure by freezing remuneration rates (despite inflation), concentrating work among specialists, forcing lawyers to bid for cases, replacing private practitioners by salaried lawyers and lawyers by laypeople, and privatising cost. Government defended concentration as the only means of ensuring quality—but then franchised most applicants and failed to validate accreditation criteria against performance. The profession accused concentration of reducing client choice, access to justice, and lawyer independence. But both adversaries acknowledged the real issues: small firms wanted to protect their market share; government hoped concentration would increase firms' dependence on legal aid and thus its ability to dictate terms. Government won this battle (like all others), cutting the medical negligence panel from 3261 to 80. This episode exposed the fatal flaw in lawyers' threats to drop legal aid if remuneration were not increased: that was exactly what government wanted. Hoon urged that lawyers be made to engage in the 'commonplace' practice of bidding for cases; Middleton wanted the Legal Aid Board to 'use its purchasing power.'

But even competitive tendering for bulk contracts was just a way station toward salaried lawyers, who offered government maximum control over costs. When a radical solicitor first proposed a Community Legal Service, Hoon denounced it as 'Orwellian', 'nationalisation', the denial of 'choice', yet another dreaded quango. Six months after taking power the Labour Government still called the CLS a 'long-term goal.' Less than a year later, however, it became a central element of the Access to Justice Bill. Now the profession protested that salaried lawyers were inherently inferior, denied clients choice, and lacked independence. The Bar even contended the CDS violated the European Convention on Human Rights! Government responded that it could offer better quality through employees (dubious in light of the CPS record and inconsistent with letting private practitioners do legal aid). But its real reasons were that employees had no incentive to create additional work, and their salaries would become ceilings for remunerating private practitioners. The profession warned that salaried services would be inadequately funded and overworked; but that was exactly what government wanted. Because laypeople were even cheaper than salaried lawyers, the CLS shifted work from private practitioners (under the Green Form scheme) to advice services (even though studies had criticised the latter's quality). Although government lost its campaign for mandatory divorce mediation, it expanded the small claims court jurisdiction (disregarding the difficulty, often impossibility, of enforcing judgments).

The Government's most radical reform was transferring the cost of litigation from the state to the parties. Lord Mackay initially proposed CFAs to give lawyers to plaintiffs ineligible for legal aid but unable or unwilling to risk paying for lost cses. The profession recoiled in horror. Barristers were inspired by a sense of 'vocation', protested the Bar, not engaged in mere trade. A radical solicitor worried that his colleagues would become 'commercial speculators and bankers first and lawyers second.' But self-interest soon converted virtually all lawyers. Both government and the profession disregarded evidence that lawyers were charging uplifts unjustified by risk. Even though personal injury cases cost the state little (since defendants paid for cases they lost) the Government's ultimate goal was clear—to eliminate legal aid for plaintiffs. Hoon shamelessly declared that 'for the first time this century, perhaps ever, access to justice for all will be a reality in this country—not just a slogan.' Lawyers should be required to put their own money at risk, as in any other 'profitable business activity.' Government then could blame lawyers and insurers for rationing justice, thereby hiding political choices behind market forces. (Insurers predictably accused lawyers of withholding winning cases; lawyers retorted that insurers demanded impossibly high win rates.)

The profession resisted Irvine even less effectively than it had Mackay. It engaged in gross rhetorical overkill. His reforms were 'Stalinist' (Law Society), 'dirigiste' (former LAG chair); the Access to Justice Act had an 'Orwellian ring', and the CDS pointed 'the way to the gulag' (Labour backbencher); 'the state prosecuting, the state defending, and the state disposing ... they don't even have that in Russia anymore' (Conservative legal affairs spokesperson). 'Noble' legal aid was 'the most efficient of all public services.' Some lawyers unwisely substantiated Irvine's charge that legal aid served lawyers rather than clients by offering Cassandra-like warnings of lawyer unemployment. The Law Society joined government attacks on 'fat cat' barristers in order to advance its own criticism of silk. It saw government efforts to cut criminal defence costs as an opportunity to wrest advocacy work from barristers. The Bar welcomed the CLS as a chance to expand direct access to lay advice services, preempting solicitors. CFAs divided the branches, plaintiffs' and defendants' lawyers, entrepreneurs and traditionalists. The Law Society's £70,000 advertising campaign against the Access to Justice Bill was derided as evidence of profligacy and desperation. The profession typically capitulated after the damage had been done: the Law Society accepted franchising in a vain attempt to forestall exclusive contracts; the Bar sought to extend fixed fees to all cases in order to dissociate legal aid from 'fat cats.'

Government confronted its own rhetorical dilemmas in juggling three mutually antagonistic constituencies. It had to convince the Treasury it was saving money, the public it was increasing access, and the profession it was preserving quality and independence. It bashed lawyers to the Treasury and the public, claimed paternalistic concern for the public in response to lawyer invocations of client choice, and sought to placate the public by denying any interest in cutting costs. Appropriating the profession's strongest trope—equal justice—the government insisted the real inequality was not between the represented and unrepresented but between legally aided and privately paying litigants (a typical 'New Labour' strategy of stoking middle class resentment of benefits for the poor). Middleton was more candid: the right of 'less well off people' to 'have access to justice on a broadly equal basis to everyone else ... has to be set against a background of limited resources.' Criticised for abridging civil liberties, the government retorted that 'professional criminals' were unentitled to the 'full panoply of a criminal trial' at 'massive public expense.' It brazenly invoked equal justice to cut criminal defence expenditures because it had reduced the CPS budget.

By replacing legal aid with conditional fees, substituting salaried lawyers and lay advisers for private practitioners, and capping the legal aid budget, Labour confirmed that it was 'New' only in its willingness to make public services permanently second-class.

Self-Regulators Serving Two Masters

Self-regulation is the profession's most jealously guarded privilege and its most tenuous achievement. The chronic crises of solicitor self-regulation became acute during the 1990s as consumerism challenged professional paternalism, economic cycles produced a dramatic spike in malpractice insurance premiums, and government became more proactive (in the roles of legal aid paymaster, managerial judges, and agencies overseeing the numerous areas into which solicitors were diversifying). Toward the end of the decade the Office for the Supervision of Solicitors complaints backlog became so unmanageable the OSS simply stopped responding; the Solicitors Indemnity Fund (SIF) miscalculated so badly it had to raise premiums to levels many could not pay. (Regulation was far less problematic for barristers, who were buffered from client complaints by solicitors and needed minimal insurance because they were immune from negligence as advocates and handled no client money. The judges who oversaw barristers in the courts and as benchers in the Inns were all ex-barristers, often members of the same chambers, who dined with their former colleagues daily.)

These trends aggravated the profession's fundamental contradiction: protecting the public from lawyers while protecting lawyers against unmeritorious complaints. Regulation requires an unattainable synthesis of expertise (claimed exclusively by insiders) and independence (claimed exclusively by outsiders). Critics of the profession called for government regulation; defenders wanted to relegate complainants to the market (whose failure was the profession's fundamental justification) and the courts (where lawyers had a clear advantage). The Legal Services Ombudsman accused the Bar of elevating its 'purity and solidarity' above pleasing consumers, a responsibility banks took much more seriously according to Lord Williams of Mostyn QC (Bar Council chair turned banker). Both the Bar Council and its lay complaints commissioner boasted of rejecting 70–80 per cent of grievances. Some lawyers wanted clients to *pay* for the privilege of complaining. Lawyers who devoted their entire professional lives to manipulating state coercion became instant converts to exhortation and conciliation when their own behaviour was in question. They condemned intrusive, petty regulation by a nanny Law Society, pointing to the collapse of several prominent disciplinary proceedings. Clients found regulation dilatory, dismissive, and excessively lenient, pointing to the exposé of notorious cover-ups. Those seeking power within professional associations appealed to members' resentment of the burdens of discipline and insurance. The intensity of these feelings was dramatically demonstrated when a Bar Council Extraordinary General Meeting rejected the proposed complaints process 2:1 and a Law Society Special General Meeting and subsequent mail ballot rejected the malpractice insurance scheme 2:1.

The contest between lawyers and clients (and the latter's champions in consumer organisations, media, and government) produced cycles of criticism, defence, grudging reform, extravagant claims of improvement, inevitable disappointment, and renewed criticism. Instead of setting and enforcing standards higher than the market or government might impose— the hallmark of a profession—lawyers did the least they could get away with. Some lawyers opposed every reform: advance fee quotations, in-house complaint procedures, compensation for inadequate professional service, open disciplinary hearings, mandatory continuing professional development, remuneration certificates for testamentary beneficiaries, liability for negligent advocacy, even rules against sexual relations with clients! The Society publicly ignored (and may have suppressed) the warning sign of two SIF premium increases after none for five years. Every external study documented the failure of firms' grievance procedures, solicitor reluctance to disclose fees, and client dissatisfaction with both solicitors and their regulatory processes. In order to control its own caseload the OSS required complainants to exhaust grievance procedures in solicitors firms knowing they did not exist. One solicitor candidly admitted that the 'learned profession ... is the stuff of sherry talk.' Solicitors should have 'the right to tell someone to bugger off if we judge it is in our interest.'

At the same time, the profession's complacency would have made Dr Pangloss blush. The Solicitors Complaints Bureau (SCB) Director pronounced that for a mere £170/year 'solicitors have a self-regulatory system which is the envy of lawyers throughout the world and of other professions in this country'—and then quit the directorship a few months later calling it 'the worst job in the world.' The OSS (the SCB's successor), severely criticised by Ernst and Young, the Legal Services Ombudsman, and a respected law professor, dealt with its growing backlog by telling complainants to try again in six months. When the *Times* blew the whistle, the Law Society President called this an opportunity to reform and tried to spin the Lord Chancellor's exasperated threat to take over regulation as an endorsement of the Society's promise to improve. The President chose this inauspicious moment to make a bid to swallow the Bar and its regulatory regime because solicitors regulated themselves so 'well.'

His successor acknowledged that the malpractice insurance premium controversy tested the profession's commitment to collectivism over individualism. A Law Society Council member and SIF director criticised City firms who wanted to opt out (since they already spent far more for excess coverage) and conveyancing practitioners who accounted for 'much of the profession's negligence' but were 'not prepared to accept collective responsibility.' Professional fractions fought over whether the purpose of insurance was to spread losses broadly or proportion premiums to risk. Advocates of the latter view were prepared to see colleagues forced to the wall, promising that most solicitors would save thousands of pounds annually. They analogised SIF to the failed command economies of Eastern Europe and may have felt that the market forces affecting so much of their professional lives should extend to insurance.

The controversies over self-regulation and insurance widened professional fissures. Many sole practitioners wanted to abandon discipline, which many firm solicitors wanted to strengthen; many firm solicitors wanted to abolish mutual insurance, which many sole practitioners wanted to preserve. Sole practitioners were targeted by the OSS, excluded by lenders from conveyancing panels, and uniquely vulnerable to rapidly rising SIF premiums. Larger firms resented that the profession's 'Sainsburys' (themselves) had to pay the same insurance rates as 'Mr Patel's excellent corner shop' (Asian sole practitioners). A solicitor acknowledged the profession's fragmentation into 'firms with widely different incomes, practices, client bases, geographical locations and needs.'

Ungovernable Professions?

The 1990s were a difficult decade for solicitors: the conveyancing market contracted sharply and was threatened by competition from the major lenders; efforts to gain higher court audience rights were stymied in battles that reaffirmed barristers' superior status; government made legal aid work less attractive and less available; and economic forces accelerated internal differentiation and stratification. Solicitors' growing frustration and resentment may explain why the Law Society's vigorous opposition to replacing legal aid with conditional fees evoked such widespread applause. A Council member exulted it had 'managed to rattle the Lord Chancellor. We need to do that more often. It will raise the morale of the members and help the Society to regain its self-respect.' The (successful) presidential candidate praised the Society for having

> fire in its belly ... for the first time in memory the Law Society was learning how to stand up for its members intelligently and confidently.

At the same time, the Society was a natural scapegoat for solicitor discontent. Financially pressed by both market and state, solicitors criticised the Society's waste and extravagance (annual meetings at foreign venues attended mostly by officials on expense accounts). Local law societies resented the national Society as a bloated bureaucracy whose activities were irrelevant to their rank and file. When the Society decided to pay officers (in emulation of the Bar), members voted more than 2:1 to cut remuneration to the level of legal aid work. The high salaries of the chief executives of the Society, SIF, and the College of Law and the generous golden handshake for the disgraced SCB director rankled with those barely making ends meet. The Council members' decision to pay *themselves* in the face of profound solicitor dissatisfaction was extraordinarily insensitive. Members also criticised incompetence: huge cost overruns for information technology unable to perform even such basic functions as issuing annual practising certificates; abandonment of the expensive but unworkable High Street Starter Kit; periodic costly public relations campaigns that were ineffective at best and sometimes seriously counterproductive.

The Society's structure was an even more intractable problem. If solicitors failed to reflect the wider population, the Council and officers were less representative of the profession. The Council fought about designating a single seat for a woman or a trainee. While Heather Hallett's chairpersonship allowed the Bar to proclaim it had transcended its patriarchal past, the Law Society saw a leading male presidential candidate forced to withdraw when decades of sexual harassment (covered up by his colleagues) was exposed and a leading Asian woman presidential candidate forced to withdraw when found to have bullied subordinates (many of them women). Other professional divisions engendered even greater tensions. The Council's geographic constituencies (a 19th century concession to the two-thirds of solicitors practising outside London) were increasingly anachronistic and embarrassingly reminiscent of rotten boroughs. Solo and small firm practitioners wanted the Society to do more *for* them and less *to* them. Sole practitioners successfully lobbied for their own section, while the British Legal Association and Solicitors Association merged, strengthening their claim to represent smaller firms. Large firm and employed solicitors found the Society so irrelevant and wasteful that many threatened to secede. Increased specialisation and its formalisation in legal aid franchising made a former president's invocation of 'one profession' (evocative of the Conservative 'one nation' ideology) more nostalgic than descriptive. Even if the Society's specialist sections replace geographic constituencies, many specialists may feel greater loyalty to their own associations.

All these conflicts fuelled power struggles. Local law societies traditionally elected Council members who chose officers served by staff. Now, however, even staff acknowledged that they dominated elected officials by virtue of knowledge and longevity (as civil servants do Ministers). When a solicitor complained that the Society claimed to know 'what is best for us', the president retorted: 'You elected the members of the Council for their expertise and at the end of the day we must use our best judgment.' Staff wanted to shrink the Council so it could again be a policymaking body, but members naturally refused. Martin Mears, who captured the presidency on a populist platform, aggressively sought more power at the expense of staff. A populist Councillor wanted a few members to be able to recall the entire body. A consultant retained by the Society proposed remaking it in the image of the companies he had run, drastically contracting democratic accountability and participation. The experience of six (often bitterly) contested elections convinced the Council (unanimously, without debate) to limit them to the single office of deputy vice president (who would succeed to the presidency over two years). But the real problem was apathy, not excessive democracy: some 12,000 solicitors declined to join the Society; few attended annual meetings; the proportion voting fell from 45 per cent to 18.6 per cent between 1996 and 2000.

Other critics identified the fundamental problem of governance as functional rather than structural: the incompatible roles of regulation and representation. Separatists hoped to relax regulation and free themselves of its cost and constraints while aggressively pursuing their self-interest. Some sought to discourage client complaints and inveighed against mandatory malpractice insurance. Opponents feared solicitors would still pay for more stringent government regulation and have fewer resources for representation. When fission was put to a vote, only 30 per cent of members were in favor. Instead, the real threat came from the government. Furious that the Society had spent £70,000 opposing his Access to Justice Bill, Lord Irvine wrote into it the power to deny the Society mandatory practising certificate revenue for such 'political' expenditures.

This was the environment in which Martin Mears and Robert Sayer won election to the Council (independently) in 1994 and as president and vice-president in 1995. Mears played on his colleagues' anxieties with fantasies of turning back the clock by limiting vocational course places (and hence entry), restoring conveyancing scale fees, and excluding cut-price conveyancers from SIF. Calling these patently unlawful proposals 'mere commonsense' (perhaps he meant Mears commonsense), he asked: 'Why is it so wrong to try to protect ourselves?' He championed small firms, making no pretence to represent all solicitors.

Contesting the presidency for the first time in over 40 years, Mears emulated Ronald Reagan, running as an outsider seeking power to shrink the Society and promptly appealing to members over the heads of the Council. Sayer forced the reporting of Council votes to expose opponents to constituent anger. Mears accused the Society of 'no-can-doism', mismanagement, and waste and disparaged opposition to his unprecedented (and unsuccessful) bid for a second term as the establishment's revenge.

His strategy was his own undoing. By creating a personal caucus within the Council, he intensified opposition. The colorful language, which ensured media coverage, also revealed his irresponsibility. All adversaries were 'leftists'; a woman he defeated for the presidency was 'the most dangerous feminist in England'; a former ally was a 'wild man ... living in a fantasy world.' Betrayed by Sayer, Mears repeated his vice-president's graphic image of him as a 'twisted little man' who kept turning up like 'a piece of dog turd on your shoe.' Although divorced and cohabiting with the mother of his two illegitimate children, Mears attacked Lord Mackay for making divorce easier. He delighted in being called 'the most dangerous lawyer in England ... a cross between Enoch Powell and Tony Benn.' He played hardball politics, exposing election scandals at the last moment so they could not be rebutted—block voting in 1996, dirty tricks in 1997— and then claiming the moral high ground. Paranoid in defeat he saw himself as 'Richard III at the battle of Bosworth. With half his forces in covert alliance with the other side, it was no wonder he lost.' It was appropriately ironic that Mears, who had made restoring the profession's good image his primary goal, was repudiated for making it a 'laughing stock', 'shambles', 'soap opera.' He succeeded in uniting local law societies, the City, LAG, the

Legal Aid Practitioners Group and five former presidents in opposition to him. In subsequent elections unity became a code word for reaction to the divisions Mears had sown. But others acknowledged the irreversible divisions by wooing particular constituencies. One presidential candidate declared 'my roots are in the high street, [my running mate's] in the City.' Another boasted that as 'the senior partner in a major department in a leading City firm' he could not be 'second best' (hardly endearing him to the vast majority of solicitors, who presumably were). A candidate accused his opponent, an employed solicitor, of not representing 'the whole profession.'

But though Mears lost two more elections, his influence was not limited to his year as president. He may have been repudiated by Sayer, but as this ex-protégé moved up the ranks from deputy vice president to vice president and ultimately president he remained firmly protectionist, criticising firms for employing law graduates as paralegals, opposing audience rights for legal executives, and condemning conditional fees for legal malpractice actions. Solicitors' acceptance of 'professional responsibilities in return for professional privileges' justified market restrictions 'in the public good.' Mears had made protectionism kosher. He mourned 'the decline in the profession's prosperity and sense of security', the loss of 'a guaranteed good income for life.' Other leaders acknowledged the dilemma of addressing both the profession and the public. 'The position we do not trumpet', said Henry Hodge, is that 'the amount of money coming from the legal aid system into the profession has doubled.' He expressed satisfaction in having delayed standard fees in magistrates' courts and urged the profession to control its numbers by limiting training contracts. Tony Girling took credit for suppressing competition from licensed conveyancers and from banks (for probate) but admitted 'we don't crow about either of those achievements because it would be counterproductive to do so.' A member of the steering committee of the Solicitors Association, established by those who felt the Law Society was insufficiently protectionist, bragged that solicitors 'would run rings around an external regulator.'

Mears may have been megalomaniacal and self-destructive, but he did transform Law Society elections from 'Buggins' turn' into political campaigns over issues, records, and personalities. Candidates recycled unrealistic promises to raise conveyancing and legal aid remuneration rates and help solicitors compete more effectively. They blamed opponents for supporting conditional fees, surrendering 'crucial areas of our reserved work', and 'politically correct posturing' about 'equal opportunities.' They waxed nostalgic about the time when solicitors were 'valued by clients' and the profession was 'appreciated and respected both by society and government.' Many distinguished their 'strong leadership', which would allow solicitors to take 'pride in the way the profession is led by the Law Society', from the embarrassments suffered under 'mavericks' like Mears and Sayer. Some called opponents liars, 'egomaniacs', whose 'rantings of yesteryear' showed they were 'living on another planet.' Others accused the vituperators of being 'incapable of avoiding personal criticisms.' Some portrayed it as a contest between 'good and evil.' As battle fatigue increased, many hoped for an end to politics. A contested election was not essential to democracy but just 'an expensive piece of spite at a cost to the profession of £100,000.' Even before elections were limited to the deputy vice president, those gaining that post once again systematically ascended to the presidency. 'Buggins' turn' was returning, but now Buggins could be a woman.

Conclusion

The 1990s fundamentally redefined the discourse of legal professionalism in England and accelerated changes in practice. A Conservative Government betrayed its loyal lawyer constituency in the name of laissez-faire. Control over supply, seriously weakened by the post-War expansion of academic legal education, was further eroded by criticism of apprenticeship and loss of the professional monopoly over vocational courses. Pride in exclusivity was replaced by chagrin at unrepresentativeness, even if the profession was unwilling to abandon its meritocratic legitimation of entry barriers and internal hierarchy. The Bar lost its monopoly of higher court audience rights but seemed likely to retain the market for most such advocacy. It threatened to by-pass solicitors and serve clients directly but was reluctant to relinquish the superior status of a consultant profession. The Lord Chancellor was under pressure to make silk and the bench more representative of the profession (including solicitors) but refused to surrender appointive power. Solicitors, who had lost almost no market share to licensed conveyancers, faced a far more serious threat from corporate conveyancers. City firms may subordinate foreign lawyers, but MDPs established by Big Five accounting firms are another matter. The future clearly favours specialists over generalists. Governmental largesse, which had fuelled the profession's expansion, has rendered the legal aid sector heavily dependent and unable to oppose cost-cutting. Government increased its control through franchising, exclusive contracts, and ultimately employment. It also privatised costs through CFAs. Crises of self-regulation threatened to expose solicitors to regulation by the market (private malpractice insurers) and the state. The politicisation of self-governance exposed fissures deep enough to split professional associations or deny them the revenue essential to effective advocacy. A profession that successfully resisted change for more than a century and a half is in the throes of a basic transformation.

3

Fighting for Survival: Unification, Differentiation and Representation of the French Bar

ANNE BOIGEOL AND LAURENT WILLEMEZ

Much has changed in the French bar since the beginning of the seventies when the question of the legal market began to be an official concern of the profession and of the state. Internationalisation of the economy, the construction of Europe, and the arrival of new competitors challenge the French bar and its position in the national and international business and financial law markets.

Because of its history, the French bar was quite unprepared to face this competition. The division of the legal profession, the division of the bar into 181 autonomous bars and the importance of the traditional way of practicing did not prepare the bar for entering the global legal market. If the bar wanted to occupy a significant position in this market, it had to change quite a lot. In order to be a stronger profession it had to begin a process of unification of the different legal professions, a process that was not easy to get under way and that is still in progress. This process of unification involved some change in the bar's jurisdiction, its organisation, and its culture. The strategy developed by the bar interferes with the strategy of other professional groups, other competitors, national or international, in the legal profession or at its border.

Such movement of unification and openness to the international legal market is connected to another phenomenon: the differentiation and fragmentation of the French bar, as in its social morphology and in its representation. On the one hand, two transformations are converging: the increasing number of lawyers and the increase of differentiation. On the other hand, the representation of all *avocats*[1] is quite fragmented, which

---

[1] In this paper will be used the French word *avocats*, and not Anglo-Saxon translations: as it will be showed, all French lawyers are not *avocats*. The *avocat* has a monopoly of pleading before the court.

causes a struggle between the disparate bodies pretending to defend the profession as a whole. Unification, openness and increasing differentiation and inequalities: those three elements seem to sum up the recent evolution of the French bar, and they combine to create a huge uncertainty within the profession about its future (Karpik 1999).

Unfortunately, apart from the work of Lucien Karpik, there are very few general studies about French *avocats*.[2] Sociological data are quite poor, and France does not have an institution like the American Bar Foundation.[3] It seems that the bar authorities have not realised yet the advantage of having such information and are often reluctant to adopt a sociological approach. Thus, this paper, based on existing studies, considers several faces of the French profession. Its aim is to analyse the transformation of the bar, in the grip of three simultaneous movements: unification, openness to the market and social-political differentiation.

First, it will be shown, through a historical view, how French *avocats* have unified and more or less established a kind of monopoly on legal activity, under the pressure of legal market openness. But such a process of unification is connected to an increase in the size of the profession, and to major social differentiation, eventually leading to inequalities. Finally, such morphological transformations are bound to precipitate a split in representation of the profession as a whole.

1. The High Price of an Unfinished Unification

Since the end of the sixties, the French bar has been trying to establish a monopoly on legal activities, more precisely on business legal counselling. It means that the jurisdiction of the bar is changing, and these changes require the unification of many professions dealing with law (Boigeol 1988). This is quite a new position, which is justified by the national and international context and by increasing competition in the legal market. The task is difficult as many professions or professional groups are involved; that is why the process of unification under the banner of the bar

---

[2] For other sociological views see Boigeol (1980, 1988) and Milburn (1991, 2002), Willemez (2003). However the field of socio-historical research on *avocats* is today developing, conducted by sociologists, politists, and historians. For instance Charle (1989, 1997), Le Beguec (2003), the Ph D of Laurent Willemez (2000) *Robes Noires, Années Sombres* (Israël, 2005), or of Sharon Elbaz on *avocats* and decolonisation.

[3] A few years ago, the department of justice produced a few data on the bar profession (Moreau, 2002). The Paris bar has published in 2001 a few data concerning its own activity (Observatoire du Barreau de Paris: statistiques 2001).

provoked such opposition and resistance, both within and outside of the bar. There are different steps in this story, each one corresponding to the adoption of a law forcing the profession into a new configuration. To understand this tumultuous story and the battles which happened at the borders of and in the profession, it is useful to consider all the professions concerned as a system (Abbott 1988) and to analyse how the interprofessional competition has affected the process of monopolisation. The French legal market has been particularly open to outsiders since the legal profession has been divided and since the legal market has not been fully exploited by the traditional legal professions.

The difficulty of establishing a monopoly of legal counselling activities is first bound to the traditional division of the legal profession into many professions, each of them being autonomous. Besides the *avocats,* who have for a long time focused almost exclusively on the traditional litigation-related aspects of legal practice, where they have a monopoly on the main courts, there are also *avoués* (solicitors), *huissiers* (bailiffs), and *notaires* (notaries).[4] All these professions are organised into and regulated by professional bodies. There were also non-lawyer practitioners who could assist people in certain types of courts, commercial courts, for instance: the *agréés* could appear in commercial courts (lay judges) on behalf of individuals. They combined the role of solicitor with that of *avocat,* whose involvement was not, and still is not, required in this jurisdiction.[5]

The difficulty of establishing a monopoly on legal counselling is also linked to the traditional jurisdiction of the bar. The activity which made the bar famous was pleading, mostly in criminal or political cases. In the early 20th century only a few *avocats* were interested in business law and legal assistance to firms. Among them were some famous *avocats* such as Poincaré or Waldeck-Rousseau. This activity is more discrete, and more lucrative. For instance, Waldeck-Rousseau's most famous trial was the *Panama Canal* affair (bankruptcy), where he acted for the engineer Eiffel. Both of them were famous political men. It has been said of Raymond Poincaré:

> Its office gives him appreciable satisfaction, which are not only moral ones; he is pleading a lot for trade, big companies. He sometimes travelled far away to plead as in Bucarest, in 1900, where he pleaded for French companies working for the harbor of Constanza. His adversary was the state of Romania (Miquel 1961:223).

Most legal assistance to middle size or small companies or corporations was given by an unofficial profession, known as *conseils juridiques* (legal

---

[4] And of course *magistrats*: judges and prosecutors.
[5] This diversity of professions belonging to the general category of lawyer is seen in the Martindale. If most of the lawyers mentioned in France are *avocats*, a few of them are notaries, or legal experts.

counsel) and also, in part, by notaries and by *agréés*. Legal counselling is not a protected activity. The *conseils juridiques* emerged, at the border of the bar, offering legal assistance to small or middle sized companies or trades. The arrival of new-comers at the borders of the bar is directly linked to the lack of interest of *avocats* in certain kind of legal matters, work and clients, which were not considered prestigious enough. Moreover, the professional rules of the bar—code of professional responsibility and exercise—do not fit with the needs of this kind of client.

A short history of these *conseils juridiques* helps to understand the problems that the bar deals with today. They arose at the turn of the 20th century, from the large entity of the *'agents d'affaires'*, a generic term used for people offering all forms of help related to business. They were a heterogeneous group that included honourable and less honourable people. The *conseils juridiques* offered many services to businesses: information about law, mainly tax law, help in relation to administrative matters, and help with financial transactions and accountancy.[6]

As the *conseils juridiques* had no traditional professional rules such as those of the bar, they faced the constraint all sellers of symbolic goods have: the need to build their social credibility (Boigeol and Dezalay 1997). In order to improve their image and make the difference with *'agents d'affaires'*, they developed two different strategies of distinction, depending on their social and cultural background.

The first was developed by the elite of the *conseils juridiques*, those who were law graduates, or had PhDs in law; they wanted to appear as professionals, following in the footsteps of *avocats*, mainly sole practitioners, with an image of integrity. They were organised in an association whose aim was to certify the competence and integrity of their members. Like the official bar, this strategy was inclined to limit the supply of labour in the face of an expansion of the demand of legal services. They promoted internal organisation in order to guarantee their members' morality and competence.

The other one was developed by people who were more prompted by the economic needs of their clients than by the ideal of the bar. Their purpose was to create customer loyalty by offering clients all the services needed. Such a strategy was mainly initiated by people whose strengths were in the experience and the knowledge acquired in a notary office or in an administrative capacity dealing with tax or real estate. They hoped to improve their position by creating a firm with several partners, in order to offer a wide set of homogenised skills to small or middle size corporations in tax law, administration and accounting. Their preoccupations were more effi-

---

[6] Accountancy became an organised profession just after World War II.

ciency oriented than deontology oriented. They were organised in the same way as the firms in which they were employed. The first firm, *La Fiduciaire de France*, was created in 1923, the second one, the *bureau Francis Lefebvre*, in 1925. They still exist today, the first one (whose name is Fidal) as a member of a multidisciplinary practice network (KPMG), the second one as an autonomous law firm specialising in tax law. The development of these practices and of these professional groups did not trouble the bar, which was not concerned by them.

After WWII *conseils juridiques* took advantage of an exceptional economic context, where firms became more and more numerous in rebuilding France. They also took advantage of the transformation of the legal field with the development of public law and the increase in social and labour law, which modified the system of professional positions. Some young law graduates did not hesitate to enter legal firms of *conseils juridiques,* which often offered better positions and opportunities than the bar. They allowed people who were not born in the *bourgeoisie* and did not have the social status usually required to enter the bar to practise law. The firms of *conseils juridique* also developed a policy of in-house training, which does not have any equivalent in the bar. With these investments, the strategy of the firms became closer to the strategy of the elite of the *conseils juridiques*. By the late sixties, the two segments of the *conseils juridiques* group seemed to have more interests in common. Their strategies partially converged. The business market was growing; their business was thriving. But they had a deficit of legitimacy, being always an unofficial profession even if its economic weight was significant.

During all this time the bar had not changed. It was mainly a craftsman's profession, with few members (Karpik 1995). Most of the *avocats* were sole practitioners, working for private people and individuals, and a few for firms. Their own organisation was homothetic of their practice. Only in 1956 were French *avocats* permitted to form collective structures of practice. Competition was limited, both by the ideology of the profession and by the limited number of *avocats*.[7]

1.1 The First Step to Unification: the 1971 Law

By the end of the sixties, the national and international context was changing. The development of an international business-law market and the construction of Europe challenged the French bar. At that time there were only a few *avocats* (and also a few *conseils juridiques*) who could pretend to own

---

[7] Which favoured the 'economy of quality'(Karpik, 1995).

an international dimension. This situation was perceived as a problem by the State and by a few *avocats* who understood that the French legal profession had to be strengthened to adapt it to these new challenges. The developing legal market in France (Dezalay 1992) and its free entry could encourage outsiders. Being aware of the danger, a few *avocats* proposed the creation of a new profession on the model of the American lawyer, ie including *avocats*, *conseils juridiques* and other professions,[8] in order to establish a monopoly on legal activities, mainly legal counselling, and to control competition.[9] A bill therefore was drafted by the department of justice.

But this strategy went against other strategies, traditions and habits of the bar. The *conseils juridiques* had a large clientele of firms and did not want to be absorbed into the bar, without any consideration for their specific nature. And a large part of the provincial bars did not have any interest in merging with people who did not share the bar's core values. Such constraints limited the scope of the project. Thus, the 1971 reform failed to integrate the *conseils juridiques* into the profession of *avocat*.[10] But the reform legally recognised the *conseil juridique* as a professional group with a protected title.

One of the main—unforeseen by the bar—results of the reform has been to strengthen two other categories of legal practitioner in France: the foreign lawyers (English and American), and the Big Eight (accountants) (Boigeol and Dezalay 1997; Nallet 1999). The Big Eight seemed to use the French legal market as a field of experiment in their attempt to include the practice of law in their multidisciplinary network.[11] The law of 1971 authorises foreign lawyers to practise in France—that means giving legal counsel and drafting acts relating to international law—on condition of being officially registered as *conseil juridique*. Henceforth they were allowed to practise in France as *conseils juridiques*, having a legal recognition and enjoying a complete autonomy from the bar and its constraining rules. The first installation of a tax law firm originating in a multidisciplinary network occurred in the early 70s with the arrival of Peat Marwick (which will become KPMG) and Coopers and Lybrand Conseils (Nallet 1999). For these firms, France appeared a 'paradise', where they could establish and develop all the more because the local lawyers were regarded as undeveloped. Hence, one of the consequences of the law was increasing competition at the borders of the bar.

---

[8] Avoués, agréés près les tribunaux de commerce.

[9] Illustration ot Abel's thesis on anti-competition practice of the bar. Cf R Abel (1982).

[10] The avoués and agréés became avocats.

[11] Report of the New York State Bar association special committee on the law governing structure and operation: Preserving the core values of the American legal profession; The place of multidisciplinary Practice in the Law governing lawyers, Albany, New-York, April 2000.

With their official title, the group of *conseils juridiques* adopted a new strategy in order to build a new profession, parallel to the bar. First of all, its elite members worked to organise and to gather all the *conseils juridiques* which were spread among many organisations into a single organisation, *l'Association nationale des conseils juridiques (ANCJ)*. This organisation welcomed all the *conseils juridiques,* including English or American lawyers who brought the association their prestige, and also lawyers coming from the legal departments of the Big Eight. To affirm their position, they insisted on their distance and difference from the bar, underlining the obsolete character of the bar's rules, which would make the profession unable to fulfil the legal expectations of business/corporate clients.

They wanted to transform the group of *conseils juridiques* into a true profession and started a process of professionalisation (Larson 1977). They controlled entry into the profession, with similar requirements to those expected of *avocats*. They organised training and teaching-specific knowledge. They created a professional organisation at both national and regional levels, which had disciplinary powers and were recognised by the law and the State. They did everything necessary to be recognised as a true profession. They were numerous, including the mass of single practitioner *conseils juridiques* and those belonging to French firms of conseils juridiques, to Anglo-Saxon law firms or to the Big Eight. One important outcome of their pursuit of honour was the development of specific training for a high level of competence. The elite of the profession made large investments in the academic field in order to improve the social credibility of *conseils juridiques* (Boigeol and Dezalay 1997). In doing so, they had an advantage over the bar which did not offer any equivalent training.

Such investment contributed to the general construction of business law in the academic field. They made alliances with new, young, law professors in commercial law, quite often newcomers to academia who had also to affirm the position of this law and their own position through the doctrine. They participated in the organisation of new academic diplomas in business law. They also offered law graduates a specialised training in the firm. The role of the *conseils juridiques* in academic life was becoming all the more important: firms of *conseils juridiques* also made big scholarly investments, editing books, some of them becoming quite famous. In the late 80's the establishment of the profession of *conseils juridiques* became a reality. And then, in 1990, although they had reached their goal, *conseil juridiques* disappeared as an autonomous profession, integrated into the new *avocat* profession. The understanding of such a radical change has to take into account the competition between the professions for the control of the business law market, and also the competition between two kinds of practices: the craftsman's practice as opposed to the practice of the firm.

1.2 The Second Step to Unification: the 1990 Law

The strategy which confered upon *conseillers juridiques* some integrity made the bar all the more anxious as the market for legal services to business grew terrifically. The bar could not let a new profession, with competence and integrity, develop in such an expanding field, when it encountered market problems. The bar was forced to react in 1985 when the signature of the 'Single European Market' allowed European lawyers to practice throughout Europe in 1993. The French bar was not ready to face this increase in international competition. The bar was not a strong profession, but one divided into many organisations, with very few big structures, but a lot of small groups (see below part 2). As in the late sixties, some *avocats* of the Paris bar decided that it was essential to promote a radical change in the profession and proposed the creation of a new profession including *conseils juridiques* and in-house lawyers, which would allow the French bar to compete on the international legal market (Soulez-Larivière 1988). Apart from establishing a monopoly of legal services, they also suggested important changes in the rules of ethics, for instance that *avocats* could be salaried (as was usual among *conseils juridiques*, but forbidden by the bar) or that the partnership of *avocats* could be organised in a commercial society (there were firms of *conseils juridiques*).

This proposition caused a big shock for the bar, producing both strong opposition (critics of the dominance of the market) and strong support (Karpik 1995). Discords also arose among *conseils juridiques* and between the professions, each of them wanting to improve their position in the business legal market.

Why did the *conseils juridiques*, who had official recognition for their profession, at last agree to disappear? The first reason was that, being organised as a profession, they were in a better position to negotiate with the bar, which was ready to recognise the specific nature of *conseils juridiques* forms of practices. The second reason was that the tactical association with the Big Six, whose size was growing, was becoming problematic for the elite *conseils juridiques* thus making it more attractive to consent to a rapprochement with the bar. Indeed, divergences appeared between the firms of legal services affiliated with the Big Six and the elite of *conseils juridiques*. The first ones disagreed with the definition of the jurisdiction of the new *avocat* and wanted to promote multidisciplinary practices, with no reference to the specific nature of legal services. The traditional elite *conseils juridiques* and the bar were opposed to multidisciplinarity practice because of questions of conflicts of interest and unfair competition, and because they were seen as a severe threat to individual practitioners. The supporters of the multidisciplinary practice left the association for a new one: *Juri-Avenir*.

The ANCJ supported the project of unification within the bar.

During the discussion of the 1990 law unifying *avocats* and *conseils juridiques*, all the professions which offered legal services fought to protect and improve their jurisdiction. The accountants fought against the establishment of a monopoly or even against the *'périmètre du droit'* (the area of professional activity reserved to *avocats*). Notaries, who feared marginalisation by the reform and were quite hostile to unification, suggested the system of *'inter-professionalité'*. That meant that each profession retained its autonomy, its independence and that nothing had to change, but they would co-exist in the same place/area, so that people could find *avocats*, notaries, and others in the same building (a situation which still exists). The lobbying of the members of the French Parliament was exceptional, the accountants reaching the highest levels.

After very severe battles, a legislative reform was adopted in December 1990 (Karpik 1995), creating the new profession of *avocat*. The new profession integrated *conseils juridiques*, but not in-house lawyers. Thus, it failed to establish a true monopoly on legal practice, for many professions which did not belong to legal professions were still authorised to give legal advice as a subordinate aspect of their activity. Nonetheless, it established a *'périmètre du droit'*, allowing *avocats* to be salaried and firms of *avocats* to be commercial firms (but whose capital came from lawyers).

But the story is not finished. Once the reform was voted on, competition between the 'law' and the 'number' *(le chiffre et le droit)* did not end. The competition was now both on the borders of the profession, with accountants who still pursued an aggressive strategy, and within the profession, between the different segments of the profession and the Big Six.

At the borders of the profession, the bar had to fight with accountants, who were not satisfied with the law of 1990. Some accountants seemed to have an extensive definition of their legal activity, supposedly ancillary to their main activity of accounting. They tended to invade *avocat*'s prerogatives, the *'périmètre du droit'*. *Avocats* had to sue accountants working in the 'field' of *avocats* (Hyest 2002), illustrating the fragility of the professional border.[12]

But the most important problem was now within the bar. By virtue of law the lawyers of those firms who were *conseils juridiques* became *avocats*. The transformation of *conseils juridiques* to *avocats* meant that the new *avocats* were ruled by the bar. The French bar had to integrate quite big law firms: former firms of *conseils juridiques*, some of them being affiliated with one of the Big Five, other law firms created by the Big Five or an

---

[12] For instance accountants have been accused of giving legal advice in social law, which is definitely not in their competence.

English or American law firm. The French bar was not sufficiently well organised to deal with such competitors. It was highly divided—there were 181 bars—with no strong organisation representing the profession. The Paris bar played a major role but a new bar sought to make its voice heard: the Nanterre bar which had 70 per cent of its membership coming from the Big Five. The new *Conseil national des barreaux* (CNB, National Counsel of the bar), created by the 1990 law, was still quite young (see below). The French bar was not in a position to impose its conception of the profession on all the new comers.

The bar focused its attention on the questions of ethics. It mainly concerned the Big Five, which, as a multidisciplinary practice, was seen as representing the most important danger for the profession. *Avocats* from multidisciplinary networks were seen by *avocats 'de souche'* (meaning those who have always been *avocats*) as non independent, accessories to auditors, receiving most of their work from auditors. For the bar it was impossible to use the title of *avocat* if the independence, secrecy and other core values of the profession were not respected. The position was quite defensive.

Very soon, divergences appeared. According to the 1990 law, a law firm belonging to one of the Big Five had to use a firm name distinct from the auditing/consulting firm. They had five years to make the change. But the wording was not perfectly clear and generated debate on its interpretation. Pricewaterhouse Coopers Juridique et Fiscal, asked by the Paris bar to change its name, adopted a new branding: Landwell and Associés. But the legal departments of the other Big Five, which were under the jurisdiction of the Nanterre bar were not urged to change their name.

However the bar was confronted with the fact that the Big Five were attractive to young law graduates—they offer good training, good pay and stable positions; when the traditional bar offers less advantageous prospects—and that well-known law firms did not hesitate to merge with one of the Big Five.[13]

For the CNB, it became urgent to deal with the multidisciplinary networks rather than to fight them. As one of its roles was to formalise the internal ethics that governed the whole bar,[14] the council drafted the amendments required by the Big Five to make their legal department conform with the ethics of the bar. That means: different names with the requirements to mention belonging to the multidisciplinary network, stringent rules of transparency, with obligations to inform the local bar about the structure and operation of each multidisciplinary network including

[13] Archibald, an Anglo-Saxon law firm merged with Arthur Andersen in 1994 and above all a French law firm Thomas et associés merged with Deloitte, Touche in 1997.

[14] Each of the 181 bars in France has got its own professional code of ethics. One of the tasks of the CNB, created in 1990, is to create a national code of ethics.

avocats, the prohibition of an *avocat* working for a client if another member of the multidisciplinary practice certifies or controls the accounts of that client. (*Avocats* have an obligation of secrecy and the person who certifies the accounts has the obligation to reveal fraud and offences on the part of his client).[15]

These rules were adopted by the CNB in 1999 as a part of the internal rules of the bar (*Règlement intéreur unifié*). Soon after this decision, one law firm of the Big Five, followed by many other affiliated firms, commenced litigation. They were reluctant to accept some of the dispositions of the code concerning the control of avocats by the local bar authorities and the CNB. They wanted to promote a way of solving internally ethical problems that might occur in multidisciplinary practice. They criticised the position of the bar as being only justified by the fear of the future.

The situation seemed intractable. But some events were about to strengthen the position of the bar. In 2002, a decision of the European Court of Justice admitted that the Netherlands were right when they argued that the integrated collaboration of *avocats* and accountants in the same multidisciplinary firm was a restriction upon competition. The *Enron* affair and the disintegration of Arthur Andersen have illustrated the danger of the proximity of the activity of certification of accounts and the activity of counsel. As a consequence, a law was introduced by the French Parliament in August 2003 on the question of 'financial security.' Among many dispositions, the law forbids the professional who certifies the accounts of a firm from giving legal advice at this very society and if it belongs to a multidisciplinary practice, from certifying the accounts of a company which receives legal advice from another member of the network, a French equivalent of the Sarbanes-Oxley law.

At last, in January 2003, a judgment of the Cour de Cassation ended the litigation against the rules decided by the CNB, saying that some of the rules of the '*règlement intérieur*' result from an *ultra vires* action of the CNB and the bars.[16] It was not in the bar's power to decide that *avocats* can be members of a multidisciplinary network only if it included a regulated profession, and to forbid an *avocat* of a multidisciplinary practice network from working for a client whose accounts are controlled by another member of the network. The Cour de Cassation retained the principle that

> the fixation of ethics rules which have a mandatory/imperative character for the profession of *avocat* belongs to the competence of the government acting with respect for the principles prescribed by the law of ....

[15] The Enron affair and the disintegration of one of the Big Five illustrate the significance of that question.

[16] Arrêt du 21 Janvier 2003. The Cour de Cassation is the highest court, which can quash the rulings of the appeal courts if errors of law have been made.

The court does not say the rules are wrong; it says that these matters must be determined by the government, recalling the role of politics in the ruling of the bar (see below).

Reacting to this decision, the CNB is once again trying to formulate new rules, reaffirming the principle that must govern the *avocats* who want to belong to a multidisciplinary practice network.[17] And in February 2004 a new law was introduced, obliging *avocats* to declare their membership in a multidisciplinary network.

The other competitors who have entered the French bar following the 1990 law are Anglo-Saxon law-firms. There is no problem of multidisciplinarity, for they are lawyers and can easily adopt the rules of the French bar. But they appear as very severe competitors, because of their organisation and their size, which make them very efficient in the market, and because of their international dimension and strategy. If the Big Five mainly specialise in tax law, those firms have a much wider competence in business law, and their organisation allows them to offer their clients very sophisticated products, particularly in financial matters. They are organised on the model of the firms they work for; they have strategies of development. Their impact throughout the world allows them to support the international strategy of their clients. For the French *avocats*, whose international dimension is underdeveloped, they represent more than serious competitors. More and more these firms tend to attract French *avocats* with an important clientele in order to increase their position in the French business law market (Nallet 1999). Moreover they import to France Anglo-Saxon methods and law, for instance in drafting contracts, which also contributes to the weakening of the French bar (Nallet 1999).[18]

Even if there is always competition outside of the profession, at its borders, the most powerful competitors are now at the bar where they play quite an important role in the prosperous, general field of business law. These competitors tend to increase their influence in the French bar by their capacity to support the international and national strategy of their clients and by their capacity to attract French *avocats*. If a partial monopoly has been established, through the '*périmètre du droit*', the French bar is not the only winner.

After the integration of the *conseils juridiques* into the bar, professional authorities have been more preoccupied with the important ethical question arising from the integration of *avocats* belonging to law firms affiliated

---

[17] CNB Rapport sur la modification de l'article 16 du règlement intérieur harmonisé, adopted by the General Meeting, 5 April 2003.

[18] Such a phenomenon can be found in many parts of the world (Dezalay & Garth, 2002).

to multidisciplinary practice network than by the development of the bar.[19] But this last task was perhaps difficult, since, as it has been suggested, their mode of government does not allow them to adopt a more offensive strategy (Karpik 1999). The very question of the existence of a French *barreau d'affaire* (business bar) is raised (Karpik 1999). But unification of the profession is not at an end. There will be a third step, with a new law, to integrate in-house legal counsel.

Such a process of unification has contributed to the remarkable growth of the bar. But the increase of its size has been accompanied by quite important changes in the structure of the profession. It has also emphasised some previous divisions and created new differentiation, which can be sources of new inequalities.

2. A Segmented Profession: Old and New Divisions

There were more than 42,000 French *avocats* at the beginning of 2004.[20] The increase in size is very impressive, since they were just more than 8000 in 1971, less than 20,000 in 1990 (see Table 1).[21] Such remarkable growth

Table 1 Increase of the Profession (1971–2000)

1971	8035	100
1975	11869	148
1980	14766	184
1985	16146	201
1990	18885	235
1995	29345	365
2000	36580	455

NB: This table counts only the *avocats* participating in an insurance and pension fund (CNBF), but whose members are 96 per cent of the whole profession.

---

[19] That is what Henri Nallet, a former minister of justice, noted when he was asked by the French government to make a report on the multidisciplinary practice in France and its conciliation with *avocats'* ethics. He concluded with propositions in order to make the French bar stronger (Nallet, 1999).
[20] More precise data are available in Vauchez & Willemez, 2002; Moreau, 2002.
[21] Such growth must be balanced by both movements of unification in 1971 and 1990. But even after the last unification, growth is still more important.

of the French bar has huge consequences on its social morphology. The social structure of the bar has changed during the last 20 years, and recent transformations of the profession, combined with its growth, has emphasised the divisions. Such divisions concern for instance: geographical location of *avocats*, their way of practising, the type of clientele and practice and the legal structures of firms. Even if these problems have always existed in the structure of the French bar, they are now increasing.

2.1. The Geographical Gap: the Domination of the Paris Bar

Fifty years ago, a social scientist wrote a book about 'France and the French desert', pointing out the huge differences between Paris, the capital, and rest of France. Such a gap between Paris and the provinces still remains in respect of the bar. If French territory is divided into 181 bars, it can be shown that the actual division is between the Parisian bar against the 180 other bars!

Statistical data are very clear about the strength of such a division within the French bar: In 2000 Paris included more than 16,000 *avocats*, while the average size of a bar is 184 *avocats*. Only nine bars include more than 500 members (see Table 2). This disproportion has increased during the last two decades: the Paris bar represents more than 42 per cent of the whole French bar whereas in 1983 it represented 36 per cent (Boigeol 1988). The Parisian *École de formation du barreau* (*EFB*, bar school) comprises more than 43 per cent of law students and more than 54 per cent of avocats *stagiaires* are in Paris.[22] These data show how attractive Paris is for young lawyers.

The weight of the Paris bar is still stronger if we add the bar of Nanterre, which is just next to Paris. This bar is important for it includes former big firms of *conseils juridiques*, which are big structures, some of them being affiliated to the Big Four. This bar and the court of Nanterre deal with the legal problems of Paris business located in Paris La Défense, in the west of the capital, one of the biggest business centres in France.

Such geographical inequalities within the profession appear easy to explain. The weight of the capital is neither new nor limited to legal professions and can be seen in every realm of French social life. For historical reasons, political power and state administration are concentrated in Paris as are the head offices of most important companies. Such a concentration

---

[22] The avocat *stagiaire* (trainee *avocat*) is a newcomer within the profession: having succeeded in a competitive recruitment procedure and having finished his (her) scholarship at bar school, (s)he is working in a *cabinet*, as a sort of apprentice.

Table 2 Main Bars in France (More than 500 *Avocats*)

Bar	Number of Avocats
Paris	16,120
Lyon	1599
Nanterre	1522
Marseille	1186
Toulouse	804
Bordeaux	751
Nice	735
Lille	660
Strasbourg	539
Montpellier	533

allows the development of a large business legal market. Concerning *avocats*, Parisian predominance is very old: Paris has always pretended to represent the whole French bar (see below); moreover, 'stars' of the bar have always been Parisian. To illustrate such a long trend of Parisian predominance, excerpts of an ironic 19th-century newspaper article can be quoted:

> Parisian *avocats* would be ungrateful if they didn't celebrate railway. Thanks to it, their eloquence, which would be reserved for Justice Palace, doesn't know any limit … Favourites of eloquence's divinity are now pleading even in France's extremities. (*La Chronique parisienne*, 18 November 1858)

Surprisingly, the situation is not so different 150 years later: Parisian *avocats* are always mobile and do not hesitate to defend people everywhere in France, facilitated by a very good centralised net of rapid train links from Paris. Logically, the role of the Paris bar, or at least of some members of the Paris bar, in the process of unification of the legal profession is obvious—because of the special situation of Paris, in a centralised state, and because the development of a French business bar concerns mainly the Parisian bar.

However, such Parisian predominance must not hide another phenomenon: an increasing differentiation between some quite big bars in the provinces and the remaining local bars, which appear very small: 84 bars have less than 50 attorneys and more than 80 per cent of the bars encompass only 25 per cent of all *avocats*. The opportunity provided by openness and globalisation of the legal market has strengthened a few legal centres, which have business clientele and, accordingly, are hugely increasing in their size and in their wealth; in the same time, smaller bars located in smaller towns are more or less stagnating.

2.2 The Unequal Rise of Women

As in most countries, one major development in the profession is the increasing number of women: in 2000, 17,000 *avocats* were women, that is to say more than 46 per cent of whole bar. This growth is important compared with 1983 where women represented 31.6 per cent of the whole bar (Boigeol 1988). Moreover, the number of women rose by 26.7 per cent between 1996 and 2000, since the number of lawyers, as a whole, increased by 16 per cent. Such evolution concerns every French bar, but in a stronger way in more dynamic bars.

Such process of 'feminisation' can be found in law schools and characterises also other legal professions (overall judges, prosecutors and in-house legal counsel) (Boigeol 2003). As a consequence women are very numerous amongst *stagiaires* (women accounted for more than 60 per cent of stagiaries in 2000) and young *avocats*: they are much younger than men: on average, women *avocats* are 36.8 years old, while make *avocats* are 42.6 years old.

Even if complete data are not available it seems clear that they occupy lower positions in the profession than their male colleagues: they are more numerous among *collaborateurs*,[23] twice more according to Karpik (1995) Also, in 2000, 53.3 per cent of salaried *avocats* were women. But the most significant difference in the position of women and men can be seen in revenues: in 2000 women earned half of that earned by their male counterparts: 37,365€ women and 79,125€ men.[24] This difference is exactly the same, as Karpik pointed out, in relation to *avocats* in the early eighties. Thus, revenue inequalities between genders have altered.

To understand the gender gap, demographic explanation is quite often used: as the large entry of women into the profession is recent, women *avocats* are younger than their male colleagues, and their revenue corresponds to their youth. But such reasoning is insufficient and there must be structural reasons to explain the weakness of the remuneration of women at the bar. First, women are mainly devoted to the less prestigious activities of the bar, sole practitioners working for individuals, or as associates, or part-time work, for family reasons. Furthermore, it appears that many women, after a few years practising, give up the bar and sometimes choose another profession like in-house legal counsel in a company or magistracy (often when they think about motherhood). As interviews women *avocats* show,

---

[23] The status of *collaborateur* (*associate*) is very specific: theoretically, it is used by newcomers into the professions, who are working at the same time for two sorts of clientele: the clientele of the 'boss' (who is a partner or an individual) and his (her) own clientele: after a few years, the weight of the second clientele is more important and the *avocat* can found his (her) own firm. Actually, a general trend in the profession is the lengthening of the duration for *collaboration*, so that many *collaborateurs* can be seen as hidden salaried *avocats*.

[24] Average revenue of French *avocats* was 52,277€ in year 2000.

combining professional life and private life (that is to say having children) is particularly difficult in the bar, especially when women hold the position of partner. But the problem in France is the same as in many other countries (Sommerlad and Sanderson, 1998; Brokman, 2001).

2.3 An Increasing Fragmentation through Clienteles and Specialities

Within the traditional concept and ethic of French *avocats*, specialisation is not allowed, and every *avocat* must be available to take every sort of case involving every sort of people, as Karpik showed (Karpik 1995). This general and non-specialised activity can be seen as a political and liberal engagement (Karpik 1995; Halliday and Karpik 1997). Such a politically and public oriented activity, whose reality can be understood only through history, is also a major self-representation, which is much used by some lawyers. Karpik shows in a recent paper that this traditional ethic is disappearing, and that 'the logic of market, with its constraints, goals and ideologies, has been asserting much beyond business bar and has provoked the disruption of most of the profession' (Karpik 1999:72). Even if such differentiation by clientele is a new phenomenon, the bar is also getting increasingly segmented according to type of law and type of practice. Such fragmentation leads to the reinforcement of a hierarchy among *avocats*, firms and even bars, since differences in revenues and other resources are linked to such different clienteles. At the top of this hierarchy is the business bar, and at the bottom the criminal, divorce and social bars.[25] Between the two, there is what Karpik (1999) called the intermediate bar, ie a bar dealing partly with individuals and partly with small companies.

The business bar appears as the prestigious bar with high remuneration and prestigious clientele. French legal firms specialised in business law are located in the major bars (mainly Paris and Nanterre, but also Lyon, Marseille), their size is quite important in comparison with the average size, their firms employ many *collaborateurs* and salaried employees and their legal form is quite new: many business *avocats* groups are organised in firms, which is in France a new development following the law of 1990 in order to create law firms able to compete with Anglo-Saxon law-firms, (other group practices do not have any commercial form). In the French bar only 5 per cent of group structures are organised as a quasi commercial firm, ie with capital (which is called: *SEL: Societé d'exercice libéral,*

---

[25] According to Philip Milburn, criminal lawyering greatly depreciated in the 1980s, partly because of the transformation of criminality (Milburn, 2002).

with different applications). There is a real connection between the size of a bar, its growth and the legal form of the groups (and its revenues): for instance, in Paris, 28.4 per cent of groups of *avocats* are organised in *SEL*. The business bar appears as the modern (and the modernising) part of the French bar for it is the most European and 'globalised' section of it. Nevertheless, compared to English or American law firms, French law firms are quite small and the big structures are not numerous: only a few firms, which are specialised in business law or tax law include more than 200 lawyers: thus, in year 1998, there were eight law firms with more than 200 lawyers in France. Among them two were independent French firms and six were affiliated to a multidisciplinary network (Nallet, 1999).

In contrast to the business bar, many *avocats* working for individuals, encounter difficulties finding clients and working, especially in huge towns, in which they lack 'social capital'. Some of them join associations (for example women protecting immigration associations) or trade-unions and are not able to specialise, even if they would like to do it.[26] Moreover, some of them need legal aid to survive. Legal aid, which is called in France *Aide juridictionnelle (AJ)*, allows poor people to be defended by an *avocat* in lawsuits: the state pays for such legal defence.[27] It appears that some lawyers are mainly paid by the state and, in that way, depend on it (which is quite paradoxical for a *profession libérale*). Many *avocats* are working for *AJ*: according to a recent inquiry, 79 per cent of French *avocats* received at least once in the year 2000 fees from the State.[28] But to such a result must be added the fact that *AJ* is very concentrated: in 2000, a quarter of *avocats* receiving fees from the state received three quarters of the whole distributed fees. In the Parisian bar, 5 per cent of *avocats*' revenues are based on *AJ*, but for a few bars, *AJ* revenues exceed 50 per cent: Those bars are quite small (for example in the bar of Avennes—in northern France—which includes 31 *avocats*, 62 per cent of *avocats*' revenue comes from legal aid), and the clientele is principally made up of small criminal cases and divorce.

2.4. The World Bar in the French Bar

Anglo-Saxon and American law firms play an important role in the business market, so it is not surprising that among the foreign *avocats* practis-

---

[26] About labour lawyers, see Willemez (2003, 2005).

[27] For a general view about the logic and the mechanisms of the judicial aid, see Boigeol, 1980.

[28] Data, studied in Vauchez & Willemez, 2002, are given by *UNCA*, the institution which is distributing and controlling state funds for AJ. It must be said that such inquiry is made only on 99 bars.

ing in France—English and American are the most numerous, (respectively 128 and 151 among 1087 foreign avocats in 2002).[29] But their number is not proportional to their weight in the legal market. Anglo-Saxon or American firms include some of the most important firms in France (eg Clifford Chance, Cleary-Gotlieb, Shearman) for they hire French lawyers in their firm. Since the introduction of a unique and free market within the European Union (EU) in 1993, the number of European avocats in France is regularly increasing (35 per cent between 1996 and 2000), particularly German lawyers. But if 45 per cent came from EU, apart from United States' lawyers, many of the remaining foreign avocats are African (30 per cent); since the process of decolonisation, there are reciprocal facilities of settlement.

Even if they are difficult to observe (partly because of the lack of data, partly because of the tradition of the profession), those combined processes of openness of new markets, growth of firms' size and internationalisation have a considerable impact on the morphology of the French bar: differences and fragmentation are increasing, making gender, revenue and status inequalities more obvious within the profession.

3. Representing the *Avocats*: the Rules of a Profession

In the French bar, differentiation and the increase of inequalities are thus combined with a very confusing and complex way of defending and representing the profession. Both movements are strengthening each other, which makes the internal relationship and the relationship toward the state relationship very complicated.

3.1. The Weight of the State

A classical image of French society lies in the huge weight of the state in every part of social life. If such assertion is somehow an overstatement, it is true that the French state is very present and tries systematically to build connections between it and representative groups, through a 'neo-corporatist intermediation' (Lehmbruch and Schmitter 1979). Representatives of *avocats*, like other groups, are associated with such 'intermediation' between state and society. But such an assertion seems to be contradicting the classical view of

---

[29] Moreau, 2002.

French *avocats* as a 'free profession' (*profession libérale*), ie as autonomous and self-ruled.[30] Actually, the state intervenes within the avocats, as it is doing for the other professions (Geison 1984; Dubar-Tripier 1998).

Indeed, for the bar as for other social groups, the state is looking for group representatives which would be able to act as intermediaries and would have a special relationship with it and when such groups do not appear the state helps to create them (Offerlé 1997). Collaborative interaction between state and the numerous groups pretending to represent and defend the profession and the creation of CNB by the state are two steps of such a narrow relationship between the state and groups pretending to defend *avocats*.

The autonomy of *ordres*, which are exercising the self-government of the profession (Karpik 1988), ruling its members and judging lapses in moral and professional ethics (except for the most serious ones), is an autonomy granted by the state; in the past, some laws have entrusted such autonomy into *ordres*' care. As the following chronology shows, the state intervened at many times to internally organise the profession, and it has intervened more and more for about 20 years.

Table 3 Short Chronology of the Interaction between State and the Profession of *Avocats*

1822:	*Ordonnance* on the organisation of the profession of *avocats*: only *avocats* are able to appear in court. Disciplinary councils are established in each bar: the council elects the *bâtonnier*, who is the president of the bar.
1830:	An *ordonnance* allowing every *avocat* to take part in the election of the *bâtonnier*.
1851:	Law introducing legal aid.
1920:	*Décret* determining the activities of the profession of *avocat*, officially protecting the title of *avocat*.
1971:	Law enlarging the profession of *avocats*: unification with *avoués* and *agréés in commercial courts*.
1972:	Law reforming legal aid.
1990:	Law reforming the profession: unification of the professions of *avocat* and *conseil juridique*, and creation of the *Conseilnational des barreaux (CNB)*: national council of bars.
1991:	Law reframing legal aid: creation of *Aide juridictionnelle*.

[30] Which is the Anglo-Saxon definition of a profession. Yet, the French term 'profession' is not equivalent.

Yet, the state is still much more present than it appears in the chronology: representatives of *avocats* can easily appear as interest groups, which negotiate with agents of the state in the name of *avocats* as a whole. Such nuances are easily missed by objective observers, because they are often unrecorded, hidden or silent. Yet, reading the professions' newspapers or talking with state officers shows the extent of their activities involving the state, inter alia: conversations with ministry or other agents of the Justice department, meeting with members of Parliament, participation in consultative commissions—the whole repertory of state action of interest groups is used by *avocats'* representatives.

There are many instances of such interest group action: in the late 90s, the bar managed to prevent a law that would allow divorce without an *avocat*. Moreover, for about ten years there have been continuous negotiations between *avocats* and the state about *Aide juridictionnelle*: a new law, which extends their scope and increases the amount of funds available for *avocats*, was at last been approved by different organisations and by Parliament in 2003. Such discussions are a good example of lobbying by *avocats'* representatives, as the following from a professional newspaper, demonstrates:

> A whole night in Justice department in 1991 for organising funds' distribution with Henri Nallet [Justice ministry in 1991] ... In 2001, more than one year of work and 500 pages of a report written by CNB ... Discussions during hours and field struggles with Justice department for the beginning of year 2002 (*Avocatempo magazine* June 2002).

On this occasion, avocats did not hesitate to engage in demonstrations and strikes, using, therefore, another but complementary repertory of collective action: social movements.

3.2. Representing the Bar: a Multiplicity of Organisations

The multiplicity of organisations representing a part of the profession and the difficulty in establishing a unique stance for the whole profession does not help to make a unified and strong profession.

Competition between Corporatist Representations: Local Ordres, Conférence des Bâtonniers and CNB

Although every French liberal profession has a national representation, which takes the form of an *ordre national*, which talks with the state, represents the profession in the media and elaborates internal rules, it was not the case for *avocats* until the last decade, and today the situation is far from being simple. Officially, the profession is ruled by local *conseils de l'ordre*, which are present in each bar and are elected by every member of the bar. At the head of this council stands the *bâtonnier*, elected by the whole bar, who is the official representative of the *ordre* and of every *avocat*. The local *ordre* governs the local bar and at the same time is the (general) official voice of the profession. Indeed, one important function of the *conseil de l'ordre* and the *bâtonnier* is to ensure that *avocats* observe the rules of professional ethics and do not exceed the bounds of their competence.

Even if the representation of *avocats* is so splintered, it has been this way since the beginning of the 20th century, providing piecemeal national representation. The oldest organisation is the *Conférence des bâtonniers*, which was created in 1902 and has always been seen by the provincial bars as a counterweight to the Paris bar: officially, it offers a voice even for small bars, since every bar is equally represented in it. Thus, the president of *Conférences des bâtonniers* appears as the major representative of smaller bars.[31] Representatives of the Paris Bar are the second institution representing French *avocats*. The voice of Parisian *ordre* and of its leader is very important in the press and at the top of the state. Such weight of the Parisian *bâtonnier* can be seen as a normal consequence of the numerical importance of the Paris bar (which represents more than 40 per cent of the whole profession) and of proximity to state power. Historically it is interesting to see how the Paris bar has always pretended to represent more than itself, that is to say the profession as a whole: since the 19th century, many struggles oppose the Paris bar and Paris *bâtonnier* to other bars and other *bâtonniers*.

Finally, a last actor has appeared in the last ten years, creating thus a triangle of national representation, that is to say the *Conseil national des Barreaux (CNB)*, created by the 1990 law, ie by the state. The 80 *CNB* members are elected every five years by all *avocats*. But the very specific ballot system is revealing: *CNB* is split into two parts, called '*collège électoral*': the first part of *CNB* is composed of *ordres* members (their weight depends on their size: bigger bars have more places than smaller bars), and the second part is composed of *avocats*' unions. Last but not least, each *collège électoral* is itself divided into two constituencies, Paris and province. Such composition shows how the representation of the profession is complex and difficult: many institutions are pretending to represent and defend the French bar, and interaction between them are often conflictual and based on an unstable equilibrium that makes collective action and unified

---

[31] Such surprising weight of small entities can be seen in other institutions in France, for example in the Senate (the second legislative assembly), whose members are elected by very small counties ('*cantons*') and then represent rural France.

representative organisations more difficult to promote. However, *CNB* has three different missions: a general one, which is 'representing the profession towards administration', and two smaller activities: contributing to the reform of professional training and creating professional rules for the whole profession (which is called *Règlement intérieur unifié*). But *CNB* knows many difficulties to impose its own authority on all bars, even on such realms.

The Weight of Unions

Such multiplicity of representation and the absence of *one* professional structure that represents avocats on a national level are again strengthened by the weight and diversity of unions which represent them. Such unions are fighting together at every election (for *CNB* or for *ordres* and *bâtonnier*). There are three main unions: the first one is the *Association nationale des avocats (ANA)*, created in 1921 which combined in 1977 with a former union *(RNAF)* to form the *Confédération syndicale des avocats (CSA)*. Again after World War I, in 1922, young *avocats* created the *Union des Jeunes Avocats (UJA: Young Avocats Association)*, representing and defending *avocats* who are younger than 40. Local organisations fused in 1947 to form the *Fédération nationale des unions de jeunes avocats (FNUJA, National Federation of Young Avocats Associations)*: quickly having huge success (Le Béguec 2003), *FNUJA* is always the largest of *avocats'* unions. But the greatest innovation occurred in 1973 with the founding of the *Syndicat des avocats de France (SAF: Union of French lawyers)*, which was created by socialist, communist and even far-leftist *avocats* who specialised in criminal law, labour law or immigration law (Willemez 2003): *SAF's* birth must be understood as an echo of the creation in 1968 of a leftist union of judges and prosecutors *(syndicat de la magistrature)* and as an element in the larger phenomenon of politicisation of the whole society during the seventies, and of the growth of left-wing parties and associations. Like many unions in France, *avocats'* unions appear as having both leanings towards corporative and internal preoccupations and towards more general and social claims (like the question of general 'access to law').

All these institutions contribute towards the fragmentation of professional representation; *CNB* remains an institution at *statu nascendi*, to use a Weberian expression. It and the other representational instances are always fighting to be the 'true' defenders of the profession, even before the state and the Justice department, which is nevertheless trying to impose a unique representation which would support an administration to govern the profession.

Conclusion

Because of its history, the French bar has been forced to change quite a lot in order to adapt to and survive the internationalisation of the legal market. The unification of the different legal professions under the banner of the bar, in order to have a stronger profession and the ability to impose a monopoly, was, from the late sixties a major piece of the process of modernisation of the profession. The process of unification has been quite long, difficult and has not yet been achieved. It has revealed the importance of competitors on the law market and also the price of unification. The division of the legal profession into many professions, and the division of the bar into 181 bars with no national representation over a long period of time, the conflict between the Paris bar and the rest of the France, and other divisions conspire to make the process of unification difficult. This process and the development of the business bar have made the profession quite attractive to young law graduates. But it has also emphasised differences in the profession, such as the fragmentation of the bar according to clientele.

The future is still uncertain and even the possibility of a French business bar has been questioned (Karpik 1999). But maybe the key question is no longer about the French bar but about a European market bar?

References

ABEL R 'The politics of the market for legal services' in PA Thomas ed *Law in balance: Legal services in the eighties*, (Oxford, Martin Robertson, 1981).

ABBOTT A The system of professions: an essay on the division of expert labour, (Chicago, University of Chicago Press, 1988).

BOIGEOL A 'De l'idéologie du désintéressement chez les avocats', 1980 No 1 *Sociologie du travail.*

BOIGEOL A 'The French Bar: the difficulties of unifying a divided profession', in Richard L Abel and Philip S Lewis, *Lawyers in society,* vol. 2 *The civil law world*, (Berkeley/Los Angeles/London, University of California Press, 1988).

BOIGEOL A 'Male strategies in the Face of Feminisation of a profession; the case of the French judiciary;' in U Schultz and G Shaw, *Women in the world's legal profession*, (Oxford, Portland (Oregon), Hart publishing 2003).

BOIGEOL A, DEZALAY Y 'De l'agent d'affaires au barreau: les conseils juridiques et la construction d'un espace professionnel', 1997, *Genèses*, 27.

CHARLE C 'Pour une histoire sociale des professions juridiques. Notes pour une recherche', 1989 *Actes de la Recherche en sciences sociales*, 76–7.

CHARLE C 'La bourgeoisie de robe', 1998 *Le Mouvement social.*

DEZALAY Y *Marchands de droit*, (Paris, Fayard 1992).

DEZALAY Y, GARTH B *The Internationalisation of Palace Wars*, (University of Chicago Press, 2002).

DUBAR C, TRIPIER P *Sociologie des Professions*, (Paris, Armand-Colin, 1998).

GEISON GL *Professions and the French State: 1700–1900*, (Philadelphia, University of Pennsylvania Press, 1984).

HYEST J-J Quels métiers pour quelle justice ? Mission d'information sur l'évolution des métiers de justice, Les rapports du Sénat 2002.

ISRAËL L 'La résistance dans les milieux judiciaires. Action collective et identités professionnelles'. 2001 *Genèses*, 49.

ISRAËL L *Robes Noires, Années Sombres*, (Paris, Fayard, 2005).

KARPIK L 'Lawyers and Politics in France, 1814–1950: The State, the Market and the Public', 1988 *Law and Social Inquiry*, vol. 13(4), 707–36.

KARPIK L *Les avocats, entre l'Etat, le public et le marché*, (Paris NRF, 1995). Translated in english in 1999.

KARPIK L 'Avocats: renouveau et crise', 1999, No 1 *Justices*, 67–82.

LARSON M *The Rise of Professionalism. A Sociological Analysis*, (Berkeley, University Of California Press, 1977).

Le Béguec G *La République des avocats*, (Paris, Armand-Colin, 2003).

LEHMBRUCH G, SCHMITTER P *Patterns of Corporatist Policy-Making*, (London, Sage, 1982).

MIQUEL P *Poincaré*, (Paris, Arteme Fayard 1961).

MILBURN P La défense pénale: une relation professionnelle, 1991 PhD university Paris 8.

MILBURN P 'Les avocats', in Mucchielli L, Robert P, *Crime et sécurité: l'état des savoirs*, (Paris, La Découverte, 2002).

MOREAU C Statistique sur la profession d'avocat, 2004 Ministère de la Justice.

NALLET H Les réseaux pluridisciplinaires et les professions du droit. Rapport au Premier ministre, (Paris, La documentation française, 1999).

OFFERLÉ M *Sociologie des groupes d'intérêts*, (Paris, Montchrestien, 1997).

SOMERLAD H, Sanderson P Gender, Choice and Commitment. Women solicitors in England and Wales and the struggle for equal status, (Aldershot, Ashgate-Dartmouth, 1998).

SOULEZ-LARIVIÈRE D La réforme des professions juridiques et judiciaires. 20 propositions, Rapport au bâtonnier du barreau de Paris 1988.

VAUCHEZ A, Willemez L Contribution à la connaissance statistique de la profession d'avocat, Research Report for the CNB 2002.

WILLEMEZ L Des avocats en politique. Contribution à une socio-histoire de la profession politique en France, Ph. D, University Paris 1, 2000.

WILLEMEZ L 'A Political-Professional Commitment.' French Workers' and Unions' Lawyers as Cause Lawyers in Sarat A and Scheingold S (eds) The World's Cause Lawyers Make: Structure and Agency in Legal Practice (Stanford, Stanford University Press, 2005).

WILLEMEZ L 'Engagement professionnel et fidelités militantes: les avocats travaillistes dans la défense judiciaire des salariés', *Politix*, vol. 16, no 62, 2003, 145–64).

4

Judges and Lawyers in the Netherlands—An Overview from 1970 till 2000

FRED J BRUINSMA

Summary

In a civil law country like the Netherlands three legal professions can be distinguished: judges, attorneys and notaries. This chapter focuses on the developments in these three legal professions in the period 1970–2000. In comparison with the surrounding countries the Netherlands is relatively non-legalistic. However, a process of legalisation (more attorneys and more cases in court) began in the mid 1970s, and accelerated at the end of the 1980s. Moreover, European integration has further undermined the Dutch legal culture of informal pragmatism since the 1990s. Despite resistance, the judicial reform of restructuring the court system and regulatory reforms regarding the lawyering professions (attorneys and notaries) have been implemented. The number of women has gradually grown in the three legal professions, thanks to the fact that there are more female than male law students nowadays.

1. Introduction

In the Anglo-American common law context the word 'lawyers' refers to all who have been admitted to the Bar. On the European continent by 'jurists' we mean all those who hold a law degree. Only one third of Dutch jurists are employed as judges, attorneys and notaries. Another third of law graduates are employed in the non-profit sector as civil servants in government or publicly financed agencies, or as instructors at universities and other higher education institutions. A final third of the law graduates will find employment in the private sector, in business, banking, and insurance companies. Table 1 shows the distribution of jurists throughout the various sectors of work in three different years of the last century.

Table 1 Distribution of Jurists

Year	Legal Professions	Public Sector	Higher Education	Private Sector	Total Number
1930	51%	15%	4%	29%	4,242
1970	30%	28%	12%	32%	14,616
1994	35%	25%	10%	30%	31,000

1.1 Secondary Socialisation in Law Faculties

As various as their work settings might be, all law graduates share a common history in a law faculty. Like in other civil law countries, legal education in the Netherlands is a privilege of university faculties. Other educational institutions offer courses in law, but their graduates lack the so-called 'effectus civilis', a statutory prerequisite for becoming a member of any of the three legal professions.[1] There are law faculties at the universities of Amsterdam (two universities), Groningen, Leyden, Maastricht, Nijmegen, Rotterdam, Tilburg, and Utrecht. In the academic year 2000–01 27,342 law students were enrolled (56 per cent female), and 3,360 took their law degree. One can also become a 'mr' at the Open University for distance learning, but most of its students take only one or a few specialised courses.

Considering their activities, most jurists working in the public or private sector could just as well have chosen any other study. Law is regarded as a very general subject. According to the German sociologist Dahrendorf (1973:294–309) 'the subject of law merely functions as an occasion for a more important social process', namely secondary socialisation for managing functions in society. With respect to the social background of the students who started their study in 1994 the CBS (Central Bureau of Statistics) reported that law and medicine are the most elitist studies. Two thirds of law students had highly educated parents. Only one out of ten had poorly educated parents as against, for example, one out of five students in economics. A similar background is the perfect condition for secondary socialisation, helped by the fact that the study of law is not very demanding. The

---

[1] A law graduate bears the title of 'master of law', shortened as 'mr' (so a *mr* might be woman who graduated in law).

study of law offers a lot of opportunities to exercise social skills outside class and in glorifying the law practise the lecturers, who are quite often part time practitioners themselves, reinforce the atheoretical and practical attitudes of law students. As a consequence the hidden agenda of the study of law might be more important than the official curriculum.

The official curriculum in continental Europe is geared towards understanding the system; it is not case- and client-oriented as in common law countries. The main areas of law—civil law, criminal law, constitutional and administrative law, and international and European Law, in their substantive and procedural aspects—are traditionally taught as systems of codified rules, principles and case law. As there are no specialised law schools, law faculties compare with the American undergraduate and graduate colleges in one and the same institution, with a focus on law from the very beginning. Students are on average 18 years old when they start, and 23 years old when they graduate. Training at the law faculties is rudimentary. Bar and Bench fill the gaps by in-service training programmes for their young recruits.

> Adoption of a system is essentially based on two main cycles, undergraduate and graduate. Access to the second cycle shall require successful completion of first cycle studies, lasting a minimum of three years. The degree awarded after the first cycle shall also be relevant to the European labour market as an appropriate level of qualification. The second cycle shall lead to the master and/or doctorate degree as in many European countries.

This is a quote from the Declaration of Bologna, as agreed upon by the ministers of Education from the different member states of the European Union in June 1999. It came out of the blue, and its implications are not fully understood yet. How can a bachelor degree in Dutch law be relevant to the European labour market? Most law faculties decided that they would ignore the content of the Declaration and would merely pay lipservice to it by some organisational reshuffling of the curriculum. It remains to be seen whether higher education institutions, rather than universities, dare to provoke the legal establishment of the law faculties by offering a three-year undergraduate legal education. If so, it will put an end to the double talk of law faculties: academic pretensions and glorification of law practise simultaneously.

1.2 The Dutch Law Machine Compared

If one considers the official court system as a machinery dealing with cases, the input in civil law suits has more than quadrupled in the time period 1965–1995, and the number of criminal sentences in serious offences has more than doubled whilst the population has increased only slightly (Table 1.2.1, indexed at 1965).

Table 1.2.1 Cases in Court in relation to Population

Year	Civil Law Suits (x1000)		Criminal Sentences (x1000)		Population (1,000,000)	
1965	113	(100)	28	(100)	12,212	(100)
1970	137	(121)	30	(107)	12,958	(106)
1975	174	(154)	30	(107)	13,599	(111)
1980	209	(185)	32	(114)	14,091	(115)
1985	280	(248)	41	(146)	14,454	(118)
1990	327	(289)	43	(154)	14,893	(121)
1995	501	(443)	62	(221)	15,424	(126)

Attorneys being the intermediaries between the population and the court system, the attorney rate, ie the number of attorneys per 100,000 of the population is a good indicator of legalisation in society (Table 1.2.2). The growth in numbers, in absolute terms and per 100,000 inhabitants, is striking. From the 1900s till the early 1970s the yearly number of attorneys registered with the Dutch Bar Association had shown a gradual growth, concomitant with the population. Since the mid 1970s however, the number of attorneys has grown out of proportion with the population and quadrupled as have civil law suits.

A process of legalisation has taken hold of the Netherlands since the mid 1970s, but the relative number of attorneys and judges per 100,000 inhabitants is still lagging behind neighbouring German Land Northrhine-Westphalia to the east and Belgium to the south (Table 1.2.3).

Table 1.2.2 Number and Rate of Attorneys

Year	Absolute Number	Rate per 100,000 Inhabitants
1900	907	17.7
1947	1509	15.7
1960	1946	16.5
1970	2063	15.9
1975	2580	20.0
1980	3726	26.4
1985	4975	34.3
1990	6368	42.4
1995	8264	51.6
2000	11,033	69.5

Table 1.2.3 Attorneys and Judges per 100,000 of the Population (1995)

	Attorneys	Judges
Netherlands	52	10
Northrhine-Westphalia	102	29
Belgium	115	20

In a circle of less than 300 kilometers around the point where Germany, Belgium, and the Netherlands meet ('drielandenpunt')—all three civil law countries and members of the European Union (EU)—such differences are not to be expected. On the contrary, it is a reasonable assumption that the baseline of legal problems[2] in the Netherlands (41,000 square kilometers, 16 million inhabitants in 2000) should be the same as in neighbouring German state Northrhine-Westphalia (34,000 square kilometers, 18 million inhabitants in 2000) and in Belgium (30,000 square kilometers, 10 million inhabitants in 2000). Blankenburg, a German legal sociologist working in the Netherlands, arrived at the conclusion that the Dutch legal system has an extraordinary rich infrastructure of out-of-court remedies (1998).

Four structural devices can be discerned in the Dutch legal system, ie diversion, dual systems, pre-trial filters, and complementary roles.

—Diversion means that the official court system is bypassed. Product arbitration is a good example. The oldest (from 1907 onwards) and most

---

[2] The baseline of legal problems is affected by the socio-economic context (BNP, demography, divorce rate, traffic density, house ownership, labor market and the number of welfare recipients, etc) and is the starting point for the process of 'naming, blaming, and claiming', (Felstiner ao, 1980).

important in the Netherlands is the Arbitration Council in Construction Disputes (Raad van Arbitrage voor de Bouw). Most of its arbitrators have a technical background, and they decide on the technical merits of the case. In almost all standard contracts for construction projects conflicts are referred to this council, thus precluding the official courts from dealing with these issues. Similar specialised arbitration boards exist in a number of other sectors in the Dutch economy, such as the steel industry, bulb growing and professional soccer. Commercial arbitration in the Netherlands forms an externalised system of private justice, while the German tradition tends to internalise as much as possible of the justice function in the courts.

—Dual systems offer the plaintiff two remedies. Employers in the Netherlands for example have a choice between a court and an administrative procedure if they wish to dismiss employees. The administrative procedure is mainly used for redundancy of groups of employees, whereas the court procedure is used for the wrongdoings of individual employees, but on paper they are substitutes. During the 1990s the share of court procedures has remarkably increased: in 1990 62,241 administrative procedures and 10,605 court cases were filed, compared to 43,000 administrative procedures and 45,000 court cases in the time period October 1997–October 1999. This shift can partly be explained by economic growth, making the administrative agency critical, and partly by the policy guidelines the Association of Local Court Judges (Kring van kantonrechters) announced. As a consequence an employer knows the price of a dismissal in advance nowadays. Labour law belongs to the competence of the 'kantonrechter', a section within the district court. No special courts as in Germany are needed.

—Disputes about rent increases provide a good example of a very effective pre-trial filter. Before being admitted to court with a complaint about a rent increase, a Dutch tenant has to file his protest with a landlord-tenant committee. The committee consists of a law graduate chair, and two representatives of the tenants' union and the housing corporations respectively. An intricate checklist is at the basis of decision-making. The committee's decision becomes binding after two months; in the meantime both parties are free to take their case to court. Only a few per cent do so, however; hence the filter keeps these cases out of court. The landlord-tenant committees in Germany do not have nationwide coverage as in the Netherlands.

—Debt collection accounts for the biggest part of the civil caseload in both countries. Contrary to their German colleagues, bailiffs in the Netherlands can combine a business as private collector with the public function of summoning a debtor to court and eventually executing a legal title (complementary roles). They use the judicial procedure as a last resort. In threatening court action, they have an effective means of negotiating terms of payment directly with debtors.

The rich infrastructure of the Dutch legal system is supported by an internal legal culture of informal pragmatism.[3] Dahrendorf connects a common training in civil law, a thrust in the state and the absence of a liberal tradition in order to arrive at the following conclusion for German society: 'It is clearly no accident that many decisions made by leaders of politics, business, and other spheres of German society are inspired by a kind of authoritarian legalism: those in power believe themselves to be experts for almost all decisions, and they often justify such presumed expertise by reference to the 'letter of the law' (oc: 307). In Dutch informal pragmatism the letter of the law is not taken for granted. A basic tenet of administrators and legal professionals is that rules should only be applied if this serves some goal, not merely for their own sake. Dutch policy-makers, civil servants and legal practitioners are very concerned about the adverse effects of too strict a rule enforcement, such as black markets, deviant sub-cultures and risks to public health. This holds true for soft drugs, prostitution, euthanasia *e tutti quanti* foreigners associate Holland with, but also for less conspicuous topics such as civil justice.

The legal system in the Netherlands is permeated with informal procedures and a corresponding legal culture supports informal practices within and outside the formal court system. The distinction between formal and informal procedures may make sense in a legal culture of (German) authoritarian legalism or (Anglo-Saxon) adversarial legalism (Kagan 2001), but it does not make sense in the Dutch legal culture of informal pragmatism. With an eye on the many quasi courts ADR Dutch style is *additional* dispute resolution, and it is *alternative* dispute resolution with an eye to the informal practices in and outside court. Take for example the 'kort geding' —even among the population at large, a well-known summary proceeding before a senior judge. It is included in all textbooks on civil procedure because it is part of the formal court system, but it allows an extent of judiciary discretion corresponding with ADR. An English critic, and a true believer in his own legal culture of adversarial legalism, writes about the 'kort geding':

---

[3] While external legal culture refers to the legal consciousness of the people at large, internal legal culture refers to the opinions about law among the legal professionals, 'the values, ideologies and principles of lawyers, judges and others who work within the magic circle of the legal system' (Friedman, 1975, p 194).

What is offered is an informal and inexpensive procedure where strict rules of evidence are not observed, enabling a quick but necessarily superficial decision. The procedure in *kort geding* is mostly of a rapid and informal manner which does not leave any room for a detailed and thorough examination of the facts. At best, all that can be expected is 'quick justice', without necessarily any proper regard to the merits of the parties' respective legal positions. At worst, one can easily find oneself on the receiving end of a truly perverse judgment which is not well balanced or considered. (Gaucci 1998)

The revised Act on Civil Procedure (2002) silenced foreign critics by means of a temporary and preliminary injunction procedure for intellectual property rights, and at the same time protected Dutch practice, contrary to the letter of the law, of considering a decision in 'kort geding' final and binding.

The foregoing is meant to inform the reader of the context of the legal professions in the Netherlands. The legal system offers various formal and informal procedures and legal practitioners are affected by a legal culture of informal pragmatism. The rest of the world, starting with the European Union, is critical, and these outside influences have occasioned some fundamental changes, or at least a discussion about the Dutch system. The Netherlands is becoming less and less a special case, less the Japan of the West that it used to be.

2. The Court System and the Judiciary

The formal court system in civil and criminal cases has three tiers. They provide the civil litigant with two different courts of first instance: a section within the district courts (*kantonsector*) hears small claims (less than 5000€) and civil cases in specific areas of law like rental and labour law; the (19) district courts (*rechtbanken*) hear larger claims (more than 5000€) and most family matters. Parties may appear without representation before the *kantongerecht*, while the *rechtbank* and all higher courts require representation by an attorney. In criminal cases the kantongerecht hears cases of petty infraction (mostly traffic offences) by a single judge, misdemeanours are decided by a single judge of the district court (*politierechter*) and felonies by a full bench of three judges. In previous times district courts consisted mostly of a full bench of three judges, but due to financial constraints, these days a single judge is more common. In criminal cases prosecutors have the prerogative of accusation, and they survey the enforcement of penal sentences. As prosecutors do not sit on the Bench, they are called the 'standing' part of the judiciary.

To each court of first instance there is an appeal instance of three judges, which reconsiders the case. There are five courts of appeal (*gerechtshof* in Amsterdam, The Hague, Arnhem, Den Bosch and Leeuwarden), which only handle appeals. Uniformity in the interpretation of the law is to be guarded by the Supreme Court (*Hoge Raad*). A full bench here consists of five judges, although most decisions are taken by a bench of three. As in the French system of *cassation*, jurisdiction of the Supreme Court is restricted to questions of law: the Supreme Court has to take for granted the facts as they have been ascertained by the trial courts in first instance and in appeal. Access to the Supreme Court is, until now, guaranteed for all kinds of cases. The growing caseload has been met with a pragmatic article in the Act on the Judicial Organisation. It permits the Supreme Court to dismiss cases without giving reasons. The percentage of rejections without further argumentation ranges from about 10 per cent in civil cases to 40 per cent in criminal cases. After the planned integration into the judicial pyramid of the specialised and now supreme courts in their area of law the Supreme Court will probably need the Anglo-Saxon device of *certiorari* or leave to appeal.

Since the 1990s a major restructuring of the Dutch court system is put into effect, on the basis of a package deal in 1983 between the Ministry of Justice and the Dutch Association of Judges (*Nederlandse Vereniging voor Rechtspraak*). In return for more judicial personnel the judges promised a more efficient and professional judiciary. The restructuring process has taken place in three stages. In the first stage the social security tribunals[4] merged with the district courts. The district courts developed administrative chambers in 1994, which are now the first instance following a complaint procedure with the administrative body that made the original decision. The second stage concerned the integration in 2002 of the front-line judiciary (*kantonrechters*) into the district courts. Thanks to effective lobbying, the original aim of full integration was not pursued, but it remains to be seen whether the *kantonrechters* will enjoy the same independent posture in the form of a special sector within the district courts. The third and final stage is now underway. A buffer between the Ministry of Justice, which is the body responsible for the budget, and the independent judiciary, which is with respect to means and (wo)manpower at the receiving end, has been established (*Raad voor de Rechtspraak,* Council for

---

[4] Judicial review of matters of social security started in 1902, when 10 tribunals of first instance (*Raden van Beroep*) were set up, supervised by an appeal court (*Centrale Raad van Beroep*). In each *Raad van Beroep* the professional judge, who was the chairman, was assisted by two lay judges, namely one representative on behalf of the employers and one representative on behalf of the employees. Research revealed that the lay judges liked their honorary job, but did not contribute much.

the Judiciary, since 2002). For no good reason the Supreme Court did not want to become involved, eg as a dual presidency. The issue at the moment of writing is what will happen to the appeal courts in special areas of administrative law. A detached view points in the direction of integration into the judicial pyramid. It would mean a position subordinate to the Supreme Court, an outcome not appreciated by the *Centrale Raad van Beroep,* now having a final say in social security matters, the *College van Beroep voor het Bedrijfsleven* with a final say in matters of economic regulation, and the *Raad van State* with a final say in all other administrative matters.[5]

2.1 A 'Bourgeois' Judiciary

There are two ways to become a judge in the Netherlands. Having completed a law degree, graduates may apply for the six-year in-service training at the magistrate's academy for judges and prosecutors. The second, and a route more often chosen, is to apply, after at least six years of law practise outside the Bench (so-called 'buitenstaanders', outsiders). One of the virtues of the Dutch judiciary is that it does not build exclusively on career judges, and with an eye to the figures, less and less so. Whereas in 1974 57 per cent of the judges had been at the magistrate's academy, in 1986 the percentage of career judges had decreased to 45 per cent, and it further decreased to a mere 27 per cent in 2001. Table 2.1.1 gives an overview of the previous work setting of the judges in percentages (including the job experiences outside the Bench of law graduates at the magistrate's academy).

Table 2.1.1 Previous Work Setting of Judges (percentages)

	1974	1986	2001
Law Firms	34	32	32
Government	19	16	35
Higher Education	7	12	13
Private Sector	10	13	8
Other	4	4	0
None	26	23	12

[5] Tax cases have their own route, starting with a complaint procedure with the Internal Revenue Service, continuing with a first instance at one of the courts of appeal, and ending with a final recourse to the Supreme Court. The proposal is to assign the first instance to the district courts, with a right of appeal to the courts of appeal.

The selection procedure for outsiders became professional in 1996 when a private assessment centre started to advise upon the suitability of the candidates. In 2000, the magistrate's academy revised its selection procedure along the outsider's model. Among the competencies tested are the ability to express oneself orally and on paper, the ability to listen carefully and to make accurate decisions, sensitivity, self-confidence and persuasiveness. Partly because of the restricted capacity (two classes per year) only 20 per cent of applicants for the magistrate's academy are selected, as against 65 per cent of outsiders. As a result a growing share of outsiders explains the increase in the total number of judges (from 778 in 1990 to 1640 in 2000). This development has influenced the age and gender distribution of the judiciary: nine out of ten of the judges are under 40 years of age, and three out of four female judges work at district court level.[6] Table 2.1.2 sets out the distribution of women at three levels of the judicial system, the so called 'glass ceiling' women look at from below.

Table 2.1.2 Female Judges at Three Levels

	1974		1986		1990		2000	
	n	%	n	%	n	%	n	%
Top	1	1.3	3	3.5	5	5.5	46	15
Middle	4	1.4	44	9.4	81	14.5	232	30
Basis	31	11.0	95	25.1	112	27.8	520	50

The ascendancy of women has halted the democratisation in social background and has strengthened the bourgeois outlook of the judiciary in the Netherlands. Most judges, and female judges even more than male judges, grew up in a traditional upper middle class Dutch family. A survey in 2001 confirmed the findings of a survey ten years earlier with respect to civil state (three-quarters of judges are married compared to half of the adult population), 70 per cent subscribe to a highbrow liberal newspaper (*NRC-Handelsblad*), and have moderate political preferences. The judiciary being the backbone of the rule of law, it is reassuring that the judiciary in the Netherlands is middle-of-the-road. However, a heated debate about the virtual absence of ethnic minorities followed the refusal, in 2001, of a district court to employ as a law clerk a law student who refused to remove her Islamic headscarf during sessions.

[6] The first function is at the basis of the district court level, and the function of *kantonrechter* is at the middle level.

2.2 The Subordinate Position of the Prosecution Services

During the 1990s two instances made clear that prosecutors are not as independent as the name 'standing magistrates' suggests.

In 1996 a particular prosecutor had disciplinary action taken against him because he refused to prosecute a case of euthanasia as the Minister of Justice, in her wish for case law, had ordered. A discussion about discretionary freedom of the prosecution versus the prosecution as a branch of government ensued. It ended in a revised paragraph in the Act on the organisation of the judiciary with an explicit opening for mandatory instructions in specific cases.

In 1998 the heads of prosecution services were forced to acknowledge their subordinate position to the Minister of Justice. One of the five chief prosecutors, who had recently formed a strong supervisory body to correct grass-roots independence, was seen to have a conflicting interest. Backed by the chairman he threatened to sue the Minister of Justice by way of injunction in order to postpone the publication of the report of an investigation. At a weekly press conference, the Prime Minister voiced his indignation saying that the '*crème de la crème* of the rule of law shouldn't behave so childishly'. After some political turmoil the chairman was forced to resign when the minister declared that she no longer trusted him.

At the end of the magistrate's academy one has to choose between the standing and the sitting magistracy, and there is a separate selection procedure for outsiders interested in a career as prosecutor. The overall gender distribution in 2000 among prosecutors is 60 per cent male (316) and 40 per cent female (214), but at district court level it is fifty:fifty (161 male and 167 female prosecutors).[7] It happens therefore that hard-headed male criminals are tried by a female prosecutor and three women judges.

2.3 Judges in the Supreme Court

A special procedure applies for nominations to the Supreme Court (*Hoge Raad*). The Supreme Court itself recommends six candidates to Parliament, Parliament submits three candidates in preferential order for appointment to the Crown, and the Crown nominates one of them.

Since 1838 Parliament's nomination policy mirrors political trends, and testifies to what holds Dutch society together: the principles of proportional

---

[7] At the intermediate level 73% (115) of the prosecutors is male and 27% female (43); at the top the gender distribution is skewed even more: 40 male prosecutors and only 4 female prosecutors.

representation and minority participation. In the first period (from 1838 to 1925) Members of Parliament who had been elected under a district majority system, served the interests of their constituencies. Until 1848 a constitutional provision provided that judges in the Supreme Court should be recruited as far as possible from all the provinces, thus disclosing the main concern in those times: the predominance of jurists living in the west of the Netherlands. Parliament frequently intervened to safeguard regional representation. In 1917 the electoral system was changed to proportional representation. Since then the Supreme Court has succeeded in achieving non-interference by Parliament by anticipating the prevailing trend. In the second period (1917–1967) the trend was religious affiliation. A minimum of one-fifth of all seats was reserved for Roman-Catholics; 12 Roman-Catholics were appointed in this way. The nomination of a Protestant in a well-known Catholic seat in 1967 clearly marked the end of this second period.

The appointment of a member of the under-represented Labour Party in 1955 was the last time Parliament intervened effectively. Since 1955 Parliament and the Supreme Court have been involved in symbolic politics. In 1975 Parliament directed the Supreme Court to pay more attention to the under-representation of women by promoting a woman from the sixth position on the recommendation list to the second position on the submission list. As number one will be appointed, this was nothing more than a gesture. In 1991, a right-wing representative of the Christian Democrat party criticised lenient sentencing in criminal cases and attributed this to a supposed majority of left-wing liberals in the judiciary in general and in the Supreme Court in particular. Although his argument was rather confused,[8] the aftermath shattered the hope of many dignified jurists on their way to the Supreme Court, that Parliament would renounce her powers in the nomination procedure. Candidates for the Supreme Court now have to present a 'curriculum vitae' to Parliament, thus making it less of a 'rubber

Table 2.3 Occupation before Nomination to the Supreme Court (Percentages)

	1838	1839–1887	1968–1987	2000
Judges	87	65	46	65
Attorneys	6	10	22	19
Prosecutors	6	10	2	3
Academics	0	2	29	13
Politics/administration	0	13	0	0
	n=16	n=48	n=45	n=31

[8] The Supreme Courts deals only with issues of law, and refers the case if the trial court's decision is found to be unlawful.

stamp' procedure than it was. It will be interesting to see what happens when the first black person appears on the recommendation list.

Table 2.3 shows occupations before nomination to the Supreme Court. The share of former judges has decreased from about three-quarters in the nineteenth century to about half since the Second World War, but in the recent past a reverse tendency can be seen. The share of academics among the newly nominated judges increased in the period 1968–1987 to 29 per cent. Most former law professors are no eggheads, however. They have been practising lawyers, and when lecturing at the university they usually served as part-time, substitute judges.[9] The change in composition reflects the changing role of the Supreme Court. In the nineteenth century the Supreme Court was the highest court in individual cases supervising the application of laws by the lower courts, while nowadays the Court's case law is also seen as another source of legal development in addition to statutory legislation.[10] For example, one of the judges in the civil chamber had been assigned by the government to prepare the way for a fundamental revision of the Civil Code (enacted in 1992). In the safe expectation that it would one day be the law, the Supreme Court, by means of a so-called anticipatory interpretation, was already applying parts of the new Code pending parliamentary approval. Anticipatory interpretation illustrates informal pragmatism at the highest level, but an even better example can be found in the haphazard, and still incomplete system of comprehensive and independent judicial review.

2.4 The Hybrid Construction of the Council of State

The traditional and reluctant point of view as to legal remedies against administrative decisions has been nicely put into words by professor Struycken, a well-known academic authority in the first half of the twentieth century: in a democracy like the Netherlands there was no need for judicial review by—essentially—outsiders to the administration. Such a review would be built upon the wrong assumption of contrasting interests between the civil service and the private citizen. Injustice should be adequately corrected via reconsideration within the administration.

[9] Substitute judges, who have their main occupation elsewhere, occasionally serve on the bench as fully fledged judges. The phenomenon survived in an adapted version despite protests about conflicting interests (attorneys as substitute judges). It is an excellent example of informal pragmatism: substitute judges are cheap and flexible, so one tried to find a way to beg the problem of conflicting interests.
[10] The recent drop to 13% may be interpreted as reflecting the diminishing importance of the Supreme Court *vis à vis* the European Courts in Luxembourg and Strasbourg. Moreover, the Supreme Court is no longer considered the top of the bill: three judges and one attorney-general resigned to take another job.

The first procedure for a (non-judicial) review of administration was institutionalised with the Crown appeal in 1861. A division of the State Council,[11] the Administrative Disputes Division (*Afdeling Geschillen van Bestuur*), was formed to advise the Crown as to how to react to complaints against his Majesty's government. One could only appeal to the Crown if the specific Act of Parliament on which the administrative decision in dispute was based, explicitly mentioned this remedy. Crown appeal was mentioned in 135 Acts of Parliament, involving 500 different administrative decisions. If the Crown wished to deviate from the advice given, it had to follow a procedure so laborious it was to be avoided, and therefore it would seek to compromise. This pragmatic solution could not satisfy the European Court of Human Rights, however. It declared the Crown appeal at variance with article 6 of the European Convention: 'The Administrative Disputes Division of the Council of State tenders only an advice. Admittedly, that advice is—as happened on the present occasion—followed in the great majority of cases, but this is only a practice of no binding force, from which the Crown can depart at any moment' (ECHR 23/10/1985). Though this verdict was anticipated, mild panic took hold of the higher circles of the administration and the State Council. There was a general feeling that the Crown appeal had been victimised on the grounds of overly legal dogmatic reasoning. In anticipation of a large-scale restructuring of the judiciary, the State Council prepared its own temporary and reactive legislation, in which it promoted the Administrative Disputes Division to independence.

In the meantime a complaints procedure had been introduced in 1976 for decisions of all administrative bodies (at local, provincial and central level) with appeal to the Council of State. The Judicial Division (*Afdeling Rechtspraak*) of the Council was established as an independent court, judging in first and last instance, alongside the advisory review of the Crown Appeal Division. The two branches developed their own style of decision-making: traditional administrative reconsideration and modern judicial review did not sit comfortably together. The Judicial Division reviewed administrative decisions according to their legal nature, whereas the Crown Appeal Division could go further by evaluating broader policy considerations. Both Divisions had their own legally qualified staff. 1993 marked the end of the peculiar Dutch mix of judicial review and policy assessment. A new Act (*Algemene wet Bestuursrecht*) assigned the first instance to administrative chambers of the district courts, while the State Council functions as court of appeal (*Afdeling Bestuursrechtspraak*). For the time being the

---

[11] The State Council (*Raad van State*) has been the Crown's main mandatory advice body for all public affairs since 1531. The council advises on all laws and by-laws, for example. State councillors are nominated with regard to their party membership.

advisory function remained intact, although another decision of the ECHR[12] required the *Raad van State* to erect Chinese walls between State Councillors in their advisory function and State Councillors in their judicial function. In its annual report of 2000, the State Council praised the mix of advising and judging, but the ECHR was critical:

> The Court is not as confident as the Government were in their statement during the parliamentary budgetary discussions in 2000 that these arrangements are such to ensure that in all appeals coming before it the Administrative Jurisdiction Division constitutes an 'impartial tribunal' for the purposes of Article 6, § 1 of the Convention. It is not, however, the task of the Court to rule in the abstract on the compatibility of the Netherlands system in this respect with the Convention (06/05/2003, in *Kleyn ao v the Netherlands*).

In the absence of a convincing rationale the Council of State muddles through. Meanwhile law practitioners complain about the inexpert handling of cases by State Councillors who are elderly statesmen, not necessarily jurists. In accordance with the traditional practice a former Minister of Defense and not a jurist became appointed as a State Councillor in 1999. Although the nomination procedure does not involve Parliament – in contrast to the nomination procedure for the Supreme Court – State Councillors are nominated with regard to their political affiliation. In the awareness that the Head of State is formally the president, and that many former politicians have found a haven in the Council of State, criticism is somewhat subdued.

3. Practising Lawyers

Dutch law recognises[13] three helping professions, namely attorneys, notaries and bailiffs. Attorneys and notaries are university educated whereas bailiffs have completed a three-year professional training. All three are private professions in the sense that they derive their income from the market, but at the same time they enjoy professional privileges because their services are also in the public interest. The end result is a rather confusing mix of professional interests, market incentives and state regulation. It creates a dilemma for policy-makers: on the one hand legal professions need to be trusted, since serving the public interest there is no real alterna-

---

[12] In the Procola verdict (ECHR 28–9–1995) Luxembourg was found to violate article 6 of the Convention because four of the five state councillors judged on the basis of a by-law they had advised on in an earlier stage.

[13] Legal advice is not restricted to lawyers or even jurists, as the law shops run by law students and the advices given by banking personnel make clear.

tive to professional privileges and self regulatory powers, but on the other hand they cannot be trusted because they are suspected of putting their own professional interests first.

3.1 Overview

The Act on attorneys at law (*Advocatenwet*) dates from 1952. From the very beginning it empowered the professional association (*Nederlandse Orde van Advocaten, NOvA*) to self regulate. One of these self-made rules was at stake in a preliminary ruling of the European Court of Justice (ECJ).[14] Reasoning on the basis of incompatible interests between the different professions the ECJ upheld the proscription on profit sharing between law and accounting firms, but it made clear that a professional body would be considered an association of undertakings, and consequently not exempt from anti-trust law (19 February 2002, C 309/99). Later in the year the CBBB (Council of the Bars and Law Societies of the European Union) advised the national bar associations to review their bylaws in the light of this ruling.

In a civil-law country one speaks of a Latin-type notary office, which means that notaries are not merely private consultants, but civil servants as well. For many transactions, such as the transfer of property, the establishment of corporate personality, drafting of wills and prenuptial agreements, a notary-authorised certificate is needed. In return for their allegedly impartial public service the number of notary offices was restricted and tariffs for the various certificates were fixed. However, the new Notary Act of 1999, which replaced the one of 1842, was inspired by a neo-liberal programme of regulatory reform. It has made serious inroads in the Latin-type of a notary office. The powers to self-regulate the professional association (*Koninklijke Notariële Beroepsorganisatie, KNB*) started to have in 1999 can be considered to be the consolation prize for the loss of some privileges.

On paper bailiffs are primarily court officials who deliver summonses and execute judicial sentences in civil cases. They have been criticised for neglecting their public duties in favour of the more profitable private practice of debt collection. The bailiff profession was upgraded in a new Act of 2001. Since then the professional association (*Koninklijke Beroepsorganisatie van Gerechtsdeurwaarders, KBvG*) has had powers to self-regulate. As they are a profession of para-legals they are treated here as a reference group.

Some key figures relating to the three legal professions are presented in Table 3.1.

---

[14] Art 177 of the EC Treaty is a preliminary reference procedure: a court in any member state of the EU may invoke the help of the ECJ for interpretation problems of EU law.

Table 3.1   Key Figures about Attorneys, Notaries and Bailiffs in 1996

	Attorneys	*Notaries*	*Bailiffs*
Net turnover (in million €)	1.085€	6591€	1211€
(Wo)man power (absolute number)	16.700	9.600	2500
Net turnover per capita (in €)	69.090€	75.0001€	50.909€
Fee earners (absolute number)	7.775	2.607	510
Net turnover per fee earner (in €)	135.000€	252.7271€	241.363€

One can deduce from these data that the leverage, ie the ratio between legally qualified personnel and other (wo)man power, is less profitable in law firms than in the two other professions. The reason is that the 'density' of attorneys (ie the number of attorneys per capita of the population, see table 1.2.2) tripled whilst the civil litigation rate (ie the number of civil law suits per capita of the population, see table 1.2.1) doubled between 1970 and 1995. In other words, a diminishing share of litigation and a growing share of consultation in the average attorney's practice have reduced the economic value of the exclusive domain. Programmes of regulatory reform are targeted at monopoly rents, and there is more for notaries and bailiffs to lose than for attorneys. These basic facts were not taken into account, however when a programme of regulatory reform was launched in 1994.

3.2 Attorneys at Law

Galanter's continuum between 'once-shooting' individuals and 'repeat-playing' organisations (1974) is reflected in attorneys' practices. At the one extreme there is a litigation practice on behalf of individuals (eg divorces, dismissals, house evictions, social security and alien law) and at the other extreme there is a consultancy business on behalf of corporations (eg company law, mergers and acquisitions, intellectual property, banking law, debt collection). 'The two kinds of law practice are the two hemispheres of the profession. Most lawyers reside exclusively in one hemisphere or the other and seldom, if ever, cross the equator', thus concluded Heinz and Laumann (1994, p 127). In the next two subsections we will see whether this conclusion holds true for the Dutch situation as well. To start with earnings, it does: the income disparity ranges from 30,000€ a year at the social end to 300,000€ at the commercial end.

3.2.1 Corporate Law Firms

In three successive waves of expansion by means of gradual growth and mergers, corporate law firms moved away from general practice, the prevailing type of law firm until the mid-1970s. In the early-1970s a first wave took place: tax consultants and notaries joined some corporate law firms. At the end of the 1980s the biggest law firms followed their business clients in the international market by establishing referral networks or branch offices all over the capitalist world. Since the end of 1990s, the third wave has concerned the invasion in the Netherlands of Anglo-Saxon, mainly London-based law firms, such as Freshfields Bruckhaus Deringer, Allen and Overy, Baker and McKenzie, and Clifford Chance.

Table 3.2.1 sets out these three waves: 100 per cent for the total number of attorneys in different years and in the last column 100 per cent for the total number of law firms in 2001. In 2001 29 per cent of all attorneys thus worked at a law firm with 6–20 attorneys (column 2001a), while only 12 per cent of all law firms had the size of 6–20 attorneys (column 2001b).

Table 3.2.1 Distribution of Attorneys Among Law Firms in Percentages

Size of Law Firm	1960	1972	1984	1991	2001a	2001b
1 Attorney	40	29	17	15	12	48
2–5 Attorneys	48	39	45	40	28	37
6–20 Attorneys	12	23	23	29	29	12
21–60 Attorneys	0.6	10	13	9	13	2
>60 Attorneys	0	0	0.1	7	18	1
Total Number	1946	2235	4825	6716	11,807	2927

At the commercial end of the continuum we find nine large multinational corporate law firms: CMS Derks Star Busmann (172 attorneys), Allen and Overy (163), Clifford Chance (121), Boekel de Nerée (116), Baker and McKenzie (116), SchutGrosheide (87), Nolst Trenité (86), Freshfields Bruckhaus Deringer (46), and Lovells (42). Partly under cover and partly indirectly four corporate law firms are multidisciplinary partnerships (including tax consultants and accountants), namely AKD Prinsen van Wijmen (211 attorneys), Holland Van Gijzen (138), Landwell (80) and Wouters/Andersen Legal (79).[15] In 1996—the most recent year we have data for—the 19 largest corporate law firms accounted for 43 per cent of the total turnover of all law firms, and they did so with a mere 23 per cent of the total number of all attorneys.

---

[15] The law firm of Wouters was the litigant party in the preliminary ruling (see n 14) who sued the local branches of the bar association because they had refused a full partnership with the accounting firm Price Waterhouse.

3.2.2 Social Advocacy

About 400 attorneys are members of the Association of Social Advocacy (*Vereniging Sociale Advocatuur Nederland, VSAN*), and about 800 attorneys are fully dependent on legal aid certificates. They are the 'die-hards' of the tradition that started in the 1970s. Responding to the international surge of the 'access to justice' movement, some law students and university graduates started what they called 'law shops' in Tilburg and Amsterdam. Within a few years about 90 law shops opened their doors. They offered easy access, an informal approach and free legal advice. They were run on a voluntary basis. Some existed on paper only, many collapsed or depended on a few individuals, but the idea of a law shop remained powerful. The improvement of legal services for the poor was placed on the political agenda. The biggest law shops (in the university towns) criticised the private profession for not paying attention to the legal problems of low-income people, and lobbied for a nationwide network of public legal services.

Socio-legal research both confirmed and refuted their criticisms (Schuyt ao 1976). The empirical results of the first Dutch legal needs study confirmed that the poor do not have fewer legal problems than the upper middle classes, but different ones, which are insufficiently met by the private profession. While the well-off go to a legal professional for a variety of problems, many of them connected with property and consumption, the lower income classes of the population need legal help to secure their welfare rights, and to deal with unemployment problems and immigrants' rights. Only divorce is evenly distributed throughout the population.

In reply to the lobbying pressures the Justice department established in each legal district, a legal aid bureau (*Bureau voor Rechtshulp*), funded from the public budget. They are staffed by (300) salaried lawyers. At first they had a dual purpose to advise people and to provide for legal aid certificates, but the latter task has, since 1994, been taken over by separate legal aid councils (*Raden voor Rechtsbijstand*) which are expected to encourage an austere use of the legal aid scheme. The Justice department was concerned about the open-ended legal aid budget: in 1970 it spent 5.9 million€ on 40,000 certificates, in 1990 as much as 156 million€ on 314,000 certificates. Taking the percentage of the population eligible for state subsidy as a yardstick, the extent of legal aid in society has varied considerably: 59 per cent in 1976, when the legal needs study was published, rising to 82 per cent in 1981, the heyday of the welfare state, and falling to 43 per cent in 1995. The new planning and control system, introduced in 1994, proved to be cost-effective, but occasioned another problem: there are fewer and fewer social advocates.

Social advocacy is a second innovation in legal services for the poor. After graduating, some of the student law shop activists started their own law firms, specialising in labour law, housing law and other problem areas of the poor. They formed the core of social advocacy, which is remunerated by legal aid certificates. In 1979 17 per cent of the attorneys spent more than 80 per cent of their time on legal aid work, while in 1993 it was a mere 9 per cent, to a large extent the same social advocates. The idealist first generation is not being followed, and the Ministry dismantled the advise function of the legal aid bureaux in 2003.

3.2.3 Proliferation of Law Practices

Probably the most significant trend of the previous decades is the proliferation of law practices. The ban on advertising was lifted in 1989, reinforcing the tendency for specialisation: 20 specialist sections within the bar have emerged. An advocate is only allowed to advertise his/her specialisation if (s)he is a member of the respective section, which has its own requirements in terms of compulsory courses and practice profile. About one-third of all attorneys are members of one or more specialist sections. Moreover, a survey in 2002 (Gunst and Bruinsma) revealed that the average attorney is no longer a general practitioner: 16 per cent practise in only one area of law, 20 per cent in two areas, 22 per cent in three and 16 per cent in four, leaving 26 per cent in general practice. This raises the question about the support the bar association has among its members. The question asked in the survey was the following: 'Does the Dutch Bar Association represent your opinions about the profession?' Table 3.2.3 presents the answers, differentiated according to the size of the law firm (the category 'agree nor disagree' has been omitted).

Table 3.2.3 Support for the Bar Association in Percentages

	1 Attorney	2–5	6–20	21–60	>60	Total
Agree	33	27	37	36	28	32
Disagree	35	28	16	15	22	22

On average the extent of agreement is not very convincing. The strongest support is from medium-sized law firms (in the categories 6–20 and 21–60). Half of the attorneys in large, corporate law seem to be indifferent and sole practitioners are divided.[16]

In his yearly address of 1999 the dean of the NOvA criticised the com-

---

[16] Dissatisfied solo practitioners and small sized law firms organized themselves in a special interest group (*Belangenorganisatie Ondernemende Advocaten*).

mercial attitude of most attorneys, and especially the multi-national and the multi-disciplinary partnership.[17] A scale analysis of five items regarding commercialism could be constructed on the basis of the survey results. It is noteworthy that partners (71 per cent) more than associates (20 per cent) and trainees (9 per cent) have a commercial attitude, and unexpectedly neither the size nor the type of the law firm showed a correlation with commercialism. In other words, the tendency towards commercialism is mitigated by a professional orientation. What makes attorneys tick? The overriding motive is solving interesting legal problems, shortly followed by helping people; building and expanding your own practice is an overall weaker motivator. Despite the differentiation in practices, there seems to be a common core of professionalism.

3.2.4 Male/Female

The percentage of women among attorneys has gradually grown from 6 per cent in 1952, to 8 per cent in 1960, 11 per cent in 1971, 19 per cent in 1981, 27 per cent in 1991 and 36 per cent in 2001. As in the judiciary, the distribution of women is skewed. Table 3.2.4 gives the gender distribution at the three levels, subdivided according to firm size (vertical count to 100 per cent).

Table 3.2.4 Gender Distribution in Percentages

	2–5 Attorneys		6–20 Attorneys		21–60 Attorneys		>60 Attorneys		Total	
	Male	Female	Male	Female	Male	Female	Male	Female	Male	Female
Partner	78	43	55	26	54	13	44	8	59	26
Associate	11	19	26	35	25	52	33	49	23	38
Trainee	11	38	19	38	21	35	23	43	18	37

In words: the larger the firm, the less female partners. If one looks deeper, and includes gender-specific variables, such as specialisation (a typically male specialisation is company law and a typically female specialisation is family law) and the time spent on management tasks (more a male than a female activity), one comes across the token female partner for family law in firms with 21 to 60 attorneys.

---

[17] The address was not very well received because the dean himself was a partner of Houthoff Buruma, 7 on the list of the large corporate law firms.

3.3 Notaries

Posner (1995:39) compares the traditional legal profession to a medieval guild. In the Dutch context notaries resembled a medieval guild very much until the mid 1990s, the essential features being the statutory limit to the number of notaries and fixed tariffs for certificates. With an eye on the absolute number of notaries, the professional association managed to function as a closed shop during a full century: in 1849 the Netherlands counted 676 notaries, in 1947 a mere 818. Pressure from within (a growing number of candidate notaries who saw their waiting period prolonged to more than 15 years) occasioned the KNB to increase the number of licensed notaries to 1056 in 1994. As the number of candidate notaries had doubled in the same time period (620 in 1947 to 1211 in 1994) this was just a drop in the ocean. Regulatory reform did the rest. The outcome of the new Notary Act is partial liberalisation: candidate notaries who have finished their six year in-service training, are still not allowed to open a notary office as advocates are after their three-year apprenticeship, but they have to submit a business plan to an expert committee in which the local notaries have a say. Table 3.3.1 reports on recent developments in the notary profession (please note the majority of female candidate notaries!).

Table 3.3.1 Growth in Numbers in the Notary Profession (1994–2001)

	Notaries	*Candidate Notaries*	*Notary Offices*	*Average Number of (Candidate) Notaries*
	(Female)	*(Female)*		*Per Office*
1994	1161 (3%)	1421 (32%)	798	3.2
2001	1401 (9%)	2135 (55%)	874	4.1

The notaries lost their battle for fixed tariffs as well. In 1996 notaries derived 94 per cent of their earnings from their professional monopoly, and in particular the conveyance of property explained 70 per cent of the net turnover. Notaries lowered the tariffs for real property transactions in 1991, 1994 and 1996, thus implicitly acknowledging their monopoly rents. Their pleas for fixed tariffs in a parliamentary hearing at the end of 1996 fell on barren ground. In October 1999 a transitional period of three years of partial price liberalisation started, monitored by an expert committee.

Table 3.3.2 shows price changes for notarial certificates since the liberalisation in 1999. In 2000 and in 2001 more than 200 notary offices chosen at random were asked what they would charge for the notarial certificates needed in different situations. The average outcome has been indexed with the fixed tariffs in 1999 as point of reference.

Table 3.3.2 Price Developments for Notarial Certificates

1999=100	2000	2001
Prenuptial agreement	113	131
Cohabitation contract	111	119
Last will	140	154
Conveyancing fee small piece of land	unknown	167
Conveyancing fee private home		
a) value 113,000€	96	105
b) value 245,000€	94	97
c) value 363,000€	unknown	94
d) value 5,900,000€	unknown	84

Contrary to the economist's expectations and in conformity with notaries' defence of fixed tariffs prices increased after liberalisation. In particular the notarial services in family law became expensive, and the disparity in conveyancing fees grew. Comparing the average fees in the lowest and the highest 5 per cent revealed large price differences. The market has not yet acquired the price transparency the fixed tariffs had. As the increase in the number of notary offices lags behind the increase in the number of notaries a concentration had taken place, another factor halting the downward trend in fees. It is expected that the market will do its restructuring work better in a less prosperous economy.

3.4 Other Regulatory Reforms

The revision of the Notary Act was part of major programme of regulatory reform that started in 1994 when a new cabinet assumed office. The political composition of this cabinet was in clear contrast with almost all previous ones because the Christian Democrats were left out. The so-called 'purple' coalition (1994–98, and 1998–2002) consisted of the Social Democratic Party (PvdA, red), the Conservative Liberal Party (VVD, blue), and the New Liberal Party (D66, green). The D66 Minister of Economic Affairs in the first purple coalition in particular took the lead to reinforce market incentives at the expense of state regulation along three lines. First of all, a renewed Competition Law (1997) established the Dutch Anti Trust Agency (*Nederlandse Mededingingsautoriteit*). Whereas the old Competition Law only outlawed abuses of market dominance, thus transforming the Netherlands into a cartel paradise, the new Anti Trust Agency is authorised to issue orders against market dominance as such. Secondly, public utilities (eg telecommunications) and public services (eg public transport) have been privatised to some extent. Thirdly, and most relevant to the regulatory reform of the legal profession, specific branches and acts were scrutinised as to their competition-hampering function.

In this context two measures targeted at attorney's privileges should be discussed. In 1999 the exclusive domain of compulsory representation in court by an attorney was restricted to money claims of more than 5000€, twice as high as before. Empirical research revealed that this new market is dominated by bailiffs (71 per cent of all plaintiffs).

Under political pressure the Dutch Bar Association has broadened the admission criteria by removing the provision that employed lawyers could not be attorneys as they were not independent *vis à vis* their employer. A new ordinance came into being in 1997, but contrary to the Bar's fearful expectations (an influx of 2000 new attorneys) less than 300 corporate lawyers and other in-house counsel made use of this opportunity. Half of them are corporate lawyers, 25 per cent are bureau lawyers, and the rest is a miscellaneous lot. Interviews and a survey made clear that personal motives prevailed over employer's considerations. More than half were attorneys reborn: they easily persuaded their employers because they had been attorneys before. A follow-up survey among corporate lawyers who did *not* apply supported these findings: the compulsory 3-year training period is prohibitive, and the added value of a corporate lawyer as an advocate is doubtful. Whereas the new ruling supposes that employers are interested in reducing attorney's costs by promoting corporate lawyers to members of the bar, employers fear they will lose control over their lawyers. The (27) employed lawyers who became attorneys in their employers' time only to leave to join a law firm are an unexpected category. The new ordinance on employed attorneys continues to be a bone of contention between the NOvA and the insurance companies. Their legal departments want to deal with their clients's cases from start to finish, whereas the NOvA sticks to the principle that any client should have a free attorney's choice.

4. Conclusion

It goes without saying that the Netherlands has a more 'legal' character than it used to have. The number of legal professionals and the number of cases going to court have multiplied. The Netherlands is catching up with the surrounding countries. The corresponding emphasis on legality and the concomitant formalism is detrimental to the Dutch legal culture of informal pragmatism, however. European integration, which is welcomed by the ruling elite, is an additional factor. In their search for 'one stop, full service' corporate law firms adopted economies of scale. Management concepts were introduced into the court system and the legal services. A distinct phenomenon is the growing share of women in the legal professions; the dissolution of the glass ceiling is a matter of time.

References

BLANKENBURG, Erhard, 'Patterns of Legal Culture: The Netherlands Compared to Neighboring Germany', *The American Journal of Comparative Law*, Vol. 46 (1998) 1–41

BRUINSMA, Fred J, *Dutch Law in Action*, (Nijmegen, Ars Aequi Libri, 2003 (2nd edn)), and see also www.law.uu.nl/rt/ (pdf-file)

DAHRENDORF, Ralf, 'Law faculties and the German upper class', in V Aubert (ed), *Sociology of Law*, (Harmondsworth, Penguin Books, 1969), pp 294–303

FELSTINER, William LF, ao, 'The Emergence and Transformation of Disputes: Naming, Blaming, Claiming …', *Law & Society Review*, 1980 (Vol 15) pp 631–54

FRIEDMAN, Lawrence M, *The Legal System. A Social Science Perspective*, (New York, Russell Sage Foundation, 1975)

GALANTER, Marc, 'Why the 'haves' come out ahead', *Law & Society Review*, 1974 (Vol 9) pp 95–160

HEINZ, John P & Edward O LAUMANN, *Chicago Lawyers. The Social Structure of the Bar*, (Evanston Ill., Northwestern Un. Press 1994 (rev.ed.))

KAGAN, Robert, *Adversarial Legalism. The American Way of Law*, (Cambridge Mass/London, Harvard University Press, 2001)

POSNER, Richard A, *Overcoming Law*, (Cambridge, Mass, Harvard University Press, 1995)

SCHUYT, Kees AO, *De weg naar het recht*, 1976; summary in English in the 1977 *European Yearbook on Law and Sociology*, pp 98–120

5

Regulated Deregulation: The Case of the German Legal Profession

ULRIKE SCHULTZ

1. A Cause for Change

Peculiarities of the German Legal Profession

In comparing the German Legal Profession—*(Rechts-) Anwaltschaft*—to legal professions in other countries two striking particularities have to be noted:

The profession is regulated in detail by federal statutes—these comprise federal acts on the structure of the profession and on fee charging.

The profession is embedded in the German model of the 'uniform jurist', the *Einheitsjurist*, embracing all university graduates who have completed the two-phase legal education which is identical for all. This united cast of jurists has been an important backbone of the modern German state, gaining in importance after the Second World War in producing and guaranteeing the legalistic culture of the German *Rechtsstaat*.

Discussions on a reform of the legal profession (*Anwaltschaft*) are as old as the profession itself. For a long time they centred round the suitability of legal education for professional work and concerned 'internal' problems like the prevention of competition from tax advisers and accountants or the legality of the code governing the profession and its implementation. However, the structure remained stable. First attempts at genuine reform took place in the 1980s. At the beginning of the 1990s signs of more profound changes began to appear, and in the past five years an erosion of the old order has started to occur.

Growth as an Agent of Change

The growing volume and speed of change went hand in hand with an increase in size of the *Anwaltschaft*, which was due to an expansion of higher education in general and growing numbers of law students and graduates in particular.

Table 1 Total Increase in Number of *Anwälte*

Year	Anwälte
1950	12,844
1960	18,347
1970	22,882
1980	36,077
1990	56,638
2000	104,067
2003	121,420
2004	126,799

The number of *Anwälte* almost doubled in the 20 years between 1950 and 1970, all but trebled in the 30 years between 1950 and 1980, and will have increased tenfold in the 55 years from 1950 to 2005.[1]

The increase in numbers which has lead to growing pressure in the legal services market is of course only one factor to spark off change, as well as itself a result of change. Other factors are: Europeanisation, globalisation with increasing exposure to market forces, commercialisation of legal practice, virtualisation, feminisation, the reunification of East and West Germany.

To give the background to these processes, the structure of the profession and its position in the German legal system are described and a short survey of its historical development is provided, the main focus being the description and evaluation of recent changes.[2]

---

[1] There were high annual growth rates in the early 1950s with the first cohorts of graduates after the war, then a steady increase at a low level of 1–2% for more than ten years, increasing to 3–4% annually between 1965 and 1975, and to 4–8% annually over the next decade; a peak was reached in 1997; since then the rate of growth in law graduates has undergone a slight decrease, but it still stood at 4.4% in 2003.

[2] Detailed descriptions of the status of the German legal profession can be found in: Blankenburg & Schultz, 1988, at 94, followed by an updated version in 1995; Schultz, 1997; and Schultz, 2003 b.

2. German Anwälte in the German System of Justice

Anwälte—a Regulated Profession

The German *Rechtsanwaltschaft* is regulated by the Federal Regulations for Lawyers (Bundesrechtsanwaltsordnung—BRAO) of 1959. It is modelled on a trial lawyer/litigator who represents clients in court. *Anwälte* have to handle the technicalities of law suits in a highly formalised system of litigation and draft the written statements in law suits. Except for criminal proceedings, oral pleading is of minor importance in German legal culture. The judge directs the proceedings, while the *Anwalt* submits the facts and a legal evaluation of the case.[3]

Anwälte have to be admitted to a court of the ordinary jurisdiction. (s18 BRAO) To be admitted they have to hold the qualification for judicial office. (s4 BRAO) The latter is regulated in the German Judiciary Act (*Deutsches Richtergesetz*). They have to run an office at the place of admission. (s27 BRAO) They charge their fees according to the Federal Regulations on Lawyers' Fees (*Bundesrechtsanwaltsgebührenordnung—*BRAGO).[4] Membership in the chamber of *Anwälte* (*Anwaltskammer*) is compulsory. Disciplinary supervision is exercised jointly by the chambers of *Anwälte* and the civil courts.

Anwalt-Notaries and Notaries

In many parts of Western Germany *Anwälte* can obtain an additional admission as notaries on presenting proof of their personal and professional aptitude (*Anwaltsnotare* s6 *Bundesnotarordnung—*BNotO). However, only a limited number of places are available. In other parts of Germany and in all of East Germany the notary is a separate profession (*Nur-Notare*).[5] The functions of the German notariat are comparable to those of the Latin notariat. Notarial certification and attestation are required to validate certain types of legal documents, eg documents concerning the purchase, sale or mortgage of land, the decisions of shareholder meetings, sale of shares in private companies, and marriage contracts and

---

[3] According to the Roman model: *Da mihi factum dabo tibi ius.* Give me the facts and I will give you the law.

[4] About 40% of *Anwälte* are also (voluntary) members of the German Lawyers' Association (*Deutscher Anwaltverein—*DAV).

[5] In Württemberg and in parts of Baden, notaries are civil servants.

wills. Notaries hold a public office. They charge fees according to a fixed scale, but they are organised as an independent profession. *Anwaltsnotare* therefore exert public power as notaries and work in private practice as lawyers.

Due to stricter entry controls, the number of *Anwaltsnotare* has slightly decreased. In 2003, there were 1654 (full-time) notaries and 8365 *Anwaltsnotare*, the latter representing around 12 per cent of the total number of *Anwälte* in those parts of Germany where dual admission to both professions is possible.

Judges

The German legal culture is thoroughly judge-centred. Germany has a highly developed court system with separate jurisdictions for civil and criminal matters (ordinary jurisdiction—*ordentliche Gerichtsbarkeit*), labour law, administrative law, social law and tax law, with three instances each, as well as constitutional courts. Among all developed legal systems, Germany traditionally has had the highest ratio of professional judges per head of population. This is also due to a combination of high litigation rates, high appeal rates,[6] and the inquisitorial system. Procedural law gives judges a dominant role: they control the proceedings, direct the inquiry, suggest settlements, pass judgments, and give detailed written reasons.

To be a judge is a lifelong career, normally starting immediately after the second qualifying examination, and often as a public prosecutor, who is formally part of the judiciary. The status of a judge resembles that of a civil servant, and promotion to higher courts is the usual expectation.

Lawyers in the Civil Service and Other Occupations

A legal qualification is particularly advantageous for public service careers. The judicial mode is deeply embedded in German administrative law: every public decision can be subject to judicial review on substantive as well as procedural grounds. Because public policy also relies heavily for its legitimation on a belief in legality, jurists play a central role in preparing new legislation.

A great number of higher civil servants with any sort of administrative responsibility are recruited from the pool of qualified lawyers. Jurists have a very strong position in both the executive and the ministerial bureaucracies.

---

[6] Civil Procedures in 2001: First instance 1,818,291; second instance 157,704; Highest Federal Court (BGH) 5386 in a population of approx 80 million.

This has created the notion of a lawyers' monopoly (*Juristenmonopol*) in German society[7] (Dahrendorf 1965; Hartmann 2002), though lawyers have to face growing competition from graduates in other disciplines. As most of these lawyers are civil servants they cannot also be admitted as *Anwälte*.

Traditionally, the lawyers' monopoly also extended to leading positions in industry. However, here law graduates have lost some ground to those with a business studies degree (Hartmann 1990; Kreizberg 1994).

With the growth of the profession, lawyers have had to move to other fields or expand their services to organisations such as companies, associations, (non-)profit making societies, service organisations, interest groups, and trade unions. Lawyers in these fields often hold an admission as *Anwalt*. If they are legal advisers they are called *Syndicus*. Information on this kind of lawyer is limited, as there is a lack of relevant statistics and systematic empirical research.

Legal Education as a Means to Create Homogeneity

A prerequisite for admission as an *Anwalt* is the qualification to hold judicial office (s4 BRAO). Therefore, *Anwälte* as well as judges, public prosecutors, notaries and lawyers in the higher civil service have to undergo the same long judge—or civil-service—centred legal education leading to the qualification of a 'fully-fledged jurist' (*Volljurist*). They have to study law at university for four years and take a first state examination set by the courts of appeal for the state ministries of justice. This is unique in Germany: all other university studies end with university examinations. Young lawyers then have to do two years of practical professional training organised by the courts of appeal. Training consists of specified placements in trial courts, a public prosecutor's office, a local government authority, and an *Anwalt*'s practice. Prior to a recent amendment to the German Judiciary Act (*Deutsches Richtergesetz*) only a minimum of four months in an Anwalt's practice was required. Since July 2003 this has risen to a minimum of 9 months—the maximum being 13 months.[8] In spite of endless discussions about a reform of legal education, the training emphasises the technical skills needed in the judiciary, in particular the composition of preparatory opinions and judgments. Only in recent years has advocacy training, such as the drafting of documents, been reinforced. Examination

---

[7] Lawyers still hold many key positions in present day German society: In 2004 Chancellor Schröder, the leader of the CSU, and the leader of the FDP are all lawyers like many other leading politicians, many top managers and leading executives.

[8] *Gesetz zur Reform der Juristenausbildung* v 11 July 2002, BGBl I, 2592. The implementation of this act varies slightly from federal state to federal state. For Northrhine–Westphalia comp Juristenausbildungsgesetz–JAG–NRW of 11 March 2003, GV NRW p 135.

papers testing the practical qualities of *Anwälte* now form part of the second examination. This again is a state examination organised by the state ministries of justice. Examination panels mainly consist of judges, public prosecutors, and civil servants, whose experience shapes the examination.[9] Examination requirements are defined broadly in ss 3–5 of the Federal Statute on Judges (Deutsches Richtergesetz—DRiG), and in more detail in the Legal Education Acts of individual federal states. During legal education considerable pressure is exerted on students by rigid marking of tests and examinations.[10] The drop-out rate is almost 50 per cent during university studies, and about 15 per cent between the first and the qualifying examination.[11] Final oral examinations have been described as a 'conformity test', ie a test to see whether the candidate's thought processes fit the appropriate pattern of 'perceiving, thinking and judging'.[12] Examinations clearly serve as a rite of passage. As s47 of the Northrhine-Westphalian Legal Training Act (*Juristenausbildungsgesetz*, JAG) states:

(1) The second state examination in law is to verify whether candidates (*Referendarinnen* and *Referendare*) have met the examination objectives (s39) and whether their subject and general knowledge and abilities, their practical skills, and *the overall impression created by their personality* [my italics, US] warrant the award of the qualification admitting them to judicial and to higher general administrative office.[13]

Career Paths

This welding process over 8 to almost 10 years[14] creates an effective socialisation in tune with the qualities expected from civil servants as well as a strong esprit de corps. Another homogenising factor is social background: German jurists traditionally come from a middle and upper middle class background with a clear overrepresentation of parents in the civil service.[15]

---

[9] In 1984 in Northrhine–Westphalia, only 9 of 235 (predominantly male) examiners in the second state examination were advocates. 20 years later, in 2004, this number had risen to 88 of 402 examiners (including 4 solo-notaries), with 47 (11.7%) of the total women.
[10] This works as a mechanism to keep the candidates on edge, and fill them with a sense of elation once they have survived the ordeal—hence the proverbial arrogance on the part of lawyers.
[11] In 2002 the failure rate was 29.91% at the first and 14.37% at the second examination.
[12] Portele & Schütte, 1983, p 32; Schütte, 1982.
[13] The act has just been reformed but this regulation has remained unaltered.
[14] The average law student takes 4½ years to graduate. This does not yet include the examination period as such (another 6 months or so). As a rule, a few months up to two years (varying from federal state to federal state) are then spent waiting for a training place as a *Referendar*.
[15] Heldrich & Schmidtchen, 1982, p 252. This represents the only quantitative research on the social background of law students so far. My own experience from teaching *Referendare* gives me the impression that nothing much has changed.

Access to a legal career is strongly determined by examination grades. A top mark (*Prädikat*, also called *Staatsnote*) opens the door to a career in the judiciary or civil service, but is achieved by fewer than 15 per cent of candidates.[16] Exceptions were made only when graduates were in short supply, that is between 1965 and 1975 when the civil service and the judiciary expanded, and at the beginning of the 1990s in the eastern states after German reunification.

In spite of the uniformity of legal education, each legal occupation has its own career path, and mobility between the different paths becomes difficult after a few years. The relatively high incomes produced by seniority and promotion practice in both the judiciary and public administration render transfer to private practice a financial sacrifice, particularly in times of a narrow legal market. Civil servants and judges rarely leave their posts to become *Anwälte*. Where mobility occurs, it tends to be a one-way movement of younger *Anwälte* into the judiciary or permanent civil service jobs. In contrast to the average *Anwalt*, civil servants and the judiciary enjoy extraordinary benefits: life tenure, health insurance, generous pension schemes, maternity leave, and the possibility to work part-time. Many young lawyers enroll as *Anwälte* with the firm intention to move into the civil service or in other fields of occupation as soon as possible (Wesel 2001:30). So in a sense, many are *Anwalt* by default only.

History Shaping the Present

The state orientation of the legal profession is rooted in history (Weißler, Bleek, Hartstang). When the German Empire was created in 1871, Prussia held the hegemony, and the Prussian order of the profession strongly influenced the imperial Regulations for Lawyers (*Reichsrechtsanwaltsordnung*) of 1879. Since 1713, the number of lawyers had been limited in Prussia as a reaction to an early oversupply, and the state had exerted entry and quality controls by setting the examination requirements. In 1781, Frederic the Great, King of Prussia, in his Procedural Code, the *Corpus Juris Fridericianum*, abolished the profession of *Anwalt*. Legal representation in court was prohibited and advocates were replaced by civil servants (*Assistenzräte*) charged with assisting the parties while helping the judges investigate the facts. Former advocates were allowed to work as judicial

---

[16] Intriguingly, the *Prädikat* includes the grade 'fully satisfactory' which is unique to law studies. In the first examination it is achieved by approx 12%, 'very good' and 'good' are awarded to fewer than 3%; approx 27% get the degree 'satisfactory', and 30% a mere pass, 25–30% fail. The failure rate is lower in the second examination, approx 15%, the distribution across the good grades is similarly low, approx 35% get a sufficient or a mere pass (Official Examination Statistics 2001 and 2002).

commissioners (*Justizkommissare*), offering advice and representation in non-contentious legal matters such as land registration, probate, guardianship, bankruptcy, drafting contracts, and notarial work.

These judicial commissioners were also civil servants, although in receipt of fees from private clients. Following pressure from jurists a revised version of the *Corpus Juris*, the *Allgemeine Gerichtsordnung* (Judicature Act) of 1783 restored the principle of representation in judicial proceedings and permitted judicial commissioners to combine both advocacy and notarial functions. This was the birth of the *Anwaltsnotar*. However, the judicial commissioners remained civil servants, appointed by the state and admitted to a court.

When the new German Empire required uniform regulations there was a strong movement in favour of freedom of the advocacy. It was partly successful. The Regulations for Lawyers removed quantitative limitations, but the state was given the right to define the standard of entry by organising the qualifying examinations and to frame the major rules governing legal practice. During the '*Third Reich*' between 1933 and 1945, state control became even stricter. Jews and women were barred from the profession by statutory regulations. (Reifner) After the war it took until 1959 for new Federal Regulations for Lawyers (*Bundesrechtsanwaltsordnung*—BRAO) to be passed. These mirrored the spirit of their predecessor of 1879.

In the early years of the German Empire of 1871 there were almost twice as many judges as *Anwälte*. After 30 years, on the verge of the First World War, both occupational groups had roughly the same numbers. Until the 1970s, the ratio remained broadly stable, with 50 per cent more advocates than judges. However, with the rapid growth of the *Anwaltschaft* in the past three decades the gap has widened. In 1989, the year before German reunification, there were about three times as many *Anwälte* as judges, by 2000 the ratio had become 5 to 1, increasing to 5.5 to 1 in 2002, and almost 6 to 1 in 2003.

Until well into the 1970s, about a third of each cohort of law graduates found a position in the judiciary or the civil service. Today this has shrunk to about 10 per cent (4 per cent judiciary, 6 per cent civil service), while ¾ are admitted as *Anwälte*. (von Seltmann 2003:227)

The number of judges has remained remarkably stable over time. Having first been expanded during the 'golden 1970s', the judiciary experienced another marked increase in membership following German reunification, when additional posts had to be created in the five eastern states to bring them up to West German standards.

Table 2 Proportion of Judges vs *Anwälte*—Judge-Centredness of the German Legal System

Year	Number of Judges in the Ordinary Jurisdiction[17]	Total Number of Judges in all Jurisdictions[18]	Anwälte	Population in millions)
1883	7,052		4,342	46.0
1909	9,798		9,608	63.7
1915	10,719		13,051	67.9
1st World War 1914–18				
1933	10,069		19,200	66.0
'Third Reich' 1933–1945 2nd World War 1939–1945				
1959	8,909		18,214	54.9
1970	9,926		22,882	60.7
1980	12,298	16,657 (1981)	36,077	61.6
1989		17,627	54,108	
Reunification				
2000	15,464	20,880	104,067	82.2
2002	15,456	20,901	116,305	82.4
2003			121,420	82.5

3. Elements of Regulation

The profession's position between state regulation and professional independence is mirrored in the Federal Regulations for Lawyers (BRAO):

S1: The *Rechtsanwalt* is an independent judicial organ.
S2: The *Rechtsanwalt* practises a liberal profession (*freier Beruf*). His occupation is not a trade.
S3: The *Rechtsanwalt* is the authorised independent adviser and representative in all legal matters.

---

[17] The ordinary (=traditional) jurisdiction comprises civil and criminal matters.
[18] For the 19th and the early 20th centuries no records of the total number of judges could be found. At that time the specialized jurisdictions were of lesser importance than the 'ordinary jurisdiction'.

Until the end of the 1990s, practising lawyers' professional autonomy was limited by state regulation in the following respects:

—Admission to the profession. Admission was controlled by the administration of justice in individual federal states, while the professional organisations, the chambers (*Anwaltskammern*), were merely consulted.

—Localisation principle. Anwälte had to be admitted to a particular court of the ordinary (civil/criminal) jurisdiction, either to a regional court,[19] or an appeal court or the Highest Federal Court. They were only allowed to represent clients in civil matters (which make up the bulk of contentious work) in these courts. The compensation for these limits to practice was the monopoly to give legal advice granted by the Legal Advice Act of 1935, and the monopoly to represent clients at particular courts as regulated in procedural codes.

—Fee charging system. The Federal Regulations on Lawyers Fees (*Bundesrechtsanwaltsgebührenordnung*—BRAO) contain a complicated system of scaled fees for all types of work. Compulsory professional organisation in 'chambers' set up alongside courts of appeal and organising Anwälte in the area of each court of appeal, headed by the Federal Chamber of Anwälte (*Bundesrechtsanwaltskammer*) in Berlin.

—Disciplinary control. *Anwalt* Courts deal with disciplinary matters. This professional jurisdiction has three levels like any other court in Germany. In the second and third instance lay judges (*Anwälte*) sit together with professional judges, in the third instance in an *Anwalt* Senate at the Highest Federal Court the professional judges have the majority vote.

—Legal education, as described above.

—Notarial functions, as described above.

Given these restrictions, German *Rechtsanwälte* cannot be regarded as an ideal-type profession in the classical Anglo-American sense. The following elements have been defined as essential (by eg Parsons; Wetterer; Kurtz):

• orientation towards social good, various kinds of altruistic behaviour
• lengthy training period
• body of technical knowledge
• control over entry and performance
• control over violation of professional discipline

---

[19] Only in some appeal court districts double admission to the appeal court and the regional court was possible.

Though the first two criteria are met, the influence on the knowledge basis, self-regulation and ethical control are limited, while control over admission is totally lacking.

For a long time *Anwälte* considered the territorial restriction as essential to their work and cherished their monopolies, guarding them jealously. Infringements were rigorously penalised, as reflected in countless court decisions. Up until the 1980s, there was no willingness on the part of the profession to consider and discuss the impact of these restrictions on competition.[20]

4. Change in Professional and Ethical Rules

First Effects of Europeanisation and Internationalisation: 1980s

The Federal Regulations for Lawyers (*Bundesrechtsanwaltsordnung*) which replaced the regulations of the *Reichsrechtsanwaltsordnung* of 1878 had been passed in 1958 after long discussions, 13 years after the breakdown of the Nazi regime and the end of the Second World War in 1945, and 9 years after the passing of the constitution of the new Federal Republic of Germany in 1949. In the 1970s it became clear that while they might well suit the requirements of the German internal legal market, they did not fit those of the emerging Europeanised and internationalised legal market. Thus, while localisation and monopolies did work within Germany, they were a definite barrier to operations in an international market. The complex and strict fee structure proved intolerable where a high value was at stake, which often applied to international cases, and was found unacceptable by foreign lawyers. Firms dealing with international cases started to break professional and also ethical rules. A gap between locally or regionally operating solo-practitioners or small partnership lawyers on the one hand and internationally oriented

---

[20] In 1987, I tried to present the results of what I had heard and learned in the context of the project 'Lawyers in Society' and the meetings of the legal profession group at the biannual meeting of the *Anwaltstag* in Hamburg. Most of my audience reacted with irritation rather than sympathetic interest, as yet unwilling to question the appropriateness of their traditional self-image as members of 'a profession under public law, regulated by the state in the service of law and legal administration'. Two years later, when it had become tangibly obvious that cross-frontier legal activities made change inevitable, I was at least listened to. Additional irritation was caused by the fact that at that time I was the only woman who dared to raise her voice in a plenary of hundreds of darkly attired gentlemen. There was an immediate disbelief that a substantive contribution could ever be made by a woman, and I was cut short.

firms on the other opened up. This led to growing tension within the profession.

Court Decisions as an Agent of Change: the Year 1987 and After

A long legal dispute had centred arround the legality of the ethical rules for lawyers, and countless cases about infringements of the rules on advertising were taken to the profession's disciplinary courts, the so-called 'honour's courts' (*Ehrengerichte*), later on called *Anwalt* courts. Until 1987 the ethical rules were laid down in so-called guidelines by the Federal Chamber of *Anwälte* (*Bundesrechtsanwaltskammer*), where representatives of the profession regularly decided on current ethical practice. Their task was to gauge and define the general opinion about what the ethical rules should be rather than making up new ones (Schultz 1997).

The first serious threat to the established system of professional law and ethics came through the Klopp decision of the European Court of Justice in 1984.[21] Until then *Anwälte* had only been allowed to have one office. If they had an office in another country, they were not allowed to have a second office in Germany; and if they had no office in Germany they were not admitted to the profession nor allowed to use the title of *Rechtsanwalt* or practise under that title in their host country. The European Court decision which overruled the one-office principle[22] was the starting-point of endless discussions in lawyers' professional associations on professional rules. The more conservative Federal Chamber of *Anwälte* (*Bundesrechtsanwaltskammer*) and the more liberal *Deutscher Anwaltverein* (a voluntary association at federal level comprising about 40 per cent of all admitted lawyers) disagreed on many aspects and rules, and failed to reach a solution. Further court decisions were needed.

Three years later, in 1987, the Federal Constitutional Court held that the Chamber 'guidelines' were unconstitutional for lack of a statutory basis.[23] From then on nobody knew what the law should be, and numerous cases concerning ethical questions were taken to the courts, both to the profession's disciplinary courts and to the Highest Federal Court, the Federal Constitutional Court and the European Court. Countless cases concerned

---

[21] European Court of Justice, decision of 12 July 1984, Rs 107/84, *Anwaltsblatt* 1984, p 608. Klopp was an *Anwalt* who had dual French and German legal qualifications and wanted to have an exemption from the rule that *Anwälte* were not allowed to have a branch office.

[22] Basically the decision was against the French rule which did not permit branch offices, but it had a lasting impact on the professional law for German *Anwälte*.

[23] Federal Constitutional Court decision of 14 July 1987, NJW 1988, p 191, and decision of 21 October 1987, NJW 1988, p 196.

questions of advertising, and each case contributed towards a redefinition of legal ethics. Many of these decisions led to liberalisation, some of the most venerable institutions of legal ethics and professional law were demolished and abolished.[24] The court decisions did the job left undone for decades by the profession.

A landmark decision of the Federal Constitutional Court followed in 1992.[25] Previously, lawyers in salaried positions were only allowed to be admitted as *Anwälte* if they held an elevated position. This restricted competition and was held to be unconstitutional as in violation of the constitutional guarantee of the right to choose and practise one's occupation or profession (*Berufsfreiheit*, Art 12, Bonn Basic Law). The Court also stated that admission as *Anwalt* could not be denied on the grounds that in a second job the lawyer was obliged to provide legal advice to third parties for an employer not bound by ethical rules.[26] This decision put *Anwälte* on the market. It spelt out:

Competition in the market is extremely tight for *Anwälte*, and is heightened by the growing number of entrants to the profession, by freedom of establishment in the European Community and by legal advice given by other professions (particularly tax advisers and chartered accountants). In this situation it is indispensable for many young advocates to have a second occupation to be able to earn their living until they have a sufficiently large clientele or the necessary publicity.

Market Pressure and the Effects of German Reunification: the 1980s and Early 1990s

Since the early 1980s, fear of growing pressure on the legal services market had spread. There were first indications of a sense of insecurity amongst lawyers. There was talk of lawyers about to flood the market. Only gradually did it dawn on German *Anwälte* that their range of options was not limited to court work but that legal advice might be equally significant in their professional portfolio. In 1988 a study was published on the situation of young lawyers in a market 'under pressure of expansion'. (Hommerich 1988) However, the empirical research carried out in 1985 showed that young lawyers still stood a good chance of successfully entering the legal services market, the latter having been regarded as defined and limited by law but proving to be expandable. Without lawyers having to increase

---

[24] This is specified below.
[25] Federal Constitutional Court decision of 4 November 1992, NJW 1993, p 317.
[26] The limits were set for cases where a danger of conflict of interest arises or the applicant does not have enough time to work as an *Anwalt*.

demand, new areas of activity as well as additional work in established areas could still be found. From the end of the 1980s pressure intensified due to the exponential growth of the number of newly admitted legal practitioners. Just before it became intolerable, German reunification in 1990 opened up a large new market. Literally hoards of lawyers qualified in the West escaped from their narrow legal home market by moving east, where a mere 600 *Anwälte* had served the needs of some 17 million people in the German Democratic Republic (GDR). From the mid-1990s, the relief afforded temporarily by vacancies in the East German legal services market had evaporated, and pressure was renewed. There was now no alternative to rethinking the market position of *Anwälte,* the operation of market forces, and new ways of ensuring a sufficient income for practising lawyers.

Reform of the Federal Regulations on Lawyers — Adjusting the Law to the Needs of Practice: 1994

In 1994, the federal legislature finally passed the *Gesetz zur Neuordnung des Berufsrechts der Rechtsanwalte und Patentanwälte* (Act to Reorganise the Law Governing Lawyers and Patent Lawyers), revising the existing Federal Regulations on Lawyers and taking into account court decisions and the solutions *Anwälte,* particularly the bigger and more influential firms, had found for themselves, thus legalising practice contra legem (Schultz 1997:68).

The GDR Act on *Anwälte* was abolished, having remained in force during the early years after unification, when the bulk of East German law had been replaced by that of West Germany.

Territorial limitations on lawyers' work by requiring admission to a particular regional court of first instance were set to be abolished from 2000.[27] However, the profession's monopoly to give legal advice as secured by the Rechtsberatungsgesetz of 1935 was upheld.

A statutory basis was created for new Chamber 'guidelines', now called Professional Regulations for Lawyers (*Berufsordnung*).

The rules on incompatibilities were specified.

Hourly fees as well as fee sharing arrangements were finally permitted.

The 'honour's courts' were re-christened '*Anwalt* courts', yet their structure and jurisdiction remained unchanged (Schultz 1997:73).

---

[27] In the Eastern states there had been no territorial limitations. In the West they were variously seen as either the backbone of German civil procedure or as a 'fossil of an antiquated guild spirit'. The salient nature of the issue is apparent from the fact that the *Berufsordnung* wanted to introduce them in the East the very moment they were abolished in the West and leave them intact until 2005, simply in order to give East Germans a flavour of what they had missed out on. Again the Federal Constitutional Court intervened.

Advertising was allowed.

Some rules previously classified as ethical were revised and transformed into legal rules, amongst them the obligation to take out insurance for professional liability and the rule on interprofessional co-operation (though multidisciplinary partnerships and interprofessional cooperation had always been allowed).[28]

Cross-regional partnerships, ie partnerships in different towns or countries, with at least one resident partner per office were allowed, as well as international partnerships. Branch offices have remained forbidden.

A Partnership Act was passed. The common form of cooperation had been—and still is—a civil law company, or an office sharing arrangement. The first private limited companies of lawyers (Rechtsanwalts-GmbH) had already been set up but not yet legalised.

This reform of the Federal Regulations on Lawyers (BRAO) has been criticised as too limited. To cite comments by an eminent author on legal ethics and professional law:

> Basic legal deficits in the professional law have been made good but the freedom of the advocacy has remained curtailed without any sensible reason (Kleine-Cosack 1994:2249).

> This shows the distrust of the legislature in the ability of advocates to make good use of the freedom of profession and occupation.
>
> There are still deficits regarding constitutional law and the European integration as well as legal policy: in particular, the rules have not been adjusted to the needs of a modern service-oriented society (Kleine-Cosack 1994:2258).

This meant that the courts would have, and indeed had, to decide on a great number of contested issues.

The New Professional Regulations for Lawyers — from Honour to Advertising: 1997

The new Professional Regulations for Lawyers were passed in 1996 and came into force on 11 March 1997. They are regularly revised by a Statutory Assembly and checked by the Federal Ministry of Justice.

The first part deals with the freedom of professional practice. S1 (Freedom of the Advocacy) states: 'The *Anwalt* is free, self-determined and

---

[28] Only part of what are considered to be cases of ethics and discipline in other countries fall within the scope of professional jurisdiction in Germany, eg disputes on fee charging, breach of professional duties (negligence) have to be dealt with by civil courts.

unregulated in his professional practice ... unless expressly bound by statutes or the Professional Regulations for Lawyers.' This regulation contrasts with the image of the *Anwalt* as an organ of justice as laid down in s1 BRAO and therefore in itself represents a sensation. It is a signal of professional self-respect as opposed to state control, and goes back to the old demand for a free, liberal advocacy voiced in the 19th century (von Gneist 1867; Blankenburg and Schultz 1995:94 n2) before the First Statute on *Anwälte* of 1879 established the German model of a state-bound advocacy. (Schultz 1997:69) Under the heading of 'From Honour to Law' it has been welcomed as a 'small but important step on the way to adapt professional law to the democratic *Rechtsstaat* of the Basic Law' (Kleine-Cosack 1997:1257).

The main practical importance of the Professional Regulations lay in the liberalisation of advertising rules, although not all relevant disputes were resolved. New court decisions followed, which interpreted the new regulations in the BRAO and the Professional Regulations. The essence of the regulations and of many judgements has been that only advertising which is misleading or the expression of a business or profit-oriented attitude is not allowed. Shocking for a traditional *Anwalt* was the argument that the question of a limitation of advertising would have to be judged by competition law.

In tandem with the Professional Regulations for Lawyers, the profession drew up its own Regulations on Specialist Lawyers. Specialist titles had been a German specialty, envied by many foreign colleagues. Until 1989 the title 'Specialist in Tax Matters' had been the most common one, while some lawyers had also been allowed to use the title 'Specialist in Administrative Law'. Specialist titles for social law and labour law were added subsequently, followed in 1998 by those for criminal law and family law, in 2000 for insolvency law, and in 2003 for insurance law. Further specialist titles are under discussion.[29] *Anwälte* have to provide proof of their knowledge and adequate experience in the field in which they are applying for a specialist title. *Anwälte* who specialise in a certain field but do not hold specialist titles may officially name fields of interest (*Interessengebiete*) or main activities (*Tätigkeitsschwerpunkte*). The rules are detailed and judicial disputes surrounding them are legion. Colleagues watch each other like hawks to see whether anyone is trying to obtain a market advantage by an overly liberal interpretation of the rules on specialisation, or, indeed, those on advertising.

---

[29] The liberal German *Anwalt* Association (DAV) is pushing for more titles, but is criticized by more conservative members of the profession for promoting an inflation of titles.

More Recent Changes — the Years 1997–2004: Europeanisation and Globalisation as Challenges

In the late 1990s the effects of Europeanisation and globalisation intensified. While numbers of newly admitted *Anwälte* grew, economic and legal transactions were increasingly conducted at European and even global levels. Traditionally, the strategy of the Anwaltschaft had been to fend off competition. Thus, when the EEC Treaty came into force and the application of the market principles of freedom of establishment and delivery of services for lawyers was discussed, the German *Anwalt* representatives were strictly opposed, declaring that Art 55 (now Art 45 of the EC Treaty)[30] had to be applied to the profession, that they were engaged in activities connected with the exercise of official authority, and consequently had to be exempted from the mobility rules. Having for a century restricted competition and protected their monopolies, the *Anwaltschaft* now began to realise that defending territories did not help any longer, that the growing profession had to extend its markets and conquer new ones. The market had finally caught up with the legal profession. One after the other its sacred bulwarks fell.

Control of admission to the *Anwaltschaft* was transferred to the *Anwalts*-Chambers.[31] This was more a symbolic act, as the *Anwaltschaft* has so far not gained in influence on the selection of candidates or the conditions of admission, but at least it underlines the profession's autonomy.

The principle of territorial limitation was abolished as of 2000. So was the admission of only a limited number of lawyers to appeal courts[32] (jurisdictional limitation). As a result, *Anwälte* may now represent their clients anywhere in Germany at first instance and appeal courts and federal court level. Yet, in 2002 the Highest Federal Court still decided that the exclusive admission of a limited number of *Anwälte* at the Highest Federal Court (for civil matters) is constitutional. The somewhat bloated rhetoric of the Court's reasoning lets one suspect that the decision may not hold for long.[33]

The organisation of Anwälte in public limited companies (*Aktiengesellschaften*) has meanwhile become accepted (Passarge; Pluskat).

---

[30] Art 55 EEC–Treaty, now Art 45 of the Treaty of Amsterdam, consolidated version of 24 November 2002.

[31] That is, chambers may, but do not necessarily, control the admission of new members. The practice differs in the federal states.

[32] Comp Federal Constitutional Court decision of 13 December 2002, NJW 2002, p 3765; one opponent even called the European Court of Human Rights for help, decision of 06 February 2003, NJW 2003, p 2221.

[33] 'It [the exclusive admission] is particularly suited to ensure that the parties are properly advised and the functionality of the dispensation of justice in civil matters at the highest level is maintained.' Decision of the Highest Civil Court of 4 March 2002, *BRAK–Mitteilungen* 2002, 132.

Even the state's seemingly sacrosanct control over legal education is showing signs of being eroded. The first inroad happened in 1993 with the admission and establishment of new programmes of study for commercial lawyers (*Wirtschaftsjuristen*) at *Fachhochschulen*, higher education institutions focusing on the applied sciences and ranking below traditional universities in the higher education hierarchy. This was the first crack in the German model of the unitary jurist, the *Einheitsjurist*. Although commercial law graduates are not (yet) regarded as having equal status with law graduates from universities, the simple fact that legal training can take place outside traditional law faculties plus the fact that the *Fachhochschule* sets the examination appeared unacceptable to many *Anwälte*. The second threat happened through the introduction of the bachelor and masters system at German universities in 2002, and specifically the launch of a qualification of bachelor in law(s) intended for positions in industry.

Everybody had agreed that the changing scope of activities of lawyers demanded at least some adjustment of the curriculum and teaching methods. As already mentioned, the reform of legal education in 2003 extended the placement in an *Anwalt*'s office, and examination questions now have to include questions specifically relevant to practising lawyers' work. The reform act also demands training in key qualifications for practising lawyers, such as negotiation skills, communication techniques, rhetoric, mediation as well as foreign language skills.[34]

Since July 2003 part of the examination, namely the chosen field of specialisation which accounts for 30 per cent of the final mark, is taken at the university, thus reducing the weight of state control.

The whole course of legal education was abridged, in order to meet the criticism that German lawyers were at a disadvantage compared to their colleagues in other countries who started in the profession several years earlier. While well into the 1990s the average age of young lawyers at admission had been over 30 years, this has gone down by approximately two years.[35]

The one-sided orientation of legal education towards civil service and judicial functions had always been criticised. Countless books and articles have been written on the subject. With less than 10 per cent of law graduates actually finding positions in these fields, and 75 per cent ending up in the *Anwaltschaft*, the German model of legal education had definitely out-

---

[34] The law faculties are still discussing what to do about it.

[35] The length of the practical training had varied over time between 3½ years and 2 years plus examination. For the past years it has been set at 2 years including the examination. Another factor which shortened legal training was the introduction of a rule that those who take the first examination after 4 years may have a first go at it without sanction in case of failure, ie without the failure being counted as such. (The examination may as a rule only be repeated once.) This has brought down the average length of law studies at university from 6 to 5 years.

lived its shelf life. Numerous new models have been invented and discussed over the past 15 years. One important question has been whether the state examinations should be abolished and replaced by a university examination as in any other subject. Also, should the practical training be split up for the different fields of practice and a specialised qualifying examination arranged by each branch of the legal profession? The reform went for the incremental, gradual modifications described above, without yet giving up the target of the *Einheitsjurist*.

Fifteen years ago the first universities started to offer practical skills training on a voluntary basis. In 2003 the German *Anwalt* Association, DAV, set up a one-year introductory course to practical work, a voluntary specialised qualification to follow on from the second state examination—possibly a forerunner of a new type of qualification. Whether the young lawyers will accept it, has to be seen.

The legal fee system is about to change. In July 2004 the *Bundes-rechtsanwaltsgebührenordnung* will be replaced by a *Rechtsanwalts-vergütungsgesetz*. As the change in terminology suggests, the idea of fees is to be replaced by one of 'payment'. The scaled fee system for contentious work is simplified, out-of court settlements will be remunerated, scaled fees for advisory work will be abolished by July 2006. Contingency fees or quota litis are still forbidden. However, the fee system is undermined by insurance firms financing law suits for clients unable or unwilling to pay. The insurance firm carries the risk and gets an agreed share (eg 30 per cent) of what is awarded[36] (Dethloff 2000).

One thing that has so far remained intact is the system of professional control by and compulsory membership in chambers. However, the German chamber principle is endangered by European legislation and court decisions.

Even the notariat is affected by market forces. Nobody in Germany had ever doubted that notaries exert public functions and are therefore exempted from freedom of establishment and service directives via Art 45. Following a complaint by a British notary the European Court has questioned the rule, sending shock waves through the profession (Shaw 2003b).

There can be no doubt that the process of liberalisation and deregulation of the profession will continue.

---

[36] Although this is only offered for cases with big values at stake.

5. The Profession Today

Economic Situation

The economic situation has deteriorated in recent years, due to increased competition and an overall weak economy in Germany. Regular statistics on the income situation of German *Anwälte* have been kept since 1993. They show that since 1999, incomes have dropped and are now lower than in 1993. The income situation is particularly poor for the average solo-practitioner. The golden times for bigger cross-regional and international partnerships with offices in several cities are over. The income in the Eastern part is still lower than in the West but more stable, and losses are less dramatic. *Anwälte* in the new federal states still have to accept a 10 per cent fee reduction compared to fees in the old federal states, but this will change from 2004.[37]

Table 3 Development of Incomes West/East between 1993 and 2001*

	Solo Practitioner West	Solo Practitioner East	Local Partnership West	Local Partnership East	Cross-Regional Partnership West	Cross-Regional Partnership East
1993	104	73	158	101	342	–
Median	84	54	142	80	300	–
1995	123	86	162	110	327	–
Median	104	65	138	90	294	–
1997	108	87	175	116	240	168
Median	80	66	142	93	180	130
1999	101	83	168	93	294	133
Median	81	65	133	83	215	101
2001	80	69	140	91	193	127
Median	58	54	116	78	150	100

* Figures are in 1000 DM and pre-tax

Although gross turnover per practitioner or partner has remained stable or has even risen in the East except for cross-regional partnerships, rising overheads have yet caused the income situation to deteriorate. In the West income stratification is greater than in the East.

---

[37] Taking account of the different economic situation and standard of living in East and West, the 1990 Unification Treaty provided for a 20% fee reduction for *Anwälte* in the East until 1996. Since 1996 the reduction has been 10%. In East Berlin it was abolished from 1 March 2002. On 28 January 2003 the Federal Constitutional Court ruled the reduction to be an infringement of the equality of treatment principle and therefore unconstitutional (Az 1 BvR 487/01).

Table 4 Turnover per Practitioner or Partner (West/East)*

	Solo Practitioner West	Solo Practitioner East	Local Partnership West	Local Partnership East	Cross-Regional Partnership West	Cross-Regional Partnership East
1993	246	179	293	219	800	–
Median	192	140	264	200	734	–
2001	205	206	289	226	425	345
Median	157	159	250	203	304	283

* Figures are in 1000 DM and pre-tax.

Overheads per practitioner or partner have risen sharply except for cross-regional partnerships. They are significantly higher in the East than in the West. Local partnerships have the most favourable income-overhead ratio.

Table 5 Overheads (in %)

	Solo Practitioner West	Solo Practitioner East	Local Partnership West	Local Partnership East	Cross-Regional Partnership West	Cross-Regional Partnership East
Overheads 1993	57.7	59.2	46.1	53.9	57.3	–
Overheads 2001	61	66.5	51.6	59.7	54.6	63.2

Data: Schmucker 2003.

For the year 2000 the average monthly net income per *Anwalt* (prior to deduction of pension and insurance costs) was calculated as 1511.51€ for solo practitioners, 3172.05€ for partners in a local partnership, 4009.25€ for lawyers in a large law firm (von Seltmann 2003a). By comparison, judges aged 50 who have been promoted once, or civil servants of that age who have been promoted two or three times (the normal expectations for that age) can expect a monthly net income of around 3500€.[38]

Salaried *Anwälte* suffered income losses too. In the West they had an average yearly income of 82,000 DM in 2001, their counterparts in the East had only 63,000 DM. Freelancers earned 78,000 DM in the West, and 61,000 DM in the East. *Syndici* (company lawyers admitted as *Anwälte*) had 141,000 DM in the West, 138,000 DM in the East.

Young lawyers in big cities are prepared to accept almost any offer and have even been known to work without pay just to get a chance to practice. Poor pay is not uncommon. Between 1996 and 1998, a young advo-

---

[38] Or even more, depending on family status.

cate was paid 1300 DM a month before taxes and social charges. The labour court saw this as an offence against moral standards (*gute Sitten*, s138 Civil Code), and the relevant clause in the employment contract was declared void. A monthly payment of 2800 DM for a 35 hour week in the first year of practice was considered to be in accordance with the 'common payment' envisaged by the law (s612 BGB)[39] (Seul 2002).

Judges have reported that young lawyers have been knocking on their doors asking for criminal work in the law courts and have labelled them 'corridor whores'.

On the other hand starting salaries for young lawyers in international firms have risen enormously. In UK based firms they run up to 100,000€ (200,000 DM), in German based firms about 70,000€–80,000€ (140,000–160,000 DM). Key criteria for high salaries include fluency in English and possibly in another foreign language, a PhD and an LLM. Top marks (*Prädikat*) in both state examinations are a *sine qua non*. In smaller or medium-sized firms a decent starting salary ranges between 30,000€ and 40,000€ (60,000–80,000 DM). All this reflects a widening of the income gap in the profession over the past 10 years, signalling a stratification process previously unheard of.

Legal aid has always made up a certain share of lawyers' work. In spite of a structural reform of the system in the 1970s, legal aid was however never much extended. This has meant that Germany, unlike other countries which have started drastically to shrink their formerly comprehensive legal aid systems, has so far not cut its public spending in this field. For a number of decades German *Anwälte* have derived an increasing portion of their income from legal expenses insurances. Germany was the first country to introduce such schemes, and today 50 per cent of households have some kind of legal expenses insurance (Kilian 2001, 2003; Kilian and Regan 2004).

Specialisation

An important factor for lawyers' economic success is specialisation. *Anwälte* who also hold a qualification in accountancy and are admitted as accountants are the highest earners, followed (in order of decreasing incomes) by specialists in administrative law, specialists in labour law,

[39] Decision by labour court of second instance (*Landesarbeitsgericht*) in Hesse of 28 October 1999, *Neue Juristische Wochenschrift* 2000, 3372. This was a very favourable interpretation of infringement of morality. In cases of mere bad pay this reasoning does not help. The Professional Regulations for Lawyers (BORA) contain a regulation that advocates may only be employed under reasonable conditions, which however does not provide a direct claim to better payment. Young lawyers could only ask the chambers for help and start ethical proceedings.

Anwälte with an additional qualification as tax adviser, specialists in commercial law (particularly competition and patent law), *Anwalt*–notaries, specialists in tax law, specialists in criminal law. The specialist groups with the lowest incomes are lawyers specialising in foreigners and asylum cases, specialists in social law, and, finally, generalists.

In 1960 only 5 per cent (= 911) of all admitted *Anwälte* held a specialist title. This figure had risen moderately to 6 per cent by 1989, jumping to 9 per cent in 1998 with the introduction of the new specialist titles, with high increase rates particularly in the areas of family law and labour law. In 2003 14 per cent (16,933) of the total (121,420) held a specialist title, breaking down as follows: tax law: 3391, administrative law: 1044, criminal law: 1326, family law: 5126, labour law: 5000, social law: 673, insolvency law: 373.

The number of *Anwälte* with a dual qualification as chartered accountants and tax advisers has recently seen a rapid growth, ie by 11 per cent in 2002 and by 10 per cent in 2003. This may be due to the rising demand from the growing number of bigger and multidisciplinary partnerships.

The number of so-called EU-*Anwälte*, ie lawyers practising in Germany and qualified in another member state of the European Union, is still low. In 2002, 293 of them had taken advantage of the right of freedom of practice under the establishment directive. By 2003, their numbers had increased by a remarkable 26.6 per cent to 371.[40]

In 2002, 1147 young lawyers between the ages of 27 and 39 left the *Anwaltschaft* (equalling 14.72 per cent of the 7790 newly admitted that year). Available statistics do not allow us to draw any conclusions as to whether this was due to lack of professional success in the advocacy or whether they were merely using the advocacy as a stepping-stone to move on to a post in the judiciary, the civil service or industry.

Feminisation[41]

Feminisation of the profession started late and only gained speed in recent years with deteriorating job prospects in the public sector which women had traditionally preferred. In 2003, of the newly admitted *Anwälte* 59.36 per cent were men and 40.05 per cent women (Seltmann 2003:227),[42] and

---

[40] In November 2003 the European Court of Justice ruled that law graduates from other states must be granted admission to practical training if they can prove the equivalence of their home qualification, representing a further inroad into national education requirements and a further deregulation of education.

[41] The story of women in the German legal profession is described in detail in Schultz, 2003b; Schultz 2003c.

[42] The missing 0.59% results from a number of lawyers' private limited companies being admitted.

the increase rate in the number of women in the profession was higher than that in the overall number of *Anwälte* (7.12 per cent as compared to 4.4 per cent from 2002 to 2003, the net increase in men in that year being 3.3 per cent). Thus women accounted significantly for the overall growth in the profession.

In the judiciary, the proportion of women among judges and public prosecutors had been rising faster for many years. With limited replacement in the judiciary in recent years, the percentage of women *Anwälte* is catching up.

Table 6 Proportion of Women in the Legal Professions

	Lawyers (Anwältinnen) %	Judges (Richterinnen) %	Public Prosecutors (Staatsanwältinnen) %
1960	>2.0	2.6	
1970	4.5	6.0	5.0
1980	8.0	13.0	11.0
1989	14.7	17.6	17.6
	= 7960 of 54,108	= 3109 of 17,627	= 661 of 3759
1991	16.1	19.1	19.5
1993	17.5	22.0	25.9
1995	19.3	26.3	28.9
1997	21.2	25.5 *	27.9 *
1999	23.7	26.3	
	= 23,139 of 97,791	= 5506 of 20,920	
2000	24.6		
	= 25,589 of 104,067		
2001	25.3	27.68	30.91
	= 27,924 of 110,367	= 5780 of 20,880	= 1559 of 5044
2003	27.9	30.1	32.99
	= 32,595 of 121,420	= 6291 of 20,901	= 1699 of 5150

Source: Federal Ministry of Justice (Judicial Statistics)
*Until 1995 the statistics for the judiciary only covered the old federal states. From 1997, data for the new federal states (the former communist part of Germany) have been included. This explains the slight decrease in the proportion of women judges and prosecutors in 1997.

The percentage of women amongst *Anwalt*-notaries is very low, only 9 per cent in 2003 (749), rising steadily but slowly. Of the solo-notaries 10.59 per cent were women (1062). The higher percentage of women in the latter group is the result of German unification, when socialist state notaries were transformed into Western-style solo-notaries. While in West Germany the share of women amongst solo-notaries has always been minute (32 = 3 per cent in 1994), in communist Eastern Germany, the German Democratic Republic, the profession of notary had been highly feminised, with low prestige and poor pay. (Shaw 2003a)

Table 7 Increase in Women in the *Anwaltschaft* and *Notariat*

	Female Lawyers (Anwältinnen) %	Total Increase In Lawyers (M And F) % and Absolute Figures	Incresase In Lawyers (F) % and Absolute Figures	Lawyer-Notaries (F) (Anwalts-Notarinnen) %	Solo-Notaries (F) (Nur-Notarinnen) Figures %
1985	12.04			4.42	
1991	16.08			4.87	14.44
1996	20.03			7.41	18.95
1997	21.21	96–97: 7.97* (6283)	14.32 (2261)	7.85	18.65
1998	22.40	97–98: 7.53 (6411)	13.53 (2442)	8.03	18.36
1999	23.66	98–99: 6.86 (6275)	12.89 (2642)	8.24	18.40
2000	24.59	99–00: 6.42 (6276)	10.59 (2450)		
2001	25.30				
2002	26.16				
2003	26.84	02–03: 4.40 (5116)	7.12 (2167)	8.95	10.59

Source: Official Statistics of the Federal Chamber of Advocates and the Federal Chamber of Notaries published annually in BRAK-Mitteilungen
* highest increase since 1976 (8.7 per cent) when training periods were cut down.

Women are generally less specialised than men, and their specialisation mainly falls into financially less rewarding fields of activity.

Table 8 Proportion of *Anwältinnen* with a Specialist Title[43]

(01.01.)	Tax Law %	Administrative Law %	Criminal Law %	Family Law %	Labour Law %	Social Law %	Insolvency Law %
1985	2.53	–	–	–	–	–	–
1990	2.89	3.28	–	–	6.57	16.31	–
1995	4.09	4.53	–	–	9.95	17.87	–
1998	5.65	7.31	7.22	47.76	13.31	21.03	–
1999	6.21	7.93	11.87	45.93	14.14	25.46	–
2003	9.67	12.16	15.46	51.74	17.68	26.45	7.24

Source: Official Statistics of the Federal Chamber of Advocates
Their income situation is less favourable.

The drop-out quota of young women is still higher than that of their male colleagues. Women try to find employment in other occupations outside the classical fields for lawyers, for instance in associations, (non-)profit making societies, service organisations, interest groups, trade unions.

The profession has hardly taken account of its female members. Professional rules ignore them, they speak—and think—of *Anwälte* (male form) not of *Anwältinnen* (female form), there are no rules on anti-dis-

---

[43] As already mentioned, the specialist titles were introduced at different times.

Table 9 Average Pre-Tax Income Per Hour of Full-Time *Anwälte* and *Anwältinnen* in the Old and New Federal States by Gender and Specialisation in 1996/97[44]

		Men DM	Women DM
Generalist	Old	45	19
	New	32	28
Specialist	Old	64	35
	New	46	31
with specialist title / Anwalt-notary*	Old	79	55
	New	57	43

* also including *Anwälte* admitted as tax advisers and as chartered accountants
Source: Schmucker/Lechner 2000

crimination, no professional recommendations on how to combine family and work, on maternity leave, part-time work, the workplace or flexible working hours. In due course, changes will be enforced by EU gender mainstreaming policies—with whatever outcome. Some of the bigger and internationally operating firms offer special working conditions for members with family obligations. But in times of a more contested market even for the big ones relevant references have started to disappear from homepages.

What cannot be discussed here is the impact of the feminisation of the profession on the scope and practice of professional work. It is difficult to measure. While women have effectively adapted to the traditional model of lawyers' practice, at least part of the deformalisation processes may well be attributable to their influence.[45]

Structure of the Profession

Germany still has a considerable number of solo-practitioners, ie about 55 per cent. Their numbers have risen in recent years due to newcomers on the market failing to find a position elsewhere. 35 per cent of lawyers are organised in local partnerships (*Sozietäten*), only 10 per cent work in large law firms with more than 10 *Anwälte*.

German civil law stipulates that in a law firm organised as (non-trading) partnership (*BGB-Gesellschaft*), each lawyer has full liability for professional negligence on the part of any other partner in any of the partnership's offices. Very recently, the organisational form of a private and a

---

[44] No newer data are available, but the situation does not seem to have changed for the better, rather the reverse.
[45] For details see Schultz & Shaw, 2003.

Table 10 Structure of German *Anwaltschaft* (2001)

Number Of Anwälte	Offices	Number Of Anwälte In Office
5,500	70	30–400
14,000	2,100	4–30
34,000	14,100	2–4
58,000	58,000	Solo-practitioner
(of these 58,000)	(8,000)	(Syndikus-Anwalt)
107,050		

public limited company (*GmbH* and *AG*) has become an option for law firms. (Passarge; Pluskat) By 2002, 38 firms had opted to become private limited companies, in 2003 their number had risen to 159, signalling further rises in future. In 2002 a total of 953 firms were practising as partnerships under the Partnership Act (*Partnerschaftsgesetz*).

The older solo- and small firm lawyers and other conservative elements in the profession deplore the passing of the good old times and anxiously watch and object to new ideas and modern forms of cooperation which have emerged in recent years: networks with joint interests and marketing strategies, even franchising with a common trademark (like *legitas*), emergency lawyers, *Anwalt*-Hotlines, internet lawyering, legal advice per e-mail, automatised legal advice (like *janolaw*). These transformation processes are as yet difficult to quantify.

As the number of admissions to the profession grows, the average age of the *Anwaltschaft* drops. Whereas in 1956 the average age was 50.7 years, in 1986 it was 44.4 years, and in 2002 it was down to 43.9 years. While in 1950 fewer than 3 per cent of advocates were under 30 years old, this percentage had risen to 8 per cent by 2002. The share of advocates over 70 years has decreased accordingly from 8.6 per cent in 1950 to 2.8 per cent in 2002.

Young lawyers face a longer wait before becoming partners than was the case only a few years ago. The classical distinction between young lawyers doing contentious work and older lawyers specialising in advisory or notarial work is blurring due to individual specialisation. In larger firms the two-part division between salaried *Anwalt* and partner is disappearing in favour of greater differentiation, as intermediate steps are inserted on the career ladder, with different voting rights and different shares in profit. Lawyers in these firms are no longer liberal professionals in a club of equals but rather professionals within organisations, no longer bosses but highly paid managers. (Hommerich 2001)

Large Law Firms — a Class of Their Own

Until ten years ago big partnerships in Germany consisted of 10–20 partners.[46] For the average partnership it is still uncommon to think of themselves in terms of a 'firm of lawyers' rather than a *Sozietät*, a partnership.
Managing partners or law firm managers were unknown until a few years
ago and are still the exception. The change occurred when Anglo-American
firms pushed on to the German legal market in the wider context of the
internationalisation of global market structures. (Henssler and Terry 2001)
Multinational firms demanded law firms of a matching profile with a broad
range of specialists. When it came to cross-border take-overs, mergers and
acquisitions, management buy-outs, and listings on the stock exchange,
traditional German law firms were out of their depth, ill prepared for
developments of this kind. They tended to be only moderately specialised,
all-knowing wise heads were considered to be important, not team-players.
Anglo-American usages did not fit the self-image of a German lawyer,
which emphasised serving rather than selling.

As time went by, German law firms had to merge with big Anglo-
American firms and have done so. They have learnt to put their heads to
beauty parades and hard bargaining. For some time they kept some of
their German identity due to the professional rule that the name of a partner had to appear in the firm's title. Since a ruling of the Highest Federal
Court has removed this requirement, German names have started to disappear from law firms' designations. There is a definite fracturing of the
market into two separate hemispheres. And there also is a gap between
large German law firms operating more along traditional lines and multinational law firms. The latter offer higher starting salaries but also operate in a climate of more acute internal competition, assessing individuals'
achievement by criteria like rainmaking, turnover, publishing etc.[47]
German firms traditionally prefer the lock-step system, ie each new lawyer
starts from the same income which is calculated upon a points scheme
with annual increments for the first ten years. After that the income
remains unchanged throughout the remainder of the partnership, which
makes for a sense of security on the part of individuals and a sense of solidarity among partners.

There are far fewer associates per partner in German law firms than in
Anglo-American firms—an average ratio of 1:1 to 1:3 compared to 1:4 or

---

[46] In a report on management concepts in the *BRAK Magazin* of 2003, firms of more than 10
lawyers are labelled as large firms. Schmucker, Alexandra, Anwaltsmarketing im
Kanzleivergleich, 3.

[47] The evaluation by the lead partner is necessarily subjective, which gives young lawyers a
feeling of insecurity and possibly unfair treatment.

1:5 or even more[48]—and income stratification was and still is much less pronounced. Until a few years ago, there tended to be a three—or a maximum five—year rule on the way to partnership. This has been extended in the multinational firms to six to seven or even eight years. Intermediate grades of participation have been introduced. Partnership has become an option, not a must. (Kilian 2002)[49] The remodelled firms have become more vulnerable to market weaknesses as they concentrate on high-end work, having off-loaded many fields of practice that guaranteed a lower, but steady income in the past, like employment law, public law, tax law. In the 1980s the bigger firms were opinion leaders in discussions of the reform of professional rules and set initiatives for reform. Today they are rather a separate class.[50]

A tedious irritation for large firms is the German rule (s10 BORA) that all partners have to appear on the letterhead.[51] Another source of annoyance is the impossibility of external ownership and multiple membership of a partner in more than one firm (*Sternsozietät*).[52] Conflict of interest was always regarded as a big problem as it extended to all members of a partnership/firm and not only to those who worked on the case. In July 2003 the Federal Constitutional Court held that the relevant rule was an infringement of Art 12 Bonn Basic Law, the constitutional right of freedom of professional practice, in that it prevented lawyers from changing firms.[53] A waiver by the clients or the use of Chinese walls was considered to be sufficient to protect clients' interests.[54]

The clash of different cultures[55] in firms leads to a degree of instability: on the one hand a so far unknown mobility of professionals from one firm

[48] Freshfields, Bruckhaus, Deringer recruited 100 new young lawyers annually over recent years, but in the past three years only promoted 40 lawyers to partnerships, a ratio of less than 1:8.

[49] Kilian gives the example that one of Germany's largest law firms proudly claimed some years ago that their ratio was 1:1—this law firm merged with an English law firm where the ratio was 1:8.

[50] They may consider themselves as 'top of the egg' (to use a metaphor coined by Avrom Sherr). This opinion is however not necessarily shared by the lawyer-middleclass.

[51] This has been upheld recently by the Federal Constitutional Court (decision of 13 June 2002, *BRAK-Mitteilungen* 2002, p 182; critical comment by Huff, Martin on p 184; NJW 2002, p 2163). The decision is based on the argument that it is important information for clients to avoid conflict of interest. In the light of a later ruling in 2002 by the same court on conflict of interest (see below), it may be possible that this decision could be overruled.

[52] Kilian states as another impediment the fact that in Germany multidisciplinary partnerships (MDPs) between advocates and accountants and/or tax advisers have always been allowed, a not inconsiderable number of German advocates holding a dual qualification. But it is foreseeable that under European competition law all member states will have to allow MDPs.

[53] German law prohibited representation or advisory work for two clients in the same or a related matter by the same firm whether or not the lawyers involved had possession of relevant information. Sec 3.2 BORA.

[54] Ruling of 3 July 2003, *BRAK-Mitteilungen* 2003, p 231.

[55] According to Hommerich, characteristics of the American style are, for instance, that the

to another has set in, on the other hand mergers in the late 1990s of German firms with English and American firms were frequently followed by break-ups, with the German part restarting its own business or looking for another international partner, or whole departments splitting off and starting a practice of their own. In recent economically tight years the German corporate clientele has begun to question the advantages of large law firms, with fear of high costs of legal services outweighing expectations of benefits resulting from lawyers' specialisation (Kilian 2002).

Range of Work

The image of the court lawyer is fading (Rabe 2004). Also for the average practitioner, work has at least partially shifted from contentious work to legal advice. There is overall less mystification of legal work, a sober service orientation is gaining ground, including reflections on quality standards and cost-effectiveness and the outer appearance of the firm. After all the fighting over advertising, marketing has now become a normal activity for a law firm, though a poll amongst clients by a lawyers' journal (called 'Anwalt') has shown that some 75 per cent still choose their lawyer on personal recommendation. Amazingly and contradicting any anecdotal evidence of poor practice being offered by many lawyers, a similar percentage of respondents declared themselves very content with their lawyer.

In a few years, publicity brochures for law firms have become much more common in Germany, representing an important factor in the process of modernisation and the promotion of a market orientation. They have helped finally to do away with the comic-image of the solo-practitioner in a small dark room with dusty books, hidden behind piles of paper files.

Rapid changes in the law owed to the prolific activities of modern legislatures and the extension of European law which permeates all fields of national law demand increasing investment in further training. Also soft skills, training in communication techniques, negotiation and mediation, are gaining in importance, but are only hesitatingly accepted.[56] The administration of justice promotes out of court settlement. Since a recent reform of the Civil Procedure Code a settlement session for minor cases has become obligatory. The policy behind it is to save public funds for con-

firm is no longer a lawyer's whole life, his family, and that job hopping, talking of money / income / bank balances is perfectly acceptable. In German firms, traditionally nobody would volunteer to reveal their income, be it only to prevent social envy. (Hommerich, 2001)

[56] My experience from training young lawyers in these skills is that they find it difficult to adjust to these alternative methods, as they are still struggling to master the techniques of legal reasoning they have only just learned in a long and painful process.

tentious matters and transfer cost to private users.[57] So far the impact of this initiative has been fairly negligible.

Ethical Questions — Still a Question of Honour?

German Anwälte still tend to know little about professional and particularly about ethical rules and do not spend a lot of time thinking about them. After all, they have their insurance against professional negligence.

There is no regular teaching of ethics. This may be partly because many of the questions which are considered to come under the heading of professional ethics and discipline in other countries, eg disputes over fee charging or breach of professional duties (negligence), do not fall within the scope of professional jurisdiction in Germany, but have to be dealt with by civil courts. Lawyers' socialisation process with its adaptation to the civil service ideal demanding high moral qualities of its members may also offer a partial explanation. A further factor is the duration and intensity of legal education. After eight to ten years of training a lot is at stake when an *Anwalt* faces the danger of disbarment. This helps to explain why statistics show that only few cases are taken to the disciplinary jurisdiction of the *Anwalts* courts. (Schultz 1997:76)[58]

The danger that discontented clients ever resort to proceedings at the professional courts is minimal. The fact that options for suing German *Anwälte* for negligence to obtain damages for breach of professional duties are clearly laid down may do a lot in the way of compensating dissatisfaction of clients. (Schultz 1997:77)

In sum, differences in this context compared to many other countries are not due to the fact that German *Anwälte* are necessarily behaving more ethically than their colleagues abroad, but that the system within which they are operating is a different one.[59]

---

[57] Even the European Commission has submitted a Green Book on Mediation.

[58] With increasing number of lawyers the percentage of *Anwälte* had started to decrease. In the 1980s approx 1% of *Anwälte* had been involved in disciplinary proceedings annually. This figure was halved by the mid–1990s. An easy explanation may be that (without any deliberate intention on their part) chambers tried to settle more cases informally as *Anwalt* courts could not cope with more work.

[59] The question is whether women are more ethical than men. German statistics are not gendered so far. Experiences in other countries, eg the Netherlands, show a lower involvement of women in ethical cases. (Schultz; Shaw, 2003)

Competitors

Lawyers' competitors in the legal market are tax advisers and chartered accountants. The latter not only dominate tax matters but also hold a significant share in advisory work for companies (company, contract, inheritance law). Solo-notaries extend the scope of their work—particularly under the pressure from the European market—to legal advice and may attract cases with big values at stake and high fees. (Shaw 2003b)

Lawyers in the civil service do not compete with their colleagues in private practice. They are barred from representing parties in most judicial proceedings, nor are they allowed a substantial side-line employment. The same holds true for most company lawyers. Though meanwhile most of them may be admitted as advocates (as so-called *Syndicusanwälte*), their workload as a rule does not leave enough time and space for more than occasional case work, and their main reason for applying for admission to the bar is to get the title of *Rechtsanwalt* and the possibility to join the profession's pension scheme The key question is how much legal work from companies is referred to *Anwälte* and how much is dealt with by in-house counsel. Company philosophies differ widely. In times of an oversupply of lawyers it may be cheaper to employ badly paid young lawyers than contract *Anwälte* who charge according to their fees scale. In recent years a growing number of young lawyers combine salaried—often part-time—work with practice as an *Anwalt*. This gives them scope to experiment how best to ensure a stable income in the longer run.

Paralegals are of almost no importance. The Legal Advice Act (*Rechtsberatungsgesetz*) outlaws unauthorised legal practice. There was a time when a small group of paralegals (*Rechtsbeistände*) enjoyed limited rights to give legal advice. However, admission to this profession terminated in 1981.

Of much greater importance are legal advisers, who, while not admitted to the bar, may give legal advice to a specific clientele on specific issues. They include trade union secretaries and advisers in consumer organisations, tenant and house-owner associations, student advice bureaux. Many of these organisations provide legal services by contracting *Anwälte* for an annual retainer who are ideologically oriented toward representing collective interests as well as individual claims.

6. The Future: Demands for Further Deregulation in the EU

The EU follows a strict policy fully to apply competition rules also to liberal professions, with the intent to establish an overall level playing field in the internal market. Regulations are only allowed when they are in the public interest. (Eichele and Happe, 2003:1215) In a speech entitled 'Competition in professional Services—new lights—new challenges', delivered on 21 March 2003 in Berlin at the Federal Chamber of Anwälte, the present European Commissioner for Competition, Mario Monti, summed up the elements of EU policy with regard to the legal professions as follows:

Member States have the right to regulate a profession. They can delegate to professional bodies as long as they retain the decision-making powers and establish sufficient control mechanisms. A regulation may be essential for the functioning of a profession even if it is against Art 81 I EC–Treaty. However, member states should refrain from establishing undue and disproportionate restrictions of competition, and regulators should also avoid unjustified restrictions to the freedom of establishment and to the freedom to provide services of practitioners from other member states. The overall goal must be to improve welfare for all users of professional services: better choice and better value for money. Any rule that is restrictive of competition and not reasonably necessary to guarantee the proper practice of the profession could be analysed by the Commission or the courts.

The Institute of Advanced Studies in Vienna has in its study 'Economic Impact of Regulation in the Field of Professions in Different Member States'[60] classified the professions in the members states according to a regulation index: regulation of market entry, regulation of conduct, overall index. The overall index ranges from 0 in case of no regulation to 12 in case of maximum regulation. In the legal profession the index ranges from 9.5 in Greece (*where the legal profession is built on the traditional German model*) to 0.3 in Finland, with many countries clustering around 6, including Germany. Monti's conclusion: Why would German consumers be less

---

[60] Institut für Höhere Studien (IHS), Vienna, January 2003. Economic impact of regulation in the field of liberal professions in different Member States. Regulation of Professional Services. Iain Paterson, Marcel Fink, Anthony Ogus *et al.* Executive Summary of a Study for the European Commission, DG Competition: http://europa.eu.int/comm/competition/publications/prof_services/executive_en.pdf
Part 1: http://europa.eu.int/comm/competition/publications/prof_services/prof_services_ihs_part_1.pdf
Part 2: http://europa.eu.int/comm/competition/publications/prof_services/prof_services_ihs_part_2.pdf
Part 3: http://europa.eu.int/comm/competition/publications/prof_services/prof_services_ihs_part_3.pdf

able to take care of their own interest than the Danish etc countries with low degrees?[61]

Monti stressed the fact that in countries with low levels of regulation, incomes per professional are lower, but the number of practising professionals generating a relatively high overall turnover is higher. This would suggest that low regulation is not a hindrance but rather a spur to overall wealth creation (and, one might add, to greater stratification). He concluded:

> You as professionals would gain from healthy competition. You may be better able to adapt your services and innovate to meet the evolving needs of the users. ... Lower regulation will expand the market: acting as forces for change is in our own interest (Hellwig 2003).

On 28 January 2004 the European Commission decided to review the professional regulations of the liberal professions. On 9 February 2004 it called upon the member states, the professions and their regulatory bodies to eliminate price-fixing and other restrictions which prevent competition, unless clearly justified by public interest considerations. The existence of price, advertisement and other restrictions, so it argued, is preventing the delivery of benefits to the economy and consumers in particular. The Commission pointed out that restrictions are still plentiful and often lack objective justification, that Germany eg continues to set minimum fees for lawyers, in some cases combined with maximum fees. It emphasised that the experience in countries which have abolished price regulations, such as France for legal services, and the United Kingdom for conveyancing, indicates that price controls are not an essential instrument for ensuring high quality standards.

The reactions of the German *Anwaltschaft* to these measures and declarations are a combination of helplessness, insecurity, irritation and anger (eg Hellwig 2003). Editorials in the legal press had headings such as 'Danger from Brussels', 'German *Anwälte* with their backs to the wall. Liberal profession status under attack from Brussels', 'Monopoly for legal advice is melting'. Repercussions are likely to include:

- The new Fees Regulations are outdated before they ever come into force. No proposed fee scale will hold in the long term.[62] (Sagawe 2002)
- The obligatory membership in chambers will have to be abolished. It is considered to be medieval corporatism.
- The regulations on specialisation are considered as advertising restric-

---

[61] Martin Henssler and Matthias Kilian have written on behalf of the German Chamber of *Anwälte* a comment on the findings of the report which was submitted to the EU Commission in October 2003. http://www.anwaltverein.de/ihs.pdf (German version).

[62] Maybe with the exception of fee scales for representation at courts, but even that is doubtful.

tions hindering competition and will at least have to be modified.
- Any remaining ban on advertising will have to be done away with.[63]
- The monopoly of legal advice for Anwälte cannot be upheld.[64]
  (Kleine–Cosack 2003)

All this represents a severe shock to the established system, the precise consequences and outcome of which cannot yet be gauged. How fast the intended changes will be brought about cannot be predicted, but obviously the Commission is pushing hard.

7. Interim Balance: Modest Adaptation to the Market

The German Anwaltschaft is still homogeneous, but centrifugal forces are gaining in strength. There is an accelerated process of internal differentiation and stratification. Members of a liberal profession conceived of as a club of equals are turning into competitors, and members of firms and partnerships into 'professionals in organisations'. (Hommerich 2001) The development in the past twenty years has been marked by a moderate but accelerating deregulation which in itself was characterised by a shift from regulation by a code of honour to regulation by law. Old crusty structures have been broken up. (Hartung 2003) The time of the gentlemen's profession is over. It is important for the profession to discuss their self-concept and self-image, to adapt to changing social conditions, to gain self-respect as an independent force, and to move towards self regulation.

The whole guild, not just the internationally oriented *Anwälte* and those in big firms, have opened up to the spirit of competition and the market in a process of slow and gradual adaptation, although even now the *Anwaltschaft* are not yet fully market-oriented. They find themselves on the threshold of a transformation from a profession to a trade. The question is what the consequences will be—for the *Anwaltschaft*, the legal and the political system, society at large, and the consumer.

It cannot be denied that the German model of *Einheitsjurist* has its merits. It provides a sense of corporate identity to a whole group of professionals, represents a kind of backbone to German society and an integral part of the German model of *Rechtsstaat*. Lawyers' long training assures

---

[63] Other countries will have to levy the ban on multidisciplinary partnerships.
[64] In 1996 the European Court of Justice had still accepted the monopoly. EuGH, SlG 1996, I–6511 (6540), comp König, Schönberger)

quality of work, and homogeneity stabilises professional ethics. As *Anwälte* have the quality stamp of state examinations, they have so far remained protected against quality controls by state agents at later stages of their practice. Whether continuing liberalisation outweighs the disadvantages of further deregulation and enhances economic benefits can be doubted, but there is no way the process can be stopped. The ultimate test should be whether professional ethics are upheld and the profession's image remains unscarred. And precisely that will be the problem.

References

BLANKENBURG, Erhard and Ulrike SCHULTZ *German Advocates: A Highly Regulated Profession.* In *Lawyers in Society,* ed by Abel, RL and P SC Lewis, (Berkeley, Los Angeles, London, University of California Press, 1988), 124.

BLANKENBURG, Erhard and Ulrike SCHULTZ *German Advocates: A Highly Regulated Profession.* In *Lawyers in Society. An Overview,* ed by Abel, Richard L and Philip SC Lewis, (Berkeley, Los Angeles, London, University of California Press, 1995), 92

BLEEK, Wilhelm *Von der Kameralausbildung zum Juristenprivileg,* (Berlin, Colloquium, 1972).

COHN, Ernst J The German Attorney: Experiences with a Unified Profession, 1960/61 9 *International and Comparative Law Quarterly* 580–99, 10 *International and Comparative Law Quarterly* 103–22.

DAHRENDORF, Ralf *Gesellschaft und Demokratie in Deutschland,* (Munich, Piper, 1965).

DETHLOFF, Nina Verträge zur Prozessfinanzierung gegen Erfolgsbeteiligung, 2000 *Neue Juristische Wochenschrift,* 2225.

EICHELE, Wolfgang and Eike Happel Verstoßen die BORA und die FAO gegen das Europäische Kartellrecht? 2003 *Neue Juristische Wochenschrift,* 1214.

VON GNEIST, Rudolf *Die Freie Advocatur,* (Berlin, Springer, 1867).

HARTMANN, Michael *Juristen in der Wirtschaft. Eine Elite im Wandel,* (Munich, Beck, 1990).

HARTMANN, Michael *Der Mythos von den Leistungseliten Spitzenkarrieren und soziale Herkunft in Wirtschaft, Politik, Justiz und Wissenschaft,* (Frankfurt aM, New York, Campus, 2002).

HARTSTANG, Gerhard *Der deutsche Rechtsanwalt. Rechtsstellung und Funktion in Vergangenheit und Gegenwart,* (Heidelberg, CFMüller, 1986).

HARTUNG, Wolfgang Das anwaltliche Berufrecht in der Rechtsprechung des BVerfG seit 1987, 2003 *Neue Juristische Wochenschrift,* 261.

HELLWIG, Hans-Jürgen Europäisches Wettbewerbsrecht und freie Berufe. Monti bläst zum Angriff, 2003 BRAK-Mitteilungen) 19.

HENSSLER, Martin and Laurel TERRY Lawyers without Frontiers—a View from Germany, 2001 *Dickinson Journal of International Law,* 269.

HESSE, Hans Albrecht, *Berufe im Wandel,* 2nd ed (Stuttgart, Ferdinand Enke, 1972).

HEUSSEN, Benno and Thomas GRIEBEL *Strukturen der Rechtsanwaltschaft in Deutschland und in den USA* 2003. http://anwaltsmanagement.anwaltverein.de/ Strukturen_Rechtsanwaltschaft.doc

HOMMERICH, Christoph *Die Anwaltschaft unter Expansionsdruck. Eine Analyse der Berufssituation junger Rechtsanwältinnen und Rechtsanwält*, (Cologne, Verlag Bundesanzeiger/Essen, Deutscher Anwaltsverlag, 1988).

HOMMERICH, Christoph and Hanns PRÜTTING *Das Berufsbild des Syndikusanwalts*, (Essen, Deutscher Anwaltverlag, 1998).

HOMMERICH, Christoph *Der Einstieg in den Anwaltsberuf*, (Essen, Deutscher Anwaltverlag, 2001).

KAUPEN, Wolfgang *Die Hüter von Recht und Ordnung*, (Neuwied, Luchterhand, 1969).

KILIAN, Matthias Legal Aid and Access to Justice in Germany. In *The Challenge of the New Century*, Vol 1, 13–29 ed by ILAG (ILAG, Melbourne, 2001)

KILIAN, Matthias *The Arrival of the Large Law Firm in Germany.* Presentation for the Legal Profession Group Conference at Aix-en-Provence 2002.

KILIAN, Matthias Alternatives to Public Provision: The role of Legal Expense Insurance in broadening access to justice: The German experience. In *After Universalism: Re-engineering Access to Justice*, ed by Moorhead, Richard and Pascoe Pleasance, (Oxford, Blackwell, 2003).

KILIAN, Matthias and Francis REGAN Legal Expenses Insurance and Legal Aid— Two Sides of the Same Coin? The Experience from Germany and Sweden, 2004, *The International Journal of the Legal Profession*, 233.

KLEINE-COSACK Michael *Berufsständische Autonomie und Grundgesetz*, (Baden-Baden, Nomos, 1986).

KLEINE-COSACK Michael Neuordnung des anwaltlichen Berufsrechts, 1994 *Neue Juristische Wochenschrift*, 2249.

KLEINE-COSACK Michael Berufs–und Fachanwaltsordnung für Rechtsanwälte, 1997 *Neue Juristische Wochenschrift*, 1257.

KLEINE-COSACK, Michael Restriktive Auslegung des Rechtsberatungsgesetzes, 2003 *Neue Juristische* Wochenschrift, 3009.

KNEER, August *Der Rechtsanwalt. Eine kulturpolitische Studie*, (Mönchengladbach, 1928).

KÖNIG, Hartmut Rechtsberatungsgesetz in Gefahr, 2001 *Zeitschrift für Rechtspolitik*, 409.

KÖTZ, Hein et al., *Anwaltsberuf im Wandel. Rechtspflegeorgan oder Dienstleistungsgewerbe*, (Frankfurt/M, 1982).

KREIZBERG, Kurt Die Juristen in den Organisationen der deutschen Wirtschaft, (Köln, Wirtschaftsverlag Bachem, 1994).

KURTZ, Thomas *Berufssoziologie*, (Bielefeld, transcript Verlag, 2002).

MONTI, Mario *Competition in Professional Services: New Light and New Challenges.* Conference paper. BRAK. Berlin, 21 March 2003 http://europa.eu.int/comm/competition/speeches/text/sp2003_007_en.pdf

MÜLLER, Lothar *Die Freiheit der Advokatur. Ihre geschichtliche Bedeutung in Deutschland und in der Neuzeit und ihre rechtliche Bedeutung in der BRD*, (Unpublished PhD dissertation, University of Würzburg, 1972).

OSTLER, Fritz *Die deutschen Rechtsanwälte 1978–1971*, (Essen, Ellinghaus, 1971).

PARSONS, Talcott Professions. In: *International Encyclopedia of the Social Sciences*, vol. 12 (New York, Macmillan/Free Press, 1968 536–547).

PASSARGE, Malte *Die Aktiengesellschaft als neue Rechtsform für anwaltliche Zusammenschlüsse. Zulässigkeit und Ausgestaltung*, (Bonn, Deutscher Anwaltsverlag. Schriftenreihe des Instituts für Anwaltsrecht an der Universität Köln, 2003).

PLUSKAT, Sorika Die Firma der Anwalts-AG, 2004 *Anwaltsblatt*, 22.

PORTELE, Gerhard and Wolfgang SCHÜTTE *Juristenausbildung und Beruf*. Hamburg, Interdisziplinäres Zentrum für Hochschuldidaktik der Universität Hamburg (AZHD Hochschuldidaktische Arbeitspapiere no 16).

RABE, Hans-Jürgen Vom regulierten Prozeßagenten zum selbstbestimmten, Dienstleister, 2004 *Anwaltsblatt*, 65.

REIFNER, Udo Die Zerstörung der freien Advokatur im Nationalsozialismus, 1984, 17 *Kritische Justiz*, 380.

ROGOWSKI, Ralf The Growth of Corporate Law Firms in Germany. In *Professional Competition and the Social Construction of Markets*, ed by Dezalay, Yves and David Sugarman, (London, Routledge, 1994).

RÜSCHEMEYER, Dietrich *Lawyers and Their Society: A Comparative Study of the Legal Profession in Germany and the United States*, (Cambridge, Mass., Harvard University Press, 1973).

SAGAWE, Christian Rechtsanwaltsvergütung und EU–Gemeinschaftsrecht, 2002 *Neue Juristische Wochenschrift*, 281

SEUL, Jürgen Advokatur und Ausbeutung—Die Missachtung des § 26 BerufsO in der etablierten Anwaltschaft, 2002 *Neue Juristische Wochenschrift*, 197.

SCHÖNBERGER, Christoph Rechtsberatungsgesetz und Berufsfreiheit, 2003 *Neue Juristische Wochenschrift*, 249.

SCHÜTTE, Wolfgang *Die Einübung des juristischen Denkens. Juristenausbildung als Sozialisationsprozeß*, (Frankfurt, Campus, 1982).

SCHULTZ, Ulrike The Practicing Lawyer in the Federal Republic of *Germany*. A Summary of the Major Rules Governing the Profession of West German Lawyers and Their Effects Upon the Manner in Which Foreign Lawyers Can Collaborate with West German Colleagues, (ed by Paul Koessler) 1980 *The International Lawyer*, 531.

SCHULTZ, Ulrike Women in Law—The Masculinity of the Legal Profession in Germany. In *European Yearbook in the Sociology of Law 1993*, ed Alberto Febbrajo and David Nelken, (Milano, Giuffrè, 1994) 229.

SCHULTZ, Ulrike Legal Ethics in Germany, 1997 *International Journal of the Legal Profession*, 55.

SCHULTZ, Ulrike Women in the World's Legal Professions: Overview and Synthesis. In *Women in the World's Legal Professions*, ed by Ulrike Schultz and Gisela Shaw, (Oxford, Hart, 2003)(2003a) 271.

SCHULTZ, Ulrike The Status of Women Lawyers in Germany. In *Women in the World's Legal Professions* , ed by Ulrike Schultz and Gisela Shaw, (Oxford, Hart, 2003)(2003b) 295.

SCHULTZ, Ulrike Women Lawyers in Germany—Perception and Construction of Femininity. In *Women in the World's Legal Professions*, ed by Ulrike Schultz and Gisela Shaw, (Oxford, Hart, 2003)(2003c).

SCHULTZ, Ulrike Die deutsche Anwaltschaft zwischen staatlicher Gebundenheit und freiem Markt. In *Festschrift für Prof Dr Klaus Röhl*, ed by Stefan Machura,

(Baden-Baden, Nomos, 2003)(2003d) 103.

SCHMUCKER, Alexandra STAR: Umsatz-und Einkommensentwicklung der Rechtsanwälte 1993 bis 2001, (BRAK-Mitteilungen, 2003) 254.

SHAW, Gisela Women Lawyers in the New Federal States of Germany: from Quantity to Quality? In *Women in the World's Legal Professions*, ed by Ulrike Schultz and Gisela Shaw, (Oxford, Hart, 2003)(2003a) 323.

SHAW, Gisela The German Notariat and the European Challenge, 2003 *International Journal of the Legal Profession*, 37.(2003b).

VON SELTMANN, Julia Umsatzeinbrüche. Einkommen der Anwälte gesunken, 2003 *BRAK Magazin*, 12.

VON SELTMANN, Julia Statistik Jurastudenten, Prüfungen, Rechtsanwälte, 2003 *BRAK-Mitteilungen*, 225–28.

WESEL, Uwe *Risiko Rechtsanwalt*, (München, Karl Blessing, 2001).

WEISSLER, Adolf *Geschichte der Rechtsanwaltschaft*, (Leipzig, Pfeffer, 1905) (reprinted Frankfurt, Sauer und Avermann, 1967).

WETTERER, Angelika *Professionalisierung und Geschlechterhierarchie*, (Kassel, Jenior und Preßler, 1993).

6

The Australian Legal Profession: Towards a National Identity*

MARGARET THORNTON

Introduction:
The Conundrum of Modernisation

The legal profession in Australia, like the profession in other parts of the world, has undergone profound change in the last quarter of a century. Australia is still a monarchy with the Queen as its Head, but the process of sloughing off imperial ties has been a distinctive feature of modernisation, which has impacted on the structure of the profession and legal practice. While the centenary of federation in 2001 was a reminder of the country's independence and autonomy as a nation, the constituent States and Territories, each with its own jurisdiction and admission procedures, norms and practices, serve as a reminder of the heterogeneity of the Australian legal landscape. The legacy of history weighs heavily, despite the imperatives to change.

Significant though it is, an exclusive focus on modernisation fails to capture the shifts and turns associated with contemporary politics. In Australia, as in many other parts of the world, there has been a marked swing away from the experience of social liberalism. In 1972, a Labor Government was elected after 23 years of Liberal (conservative) government. This period, under the Prime Ministership of Gough Whitlam (1972–75), represents the high point of social liberalism. Since the 1980s, but particularly since the 1990s, there has been an unravelling of the welfare state, inchoate though it was in Australia, as in other Western liberal capitalist democracies.

* Thanks to Jo Bagust and Judith Dickson for commenting on the manuscript, and to Dennis Warren for library assistance.

While liberalism has not been abandoned altogether, it is a particular form of neoliberalism, or market liberalism that is in the ascendancy. The principles in favour of a regulated economy, a strong public sphere, social justice and the common good, have generally been jettisoned in favour of deregulation, privatisation, market choice and individual good. This trend boosts the work of legal practitioners. Nevertheless, it is one that has not been consistently followed in respect of the profession itself. Instead, a paradox is apparent in that, while neoliberalism favours deregulation, neoliberal governments have been the most assiduous in seeking to regulate the legal profession (McQueen 2000). Such contradictions highlight the complexity of social change, as well as the limitations of structural theories predicated on clear lines of demarcation between different incarnations of liberalism.

All State jurisdictions have enacted new Acts to replace their Nineteenth Century Acts.[1] Reforms include moderating the rigid division between barristers and solicitors. Historically, colonial New South Wales, Queensland and Victoria retained a formally separate bar, while barristers and solicitors' branches were fused in South Australia, Western Australia and Tasmania, as well as subsequently in Victoria, even though a 'voluntary bar' existed in those jurisdictions (Weisbrot 1988). Lawyers are now generally admitted as 'legal practitioners', rather than having to choose whether to become barristers or solicitors *ab initio*. Separate applications are made to the relevant Law Society or Bar Association in order to practise as either a solicitor or a barrister, although some overlap exists in the provision of advocacy services and advice. Admission to a State or Territory court permits practise in a federal court.

The steps towards unification, rationalisation and consistency between jurisdictions have been halting and uncertain. Nevertheless, the pro-market and pro-competition imperatives of neoliberalism are hastening the propulsion towards a national 'market' for legal services. The Mutual Recognition Act 1992 (Cth) was enacted in order to facilitate the free movement of lawyers between States and represents an important step towards the development of a national regime. The Act does not guarantee interstate practitioners an automatic right of practice. To be recognised, they must still apply to a specific jurisdiction, pay admission fees and maintain practising certificates. The Trade Practices Commission recommended an integrated national legal services market with formal recognition in each State and Territory of the practising rights of lawyers admitted in any other jurisdiction (ALRC 2000). The former Attorney-General, the Hon Daryl

---

[1] Legal Profession Act 1987 (NSW); Legal Practice Act 1996 (Vic); Legal Practitioners Act 1995 (Qld); Practitioners Act 1981 (SA); Legal Practice Act 2003 (WA); Legal Profession Act 1993 (Tas).

Williams, in supporting a national regime, advocated uniformity in the fundamentals of legal practice, including trust accounting, professional indemnity insurance, conduct rules and disciplinary procedures (2001). These principles have been incorporated into a draft Model Bill for a national legal profession (Standing Committee, 2003). Thus, it is the market, with some prodding from government, rather than philosophical commitment or self-direction by professional associations, that is providing the primary impetus for the development of an 'Australian' professional legal identity.

The rapidity and multifaceted character of change is compelling lawyers to re-invent themselves in ways previously unimaginable. Many of the restrictive practices of the past, such as those relating to advertising and contingency fees, have been liberalised as a result of greater responsiveness to the market. Exclusivity of role has been eroded by competition from outside the profession, as well as by increasing mobility between jurisdictions. The multiple incarnations of what it is to be a lawyer in Australia today suggest that the profession is experiencing the postmodern turn at the very moment that it is entering the modern age. As Australia has moved away from reliance on primary production to the tertiary sector for its economic wellbeing, legal services have become a pivotal resource in facilitating the knowledge economy, which has everywhere replaced land as the new site of contest between nation states (Lyotard 1984). Within this new global paradigm, legal services are treated as market commodities in their own right. The export of legal services has developed rapidly since the 1990s with the assistance of the International Legal Services Advisory Council (ILSAC), a body that operates under the auspices of the Attorney-General.

It must also be pointed out that an altogether different pressure, namely, an increasing public cynicism towards lawyers, has hastened some aspects of change. While cynicism about lawyers is by no means a new phenomenon, it is no longer countered by an aura of mystique or the service ideal of lawyering. Deprofessionalisation, coupled with greater scrutiny and accountability, graphically signals the declining status of lawyers. Other change agents include the 'massification' of higher education and information technology.

Against this kaleidoscopic backdrop, I will present an overview of an increasingly heterogeneous profession, including changes in areas of work, practice and procedure, professional bodies and regulation, the development of a pro bono culture and legal education.

Mapping Legal Practice

Private practice remains the core of the legal profession in Australia, as in other common law countries. This characteristic has become even more pronounced with neoliberalism's propensity to privatise public goods. The Australian Bureau of Statistics (2003) revealed that there were 36,124 qualified legal practitioners working in the legal services industry in 2001–02. This figure included 29,159 solicitors and 3,670 barristers. These practitioners were distributed over 11,493 practices, 7,566 of which were solicitor practices and 3,670 barrister practices.[2] In addition, they employed 57,628 general staff.

Table 1 Number of Legal Practitioners in Legal Practices 2001–02

	Solicitors	Barristers	Patent Attorneys	Govern- ment	Legal Aid Authorities	Community Legal Centres	Total
Practices Solicitors/	7566	3670	41	18	8	191	11,493
Barristers	29,159	3,670	37	1,935	770	553	36,124
Patent Attorneys	98*	0	324	0	0	0	421

Source: Australian Bureau of Statistics 2003
*Estimate and should be used with caution.

The legal services industry generated income of more than AUD10m and contributed 1.1 per cent to the Australian GDP in 2001–02. Allowing for labour costs and other operating expenses, the total operating profit before tax was AUD3335 million. Commercial, property and personal injury law were the major sources of income. More than 80 per cent of the total revenue was accounted for by solicitor practices.

Table 2 Income from Legal Services 2001–02 (AUDm)

Solicitor Practices	Barrister Practices Businesses	Patent Attorney	Government Solicitors	Legal Aid Authorities	Community Legal Centres	Total
8378.6	1146	287.6	413.6	325.5	84.8	10,636

Source: Australian Bureau of Statistics 2003

[2] Solicitors normally practise within firms, whereas barristers are more likely to practise alone. The generic term 'practices' is used to encompass both and to conform to the Australian Bureau of Statistics nomenclature.

Australia is a highly urbanised society, with approximately 85 per cent of its total population of 20 million living on its eastern coastal fringe. Legal services are disproportionately concentrated in the most populous States of New South Wales (together with the Australian Capital Territory (ACT)) and Victoria, which generate more than 70 per cent of the total income. The average income per solicitor practice in both New South Wales and the ACT was more than AUD1315m in 2002.

Table 3 States and Territories, Solicitor Practices 2001–02

	Practices		Practitioners		Total Income	
	No.	%	No.	%	AUDm	%
New South Wales	2,894	38.3	11,900	40.8	3,810.7	45.5
Victoria	2,430	32.1	7,678	26.3	2,049.3	24.5
Queensland	1,049	13.9	4,415	15.1	1,221.8	14.6
South Australia	413*	5.5*	1,752*	6.0*	394.1*	4.7*
Western Australia	649*	8.6*	2,104	7.2	599.4	7.2
Tasmania	116	1.5	444*	1.5*	84.0*	1.0*
Northern Territory	56*	0.7*	210	0.7	42.4	0.5
Australian Capital Territory	133	1.8*	656	2.3	176.9	2.1
Australia	7,566	100.0	29,159	100.0	8,378.6	100.0

Source: Australian Bureau of Statistics 2003
*Estimate and should be used with caution.

Table 4 States and Territories, Barrister Practices 2001–02

	Practices		Practitioners		Total Income	
	No.	%	No.	%	AUDm	%
New South Wales	1612	43.9	1612	43.9	664.4*	58.0
Victoria	1202	32.8	1202	32.8	292.4	25.5
Queensland	431	11.7	431	11.7	97.5*	8.5
South Australia	190*	5.2	190*	5.2	35.9*	3.1
Western Australia	147	4.0	147	4.0	40.3*	3.5
Tasmania	13*	0.4	13*	0.4	2.1*	0.2
Northern Territory	26	0.7	26	0.7	5.6*	0.5
Australian Capital Territory	47*	1.3	47*	1.3	7.7*	0.7
Australia	3670	100.0	3670	100.0	1146.0	100.0

Source: Australian Bureau of Statistics 2003
*Estimate and should be used with caution.

While the 1970s might be identified as the high point of social liberalism, this period is also associated with the emergence of the corporate law firm, which has transformed legal practice. In no time at all, the corporate law firm became the mega-firm through mergers and takeovers. By the 1990s, the trend was for these big firms to become even bigger. The 1999 rankings (based on the number of lawyers) projected by the International Financial Law Review 1000 indicated that 6 of the world's 40 largest firms are from Australia. In the Asia Pacific region, Australia has 10 of the top 15 firms. Increasing overheads, including costly information technology, has boosted the trend towards amalgamation. The neoliberal turn would also seem to have engendered a greater emphasis on the maximisation of profits. It is notable that the top six or eight Australian firms have shed areas of practice that do not command premium billing, including wills, probate, family law and criminal work (Law Council 2001).

One per cent of solicitor practices employ more than 100 persons. These large firms employ 30 per cent of all solicitors and account for 42 per cent of the operating profit before tax. The phenomenon of the employed solicitor in the corporate law firm is challenging the popular image of the autonomous lawyer as sole practitioner or partner in a small firm as the norm. Nevertheless, despite the propulsion towards the creation of ever-larger national firms, corporatism did not signal the end of the small solicitor practice, an organisational form that had already withstood the challenges of post-War growth (Mendelsohn and Lippman 1979). About 70 per cent of all legal practices in Queensland, for example, are conducted by a sole principal (<http://www.qls.com.au/qls/function.htm>). Small solicitor practices are found in myriad small towns around the country, although they comprise only about ⅓ of all practising solicitors. At the same time, the increasing trend towards specialisation has created a need for small boutique practices (ALRC 2000).

In addition to the trends in favour of both large and small firms, there is also a third trend of a more destabilising nature. This is the emergence of multi-disciplinary practices (MDPs), a new form of partnership business effected between lawyers and non-lawyers. Although so far permitted only in New South Wales, they are set to become much more widespread with their inclusion in the national Legal Profession Bill (Standing Committee 2003). MDPs offer integrated services in the interests of clients because they facilitate 'one stop shopping', but they also represent an attempt to staunch the haemorrhage of business away from law to other professions. In establishing MDPs, accountants and business consultants are the favoured partners, although law firms themselves are establishing a wide range of 'spin-off' specialist services (Warnecke 1998). These developments are further eroding the exclusiveness and autonomy of the legal profession. The new deregulated environment also poses unresolved ethical, regulatory and disciplinary questions, in respect of which prevailing legal norms afford little guidance.

Despite the rhetoric emphasising service, ethics and professionalism, law firms are businesses devoted to profit making, just like the business interests they serve. While the practice of law has always had a business and profit-making dimension, this factor has become more pronounced as a result of the corporatisation of the law firm. Gone are the days when a few partners controlled the day-to-day operations of a firm. The emphasis on business activities is apparent in the type of publications and professional advice, which has emerged since the 1980s. The opening line of a management guide for practitioners prepared by the Law Institute of Victoria states baldly: 'Your practice is a business ...' (1985; cf. Barker 1994; Fenton and Grutzner 1996; Balls 1998). In an age dominated by the market, there is now concern that the business imperative may have supplanted the service ideal of the profession.

The corporate law firm as business proposition is further supported by moves to incorporate legal practices. In Victoria, South Australia, Tasmania and the Northern Territory, incorporation is permitted on an unlimited liability basis, whereas New South Wales permits incorporation on a limited liability basis, which included public listing from 2001. Individual lawyer directors and employees, not the company, are subject to the Solicitors' Rules (Law Council 2001; Standing Committee 2003).

Within firms, there is much more focus on strategic planning in order to deal with the reduced share of the market and increased competition arising from deregulation and the abolition of monopolistic practices (Stein and Stein 1994). Competition is no longer restricted to the local or national level. The high demand from transnational corporations for cross-border legal services to facilitate global business is further eroding jurisdictional practices of exclusiveness. Anti-competitive barriers are being lowered to make it easier for foreign lawyers to be admitted to the practice of law in Australia in recognition of the trend towards the globalisation of legal services. Greater regard is being paid to experience, as opposed to credentialism, although lawyers from common law countries still need to satisfy the admitting authorities that they have completed certain course requirements, such as Constitutional Law, Property and Ethics. Transcending the individual level, it is notable that a small number of North American firms have established branches in Australia. Legislation relating to the practice of foreign law in Australia has been enacted in all jurisdictions, except Queensland and Western Australia (see also Standing Committee 2003). Despite this increasing receptiveness within Australia, the Law Council has observed that there is no sign that reciprocal rights have been extended to Australian lawyers overseas (Law Council 2001), although overseas law firms are happy to recruit lawyers trained in Australia. The fact that Australian law partners earn less than their European counterparts has been a disincentive in respect of international amalgamations. It has, however, proved advantageous in respect of tendering, and Australian firms are beginning to tender successfully in Europe (Law Council 2001). The main area of dynamism offshore is in Asia, where Australian law firms have established offshore alliances.

Despite the increasing heterogeneity of the Australian legal profession, corporate law firms continue to exercise a disproportionate amount of power over both the legal profession and legal education (cf. Kronman 1993). The homologous relationship between big business and law is clearly apparent. A cognate area of growth is that of in-house lawyering for large corporations. The Law Council (2001) estimates that there are at least 2700 of these corporate lawyers but, because they are not necessarily members of law societies, they do not appear in statistics. The calibre of corporate counsel has improved as their salaries have risen. They are cost effective for companies, costing 41 per cent of the fully loaded costs of lawyers from private practice (Law Council 2000).

In the face of neoliberalism's apparent antipathy towards the public sphere, the contraction of the public service and a propensity to engage in outsourcing, it is notable that public law practice has also expanded. The increase in government lawyers, including community legal centre and legal aid lawyers, over the decade 1988–98 was reported to be 43 per cent overall, with a 27 per cent increase at the federal level (ABS 2000).

Solicitors

Stein and Stein (1994) liken the impact of change on legal practice to that of a tornado. Rather than being sole practitioners or partners in small firms, the majority of lawyers are employed associates who are accountable for what they do with their time and the generation of income through billable hours. In recent years, however, there has been a reaction against the 'tyranny of billable hours' with moves towards a more realistic task-based billing, at least on the part of Sydney's largest law firms (Law Council 2001).

Despite changes in the nature and substance of practice, traditional fields continue to be the most prevalent. Thus, property remains the most prevalent field of work, being carried out by 86 per cent of solicitor practices. Small practices (less than five persons) generated 29 per cent of income from this source, compared with 19 per cent for all solicitor practices. The bulk of property work continues to be conveyancing, despite the trend towards deprofessionalisation. Wills, probate and estates were the second most prevalent field of work, which was carried out by 73 per cent of practices, although generating only 4 per cent of practice income. Large practices generated more than 39 per cent of their income from commercial work, compared with 28 per cent overall.

Table 5 Sources of Income, Solicitor Practices 2001–02

	Practices (No)	Value (AUDm)	Proportion of Total Income (%)
Property	6585	1756.1	21.0
Wills, probate and estates	5701	299.0	3.6
Banking and finance	1365*	528.0	6.3
Commercial	2975	2074.0	24.7
Family	4069	484.7	5.8
Criminal	3091	146.0*	1.7*
Environmental	537*	80.2	1.0
Intellectual property	652*	212.0*	2.5*
Industrial relations	1297*	238.8	2.9
Personal injury	3215	1304.8	15.6
Administrative/Constitutional	584*	78.6*	0.9*
Other fields	2564*	782.2	9.3
Total	7566	5984.2	95.3

Source: Australian Bureau of Statistics 2003
*Estimate and should be used with caution.

The conventional congruence between women lawyers and the affective side of practice persists (Thornton 1996) but has become less pronounced. A survey of New South Wales solicitors revealed that 17 per cent of women and 14 per cent of men were engaged in family law practice (Israel 2001). Nevertheless, the stereotypical assumptions that money and masculinity are imbricated with one another are still reflected to some extent in commercial law practice in which 33 per cent of male lawyers are engaged, compared with 26 per cent of women. In the cognate area of property, 39 per cent of male solicitors are to be found, compared with 26 per cent of women.

Lawyers in private practice work long hours—often as much as 50 or 60 hours per week, resulting in professional associations investing effort on time management and stress because of 'burnout' (ALRC 2000). Increased pressure can be attributed to the uncertainty resulting from the excessive demands and fickleness of clients, coupled with stiff competition, which is compounded by the trend in favour of having to tender for work (Nosworthy 1995).

High remuneration is the hoped-for recompense for long hours of work. The average income for solicitors in private practice was AUD129,000 in 2002 (ABS, 2003), whereas the average income for partners varied between

AUD300,000 and AUD1 million per annum, depending on the size of the firm and whether they are salaried or equity partners (Lawson 2001). A gender-based earnings differential persists, which means that men figure disproportionately in the high earnings bracket and women in the low. A New South Wales survey found that 13 per cent of women solicitors, compared with 30 per cent of men, reported incomes of AUD100,000 or more. On the other hand, 45 per cent of women compared with 27 per cent of men, reported incomes of AUD50,000 or less (Israel 2001).

The effects of technological change, particularly modes of communication and transmission of documents, as well as the conduct of searches, have revolutionised legal practice. The new technology enables lawyers to engage in routine work while away from the office, whether travelling or at home. The trend towards outsourcing and 'virtual staff' underscores the idea of the law firm as business proposition, in which a small core of staff are employed to manage non-core outworkers.

Although home-based work, or 'telecommuting', is touted as a flexible option for lawyers with parenting responsibilities, it can induce a degree of invisibility for legal workers. Deviations from the normative *in situ* model of full-time work are perceived as aberrant and can deleteriously affect applications for promotion. The Women Lawyers Association of New South Wales draws attention to the advantages and disadvantages of telecommuting on its website (http://www.wlansw.asn.au/workfrom.htm).

Barristers

11 per cent of practitioners (3,670 in 2002) hold themselves out to be barristers, or courtroom advocates. Those from a fused profession who wish to engage in advocacy may choose to practise as a barrister at the bar, which gives them the independence associated with barristers, or they may choose to operate through a law firm. Those who choose membership of the Bar are, with the exception of Western Australia, required to practise as sole practitioners (Law Council 2001).

Barristers' practices were responsible for 11 per cent of the total income generated by the legal services industry in 2001–02 (AUD1146m). The main sources of income were personal injury and commercial law, although significant income was also generated from criminal law, administrative and constitutional law, family law, banking and finance, property and intellectual property.

With a 66.5 per cent operating profit margin (compared with 30 per cent for solicitors), the average income for barristers was AUD206,900 in 2002, although senior counsel, like senior partners in corporate law firms, can earn more than a million dollars per annum. The normal equation is: the longer at the bar, the higher the income.

Table 6 Barrister Income 2001–02

Barrister Type	Senior Counsel	Junior Counsel	Total
Practices	386	3286	3670
Estimated return per barrister AUD '000	519.4	170.4	206.9

Source: Australian Bureau of Statistics 2003

The most remunerative areas of practice for barristers were property, tax and commercial work. As for solicitors, the more human-centred cluster of personal injury, crime and family law are associated with the lower end of the remuneration spectrum.

The bar has traditionally been regarded as the élite branch of the profession, although it has been suggested that its status is being threatened by the big corporate firms (Weisbrot 1988). These firms woo the top law students, offering them the opportunity to work as summer clerks ('Christmas beetles') before they graduate. They are then tantalised with generous remuneration packages and the prospect of lucrative partnerships. It is difficult to renounce these rewards for what could be many years of insecurity of life at the bar, which may also involve considerable outlay in the purchase of chambers, particularly if one is proposing to set up practice in Sydney. Nevertheless, it is clear that barristers are doing very well financially. Not only is their average income well above that of solicitors, the data reveals a 40 per cent increase in annual income per barrister between 1999 and 2002.

In a move away from the imperial and monarchical ties of the past, Queen's Counsel (QC's), the senior branch of the bar, or 'silks', are now known as Senior Counsel (SC's) in most States. The '⅔ rule', in which a QC was always assisted by a 'junior', who charged ⅔ of the fee charged by the QC has become less rigid, again in response to the market. The term 'junior' itself may carry pejorative overtones, since it applies to all counsel who are not SC's, even if they have been practising for twenty years or more.

Barristers continue to be overwhelmingly male and their support staff overwhelmingly female. Women constitute 15 per cent of barristers, and face greater resistance as advocates than practitioners in other branches of the profession. The gender discrepancy between SC's is most marked. In New South Wales, 18.5 per cent of men but only 0.75 per cent of women belong to the Senior Bar (NSW Bar Association 2001). Although the discrepancy is somewhat less egregious in the Junior Bar, where 81.5 per cent are men and 12.3 per cent are women, it continues to be a cause for concern. There has long been unwillingness on the part of solicitors to brief women, perhaps because of the authoritative and public nature of advocacy (Thornton, 1996). Bar Associations and some Attorney-Generals have begun to address the issue and develop strategies for effecting gender equity.

Judges

Traditionally, judges have been selected from the ranks of the senior Bar. As in the United Kingdom, they are normally appointed by the government of the day, on the basis of informal recommendations. Judges may be appointed from the ranks of solicitors and public lawyers, although such appointments are still relatively uncommon. When a solicitor was appointed to the Victorian Supreme Court for the first time in 1987, there was an outcry. Possibly because of a residual distrust of the academy, it has been even rarer to appoint academics as judges, although specialist jurisdictions, such as Family Law, have been more receptive than general jurisdictions. However, this bias is also receding, as can be seen from the appointment of law professors to both the Federal Court and the New South Wales District Court in the 1990s.

Women constitute approximately 15 per cent of the judiciary. Most of the women who are judges have been appointed subsequent to the ventilation of public concern about the extent of gender bias in the judiciary in 1993 (Parliament of the Commonwealth of Australia, 1994). The gender bias critique prompted debate about the general absence of transparency in the criteria for appointment of judges (Law Council of Australia 2000). Victoria was the first jurisdiction to advertise a vacancy in a superior court. As a result, the Victorian Government was able to claim in 2003 that the appointment of Marilyn Warren as the first Chief Justice of an Australian superior court had been made after an unprecedented search for the best candidate.

Demographic Profile of the Profession

The composition of the Australian legal profession formerly displayed a high degree of homogeneity, as it was dominated by Anglo-Celtic, middle class men. It now evinces greater diversity, although precise demographic data is unavailable. While data in respect of sex is generally collected and data in respect of race, class and age is occasionally collected, data in respect of religion and sexuality is not collected at all. The Law Council of Australia relies on a range of sources in respect of its data, including State and Territory professional associations, but consistent criteria are not used, partly because there is 'no definitive definition of the legal profession' (Law Council 2001:17).

Sex

The most striking change in the profile of the profession in recent years relates to the increase in the number of women practitioners. In the early 1970s, women constituted approximately 20 per cent of law students and 6 per cent of practitioners. They now constitute more than 50 per cent of law students[3] and more than 30 per cent of the practising profession. However, these figures belie the fact that women still encounter resistance in the more authoritative areas of practice. This is reflected in all areas of the profession. For example, women represent 9 per cent of principals/partners in large law firms, 15 per cent of judges and 20 per cent of the professoriate, but only 1 per cent of senior counsel. In solicitor practices generally, women constitute 48 per cent of employed solicitors but less than 20 per cent of sole practitioners and partners.

Table 7 Gender of Lawyers in Solicitor and Barrister Practices 2001–02

	Males	*%*	*Females*	*%*	*Persons*	*%*
Sole Practitioners/ Partners	11,508	82.2	2494*	17.8*	14,002	100.00
Employed Solicitors	7859	51.9	7299	48.1	15,157	100.00
Barristers	3129	85.3	540*	14.7	3670	100.00
Total	22,496	68.5	10,333	31.4	32,829	100.00

Source: Australian Bureau of Statistics 2003
*Estimate and should be used with caution.

The gender breakdown for all employees within legal practices is illuminating. 66 per cent of those working in solicitor practices are women, of whom 12 per cent are paralegals, 65 per cent are other non-professional support staff, and less than 20 per cent are qualified practitioners. The gender disproportionality is even more striking in the case of barrister practices, where 79 per cent of support staff but only 15 per cent of barristers

[3] In a study of law students conducted in 1994, women constituted the majority of students in 19 out of the 24 law schools, and a majority of the final year students in 12 of the 18 law schools with final years (Roper, 1995).

are women. It would seem that the stereotype of women as ancillary workers has contributed to their non-acceptance as authoritative legal practitioners.

The liberal progressivist hope that it would simply be a matter of time before women secured equality within all branches of the profession, including its most prestigious areas of practice, has not been realised. While advances have undoubtedly emanated from numerosity, women continue to be fringe dwellers of the jurisprudential community (Thornton 1996). They tend to be paid less than men, to be offered less favourable assignments and to be subjected to disparagement and sexual harassment, particularly in private practice. They tend to be more comfortable as government lawyers and corporate counsel. Indeed, women are almost twice as likely as men to work in the public sector (Israel 2001). A 'boys' club' mentality, fostered by sport, coarse humour, lunching and drinking, has created a culture of camaraderie between lawyers and corporate clients that is designed to facilitate business, but operates to exclude women. Legal careers in the public and corporate sectors are less dependent on homosociality.

The ideal lawyer is constructed not only in masculinist terms, but also as one who is autonomous and uncompromisingly committed to the workplace, including the 'long hours culture', a culture that is encouraged by practices found in some of the big firms, such as the provision of meals and weekend retreats in out-of-town locations. Regardless of child bearing and rearing responsibilities, women are expected to conform to the same autonomous worker ideal. Although initiatives to accommodate family responsibilities, such as flexible working hours, part-time work, and home-based work have made a limited appearance, women still encounter the ubiquitous 'glass ceiling' and less favourable treatment than men. Indeed, 37 per cent of women solicitors surveyed in New South Wales reported that they had been subjected to discrimination on the ground of sex (Israel 2001).

Women lawyers are cautious about complaining to anti-discrimination agencies about discrimination or sexual harassment because of fear of reprisal. Their concerns relate not just to the firm, which they normally leave once the workplace has become hostile, but the possibility that they may be 'blackballed' within the profession and find that they are unable to obtain another position. The only reported discrimination complaint that proceeded to public hearing is *Hickie v Hunt and Hunt* (1998) EOC 92–910, a complaint that involved a solicitor on a contract partnership who took maternity leave and returned to work on a part-time basis, when her contract was not renewed. Her claim of indirect discrimination on the ground of sex was successfully made out, and damages were awarded because of the unreasonableness of the requirement or condition that she would have had to work full-time in order to maintain her practice.

Race

Australia abandoned its notorious 'White Australia' policy in the 1960s and consciously embraced a policy of multiculturalism from the 1970s. A study of Australian graduates in 1997 reveals how the predominantly Anglo-Australian image of the typical lawyer has become more varied. The study found that 68 per cent identified themselves as Anglo-Saxon (down 9 per cent from 1991), 17 per cent as European and 11 per cent as Asian (up 4 per cent from 1991). Only five of the 1997 cohort identified themselves as being of Aboriginal/Torres Strait Islander background (Karras and Roper 2000).

Issues pertaining to Aboriginality have been on the Australian political agenda since the 1970s, as evidenced by the enactment of the Racial Discrimination Act 1975 (Cth) and the development of social justice policies. The bicentenary of white settlement in Australia in 1988 represented a high political moment, which was a cause for both celebration and regret. The struggle for land rights culminated in two controversial High Court cases: *Mabo v Queensland* (1992) 66 AJLR 408 and *Wik Peoples v Queensland* (1996) 141 ALR 129, but the *Wik case* coincided with the neoliberal turn, which signalled a harsher stance on race and reconciliation. Somewhat ironically, however, such cases have led to race and native title issues emerging as new areas of specialisation for legal practitioners. In *Yorta Yorta Aboriginal Community v State of Victoria* [1998] 1606 FCA, there were more than 400 non-claimant parties. The millions of dollars expended on legal fees in such cases have resulted in disparaging references to 'the native title industry'.

To redress the dearth of Aboriginal lawyers, initiatives to encourage and support indigenous students have been fostered by law schools, such as the University of New South Wales, from its inception in the early 1970s. Aboriginal legal services were also established at that time. Aboriginal magistrates have been appointed in New South Wales, Queensland and Western Australia, as has a judge in New South Wales. Legal professional bodies and the private profession have been slow to offer support to indigenous students and lawyers. In Victoria, however, a mentoring scheme has been developed by the Supreme Court Aboriginal Cultural Relations Committee to facilitate training for students and lawyers in major law firms.

Class

With the collapse of communism, class has declined worldwide in importance as a category of analysis, despite valiant attempts to revive it (Seron and Munger 1996). Class has always been a problematic concept for lawyers, as the legal profession is a middle class occupation that relies upon a middle class client base. The data reveals that law students tend to enter law school with the cultural capital derived from the middle class occupations of their parents, as well as their own educational experience at selective schools (private independent, Catholic and state selective) (Ziegert 1992; Karras and Roper 2000). Conventionally, law students have had the most élite social background of all Australian university students (Weisbrot 1988). Hence, there is a well-established homology between law students, high status areas of practice, and business and professional interests.

More recently, the 'massification' of higher education, together with the establishment of regional law schools and alternative modes of entry, has contributed to the creation of a somewhat more diverse legal culture. Nevertheless, even if a neonate lawyer comes from a modest working class background, the legal acculturation undergone at law school and in the profession, particularly the likelihood of acting only for wealthy individuals and corporations, can alter a lawyer's class orientation. A biography of Sir Garfield Barwick, a former Chief Justice of the High Court, shows how a person with comparatively humble beginnings can quickly become an advocate for the privileged (Marr 1992).

While the proportion of politicians who are lawyers is relatively small—about 15 per cent over all—these lawyer-politicians exercise a disproportionate amount of power, because of their domination of leadership positions, including that of Prime Minister, State Premier, and opposition leader (cf. Weisbrot 1988). Sir Garfield Barwick held the key position of federal Attorney-General before he was appointed Chief Justice of the High Court in 1964.

The legal profession exudes an aura of conservatism even though there are many lawyers who are supportive of progressive politics. Indeed, a strand of political radicalism has been associated with Australian law schools since the 1960s (Chesterman and Weisbrot 1987). Neoliberalism, however, has revived an interest in property accumulation and individual profit-making at the expense of common good, a factor that has served to augment the profession's conservative image. It is a primary function of lawyers to protect private interests of this nature, which ensure continuing class privilege. The concept of class is certainly not passé, despite the enduring myth that Australia is an egalitarian and classless society.

Age

Although comprehensive national figures are not available, the NSW Bar Association, the Law Society of New South Wales and the Law Institute of Victoria collect data. The increase in the number of new graduates to the profession is dramatically affecting the age profile of the profession. One survey found that 50 per cent of lawyers working as corporate counsel had graduated since 1990 (Law Council 2001). Another found that 47 per cent of solicitors in New South Wales are under 40.

The Law Council of Australia (2001) avers that 'Generation X' lawyers are exerting an impact on the profession because they are generally more concerned with doing interesting work than earning huge salaries. This new wave of lawyers may find the culture of the big firms unattractive, preferring 'dotcoms' to the stability of a firm. The conjunction of age and femaleness is the most striking feature of this data. The Victorian figures show that while women represent 57 per cent of practitioners under 30, and 44 per cent of those between 30 and 39, the numbers drop to 12.8 per cent for those who are over fifty (Brown 2000). The New South Wales gender profile is similar.

Table 8 Age Distribution by Gender: NSW Solicitors 1999

	Male	*Female*	*Total*
Less than 30	12.1	26.2	16.7
30–39	26.2	39.8	30.7
40–49	33.2	23.0	29.8
50 and over	27.4	9.0	21.3
Unknown	1.2	2.2	1.5
Total (%)	100	100	100

Source: Law Society of NSW 2000; Law Council of Australia 2001

At the upper end of the age spectrum, there is a population of older lawyers who do not wish to be involuntarily retired when they need to maximise their income to accommodate increasing longevity. There are reports of a trend to 'bully' older employees out of jobs (Law Council 2001). While sole practitioners are unlikely to be 'bullied' out of a job, they also see the future as bleak. The 1999 Victorian Annual Practising Certificate Survey found that solicitor sole practitioners tended to be older men who had been in the job for many years and 'were pessimistic about the future' (Brown 2000:21). In contrast, the survey found that most young lawyers, who were predominantly female and worked in the city, were optimistic about the future. The suggestion is that 'Generation X' lawyers are coping with the turbulence of change better than older lawyers in conventional legal practice.

Practising Trends

Substance

Deprofessionalisation is transforming legal practice. Lawyers may now find themselves in competition with accountants, mediators, insurance companies, migration agents and banks. The legal monopoly over conveyancing, long the lucrative mainstay of legal practice, has virtually come to an end. The amount of personal injury work that solicitors do has declined overall with the advent of no-fault schemes, although common law actions are still a prominent source of income, particularly for barristers.

Lawyers, as the *'par excellence* legal inventors'* (Cain 1994) have substituted new areas of practice for those that have contracted. As we inhabit an age of statutory regulation, this has not been difficult. Human rights, discrimination law, and environmental protection, for example, are areas of practice unknown to the common law, but which received a boost during the Whitlam years. This period was also marked by an increasing tendency to centralise regulatory power to accord with a new notion of nationhood, as well as to rationalise the plethora of inconsistent State and Territory laws, all of which were grist to the mill of lawyers.

Deregulation has not hurt lawyers either. The movement away from a centralised wage-fixing system to enterprise bargaining and private workplace contracts has caused an explosion of work in the areas of industrial and employment law. Sports law has been described as 'a spectacular growth area' (Sexton 2000), but biotechnology, patents and all forms of intellectual property have superseded it. Trade practices, taxation and corporate law are also areas of practice that have mushroomed with the growth of the global economy.

Dispute Resolution

Courts and tribunals, including the establishment of a federal jurisdiction, expanded to accommodate the increase in regulation and the social justice initiatives of the Whitlam Government. The Family Court, which allowed no-fault divorce for the first time, was established by the Family Law Act

1975 (Cth). The ratification of United Nations Conventions on human rights, civil rights and discrimination resulted in the establishment of the Human Rights and Equal Opportunity Commission, while specialist anti-discrimination tribunals were established at the State level. From the late 1990s, however, there has been a tendency to rationalise these tribunals in favour of generalist bodies.

The burgeoning of intellectual property and contract disputes is posited as a reason for the dramatic growth in litigation, as in the United States and the United Kingdom (Haigh 2000). A federal Magistrates' Court was established in 2000 to take pressure off the Federal Court. The High Court (2000) reported a significant increase in its judicial workload, with special leave applications heard by the Court rising by 64 per cent in 1999–2000 compared with the previous year. The conservative underpinnings of neoliberalism have also evinced a tendency to criminalise matters that may have formerly given rise to a welfare solution. The Law Council (2000) notes that whereas there were 14 special leave applications in criminal matters to the High Court in 1977, this had risen to 114 by 2000.

While adversarialism remains central to the common law system of adjudication, it has been the subject of scrutiny and critique, particularly because of the high public cost of allowing litigants to determine the ambit of their own litigation (ALRC 1999). The possibility of introducing private courts has been mooted, but the issue is not yet formally on the official agenda (Parker 2001). Such a development would nevertheless comport with the 'user pays' philosophy of neoliberalism. Electronic courtrooms and on-line dispute resolution are also being developed in many Australian jurisdictions in an effort to reduce costs (Law Council 2001).

Paralleling the increase in litigation has been a move towards cheaper and less formal measures of dispute resolution. Mediation, for example, is used across the entire spectrum of civil litigation, as well as within diversionary criminal law programmes (Astor and Chinkin 2002). Mediation is one of the new areas of non-traditional work being undertaken by lawyers.

Regulation of the Profession

Attempts to regulate the profession and make its practices transparent and accountable are an ongoing aspect of modernisation. Hence, inquiries into the legal profession have proliferated since the late 1970s, as the New South Wales experience reveals (eg, NSW Law Reform Commission, 1979a, 1979b, 1979c, 1981a 1981b, 1981c). The propulsion in favour of law as business has been constrained by measures requiring lawyers to be more accountable. Clients have been voicing concerns for years regarding the 'turn around' time involved in the handling of matters, the quality and cost of legal services, the extent of over-servicing and the handling of complaints. Government regulation has sought to respond to public criticism by reining in the profession and curtailing its autonomy. Barristers and solicitors are now subject to common admission systems, external disciplinary procedures and scrutiny from the Trade Practices Commission in regard to price fixing and other restrictive practices.

The profession itself generally prefers self-regulation based on industry codes of practice (ALRC 2000). Both barristers' and solicitors' associations advocate compiling professional practice rules pertaining to procedure and professional conduct. While State Bar associations (representing barristers) adopted the uniform rules developed by the Australian Bar Association in 1993, law societies (representing solicitors) have compiled State-based comprehensive rulings and decisions, particularly relating to trust accounts. The Law Society of Western Australia issues certificates to firms that have successfully undergone an independent assessment and authorises them to use the logo 'Approved Quality Practice' on their stationery and publications (<http://www.lawsocietywa.asn.au/qps.html>). All sections of the profession are anxious to secure compliance with acceptable ethical standards in view of the deleterious impact of defalcations and instances of incompetence on the standing of the profession.

Government regulation of the profession nevertheless continues to be contentious, with some legal professional bodies still vainly hoping for a return to more traditional forms of self-regulation, and community organisations advocating the establishment of independent regulatory schemes. The tension is apparent in relation to the revised Victorian regime, about which concerns continue to be raised regarding complexity, conflict of interest and cost (Sallman and Wright 2001). The appointment of a statutory legal ombudsman, a non-lawyer, empowered to investigate complaints against lawyers, highlights the move away from self-regulation, which has been bitterly opposed by the professional associations (Shiel 2003). Nevertheless, self-regulation is no longer the reality in any Australian jurisdiction and a reversion to it is highly unlikely. Instead, a limited form of co-regulation has become the norm.

Typically, if a matter cannot be resolved by the relevant law society or bar association in the first instance, it is referred to an independent complaint handling body, such as a legal services commissioner or ombudsman, and then, perhaps, to a body such as a complaints tribunal, which has the power to make orders. The tribunal includes lay members on its panel, signifying the more active community role in the regulation of the profession. The power to strike the name of the errant practitioner from the Roll is usually reserved for the Supreme Court.

Needless to say, professional bodies are anxious to foreclose the possibility of complaints going 'outside' with their adverse publicity. A muted approach towards possible infractions is adopted by the Queensland Law Society, which refers, somewhat euphemistically, to its complaint handling section as the 'Client Relations Centre' <http://www.qls.com.au/complaints/complaints.htm>. In New South Wales, in contrast, members who have been disbarred are named on the homepage of the Bar Association's website <wysiwyg://26/http://www.nswbar.asn.au>. There was a public outcry in that State when it was revealed that a barrister had failed to pay tax for 38 years and a number of other barristers were declared bankrupt (Videnieks 2001). To counter criticism of the profession, the NSW Legal Profession Act was altered, requiring practitioners declared bankrupt to be either suspended or disbarred.

State and Territory law societies and bar associations have been reluctant to cede power to a centralised body to rationalise the handling of complaints, although such a step would make sense for a national profession. The Commonwealth could rely on its constitutional power relating to corporations to establish such a body, but prefers not to be heavy handed in a regime dependent on cooperation. The resistance of State bodies may have influenced the Law Council of Australia to change its position from one of support for a single national body to govern the legal profession to a regime involving schemes specific to each jurisdiction. In line with its support for a national profession, the Australian Law Reform Commission (2000) encourages the adoption of cooperative regulatory models within the States and Territories. While the moves towards a unified national profession are becoming more definite, the fragmentation and rivalries of the past have frustrated and slowed the process.

Professional Bodies

As the discussion of regulation of the profession makes clear, the States have their own professional organisations, with separate associations for barristers and solicitors. Whereas the Queensland Law Society is incorporated under its own special Act of Parliament (Queensland Law Society Act 1952), most organisations are less formally constituted, although their powers may be mandated by statutes governing the legal profession. Professional associations perform a range of functions, including regulation and complaint handling although, as pointed out, community dissatisfaction has sought greater independence in the performance of these roles. Prudential supervision is nevertheless seen to be of crucial importance, particularly when the associations stress their commitment to justice, not just the interests of members (eg, <wysiwyg://28http://www.nswbar.asn.au>; http://www.vicbar.com.au>). Supervision includes the maintenance of ethical standards, control over practising certificates, regulation of trust accounts and administration of guarantee funds.

The associations also offer assistance and support to members on both substantive and professional aspects of practice. They are major providers of continuing legal education (CLE) programmes. In a conscious endeavour to improve the standing of the profession, the associations organise community activities, such as Law Week, when they participate in educational programmes. For example, the Law Institute of Victoria runs an Extension Education Service to provide assistance in the teaching of legal studies and law-related subjects in secondary schools and technical colleges.

At the national level, the Law Council of Australia (<http:www.law-council.asn.au>) provides a national voice on law and justice. It liaises with State bodies and increasingly plays a role in representing the Australian profession in the international arena (Law Council of Australia 1992). The Council maintains links with foreign professional associations, including the International Bar Association, LAWASIA, the Commonwealth Lawyers' Association and the Union Internationale des Advocats. It also pursues professional interests, such as advocating liberalisation of market access for Australian lawyers in foreign jurisdictions through both the Council's International Trade and Business Law Committee and ILSAC. In addition to pursuing professional interests, the Council has taken an ethical stance on a range of issues pertaining to overseas jurisdictions, such as the independence of the judiciary, deviations from the rule of law and violations of human rights.

Despite playing an increasingly proactive role in supporting the profession and recognising the necessity of speaking with one voice, professional associations are becoming increasingly fragmented. The disparity between the large national corporate law firms, which see themselves as the drivers of policy, and the more traditional small firms has caused some of the former to withdraw, giving rise to 'two hemispheres' in the practice of law (Arup 2001). As suggested, the nature of the work is also quite different: business and commercial versus personal legal assistance. This fissure between practitioners is a sign of the increasing heterogeneity of the profession. It may well be that the growth of MDPs will cause a further rift, leading to the creation of breakaway associations.

Women lawyers' associations have worked assiduously to improve the profile of women within the profession. Each jurisdiction has a women lawyers' association, and there are also women barristers' and feminist lawyers' associations (<http://wlansw.asn.au/womenlaw.htm>). Victoria convenes a national organisation: Australian Women Lawyers. Separate associations for women lawyers were nevertheless opposed by mainstream organisations in the outlying States of Queensland, Western Australia and Tasmania as late as the 1980s (Thornton 1996).

From Legal Aid to Pro Bono

The idea of a 'right' to state-funded legal aid for people unable to afford lawyers' fees is a marked casualty of neoliberalism and the contraction of public expenditure. The principle of Commonwealth responsibility for legal aid, which was established by the Whitlam Government in 1973, began to unravel soon afterwards (Noone 2001). Responsibility reverted to the States alone in the 1990s, and the trend in favour of user-pays has left virtually all but the most serious criminal offences and some family law matters without legal aid.[4] There are also a number of court-based and bar association-based legal assistance schemes in operation. Several organisations, which are partly sustained by the interest on solicitors' guarantee funds, such as the Public Interest Law Clearing House (Vic) and the Public Interest Advocacy Centre (NSW), support cause lawyering and pro bono work.

The main responsibility is now expected to be assumed by the profession itself in the form of pro bono work, a strand of lawyers' work that has received little systematic scrutiny in Australia, despite the substantial value put on such work by professional associations (Western, Makkai and Natalier 2001). Pro bono is widely understood as the provision of legal services to the community on a voluntary basis, but it is impossible either to define or to quantify precisely. The Australian Bureau of Statistics collects data from practitioners based on estimates.

Table 9 Estimated Pro Bono Work undertaken by Solicitor Practices according to Size of Practice 2001–02

Principals/partners	*1*	*2*	*3–5*	*6–9*	*10 or more*	Total
No Practices	3032	1019	528	90	75	4744
Time spent '000 Hours	736.5	311.3	350.4	85.8	206.4	1690.4

Source: Australian Bureau of Statistics 2003

---

[4] The High Court has held that the trial of a person charged with a serious crime cannot proceed if the accused is not legally represented: *Dietrich v The Queen* (1992) 67 ALJR 1. The principle does not extend to appeals, or applications for leave to appeal.

156   *Margaret Thornton*

Table 10 Estimated Pro Bono Work undertaken by Barristers according to Type of Practice 2001–02

Barrister Type	Senior Counsel	Junior Counsel	Total
Practices	301	2577	2878
Time spent '000 Hours	79.2	534.9	614.1

Source: Australian Bureau of Statistics 2003

The vagueness surrounding the meaning of pro bono is compounded by the legal profession's tendency to conflate it with paid legal work under legal aid schemes (Arup 2001; Weisbrot 2001). Discounted legal fees may be characterised as pro bono, as well as the more familiar provision of service without fee. Community legal education and law reform work are also included in the Australian Bureau of Statistics data. Pro bono service is not presently an ethical requirement of Australian lawyers, but the Australian Law Reform Commission has recommended that it should be. There is nevertheless an expectation that all lawyers donate a certain proportion of their time to pro bono work. New South Wales barristers, for example, are supposed to devote at least five days a year to it.

The potential for clash between the market values of competition policy and the service ideal of lawyering poses further problems for the construction of pro bono (Weisbrot 2001). The service ideal has tended to be associated with sole practitioners and small firms. Corporate practice with its billable hours targets and obsession with profit margins allows little space for the service ideal, causing some practitioners to feel dissatisfied and leave. Perhaps, in response, together with the more general concern about the profession's public image, some large corporate firms have led the way with visible pro bono initiatives, such as providing the services of an associate to a community legal centre. To systematise and harness the present ad hoc and privatised nature of pro bono work, the Australian Pro Bono Resource Centre was established in 2002 (National Pro Bono Task Force 2001). The Centre is also intended to foster a pro bono culture and the conduct of research (www.national probono.org.au).

As a corollary of the intention to transfer responsibility for legal aid from the public purse to the private practising profession, publicly funded agencies are changing their orientation. Legal aid commissions and community legal centres are moving away from aiding individual applicants to self-help through the general provision of information, such as workshops, do-it-yourself kits and on-line information (Giddings and Robertson 2001). In accordance with the prevailing user-pays philosophy, not all information is free; some websites provide do-it-yourself solutions for a fee. The Law and Justice Foundation of New South Wales is conducting research into how users access and use electronic information, as well as investigating the broader ethical implications associated with the new modes of delivery (<http:www.lawfoundation.net.au/olap/about/initiatives.html>).

Legal Education

Law Schools

The most striking change that has occurred in the legal education landscape is the number of new law schools. In 1970, there were 8 law schools; in 1985, there were 12, and by 2001, there were 29 (within 37 universities), and there are thought to be several more waiting in the wings. The proportion is much higher per capita than that of Canada, for example, which has 21 law schools (within 91 universities) for a population of 30 million (ALRC, 1999). The fact that there are approximately 30,000 law students in Australia compared with approximately 36,000 qualified practitioners, underscores the dramatic change occurring in the profile of lawyers in training.

Eight of the post-1988 law schools are in regional areas, which represents a marked departure from the traditional metropolitan location. Some metropolitan universities have also established regional programmes. La Trobe University, for example, established an LLB programme at its Bendigo campus in regional Victoria in 2004.

Two of the new metropolitan law schools (University of Western Sydney and Victoria University in Melbourne) are intended to cater specifically for less economically privileged urban students. It remains to be seen whether these institutions will disturb the class bias conventionally associated with law, particularly as Victoria University advertises strengths in commercial and corporate law, and has moved its law school to the city legal precinct.

Almost all Australian universities are public institutions, which are incorporated under State Acts, but regulated and funded by the federal Government. Two private universities, Bond University in Queensland and Notre Dame in Western Australia, also have law schools. In 1988, the public university structure was dramatically altered when the binary system came to an end and Colleges of Advanced Education were incorporated into the university structure, as occurred with polytechnics in the United Kingdom. In the new system, centralised regulation gave way to a more laissez-faire arrangement, in which responsibility for all courses, other than medicine, was devolved to universities. Many Vice-Chancellors seized upon law with alacrity. There was a high demand for places, and law was thought to be cheap to offer, having being placed in the lowest cluster of the Relative Funding Model. Law also had the added advantage of being a prestigious professional degree with a high tertiary entry score and it fitted in with the government's aim of improving the low rate of credentialism to make Australia competitive within the global new knowledge economy.

The Bachelor of Laws (LLB) is accepted as the basic prerequisite for admission to practice, although State and Territory admitting authorities do not automatically accredit new LLB programmes. The proliferation of new law schools has prompted closer scrutiny of proposed programmes because of concern about quality assurance, as well as the impact of over-supply on the standing of the profession. Although no law school has been rejected to date, the Law Council of Australia has raised the question of the desirability of developing uniform accreditation standards for all law schools. While recognising that the support of the Law Council could act as a valuable lever in securing better resources, the Committee of Australian Law Deans has been resistant to ceding power over legal education to the practising profession.

Law is not formally a graduate degree, as in North America, although 19 per cent of 1997 law graduates already had at least one degree when they commenced their law studies (Karras and Roper 2000). The favoured model of legal education in Australia is the double degree, whereby students enrol simultaneously in a combined programme, such as Arts/Law, Commerce/Law or Science/Law. Of the 1997 graduate cohort, 68 per cent completed combined degrees (Karras and Roper 2000). The combined degree, particularly so far as the BA/LLB is concerned, was designed to satisfy the liberal arts aim of a university education and to enhance the professional training offered by the law degree. It represented a reaction against the 'trade school' image of legal education of the past (Chesterman and Weisbrot 1987). The inclusion of Commerce, Science and other degree options, signifies the more vocational orientation of contemporary higher education. The concurrent nature of the programme also meant that law teachers did not have to worry unduly about interdisciplinarity; this was conveniently seen to be the responsibility of the other programme (cf. Chesterman and Weisbrot 1987).

Alternative routes to admission include the apprenticeship system, which has all but disappeared, other than in respect of articling as a form of practical legal training, and the law extension course in New South Wales run by the Solicitors' and Barristers' Admission Boards. It was hoped that this system would be phased out when Macquarie University and the University of Technology, Sydney, Law Schools were introduced in the mid-1970s. This did not occur, and the demand for what is now the Joint Admission Board course is greater than ever, although those who successfully complete the course receive a diploma, rather than a degree. While the majority of university law students study full-time, the Admission Board caters specifically for part-time students by providing lectures at the end of the working day. In addition, external study is offered by a few law schools, and the move to on-line learning and other flexible forms of delivery recognises that participation in paid work is a priority that takes up a greater proportion of students' time than in the past.

A degree of uniformity was formally introduced into the LLB core curricula in 1994 when a Consultative Committee of State and Territorial Law Authorities developed the Uniform Admission Rules. Eleven areas of study were agreed upon as prerequisites for admission, colloquially known as the 'Priestley Eleven'.[5] Unlike the McCrate Report, the major review of legal education conducted in the United States in 1992, the 'Priestley Eleven' focuses on substantive knowledge rather than the professional skills a lawyer might need (ALRC 1999).

A comprehensive review of Australian law schools and the discipline of law was undertaken for the Commonwealth Government in the mid-1980s (Pearce 1987). The report considered the aims and objectives of legal education in conjunction with issues of resource allocation, and community and professional needs. The substantial four-volume report was critical of a narrow doctrinal approach to legal education and advocated a broader contextual approach, which took account of theory, critique and the perspectives of other disciplines. It suggested that the LLB was replacing the BA as the favoured generalist degree. At the same time, it stressed the importance of 'solid legal substance' deemed essential for practice.

A follow-up report seven years later sought to gauge the effects of the Pearce Report, and found that it had acted as an important catalyst in the way that it encouraged law schools to define and articulate their aims and objectives (McInnis and Marginson 1994). The shift to a law-in-context approach by a number of law schools was attributed to the impact of the Pearce Report. This was an overt aim of some of the new law schools, which expressly rejected a narrow, 'black letter' approach to legal education (eg Thornton 1991).

The Pearce Report's criticism of traditional legal pedagogy as a series of dry lectures, the content of which was regurgitated in examination, led to the development of more effective teaching methods, particularly small-group teaching and more favourable staff:student ratios. The impetus to improve classroom teaching was spearheaded by the Association of Law

---

[5] Justice Priestley chaired the committee. Rule 3(b) specifies Criminal Law and Procedure, Torts, Contracts, Property (Real and Personal), Equity (including Trusts), Federal and State Constitutional Law, Civil Procedure, Evidence, Company Law and Professional Conduct.

Teachers of Australasia (ALTA), which ran workshops and instituted a journal devoted to teaching and learning—the *Legal Education Review* (see also Le Brun and Johnstone 1994). In addition, the Pearce Report acted as a lever to improve the resourcing of law schools, in the area of library development, as well as staffing and clinical programmes. While contentious and expensive to run, clinical programmes have a strong following because it is believed that they promote a public interest and social justice orientation among students, in addition to enhancing practical skills (Styles and Zareski 2001).

In the years since the report of McInnis and Marginson (1994), there has been a renewed emphasis on training law students to be good technocrats in order better to serve the market and the new knowledge economy (Thornton 2001). Within the contemporary neoliberal market economy, what is taught is expected to have use value—either as a commodity in its own right or as a facilitator of business. There has, therefore, been something of a resiling from the social liberal smorgasbord of offerings. Even legal studies programmes, which have tended to occupy a position on the margins of the law school because they usually do not prepare students for legal practice, have suffered a contraction in light of contemporary agendas (Duncanson 1997). It is notable that a number of law schools, including several of the newer ones, have moved to offering 'straight' law degrees once again, comparable to the United Kingdom undergraduate model of legal education. This is despite the fact that the evidence suggests that the sloughing off of context and a social justice orientation contributes to an increase in cynicism among law students (Styles and Zariski 2001).

Corporate law practice, seen as the most prestigious destination for graduates, exercises a centripetal pull on them, although the evidence suggests that it is not their favoured destination before they graduate. A national survey of final year students revealed that only 48 per cent wished to work in the private profession as their first preference (Roper 1995). The majority considered public sector work to be more desirable. Nevertheless, to make themselves look attractive in the contemporary labour market, students overwhelmingly choose offerings that are business-related, particularly in the areas of corporate law, taxation and intellectual property.

A recent study has challenged the Pearce Report's asseveration that the law degree has become the new generalist degree (Karras and Roper 2000). Even though graduates may not engage in traditional legal practice, Karras and Roper found that 80 per cent were going to a widening range of jobs with a significant legal component. Accounting firms, for example, have been engaged in a concerted attempt to recruit lawyers, and merchant banks offer substantial salaries, which law firms cannot match. Lawyers also go into publishing, research, the retail industry and a range of other positions. Karras and Roper found that using the practising certificate as a test of whether the work was legal or non-legal was unduly narrow and simplistic. While 58 per cent of the 1997 graduate cohort went into the private profession, 70 per cent of those working in the public sector and 32 per cent of those working in the private (non-legal) sector were engaged in legal work.

Like the UK, Canada and New Zealand, Australia has traditionally regarded higher education as a public good, not a commodity to be purveyed in the market. The emphasis on generating fee income has caused a change in the nature of the law curriculum, with an increased focus on business-related offerings (Thornton 2001). There also appears to have been some resiling from the diversity that developed in the curriculum of the 1970s and 1980s, despite the increase in the number of law schools. Paradoxically, the market encourages a degree of curricular homogeneity as law schools compete with one another. Reliance on fee income and other sources of private income is also causing a marked stratification to occur between law schools. While the older 'sandstone' universities are able to capitalise on their age and the fact that judges, partners and other senior members of the profession are their alumni, the second and third generation law schools have sought to compensate by appointing legal academics with a commitment to quality in teaching and scholarship. The inclusion of a fourth tier of law schools within the Unified National System has thwarted this trend to some extent. Not only are resources not available to support the core activities of the new schools to the extent recommended by the Pearce Report, but the existing schools have also been confronted with the harsh reality of having to do more with less, as funding has contracted.

University fees were abolished by the Whitlam Government in 1974, but are creeping back in accordance with the user-pay philosophy of neoliberalism, although the language of 'fees' has been largely restricted to coursework postgraduate programmes and international student candidature. International exchange students, mostly from Europe and the United States, may opt to spend a year of their law degree at an Australian law school.[6] Instead of fees, most domestic undergraduate students pay a levy under the Higher Education Scheme (HECS), which for Law was AUD6283 per annum (the highest rate) in 2004. Students may pay the levy up-front or defer payment, whereupon a low rate of interest accumulates until a specified income threshold is attained. This system, coupled with a

---

[6] Credit is contingent upon the existence of reciprocal institutional exchange agreements. The University of Sydney Law Faculty, for example, has exchange agreements with United States law schools at New York, Cornell and Duke Universities, and the University of Texas at Austin, as well as with a number of Scandinavian law schools.

means-tested living allowance, was designed to facilitate broad access to higher education. The marketing of legal education is likely to put paid to such aspirations. Melbourne University has established a private arm—Melbourne University Private—that offers a two-year graduate law degree at a cost of approximately AUD78,000, for which students receive a JD (Juris Doctor) rather than an LLB. In addition, Melbourne University, the University of Sydney, and a small number of other public universities, also offer a proportion of full-fee places in their undergraduate LLB programmes, designed for students who fail to satisfy the tertiary entry quota, but can afford to pay (approximately AUD16,000 per annum). Provided they do well in the first year, these full-fee students may then be able to transfer into HECS-based places. Such initiatives are highly contentious as they are regarded as attempts to privatise public education by stealth. Nevertheless, all universities will be able to offer full-fee places to 35 per cent of domestic undergraduate students in 2005 as a result of a major policy shift in the funding of universities.

Within coursework LLM programmes, taxation law, intellectual property and international business law are currently favoured offerings. Again, it is the older sandstone universities that are able to capitalise on their 'brand' names in the market and attract large numbers of full fee-paying students—international, as well as domestic. A proportion of research Masters and PhD programmes are presently HECS-based, provided that candidates complete in minimum time, otherwise full fees are levied, although scholarships and government loans are available. While the number of research degrees in law has increased, it remains small compared with other disciplines, and there is a high attrition rate. The lure of highly paid employment, and/or the demands of practice, proves too much for most students. In addition, few law schools are able to provide a supportive research culture (Goldsmith 1999). A small proportion of students continue to pursue postgraduate study overseas, mainly in the United Kingdom, the United States and Canada.

The commodification of legal education coincides with the increasing importance of the market everywhere. Rather than concentrate on the traditional curriculum of the past (Haigh 1999/2000), law schools are being exhorted to rethink what should be taught for a global world. The pressure is on law schools not to be 'too jurisdictionally bound' (Clark and Blay 1999). The LLB (International Studies) offered by the University of Technology Sydney is an example of a programme that has taken the challenge seriously (<http:www.uts.edu/au/study/courses.htm>). What is lacking, according to Clark and Blay (1999), is a co-ordinated strategy for internationalisation among law schools.

While it is impossible to expect the same degree of rough parity to continue between 30 law schools as existed between 12, in light of the resource differentials, the ability of the élite, older law schools to attract substantial full-fee income is already resulting in stratification between law schools. Inequality is an inevitable corollary of the market and one that is likely to affect the character of both Australian legal education and the legal profession in ensuing years. More troubling is the way that the market privileges business law over those areas that sustain the dignity of the individual, such as human rights and social justice. The commodification of legal education is insidiously transforming legal knowledge in Australia, as elsewhere.

Pre-admission Requirement

There is no separate bar exam to be passed in order to be admitted to the practice of law in Australia. Nevertheless, in addition to satisfying the academic requirement (normally the LLB), it is necessary to have completed a formal pre-admission course or a period of apprenticeship (articles of clerkship) in a law firm or other approved site. Completion of a pre-admission course or articles leads to a restricted practising certificate, which entitles the neonate lawyer to practise under supervision for a period of up to three years when an unrestricted practising certificate is issued. In the 1970s, the favouring of those with family or class connections for articles, together with the ad hoc nature of training received in-house, led to the development of institutional practical legal training (PLT). In 1997, 60 per cent of graduate lawyers surveyed had completed a PLT course and 39 per cent had completed articles of clerkship (Karras and Roper 2000). However, in Victoria and Queensland, which retain a choice, 75 per cent completed articles. The figure is even higher for the older law schools, with 89 per cent of University of Melbourne graduates completing articles (Karras and Roper 2000). The inference is that personal connections continue to be a factor in securing articles. However, the phasing out of articling for Victoria is being considered, which poses a major logistical problem for PLT providers in light of what has been described as 'a massive oversupply of graduates' (Shiel 2003).

The contraction in government funding for higher education post-1988 led to the withdrawal of support for professional programmes. Like postgraduate law programmes, pre-admission courses are now offered on an up-front, full-fee paying basis by a range of providers. In order to lessen the financial burden on students, as well as to make them more attractive in the labour market, most law schools have moved to incorporate at least some practical skills into their LLB curricula. Thus, interviewing skills, negotiation, advocacy and dispute resolution, as well as placement experience, are likely to be found within the law degree itself. Some law school curricula, such as that of the University of Newcastle, include such a range of skills and clinical experience that it satisfies the pre-admission requirements for admission, and students graduate simultaneously LLB/DipLegPrac. Some of the large national firms, such as Mallesons Stephen Jaques, offer short, customised pre-admission courses for their graduate recruits. Flexible delivery modes are also available, including 'sandwich' courses and on-line delivery (Council of Australian Law Deans 2001).

A set of national minimum competency standards for practical skills, comparable to the substantive 'Priestley Eleven', were agreed to in 2001 by the Law Admissions Consultative Committee (LACC) and came into effect in 2003. These standards are to apply to all courses, regardless of approach and mode of delivery.

Continuing Legal Education (CLE)

While professional associations generally encourage CLE activities, they are mandatory for practitioners only in New South Wales, requiring the completion of ten hours per annum in order to maintain a current practising certificate. CLE providers include law schools, pre-admission institutions, professional bodies, government bodies and agencies, and private companies, as well as law firms. The quality of these programmes varies considerably (ALRC 1999). Specialist accreditation schemes are also available in the various jurisdictions in a range of fields (Law Council 2000).

In light of the rapidity and the unevenness of change in legal education and training, the Australian Law Reform Commission has proposed the establishment of a broadly constituted national Council of Legal Education. Under the auspices of the federal Attorney-General, such a body would have responsibility for undergraduate legal education, pre-admission and CLE, as well as ancillary issues of accreditation and training (ALRC 1999).

The issue of gender bias has been the major catalyst for prompting debate about judicial education, which, until recently, has been largely *ad hoc*. However, in accordance with the impetus in favour of an Australian identity, the Australian Judicial College was established in 2002 (www.njca.anu.edu.au). It is an independent body, housed at the Australian National University in Canberra, and responsible for the education and professional development of judges, magistrates and tribunal members. It is incorporated as a company limited by guarantee; it is not a statutory authority, like the Judicial Commission of New South Wales or the Judicial College of Victoria.

Conclusion

The Australian legal profession is beset with contradictions. Each trend or trait contains the seeds of its antinomy. Even the descriptor 'Australian' is something of a misnomer, given that there are six States and two Territories, as well as a federal jurisdiction, all valiantly clinging to their historic monopolies and privileges, while simultaneously recognising that the freedom to practise throughout Australia, as well as overseas, requires the relinquishment of power to enable representative bodies to speak with one voice. Many of the moves towards unification are inchoate, but market forces are an important driver for change. The large corporate firms that are already influential in establishing the norms for practice and legal education, albeit indirectly, are likely to be the strongest supporters of national regulation as divisions and differences between jurisdictions represent impediments for them. They also want support for their offshore ventures in order to be competitive within global markets. Accordingly, they are more likely to seek alliances with the federal Government to effect a national regulatory regime, rather than resist it. A neoliberal government is likely to be highly receptive to such overtures in the interests of facilitating business and the new knowledge economy.

The singular form, 'profession' is also something of a misnomer. In the propulsion towards MDPs and new forms of practice, it may be more accurate to use the plural, as 'profession', like 'Australian', suggests a non-existent homogeneity. The inclusion of legal academics as members of the legal profession, for example, has always been problematic. Sometimes, they (we) are included, sometimes not. The judiciary occupies a similarly ambiguous position. It seems that the categorisation of a range of other legal workers has also now become uncertain. Legal workers have become increasingly fragmented and insecure, always eyeing off competitors within fickle markets. While qualified as legal practitioners, they may no longer be members of a professional association or possess a current practising certificate, and are consequently not subject to the normal regulatory and ethical controls of the profession. Their loyalties are to public sector employers, private companies or, as self-employed consultants, to no one but themselves and their clients. These fringe dwellers of the legal services industry are nevertheless able to exert a discursive power in corroding professional norms by challenging, competing with and undercutting more conventional legal practitioners.

Thus, it can be seen that the Australian situation presents something of a paradox. On the one hand, we see tentative moves towards a unified national profession. On the other, we see that the unitary concept of a 'profession', if not exactly disintegrating, is becoming more friable. It would appear that the idea of a fixed identity for the Australian legal profession is likely to continue to remain elusive.

References

ABS (Australian Bureau of Statistics), Legal Services Industry Australia 1998–99. 8667.0. Canberra, Australian Bureau of Statistics, 2000.

ABS (Australian Bureau of Statistics), Legal Practices: Australia 2001–02. 8667.0. Canberra, Australian Bureau of Statistics, 2003.

ALRC (Australian Law Reform Commission), Managing Justice: A Review of the Federal Civil Justice System. Canberra: Australian Government Publishing Service, 2000.

ALRC (Australian Law Reform Commission), Review of the Federal Civil Justice System. Discussion Paper 62. Canberra: Australian Government Publishing Service, 1999.

ARUP, Christopher Pro Bono in the Post-Professional Spectrum of Legal Services. In For the Public Good: Pro Bono and the Legal Profession in Australia, edited by Christopher Arup and Kathy Laster. Special Issue 2001, 19 *Law in* Context, 190–213.

ASTOR, Hilary and Christine M CHINKIN *Dispute Resolution in Australia*, (Sydney, LexisNexis, Butterworths, 2002).

BALLS, Ashley *Law Firms: Managing for Profit*, (Sydney, Federation Press, 1998).

BARKER, Peter *Winning Tenders and Business Proposals for Lawyers*, (Sydney, PB Marketing and Media, 1994).

BROWN, Melinda Annual Practising Certificate Survey, 2000, 74 *Law Institute Journal*, 20–22.

CAIN, Maureen 'The Symbol Traders' in Maureen Cain and Christine Harrington, *Lawyers in a Postmodern World: Translation and Transgression*, (London, Open University Press, 1994).

CHESTERMAN, Michael and David WEISBROT Legal Scholarship in Australia, 1987, 50 *Modern Law Review*, 709–24.

CLARK, Eugene and Sam BLAY The Internationalisation of Legal Practice and Education. 1999, 73(11) *Australian Law Journal*, 791–95.

COUNCIL OF AUSTRALIAN LAW DEANS 2001. Studying Law in Australia 2002. http://www.law.newcastle.edu.au/cle/cald/slia/html.

DUNCANSON, Ian The Ends of Legal Studies, *Web Journal of Current Legal Issues* http://webcli.ncl.ac.uk/1997/issue3/duncan3.html.

FENTON, Jane and Anna GRUTZNER *The Rain Dance: A Marketing Book for Lawyers*, (Melbourne, Fenton Communications, 1996).

GIDDINGS, Jeff and Michael Robertson 'Informed Litigants with Nowhere to Go': Self-help Legal Aid Services in Australia, 2001, 26 *Alternative Law Journal*, 184–90.

GLASBEEK, Harry and Reuben HASSON Some Reflections on Canadian Legal Education, 1987, 50 *Modern Law Review* 777–803.

GOLDSMITH, Andrew Standing at the Crossroads: Law Schools, Universities, Markets and the Future of Legal Scholarship, in *The Law School—Global Issues, Local Questions*, edited by F Cownie. (Aldershot, UK, Ashgate/ Dartmouth, 1999).

HAIGH, Richard Of Law, Lawyers, Globalisation and Millennia, 1999–2000, 4 *Deakin Law Review*, 93–104.

HIGH COURT OF AUSTRALIA Annual Report 1999–2000. Canberra: Commonwealth of Australia, 2000 http://www.hcourt.gov.au.annual_reports

ILSAC (International Legal Services Advisory Council)1999. Australian Legal Services Export Development Strategy Outline 1999 to 2002. Canberra: http://law.gove.au/aghome/advisory/ilsac/exportreport/exportreport.htm

ISRAEL, Susan Disparities continue between Women and Men in the Legal Profession: Gender Issues in the 1999–2000 Practising Certificate Survey, 2001, 39 *Law Society Journal*, 63–6.

KARRAS, Maria and Christopher ROPER *The Career Destination of Australian Law Graduates*, (Sydney, Centre for Legal Education, 2000).

KRONMAN, Anthony The Lost Lawyer: Failing Ideals of the Legal Profession, (Cambridge, Mass, Belknap, 1993).

LAW COUNCIL OF AUSTRALIA 2010: A Discussion Paper: Challenges for the Legal Profession. Canberra: Law Council of Australia, 2001.

LAW COUNCIL OF AUSTRALIA Policy on the Process of Judicial Appointments. Canberra: Law Council of Australia, 2000.

LAW COUNCIL OF AUSTRALIA Statement on International Legal Practice. Canberra: Law Council of Australia, 1992.

LAW INSTITUTE OF VICTORIA Law Office Management: A Guide for Practitioners. Melbourne: Law Institute of Victoria, 1985.

LAWSON, Valerie Laws unto Themselves. Sydney Morning Herald, 17–18 November, 2001: News Review, 29.

LE BRUN, Marlena and Richard JOHNSTONE *The Quiet (R)evolution: Improving Student Learning in Law*, (North Ryde, NSW, Law Book, 1994).

LYOTARD, Jean *The Postmodern Condition: A Report on Knowledge*, (Manchester, Manchester University Press, 1984).

MARR, David *Barwick*, (Sydney, Allen and Unwin, 1992).

McINNIS, Craig and Simon MARGINSON Australian Law Schools after the 1987 Pearce Report. Higher Education Division Evaluations and Investigations Program, Department of Employment Education and Training. Canberra: Australian Government Publishing Service, 1994.

McQUEEN, Rob Comment: The Darker Side of the Profession? In For the Public Good: Pro Bono and the Legal Profession in Australia, edited by Christopher Arup and Kathy Laster. Special Issue 2001, 19 *Law in Context*, 54–64.

MENDELSOHN, Oliver and Matthew LIPPMAN, The Emergence of the Corporate Law Firm in Australia, 1979, 3 *University of New South Wales Law Journal*, 78–98.

NATIONAL PRO BONO Task Force Recommended Action Plan for National Coordination and Development of Pro Bono Legal Services. In For the Public Good: Pro Bono and the Legal Profession in Australia, edited by Christopher Arup and Kathy Laster. Special Issue 2001, 19 *Law in Context*, 228–46.

NEW SOUTH WALES Bar Association Statistics. Volume I. Sydney: NSW Bar Association, 2001.

NEW SOUTH WALES Law Reform Commission General Regulation: Legal Profession Discussion Paper No 1. Sydney: NSW Law Reform Commission, 1979a.

NEW SOUTH WALES Law Reform Commission Complaints, Discipline and Professional Standards Discussion Paper No 2. Sydney: NSW Law Reform Commission, 1979b.

NEW SOUTH WALES Law Reform Commission Professional Indemnity Insurance Discussion Paper No 3. Sydney: NSW Law Reform Commission, 1979c.

NEW SOUTH WALES Law Reform Commission The Structure of the Profession Discussion Paper No 4. Sydney: NSW Law Reform Commission, 1982a.

NEW SOUTH WALES Law Reform Commission Advertising and Specialisation Discussion Paper No 5. Sydney: NSW Law Reform Commission, 1982b.

NEW SOUTH WALES Law Reform Commission Solicitors' Trust Accounts and the Solicitors' Fidelity Fund Discussion Paper No 6. Sydney: NSW Law Reform Commission, 1982c.

NOONE, Mary Anne The State of Australian Legal Aid 2001, 29 *Federal Law Review*, 37–56.

NOSWORTHY, Elizabeth Ethics and Large Firms. In *Legal Ethics and Legal Practice: Contemporary Issues*, edited by Stephen Parker and Charles Sampford (Oxford, Clarendon, 1995).

PARKER, Stephen A Case for Private Courts, 2001, 26, *Alternative Law Journal* 161–66.

PARLIAMENT OF THE COMMONWEALTH OF AUSTRALIA, Report by the Senate Standing Committee on Legal and Constitutional Affairs Gender Bias and the Judiciary. Canberra: Commonwealth of Australia, 1994.

PEARCE, Denis, Enid Campbell and Don Harding Australian Law Schools: A Discipline Assessment for the Commonwealth Tertiary Education Commission. Canberra: Australian Government Publishing Service, 1987.

ROPER, Christopher Centre for Legal Education, Career Intentions of Australian Law Students, Department of Employment, Education and Training. Canberra: Australian Government Publishing Service, 1995.

SALLMAN, Peter and Richard WRIGHT, Legal Practice Act Review: Discussion Paper. Melbourne: Victorian Government–Department of Justice, 2001.

SERON, Carroll and Frank MUNGER Law and Inequality: Race, Gender ... and, of Course, Class, 1996, 22 *Annual Review of Sociology*, 187–212.

SEXTON, Michael Uncertain Justice: Inside Australia's Legal System, (Sydney, New Holland, 2000).

SHIEL, Fergus Ombudsman seeks advocates of her own. Melbourne: *The Age* 26 July 2003.

SHIEL, Fergus Articled clerks may become a thing of the law's past. Melbourne: *The Age* 20 November, 2003.

STANDING COMMITTEE OF ATTORNEYS-GENERAL Legal Profession–Model Laws Project Consultation Draft. Canberra: Office of Attorney-General, 2003.

STEIN, David and Charis STEIN *Legal Practice in the 90s*, (Sydney, Law Book, 1994).

STYLES, Irene and Archie ZARISKI Law Clinics and the Promotion of Public Interest Lawyering. In For the Public Good: Pro Bono and the Legal Profession in Australia, edited by Christopher Arup and Kathy Laster. Special Issue 2001, 19 *Law in Context*, 65–88.

THORNTON, Margaret The Demise of Diversity in Legal Education: Globalisation and the New Knowledge Economy 2001, 8 *International Journal of the Legal Profession*, 37–56.

THORNTON, Margaret Among the Ruins: Law in the Neo-Liberal Academy, 2001, 20 *Windsor Yearbook of Access to Justice*, 3–23.

THORNTON, Margaret *Dissonance and Distrust: Women in the Legal Profession*, (Melbourne, Oxford University Press, 1996).

THORNTON, Margaret Portia Lost in the Groves of Academe wondering what to do about Legal Education, (Melbourne, La Trobe University Press, 1991).

VIDENIEKS, Monica Barrister fights Expulsion over Tax. The Australian, 21 November, 2001:3.

WARNECKE, Andrea Legal Profiles: A Client's Guide to Australia's leading Law Firms and their Practices 1998–1999, 5th edn (Sydney, Profiles Publishing, 1998).

WARNEMINDE, Martin People v Lawyers v Money. Bulletin, 11 June, 1991:32.

WEISBROT, David Introduction to Report of the National Pro Bono Task Force and Recommended Action Plan. In For the Public Good: Pro Bono and the Legal Profession in Australia, edited by Christopher Arup and Kathy Laster. Special Issue 2001, 19 *Law in Context*, 214–27.

WEISBROT, David *Australian Lawyers*, (Melbourne, Longman Cheshire, 1990).

WEISBROT, David The Australian Legal Profession: From Provincial Family Firms to Multinationals. In *Lawyers in Society: The Common Law World, Vol. 1*, edited by Richard L Abel and Philip S Lewis, (Berkeley, University of California Press, 1988).

WESTERN, John, Toni Makkai and Kristin Natalier Professions and the Public Good. In For the Public Good: Pro Bono and the Legal Profession in Australia, edited by Christopher Arup and Kathy Laster. Special Issue 2001, 19 *Law in Context*, 21–44.

WILLIAMS, The Hon Daryl Address to 32nd Australian Legal Convention. Law Council of Australia, 14 October, 2001. <http:lawcouncil.bris.binke.com.au/release.html>.

ZIEGERT, Klaus A Social Stratification, Educational Attainment, and Admission to Law School, 1992, 3 *Legal Education Review* 155–234.

7

A Legal Profession in Transformation: The Korean Experience

DAI-KWON CHOI

1. Introduction

This chapter mainly traces the transformations which the Korean legal profession has undergone over the last few decades and explores their future. South Korean society has been tremendously transformed from a war-torn, predominantly agricultural state up to the 1960's into an industrialised and globalised information society today. The per capita national income was around $100, and 60 per cent of the population was in the agricultural sector in the 1960s, but now the figures are respectively around $10,000 and 10 per cent in the 1990s and in the 2000s. There were between 400 to 700 practising lawyers relative to a population of around 25 million in the 1960s, but their number has now grown to around 5000 relative to a population of around 40 million in the 2000s.

Table 1 Population Size, Farm Population, Per Capita GNI and Number of Practising Lawyers

	Estimate of Mid-Year Population (thousand persons)	Percentage of Farm Population to Total Population (%)	Per Capita GNI($)	Number of Lawyers Practising
1960	25,012	58.2	79	450
1965	28,705	55.1	105	662
1970	32,241	44.7	249	719
1975	35,281	37.5	592	809
1980	38,124	28.4	1,598	940
1985	40,806	20.9	2,229	1,179
1990	42,869	15.5	5,886	1,803
1995	45,093	10.9	10,823	2,852
2000	47,008	8.6	9,628	4,228

(Sources: Korea National Statistical Office, 2001; Korean Federation of Bar Association)

Diagram 1: Production Structure at Current Basis

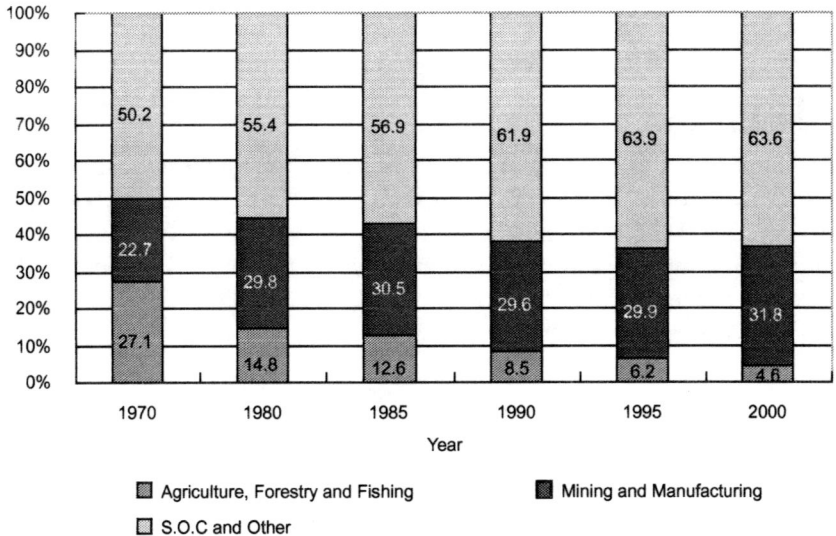

(Sources: Korea National Statistical Office, 2001)

The prevailing form of government was largely authoritarian throughout the 1960s, 1970s, and much of 1980s. Since 1987, however, it has become undoubtedly democratic. The questions that follow include: How is the Korean legal profession structured today? How has it evolved from what state of things? Are changes which it underwent a reflection of the societal transformation? Were Korean lawyers agents, or reluctant followers of social changes? What are their future prospects? An attempt will be made to take a look at what has happened to the legal profession in the last few decades, and what might come next and how or what should be done in the future. In the process, the questions raised above will also be tackled.The legal profession of North Korea is outside our remit.

2. Present State of Legal Profession in Korea

Korea's present legal system belongs to the civil law family. With the adoption of the Court Organisation Act in 1895, the idea of a legal profession alongside a Westernised court system was introduced for the first time in Korea. Until then, Korea belonged to the ancient Far Eastern Asian legal system in which the idea of lawyer as an intermediary between the court and parties to a case had been an alien concept.[1] During the Japanese rule (1910–1945), there were only a few hundred lawyers (the majority of whom were Japanese).[2] When the Japanese left Korea following the end of the Second World War, there were such a small number of lawyers left in South Korea (statistics for which are not available today) that special measures (like recruiting former court clerks as judges) were taken to fill the judges' and public prosecutorial positions in the newly established court system and in the public prosecutors offices when the Republic of Korea was founded in 1948. A similar shortage of formally licensed lawyers was faced during the Korean War (1950–53) and immediately afterwards when other special measures were introduced to meet the immediate needs of the time, that is, to fill the vacant judges' and public prosecutors' positions,

---

[1] D-K Choi, 'Development of Law and Legal Institutions in Korea', in B Duck Chun, W Shaw and D-K Choi, *Traditional Korean Legal Attitudes*, Korea Research Monograph 2, (Berkeley, CA, Center for Korean Studies, Institute of East Asian Studies, University of California, 1980) 54–101, esp 69–70; P-h Pak, *Hankukbopjaesago* (Studies on Legal History of Korea), (Seoul, Bopmunsa, 1974) 315–19; P-h Pak, *Hankukui Jontongsahoewa Bop* (Traditional Korean Society and Law), (Seoul, Seoul National University Press, 1985) 262–64. For further information on the traditional law of Korea, see also B Duk Chun, 'Legal Principles and Values of the Late Yi Dynasty'; and W Shaw, 'Social and Intellectual Aspects of Traditional Korean Law, 1392–1910' in *Traditional Korean Legal Attitudes*, and Pak's two books above; W Shaw, *Legal Norms in a Confucian State*, Korea Research Monograph 5, (Berkeley, CA, Center for Korean Studies, Institute of East Asian Studies, University of California, 1981); Hi-ki Sim, *Hankukbopjesakangui* (Lectures on Legal History of Korea), (Seoul, Samyongsa, 1997).

[2] For the statistics of lawyers during the Japanese period, see D-k Choi, 'Development of Law and Legal Institutions in Korea' 86. In 1910, there were 183 Japanese and 71 Korean judges, 54 Japanese and 6 Korean prosecutors, and 30 Japanese and 51 Korean practising lawyers in Korea. Those figures in 1935 were respectively 146 Japanese and 38 Korean judges, 74 Japanese and 7 Korean prosecutors, and 172 Japanese and 217 Korean practising lawyers.

because many either voluntarily went north or were forcefully taken north and many others were killed, and also to fill the judge-advocates' positions in the greatly expanded army.

Presently, legal education is conducted at a college of law or department of law of a university with a four-year programme (one year prelaw and three years law studying).[3] Neither a law degree nor a university degree is required to become a lawyer, however, although more than 95 per cent of new lawyers are college graduates. The passing of the bar examination is practically the only barrier to the world of the legal profession. For the bar examination there is a quota of those who pass. To be a lawyer, those who pass the bar examination are further required to undergo a two-year practical training at the Judicial Research and Training Institute (JRTI) administered by the Supreme Court, the only one of the kind in the nation (one year of class-room instruction and one year of practical training in court, the public prosecutor's office, lawyers' offices and others). Now, those who complete their training achieving the top grades at the JRTI alone are recruited either to be judges or public prosecutors while the rest go into practice, either after three years of military service as a judge-advocate, or immediately following their graduation if they have already finished their compulsory military service. Those who choose to be judges are further required to undergo an apprentice judgeship for two years in order to become fully-fledged career judges.

Those who want to become law professors usually take a university academic course only, while tending to avoid the bar examination.[4] Today a doctoral degree is a necessity for them. Consequently, only a tiny minority of law professors are licensed lawyers. The small number of law professors with a lawyer's license are usually those who have successfully taken both the practitioners course (the bar exam, JRTI, etc) and the academic course leading to a doctoral degree. Usually, they will begin an academic career after a few years of practical experience as a young judge, public prosecutor, or practising lawyer. The problem of whether law professors who have undertaken a full-time academic career at an accredited university for a certain period of time (say, fifteen years, perhaps five years of which were in Japan) should be qualified to practise as lawyers has been hotly debated and remains unresolved. Consequently, no law professor has ever been appointed to a judicial career such as a Supreme Court or Constitutional

---

[3] D-k Choi, 'Legal Education in Korea: Problems and Reform Efforts' (1988) 29(2) *Seoul Law Journal* 104; D-k Choi, 'Hakbukyoyukkwa bophakkyoyuk' (Undergraduate and Legal Education in Korea) (1996) 37(2) *Seoul Law Journal* 81.

[4] In the College of Law at Seoul National University, only 8 out of 42 full-time faculty members are licenced lawyers. The figures for the other 4 of the nations' top 5 universities are as follows: Korea University: 5 out of 28 full-time members; Yonsei University: 1 out of 24; Sungkyunkwan University: 3 out of 25; Hanyang University: 7 out of 37.

Court Justice, since he or she is not considered a lawyer in the technical sense. The legal profession in Korea (*Bopjoin*) is regarded as composed of judges, public prosecutors, and practising lawyers, that is to say, 'the three wheels of legal profession' (*Bopjo samryun*) alone. There has been little interaction between legal practitioners and professors, although they both serve as equal members on many governmental and non-governmental commissions and committees such as major law revision committees.

Today, there are about 1,700 judges, about 1,400 public prosecutors and about 5,559 practising lawyers whereas there are about 900 law professors nationally. More than two-thirds of practising lawyers (4,190) practise in the metropolitan area of Seoul, the capital city, including Inchon and Suwon, where half of the nation's population live, while about half of the nation's judges are sitting in the courts including the Supreme Court and Seoul High Court in the same metropolitan area.

Table 2 The Number of Judges, Prosecutors, and Practising Lawyers

	Judges		Public Prosecutors		Practising Lawyers	
	Total	Female	Total	Female	Total	Female
1950	149		163		*	
1955	157		163		293	
1960	296		190		456	
1965	372		300		662	
1970	413		343		719	
1975	517	2	377		809	3
1980	562	4	437	2	940	3
1985	769	11	545	2	1179	3
1990	1028	27	761	1	1803	18
1995	1212	63	986	10	2852	43
2000	1341	88	1190	29	4228	132
2001	1467	102	1272	50	4618	174
2002	1578	114	1353	67	5073	238
2003	1708	137	1437	87	5533	303

Source: Ministry of Court Administration (the Supreme Court), Yearbook of the Ministry of Justice, and Korean Federation of Bar Associations.
* Information is not available

The percentage of female lawyers among the nation's practising lawyers is 5.5 per cent whereas that of female judges is 8 per cent today. Korea has one national judicial system consisting of three tiers of courts: the Supreme Court, High Courts and Districts Courts and their Branch Courts. There is a semi-legal profession of judicial scrivners in Korea (4,820 of them as of 2002) roughly equivalent to solicitors, who are qualified to draft a range of litigation-related papers including briefs and affidavits to be filed at courts and public prosecutors' offices on behalf of their clients for monetary remuneration but they are not allowed to represent parties at court. However, they are not regarded as members of the prestigious, learned legal profession.

3. Transformation of the Legal Profession in the Last Few Decades

The quota system[5] for those passing the annual bar examination has proved to be one of the major factors related to the transformation of the Korean legal profession over the last few decades. In fact, the quota has been utilised as an effective barrier to entrance to the legal profession, particularly in the interests of lawyers who are strategically located in Korean society,[6] the 'natural' aristocrats in Tocqueville's terms. Until the year 1980, the number set for the quota was unpredictable, ranging from a single digit number to 150, several tens for most of time. The quota was set at 300 for the first time in 1981, and remained so until 1995. A drastic increase in the size of the quota, as compared with that of the previous years, has been in place since then. The number was 500 in 1996, 600 in 1997, 700 in 1998 and in 1999, 800 in 2000, and then 1,000 in 2001 and in 2002. The quota of 1,000 will remain for the time being. The battles that were waged with the annual quotas have tended to take the form of lawyers yielding to strong social pressure for legal reform, especially to the social demand for legal education reforms. No doubt, their small numbers, that is, their scarcity, has best served the interests of lawyers in society as well as in the legal services market. Law professors have been in favour of an increase in their numbers, however, in that this would lead to a greater number of their students becoming lawyers, as a result of which their social power would also increase. Nationally about 9,000 law students graduate from universities each year but only a fraction of them pass the bar exam-

[5] In the determination of the quota, the legal profession is structured to have the strongest voice. Presently the Minister of Justice determines the quota for the bar examination each year in consideration of the opinions presented by the Supreme Court and the Korean Federation of Bar Associations (the Bar Examination Act, Art 5). The Minister of Justice administers the bar examination today. In the past, the Minister of Government and Home Affairs administered the bar examination. Still he was to determine the quota only in consideration of the opinions tendered by the Supreme Court and the Minister of Justice.
[6] The fact that today 38 are licensed lawyers in the 269 member National Assembly, the Korean parliament, may be suggested as a rough indicator of their strategic position in society. The number of 38 is proportionally a large one, that is, 14.1 % of the total 269 member of the National Assembly in consideration of the size of the legal profession (5,533 practising lawyers plus 1,708 judges and 1,450 prosecutors as of 2003) against the national population of 47 millions.

Table 3 Statistics of the Bar Examinations

Year	1951	1952	1953	1953	1954	1955	1956	1957	1958	1959	1960	1961	1962	1962	1963
Applicants	457	258	711	842	1,141	1,999	2,855	3,414	3,047	3,416	5,557	4,450	3,036	3,825	3,194
Passed	39	21	16	12	17	30	108	51	50	24	31	110	50	56	36
Success Rate	39:1	12:1	44:1	70:1	67:1	67:1	26:1	67:1	67:1	142:1	179:1	40:1	61:1	68:1	89:1

Year	1963	1964	1964	1965	1966	1967	1967	1968	1969	1970	1970	1971	1972	1973
Applicants	2,318	3,450	3,770	3,251	2,141	1,858	2,304	1,837	2,070	2,363	2,326	2,531	2,629	3,614
Passed	45	41	10	22	16	19	5	83	37	34	33	49	81	60
Success Rate	52:1	84:1	377:1	148:1	134:1	98:1	461:1	22:1	56:1	70:1	70:1	52:1	32:1	60:1

Year	1974	1975	1976	1977	1978	1979	1980	1981	1982	1983	1984	1985	1986	1987	1988
Applicants	3,311	3,344	3,625	4,011	4,153	4,506	4,868	6,173	7,386	8,450	12,221	12,449	14,303	14,963	14,245
Passed	60	59	60	80	100	120	141	289	300	300	303	298	300	300	300
Success Rate	55:1	57:1	60:1	50:1	42:1	38:1	35:1	21:1	25:1	28:1	40:1	42:1	48:1	50:1	47:1

Year	1989	1990	1991	1992	1993	1994	1995	1996	1997	1998	1999	2000	2001
Applicants	14,201	15,041	16,311	17,131	18,991	19,736	20,737	22,771	20,551	20,755	22,964	23,249	
Passed	300	298	287	288	288	290	308	502	604	700	707	801	
Success Rate	47:1	50:1	57:1	59:1	66:1	68:1	67:1	45:1	34:1	30:1	32:1	29:1	

(Source: Korea Institute of Public Administration(KIPA) Data Base).

ination precisely because of its stringent quota. The small numbers restrict access to lawyers' services and lead to greater expense for the mass of the population. An increase in numbers would naturally serve the interests of many in terms of access to and lowered costs for legal services.

The newly-hatched lawyers size of 300 or more has proved to be significant in terms of changes in the patterns of legal practice. Previously the prevailing pattern of practice was that the most young lawyers became either judges or public prosecutors following their training at the JRTI. Many of them then left their positions and went into practice after having acquired several years' practical experience as a judge or public prosecutor. To some extent, this pattern still continues, but with numbers set at 300 in 1981 a significant number of young lawyers, at least a third of them, went into practice immediately after graduation from the JRTI without gaining any practical experience as a judge or public prosecutor. Each year only about 200 graduates from the JRTI found their position either in courts as a judge or public prosecutors office as a public prosecutor. Today, four-fifths of the yearly graduates from the JRTI have either to go into practice or find a position in a law firm, a law department of a big corporation, or other offices. Besides, the predominant pattern of practice was a sole practice for litigation (advocacy) in typical civil and criminal cases. With the increased size of the quota since the 1980s, however, practice patterns have diversified into other fields of legal work such as labour law rather than typical civil and criminal cases, and into other activities such as counselling and drafting in law firms rather than litigation, and in the position of in-house counsel, employed lawyer, and others. For the first time in the legal services market, there emerged in the 1980's a group of lawyers who specialised in labour law. It is no surprise that with the increase in their numbers, lawyers began to take mostly labour cases and still earn enough to meet their expectations as a labour law specialist located in or near the nation's major industrial sites. It is equally no surprise that law firms[7] began to appear on the Korean social scene from the early 1980s. No doubt, the emergence of law firms was much facilitated with the adoption in 1982 of the statutory provisions, precisely in their interests, in the Attorneys-At-Law Act (*Pyonhosabop*). It is only natural that the very nature of the JRTI should have been seriously questioned over the last few years, particularly since it started as, and still is primarily, the government lawyers' (judges and public prosecutors) training institute in its orientation, structure, and the financial support it receives; thus is not necessarily suited to the training of future practitioners, which today make up four-fifths of its students.

---

[7] There are 252 law firms nationally as of May 2003. Seoul alone has 144 law firms. *The Korean Bar Association News* 26 May 2003 issue, p 8. The largest law firm Kim & Chang has 200 or so lawyers (around 150 Koreans and around 50 foreign nationals).

Moreover, the changes described above which the legal profession underwent, can meaningfully be related to the pace of industrialisation that has taken place over the last few decades. In Korea it took just a few decades to reach the level of industrialisation which occurred over two centuries in the West. This rapid industrialisation has been accompanied by an equally rapid rural emigration, urbanisation, globalisation, and increasingly greater social complexity. Small and large-scale industrial firms, business corporations, labour unions, political parties, mass-media associations and other organisations have arrived and flourished on the Korean social scene along with or in place of traditional rural communities, guilds, clans and other primary organisations. It seems clear that these social changes have been in a large measure followed by the transformation of the legal profession in terms of the increase in its numbers and the diversifications of its practice patterns, although the latter changes have, for most of the time, lagged behind the former, as best seen in the case of legal education reform efforts.

The informal traditional ways including traditional organisations and personal ties[8] have been dying out as older generations have passed on and became increasingly irrelevant to industrialised and urbanised social relations and to the invisible market in which large-scale business firms and organisations have emerged as more important. It is only natural that the law and, at the same time, lawyers should play an increasingly important, diversified role in Korean society. Until the 1960s, perhaps until the 1970s, Korea was once described as an 'alegal' society[9] where litigiousness was looked down upon and harmony was particularly emphasised as Confucian teachings were instilled in the mind of Koreans. Now Korean society has been experiencing a litigation explosion through the 1970s, 1980s and particularly the 1990s. According to a sociological study, Koreans are today far more litigious (4.6 times more) than the Japanese: 1 out of 52 Koreans filed a civil or administrative suit while 1 out of 241 Japanese did so in 1999 (compared with 3.4 times more in 1995).[10] The growth of business transactions involving large corporations including international transactions calls for the involvement of lawyers in drafting contracts and giving legal advice as well as litigation in many other areas of law such as corporation, security, tax, environment, patent law, and

---

[8] D-K Choi, 'Informal Ways Versus the Formal Law in Korea' (1995) 36(3–4) *Seoul Law Journal* 51, to see how informal ways make the formal law complicated.

[9] Pyong Choon Hahm, *The Korean Political Tradition and Law* (Seoul, Hollyym, 1967) 6; Pyong Choon Hahm, *Korean Jurisprudence, Politics and Culture* (Seoul, Yonsei University Press, 1986) 95.

[10] Do-hyon Kim, 'Hankukui minsasosong jungkachu-iwa woninpunsok' (Increase Trend of Civil Litigation in Korea and Causal Analysis) (2000) 1 *Bopsahoehakyonku* (Sociology of Law Studies) 183, 186–87.

anti-trust law rather than in areas of civil and criminal law. The appearance of law firms and in-house counsel in law departments of large corporations are but a few features of the legal profession's response to the developments produced by industrialisation and globalisation. Today Korea is the 12th largest trading nation in the world.

4. Democratisation and the Legal Profession

With the adoption of the Constitution of the Republic of Korea in 1948, a liberal democratic document, a democratic form of government was introduced in the South for the first time in Korean history under the auspices of the UN. Koreans had lived under monarchical rule for many centuries until 1910 when Korea was forcefully annexed to Japan as part of its extortionist colonial rule. Under Japanese rule Koreans experienced totalitarianism by foreigners. It is interesting to observe that the exiled government of Korea in China took, as part of nationalist independent movements, a free democratic form of government, not the form of a revived monarchical rule. Before its fuller consolidation, however, Korean democracy underwent the harsh test of the three years war (1950–53) started by the North Korean communists. It then suffered more than two decades of authoritarian rule by army generals until 1987 when democratisation took place in the form of a people's revolution, by yielding to which the so-called military dictatorship finally came to an end. In Korean history, the year of 1987 is recorded as the watershed separating the authoritarian past and the democratic era that followed. In any case, the leadership was more or less democratic throughout the 1950s up to 1960, although it had no doubt authoritarian features in its practice as well. It was then followed by an army-general-led coup d'etat in 1961 and the rule by the junta. From 1962 until 1972 when the world-wide oil shock took place and the leadership resorted to a definitely authoritarian form of government, the leadership bore the appearance of democracy mixed with authoritarian practices. From 1972 until 1987, the rule was definitely that of a military dictatorship.

Interestingly enough, however, Korean industrialisation, especially its beginnings in the 1970s and the growth of heavy industry in the 1980s, went hand in hand with authoritarian rule. To a great extent, democratisation appeared alongside the growth of the economy, and particularly the emergence of a middle class which accompanied industrialisation. In that sense, authoritarianism has caused its own demise in Korea. At the same time, it should be noted that Korean authoritarian rule was characterised by a disparity between the authoritarian political reality and the formal law as it was practised under one of the liberal democratic written constitutions since 1948. Authoritarian rule in Korea was, at least in terms of formal norms, in violation of constitutionalism incorporated in the written liberal constitution, of which the principles of separation of power including that of the independent judiciary and the protection of fundamental rights including freedom of speech and rights of workers were integral parts from the outset (1948), in contrast with the situation in the former and still remaining socialist states like China today. Thus it was because of the disparity between the authoritarian political reality and the formal law that Korean lawyers could contribute to the democratisation process simply by standing up to the letter and spirit of the written constitution. Democratisation in Korea took the form, more than anything else, of realising the democratic ideals declared in the formal constitution.

Throughout the authoritarian rule, there had emerged long lines of both democratic and labour movements that included demands for the protection of such fundamental constitutional rights as freedom of speech and assembly and workers rights to join unions, to take part in collective bargaining and to strike in defiance of governmental interdictions and intimidations. In many cases, both movements were intermingled. The origin of labour movements goes back to Japanese rule. In any case, pro-democratic, anti-regime activism was suppressed. Labour was also suppressed. Thus many were silenced or acquiesced. Naturally, however, a number of lawyers became active participants in the both pro-democratic and/or labour movements. Other lawyers bravely came forward to defend pro-democratic activists and/or workers who were arrested on various criminal and other violations of law charges. A few became champions of democratic or pro-labour causes in nationally, high-profile court cases. Lawyers' constitutional principles and professional privileges were their weapons in the fight for pro-democratic and/or labour causes. At times some were imprisoned because of their actions.[11] Out of the pro-democratic and pro-labour activism of the 1970s and 1980s, there emerged a loosely organised, pro-human rights group of lawyers called *Minbyun* (Lawyers for a Democratic Society).[12] This group of lawyers became a force with a voice in society even today.

Along with *Minbyun*, Korea has experienced an explosion of civic movement organisations and NGOs occasioned by democratisation in 1987.

[11] See Won-soon Park, *Yoksaga idulul mujoero harira* (History will Acquit them), History of Advocacy for Human Rights in Korea, (Seoul: Durae, 2003), 209, 253; Minchonghakryonundongkyesungsaophoe, (ed) *1974 Nyon sawol* (April 1974), Silrok Minchonghakryon, '*History of Democratic Youth and Students League*' (Seoul: Hakminsa, 2003), vol 1 304, 311, 325, vol 2 243, 295.

[12] For information on their organization and activities, see *Minbyun baekso* (Minbyun White Paper), (Seoul, Minbyun, 1998).

Kyongsilyon (Citizens' Coalition for Economic Justice), *Chamyoyondae* (People's Solidarity for Participatory Democracy), *Hwankyon-gundongyonhap* (Korean Federation for Environmental Movement), *Noksaekyonhap* (Green Korea United), *Hankuksobijayonmaeng* (Consumers Union of Korea), and *Bopyulsobijayonmaeng* (GOODLAW) are some of the well-known civil movement organisations today. The areas of civic activities carried on by these organisations are quite broad and varied including those of human rights protection, citizens watching governmental, legislative and judicial processes, environmental protection, consumer protection, legislative initiatives, filing of strategic law suits, and educational campaigns for the heightening of citizens' awareness. And naturally lawyers, especially many young lawyers, are actively participating in the varied civic movements individually and/or as leading members of the organisations. Out of active participation in the various civic movements, there have naturally emerged specialist lawyers in many fields of public interest law including, inter alia, human rights protection and labour law, environmental protection, consumer protection and education, all matters in keeping with the needs of a contemporary industrialised and globalised society. Moreover, lawyers are now statutorily required to engage in public interest law service for a period of hours as organised by the bar association (Attorneys-At-Law Act of 2000 Art 27).

Legal aid has also become an integral part of lawyers' activities today. Until the 1960s little was known of systematically-provided legal aid. For the first time in 1972, a legal aid corporation was founded to provide legal aid on a regular basis. Its local offices were, however, organisationally integrated into the public prosecutors' local offices for the sake of convenience. The bar associations began to promote *pro bono* activities in their charters as part of their activities which involved mainly legal counselling for the poor; yet overall legal aid activities were largely passive. With the enactment of the Legal Aid Act in 1986, however, the Korea Legal Aid Corporation, a separate entity funded by the government, was established to provide legal aid for the poor on a systematic basis. There then emerged a group of lawyers who were employed by the legal service corporation—and another group of lawyers fresh out of the JRTI who were able to do their first practical training as legal aid lawyers of the corporation. This second group of lawyers are to complete their compulsory military duty at the same time by serving as a legal aid lawyer with the corporation for three years.

The social status of women has improved significantly even in the legal profession. Women's progression, especially in recent years, is on a par with men's, as compared with the 1960s, 1970s and even 1980s when traditional Confucian values were still strong. Gender equality has been reflected in their ever-increasing, large-scale entry into universities and higher educational institutions, employment, and professions of women. It has been much facilitated by feminist activities on the one hand and by legislation particularly designed to facilitate gender equality in Korean society on the other. For example, *Hankukyosongkyebalwon* (Korean Women's Development Institute) was established in 1983 to conduct studies on women-related issues from broad perspectives and to develop policies therefrom; *Namnyogoyong-pyongdungbop* (Gender Equality in Employment Act) was adopted in 1987; the ministry without portfolio was established in 1988 to be responsible for women's issues with a broader perspective than in previous years when they were handled as part of women's welfare by the Ministry of Health and Welfare; *Namnyochabyolkumjimitkujae-e-kwan-hanbopyul* (Act for Elimination of Discrimination against Women and Relief) was adopted in 1999; the Ministry of Gender Equality was established in 2001 and a woman has been appointed as its minister; the National Human Rights Commission of Korea was established in 2002; and *Nyosongbaljonkibonbop* (Basic Law for Women's Development) was adopted in 2003. A female former judge-practising lawyer was appointed Minister of Justice in the new Korean administration in 2003.

As shown in Table 4 below, there were no women judges until 1972, then between 2 and 8 by 1984. With 11 women judges in 1985, their number increased slowly but steadily until the mid-1990s. The increase in their numbers from the mid-1990s, however, has been explosive. There were 137 female judges out of a total 1,708 judges in 2003; there were 90 female apprentice judges out of the total 224 apprentice judges in 2003. The trend of this sharp increase is expected to continue for the time being. The proportion of women among the total number of those who passed the bar examination increased from 4.0 per cent in 1990 to 18.9 per cent in 2000 and to 23.7 per cent in 2002 whereas in the case of the Higher Civil Service Examination the proportion of women has risen from 1.7 per cent in 1990 to 25.1 per cent in 2000 and 25.3 per cent in 2001. Today about 30 per cent of law students are female. The picture of women lawyers in practice is perhaps less impressive but has shown a steady increase. The number of women lawyers in practice has risen from 43 (1.5 per cent) out of the total of 2,852 in 1995, to 303 (5.5 per cent) out of the total of 5,533 in 2003. Naturally there are quite a number of active feminist lawyers who struggle for the cause of women in legislation, litigation, NGO activities, as well as in the academic world.

With women, particularly in the legal profession, adopting a strategic position in society, many of the traditional social institutions that have been valued without question have been challenged by feminists, usually led by feminist lawyers within and outside of government, particularly in

Table 4 Female judges and apprentice judges against total numbers

Year	Judges		Apprentice Judges	
	Female	Total Number	Female	Total Number
1950~60		149~296 (216~301)		
1961~70		250~413 (350~471)		
1971		406 (471)		
1972		437 (471)		
1973~77	2~2	451~522 (471~580)		
1978	4	547 (610)		
1979	3	546 (640)		
1980~85	4~11	562~769 (640~887)		
1986~90	12~27	824~1028 (887~1138)		
1991	34	1048 (1184)		
1992	41	1089 (1238)		
1993	46	1115 (1288)		
1994	54	1170 (1338)		
1995	63	1212 (1388)		
1996	76	1293 (1448)		
1997	90	1362 (1508)		
1998	88	1341 (1578)	12	79
1999	85	1327 (1658)	18	150
2000	96	1393 (1738)	23	176
2001	102	1467 (1738)	40	207
2002	114	1578 (1808)	60	221
2003	137	1708 (1888)	90	224

Source: Ministry of Court Administration(the Supreme Court)
The Numbers without parentheses are actual numbers and the numbers in parentheses are those of the Full Strength. The table shows that the full strength are always undermanned. The reason why the actual numbers of male and female judges in 1979 and 1999 are less than those in the previous year (1978 and 1998) despite the general trend of increase is probably due to the early retirement of a number of judges who decided to enter into law practice.

the very recent years. In 1997, a traditional ban on marriage between broadly-defined family members bearing the same family name and the same place of family origin provided for by a civil code, was challenged and finally declared as repugnant to the Constitution by the Constitutional Court.[13] Traditionally one's family name, which is passed along the patriarchal line, has been regarded as unchangeable so that women have been required to keep their maiden name upon marriage. Any number of people who bear the same family name and the same place of family origin (eg Kim of *Kimhae*) have traditionally been regarded as family members however remotely they might be related to each other so that a marriage

[13] Constitutional Court Decision of 17 July 1997 (95 Honka 6·13).

between members of the same family was banned as almost incestuous.

In 1999, the favourable treatment (3 to 5 per cent of the total grade points in state-conducted examinations) statutorily given to those, usually males, who have completed their military service, was challenged and declared unconstitutional by the Constitutional Court.[14]

Today a civil code-provided institution of family headship in the family registry has been challenged as a male-centered institution discriminating against female members. Traditionally Koreans are registered with members of a family as a unit in the family registry, which is a civil code matter. The institution of family headship is likely to be abolished by special legislation despite strong resistance from traditional sectors of society.[15] Along with the institution of family headship, the traditional principle that one's family name never changes has also been challenged recently in various ways and with increasing force. Examples include a legislative proposal, a radical one in the Korean social contexts, that when a divorced woman takes her child from her previous marriage to her newly-married husband's family the child should be allowed to take the family name of his or her mother's second husband. Another radical proposal is that a child should be allowed to choose between the family names of his or her father and mother. These are only a few reflections of the industrial and democratic transformations that Korean society—along with law and the legal profession—has undergone in the last few decades.

The introduction of the Constitutional Court in 1987[16] and the constitutional developments thereafter in Korea should be also noted along the route of democratisation. From the outset, the Constitutional Court can be characterised by its activism in judicial review of legislation, particularly compared with Japanese judicial review which has been passive.[17] From 1987, democratisation in politics, economy and society including human rights and the feminist issues mentioned above, have definitely been facilitated by the Constitutional Court's review of legislation. Before 1987,

---

[14] Constitutional Court Decision of 23 December 1999 (98 Honma 363).

[15] The institution of family headship is held as inconsistent with the Constitution by the Constitutional Court in 2005. See Constitutional Court decision of February 3, 2005 (2001Honka9.) 10·11·12·13·14·15, 2004Honka5).

[16] D-k Choi, 'The Structure and the Function of the Constitutional Court: The Korean Case' in G Hassall and C Saunders (eds), *The Powers and Functions of Executive Government* (Carlton, Australia, Center for Comparative Constitutional Studies, University of Melbourne, 1994) 104.

[17] For Japan's judicial passivism, see Ito Masami, *Saibankanto gakusya aida* (Between the Judge and the Scholar), an autobiography by a former Japanese law-professor-turned Supreme Court Justice, (Tokyo, Yuhikaku, 1993) 106–44; M Ichikawa, T Sakamaki and K Yamamoto, *Gendaino Saiban* (Contemporary Judicial Decision-Making), 2nd edn (Tokyo, Yuhikaku, 2001) pp 227–33; M Ichikawa, 'Ikensinsaseino Kiisekito Denbou' (The Conducts of the Judicial Review System and its Prospect) in M Kamiya (ed), *Nihonkokukenpo o Yomizikisu* (Correct Readings of the Japan's Constitution), (Tokyo, Nihonkeizai Sinbun, 2000) 167.

lawyers did not have to learn constitutional law, except as university law students and when taking their bar examination, because their law practice did not and could not involve constitutional law issues under the authoritarian regimes. Since 1987, however, there has emerged literally an explosive development of constitutional jurisprudence and an equally explosive growth of constitutional law specialists including both constitutional scholars and practitioners, especially among young lawyers.[18] Probably both the dynamism of Korean society and bad legislation made under the authoritarian regimes have contributed to this constitutional activism since 1987. The institution of judicial review by constitutional courts rather than ordinary courts having the power of review may also have partly contributed to the activist constitutional developments.[19]

5. Legal Education, the Bar and the Judiciary at the Crossroads

Korean society has undergone rapid social, cultural and political transformation accompanied by industrialisation and democratisation. So have legal education, the bar and the judiciary. Some legitimate questions about all these changes in law and society include whether the changes in the present legal education, the bar and the judiciary are closely related to social changes or whether they lag behind them. Another way of raising the same question would be to ask whether legal education, the bar, and the judiciary are sufficiently fulfilling what is expected of them in the changed social and political environment. Our observations seem to indicate that usually change in the law takes place after change in society and that there still remain unfulfilled social expectations in respect of legal education, the bar and the judiciary which will be considered below.

---

[18] As of 30 April 2003 from September 1988 when it began its function of judicial review, 8765 cases were filed at the Constitutional Court (average around 550 cases a year). Among them, statutes or statutory provisions in question were declared outright unconstitutional in 233 cases, 'inconsistent with the constitution' (practically unconstitutional) in 70 cases (meaning that the legislature was required to amend the statutes so as to be consistent with the constitution until a certain deadline. Otherwise, from that time they become *null and void*), partly unconstitutional in 42 cases, and partly constitutional (meaning that other part was unconstitutional) in 28 cases and constitutional complaints were 'accepted' as constitutionally well-grounded in 186 cases. Altogether legislation was declared unconstitutional wholly or partially in 559 cases after all whereas it was declared constitutional in 714 cases and 6597 cases were dismissed either as ungrounded or on procedural grounds. See *Honbopjepanso Kongbo* (the Constitutional Court Gazette) no 80, p 355 (20 May 2003).

[19] D-K Choi, 'Honbopjepansoui jongchihak: ku kujowa kinungul jungsimuso' (Politics of the Constitutional Court: With the Focus on its Structure and Functions) (1993) 34(1) *Seoul Law Journal* 106.

Koreanisation of legal terms has been and still is one of the major issues facing the judicial department. An initial stage was to change Japanese legal terms including Japanese jargon into the Korean language. The next stage was to express Chinese characters in legal terms with Korean alphabets. It has been some time since all official documents including judicial opinions were written in Korean alphabets alone except where the use of Chinese characters was necessary, for example, to distinguish a person. Today, a governmental plan is underway to use Korean alphabets alone in all laws and regulations, because there are still many of them in which Chinese characters are used for legal terms. Legal concepts are defined mostly by using Chinese characters which are ideographic. Chinese characters in Korea and Japan are a functional equivalent to Latin in Western language. To a great extent, Koreanisation of legal terms has been both necessitated and facilitated firstly by and with the wide use of typewriters and then word processors.[20] Koreanisation of legal terms has also meant easier access to justice for ordinary people. In recent years the introduction of either a lay person jury or assessor judge system has been under a serious consideration as a measure for democratisation of the judicial process. These examples are only an indication of the conscious efforts to narrow the distance between the judicial department and the masses. The court has not been one of the major places in which the social life of ordinary people was shaped, however. Equally lawyers are not the people to whom you turn for help except for litigation, which is to be avoided as much as possible. In the popular perception, access to lawyers' services has been financially and culturally out of reach. Lawyers still do little in government or other major policy-making beyond advocacy in litigation.

Among others, the present legal education and training institutions have been more seriously challenged in Korea. The challenges have come basically from three or four fronts of concern: the need for a professional legal education, the need for legal specialists and training for legal specialists, the concern with professional ethics, and the proper size of the legal profes-

---

[20] Before the arrival of personal computer's word processors, Korean typewriters were widely used at the courts and the practising lawyers offices. Use of typewriters was possible in Korea because the Korean language has 24 phonetic alphabets whereas it was impossible with ideographic Chinese characters whose number is over a few thousands even for everyday use. Today Korean word processors are far more widely used along with the wide spread of personal computers. With personal computers, use of Chinese characters is also possible today. But it makes it far more complicated to use Chinese characters than to use Korean alphabets alone. The younger Koreans are the less command they have over Chinese characters today. With Koreanization of legal terms and with the wide use of personal computers, access to judicial information including litigation related information is made far easier for ordinary citizens, particularly because of the conscious efforts on the part of the judicial department to computerize toward an electronic court system.

sion. Generally speaking, the basic nature of legal education and training, and the very framework within which they were conducted, have not changed for the last half century or more although the society in which lawyers work has been greatly transformed. Of course, there have been some changes and innovation in legal education and training but they were more piecemeal than structural changes as manifested in the addition to the traditional university law curriculum of new legal subjects such as labour law, environmental protection, intellectual property law, science-technology and law and human rights, the substitution of the JRTI in place of the former unsystematic training, the institution of the apprentice judgeship and others. Legal education in universities remains basically that of a liberal education. It consists more of lectures than anything else. A law degree is not required in order to take the bar examination and to become a lawyer. Consequently, lawyers are recruited by way of the written bar examination alone, not by education. Previously self-education was all that was required for preparation for the bar examination. Today cramming courses in exam skills and technique are flourishing almost to the point of replacing university law classes for preparatory studies for the bar examination, especially for those whose majors are not in law.

The JRTI has been oriented principally towards the training of *bop-kwan* (governmental lawyers), that is, judges and public prosecutors. There is far more emphasis on training in drafting judicial opinions and indictments than anything else in the JRTI's education. The grades given in drafting classes at the JRTI determine a student's chance of becoming a judge or public prosecutor. Only those graduates who are in the top 20 per cent or so are likely to succeed. Consequently, the kind of orientation of the JRTI as the training body for future government lawyers and the associated characteristics of its education have recently been criticised as unsuitable for the training of future lawyers, the majority of whom will become practising lawyers. Demands for the expansion of training programmes for future practising lawyers or for the transformation of the JRTI into a practising lawyer's training institution have been voiced even by trainees themselves.[21] The very wisdom and efficiency required to manage the single, state-run JRTI's training programmes uniformly for 2,000 trainees began to be questioned by many onlookers. The JRTI's practical training and professional ethics programmes are also seen as deficient.

Two embarrassing incidents involving one former-judge and another former public prosecutor attorney that took place respectively in 1998 and in

---

[21] For example, Byong-Chun Song, 'Sabopyonsuwonkyoyuk iroke dallajoyahabnida' (Ways in Which the JRTI Should Change) [2003] (April) *Siminkwa Pyonhosa* (Citizens and Attorneys) 74–77. Song is himself a trainee of the JRTI presently.

1999[22] have occasioned those in the legal profession publicly to reappraise the state of their professional training and ethics. The two, who followed the general pattern of becoming practising lawyers upon their retirement from government positions, became rising stars in the legal services market in a short period of time. It transpired that the secret of their quick success lay in building up and managing a group of the courts' and prosecutors offices' clerical officials and policemen as a network of brokers for their law business. These individuals were willing to refer cases to the lawyers for money, potential clients whom they came into contact with in the line of their official duties. To public outrage, they also managed consciously to cultivate, on their arrival or departure, a friendly relationship with judges and public prosecutors in their area of practice, by issuing invitations to top-class restaurants and other places of entertainment and/or offering gifts of holidays. With the two incidents came a new starting point, with the judiciary, the public prosecutors, and the bar associations reviewing their code of conduct and tightening their ethical standards, by for example, prohibiting acceptance of even innocent friendly invitations and gifts. Professional ethics programmes are reinforced in the JRTI as well. Another practice deemed to be unethical is that of 'deferential treatment' (*Jonkwan ye-u*) by judges or prosecutors of former-colleague lawyers opening their new law offices upon retirement from the position of judge or prosecutor.

In fact, professional ethics has been one of the serious issues that the legal profession has had to face squarely. The real issue seems to be that of how to build up its own identity as a learned profession in society beyond the image of a state-licensed interest group or simply a group of traders or businessmen. Naturally professional ethics is one of the crucial issues that the Korean legal profession has successfully to deal with. Its ability as a profession to self-discipline is still doubted by the public. As part of a society-wide democratisation process, the bar association came to acquire a bigger voice in the disciplinary matters of practising lawyers with the introduction of the disciplinary committee at the Korean Federation of Bar Association in 1993. Previously the ministry of justice had played a major role in lawyers' disciplinary matters. The judiciary and particularly public prosecutors, as well as practising lawyers, have come under strong pressure to raise ethical standards including those of fairness, political neutrality and accessibility, in the name of 'reform.'

Consequently, serious doubts have for some time been raised about the ability of the present legal education and training institutions to produce the capable and responsible lawyers that Korea needs to service a com-

---

[22] See D-k Choi, 'The Judicial Functions and Independence in Korea', *Seoul Law Journal* 1999 vol 40 (2), 53, 62-4.

plex, contemporary society and one of the world's leading economies. Perhaps the present education and training institutions might have been adequate in terms of what was expected of lawyers in the 1960s and 1970s when Korean society was less complex and far less litigious and its economy was still in an agricultural and far less industrialised, initial stage under authoritarian regimes. But they may no longer be so, in that they are still producing lawyers whose orientation is limited mainly to litigation advocacy and whose intellectual and educational backgrounds are too deficient to allow them to become legal specialists in various areas of complex, contemporary law such as banking, securities, corporate reorganisation, insolvency, composition, acquisition and merger, anti-trust law, patent, and environment. Because of their limited orientation and education and also because their numbers are still limited, lawyers produced under the present system have a small part to play in counselling, negotiation and drafting in major economic, industrial and world trade policy-making processes, in which the administration's non-lawyer officials dominate.

Looking at the picture of the legal profession described above, it is only natural that the attempted drive towards the professionalisation of university legal education and training , while phasing out the JRTI training stage, has twice in the past been undertaken, following the American model, once in 1995–96 and then in 1998–99. Each time, the drive, spearheaded by reform-minded law professors, failed because of vehement resistance on the part of the established legal profession joined by conservative professors many of whom have been trained, interestingly enough, in Germany. The resistance was rationalised among others on the ground that the American model was not suited to Korea, whose legal system was that of the civil law. No doubt, however, their hidden motive was to keep the profession small and privileged by limiting access, in order to prevent a nation-wide law school system from being introduced. The proper size of the legal profession has been one of the most hotly-debated topics.[23] A consensus is unlikely to be found in the near future because of the disparity of views about its proper size but also about the proper functions that lawyers are supposed to fulfill in society. As would be argued by conservative lawyers, if their proper function is confined largely to litigation advocacy, with 1,000 new members each year, their numbers may become too large. Their numbers would not be too large if their functions were broadened to include counselling and drafting as well as litigation advocacy and

---

[23] For a serious discussion on the proper size of the practitioners in Korea, Sang-hi Han, 'Pyonhosaui jokjongsu' (The Right Size of the Practising Lawyers) (1995) 11 *Bopkwa Sahoe* (Law and Society) 38–70; U-hyon Cho, 'Bopjoin jokjongsuae daehan sogo' (A Study on the Proper Size of the Practising Lawyers) (1995) 11 *Bopkwa Sahoe* (Law and Society) 71–81.

extended into legal specialist roles beyond typical civil and criminal law, as required by a contemporary economy. Consequently, a graduate-level law school has been argued as more than justified in Korea, in that it would offer lawyers far better training in terms of their knowledge and skills and also in terms of the professional ethics expected of them today and in the future world.[24]

An attempt was made to develop a law school in 1995–96 with the formation of a presidential commission as part of an anti-unethical practice, judicial reform drive, which was again a part of the new administration's reform campaign.[25] The attempt failed, but succeeded in setting in motion the increasing of the size of the quota for the bar examination to 1,000 a year. In the second attempt in 1998–99, two presidential commissions were formed: one for educational reform and another for judicial reform. The former commission recommended law school,[26] the latter the strengthening of the JRTI,[27] and no agreement was reached between them. Eventually no action was taken although the yearly quota of 1,000 for the bar examination was confirmed. Ironically, the two earlier attempts by Korea to introduce law schools have provided the impetus for Japan to take steps to introduce law schools in their country. The presidential commissions' reports, in particular that of the Presidential Commission for New Education Community, were widely consulted with by Japanese special-

---

[24] See D-k Choi, 'How is Law School Justified in Korea?' (2000) 41(1) *Seoul Law Journal* 25; D-k Choi, 'Legal Education in Korea: Toward Professional Model' (2000) 13 *Dokkyo International Review* 35; D-k Choi, 'Proposed Legal Education Reform in Korea: Toward Professional Model' (March 2001) 18 *Ritsumeikan Law Review* 93.

[25] See *Saekyehwa Jongbohwa Sidaelul Judohanun Sinkyoyukchaeje Suripul Wihan Kyoyukkyehyok Bangan* (II) (Education Reform Proposal for Establishment of the New Education System that Shall Lead the Era of Globalization and Information II), 3rd Presidential Report, (Seoul, Presidential Advisory Commission for Education Reform, 9 February 1996) pp 57–59; *Bophakjonmundaehakwon Solipbangan Yonku* (Study on Establishment Plan for Law School), the 1997 report of the task force headed by Yang Sung-du. See also O-sung Kwon, *Sabopdo Service-da* (Administration of Justice is also a Service), (Seoul, Miraemedia, 1996); Chamyoyondae, *Kukminulwihan Sabopkyehyok* (Judicial Reform for the People), (Seoul, Pakyongyul Press, 1996).

[26] See *Bophakkyoyuk Jedokyeson Yonku: 'Haksahu Bophakkyoyuk'ui Doip* (Study on Legal Education Institution Reform: Introduction of 'Post-Undergraduate-Degree Legal Education'), the report to the Presidential Commission for New Education Community by Daehakjedoyonku Wiwonhoe (the task force headed by the author), (Seoul, Presidential Commission for New Education Community, 1999).

[27] See *Minjusahoelul Wihan Sabopkyehyok: Daetongryong Jamunwiwonhoe Bogoso* (Judicial Reform for Democratic Society: Presidential Advisory Commission Report), (Seoul, Presidential Commission for Judicial Reform, 2000) pp 391–430. The commission's legal education reform proposal largely reflected the opinions and sentiments of the legal profession then. It retained basically the structure and concepts of the present legal education and training institution with a few minor changes adopted from the proposal of the Presidential Commission for New Education Community such as a proposed educational requirement that only those who earned an undergraduate law degree or a certain number of credit units in university law courses should be entitled to take the bar examination.

ists.[28] In any case, Japan decided to introduce a graduate level law school, at a level above the previous undergraduate-level law departments, a compromise measure in the name of the Japanese version of law school.[29] The attempts at a Korean version saw a graduate-level law school idea with undergraduate law programmes being phased out. It is also certain that the Japanese action in turn gave the impetus back to Korea to go forward with the law school. Now, a sense of inevitability that Korea will introduce a graduate-level professional law school has begun to set in among lawyers and law professors, even those who were previously opposed to it. The JRTI is now widely seen as an inefficient institution for the training of the future lawyers in one place. With the establishment of a law school,[30] the legal profession is expected to be more professional and diverse in its functions and Korea will be in a better position to produce specialists in various areas of contemporary law.

6. Concluding Remarks

At this juncture of social development, Korean lawyers are placed in a schizophrenic situation; they are caught between two different elements of the legal culture, one a cognitive and the other an emotional element. The proposition that the rule of law is not only useful but also necessary for a well-functioning market economy and democracy has been widely accepted. This has been further reinforced by the recent experience of the economic crisis of 1998 and the restructuring efforts to overcome it, and with the eruption of social and political forces including labour and other organised interests that were previously suppressed under the authoritarian

---

[28] The Presidential Commission for New Education Community's *Bophakkyoyuk Jedokyeson Yonku: 'Haksahu Bophakkyoyuk'ui Doip* (see n 26) is promptly translated into Japanese and carried with translators' introduction in a well-known Japanese law journal. See (Siryo) Kankoku Daitoryo Simon Sin Kyoikukyodotai Iinkai Hogaku Kyoikuseidokenkyu Iinkai, Setsuo Miyazawa and Dong-Hi Yi (trs), 'Hogakukyoikuseidokaizenno Kihonhoko-'Gakusigo Hogaku Kyoiku'no Donyu', (Study on Legal Education Institution Reform: Introduction of 'Post-Undergraduate-Degree Legal Education), (1999) 49(2) *Kobe Hogaku Zassi* 153.

[29] See Recommendations of the Justice System Reform Council—For a Justice System to Support Japan In the 21st Century, by the Justice System Reform Council, 12 June 2001, esp p 83 ff.

[30] As of Augusr 2005, introduction of the graduate level law school has become ever more certain in Korea, with its recommendation by two government commissions, one Judicial Reform Commission organized by the Supreme Court in 2004, and another Presidential Commission for Judicial Reform in 2005 upon the proposals by the former commission. Both law school and lay participation stand out among many other recommended judicial reform proposals by the two commissions. These are now up for realization through legislation and other related governmental measures.

regimes but now unleashed by democratisation. Since the economic crisis, the terms 'legal principles and transparency' have become the catch phrases of the prescription for a robust economy in Korea. Along with knowledge, the rule of law in Korea has made great strides in the recent decades. As we have seen, so has the legal profession.

Perhaps as a cultural lag phenomenon, however, there also remains the traditional Confucian sentiment that the best policy is to cultivate people to behave well and be upright by *ye(li)*, and that law is necessary only to make society one that needs no law. Popularly a good neighbour is described still as 'a person who can live without law.' Certainly, the Confucian tradition has considerably faded away. But political expediency has coalesced with the remaining elements of the traditional aversion to the law. Emotionally, law is still not well accepted but something that people want to shy away from. This dichotomous situation has been utilised to its utmost, however, by various players for their own benefit in the market and in democratic games. There is a tendency then to use law only as a convenient, strategic tool. The law is relied upon when its observance is advantageous. Otherwise, those players readily resort to personal ties and traditional sentiments and/or ideological bonds in support of their claims, which, in may cases, easily amount to an evasion or violation of laws and principles. Such social stability and predictability as are necessary for further advancement of the economy and democracy in Korea may not be achieved with law as a means of strategic use alone, however, unless law becomes the more relevant basis of the rules of the economic and democratic game.

In this situation, it seems clear that their prevailing litigation-centered orientation tends to keep lawyers a step apart from the mainstream movements in Korean society. Korean lawyers are either destined to find their position as a positive player in the mainstream of economic, social and political transformation by making law a more relevant element in socio-economic and political processes, for example, by finding a policy-making or a mediator's role in international as well as domestic theatres, or to remain in the litigation lawyer's position, of passive after-the fact carer for social dynamism. The globalisation of the Korean economy and the scheduled opening of the legal services market under the WTO regime makes matters more complicated. The defensive posture that the Korean legal profession has been taking thus far toward the opening of the legal services market alone does not solve their problems at their roots. It is our opinion that the transformation of Korean society in the globalised world requires law to be made a more relevant force and lawyers to play a more active role in the economy and in society.

It is indeed doubtful whether the present legal education and training system is adequate to prepare lawyers sufficiently for the complex tasks expected of them in the transformed contemporary society. The proposal of graduate-level law schools is only a natural response to the appreciation of the situation in which the present legal education and training system finds itself. Society has changed but the methods by which future lawyers are selected and prepared for the role expected of them in the changed society has not. Legal education reform is one of the most pressing agenda items that the Korean legal profession has to squarely face in years to come. The Korean legal profession is situated at a crossroads in terms of the future of its legal education and training, its orientations and functions, its size, and its position in society and the globalised world.

8

Lawyers in Late Twentieth-
Century Latin America*

ROGELIO PÉREZ-PERDOMO

Imagine looking at a figure and thinking you saw an old woman and then sud-
denly the same figure turned out to be an elegant young lady—lawyers in late
twentieth-century Latin America represent a similar form of ambiguous perception. You might see an old profession, wanting to be connected with the
Roman tradition. Latin words and old heraldic signs might be found in the
coat of arms of the *colegios de abogados*. But, at the same time, they might be
proud of ultra modern offices in glass skyscrapers, full of computers and modern equipment. They might be discreetly talking in English on cellular phones.
How old or how new is the profession at the turn of this century?

The time frame we will use is the last third of the twentieth century and
these very first years of the twenty-first century. It is a period of change,
seen even in the likes of Fernando Henrique Cardoso. In the 1970s he was
a young scholar, very representative of the dependency theory. Cardoso
and other scholars thought that national development was the collective
challenge. Multinationals and other foreign investors were the great danger; only an interventionist state could protect the national industry and
promote endogenous growth. In the late 1990s Cardoso became Brazil's
President. He is the champion of open markets. Foreign investments are
welcome and the world is a place of opportunity. We can call these opposing views of societal ends, national development and globalisation. We are
not talking about Cardoso's personal conversion. Many other leading
political figures have similar histories, and political parties like the Argen-
tinean Justicialist, Mexican PRI, Venezuelan *Acción Democrática*, and
Chilean Socialists and Christian Democrats have made similar conversions.

* From *Latin American Lawyers, A Historical Introduction* by Rogelio Pérez-Perdomo, ©
2006 by the Board of Trustees of the Leland Stanford Jr. University, all rights reserved. By
permission of the publisher, www.sup.org.

In the last 30 years, the change has not only been in terms of ideology. Social and political change has been very important. In the 1970s most Latin American countries had terrible dictatorships. In the 1990s to the present day, the trend has been one of democratisation. The picture is not entirely rosy, however: recent troubles in Argentina, Colombia and Venezuela show that these political systems are still unstable. Economic crisis shakes every Latin American country from time to time—but, with all the difficulties, the direction of social change has been clear: increased urbanisation, expansion of education, deepening social inequality.

Social and political change has had an important impact in the law. We will look only at lawyers and two aspects of the legal profession: the selection and the occupation.

The Selection of Lawyers: the Law School

In Latin America, lawyers are mostly selected through university legal education. Universities date back to the colonial past for most countries, or, in the case of Brazil and some central American countries, from a period of early nineteenth-century independence. Traditionally law schools have been the principal place from which lawyers were selected, but in some countries bar exams and other requirements have been established.

Law schools appear to be the most traditional part of the legal profession. Their curricula have changed little in the last 30 years. At their core continue to be courses in constitutional law, civil law, penal law, commercial law, civil procedure, and criminal procedure. The references for these courses are the constitution and the main codes, documents that in their structure and most of their content originate in the nineteenth century. In the 1970s there was a movement for renovation of the curriculum, generally referred to as 'law and development'. The common opinion is that it was a failure and that legal education changed little. We will discuss this opinion and we hope to show a more complex panorama. There is more change under the appearance of immobility, but before we analyse these changes in curriculum and methodology, we shall analyse the demographic trends and their social significance.

How Many Students Are There, and Who Are They?

Most students enter at approximately the age of 18, immediately after completing their secondary education. University studies usually last for five years. In the predominantly agrarian societies of the past, the fact that law was studied in universities was a barrier to the number of people who could aspire to enter into that career. There were few universities, and the cost of moving to and living in the capital or a city with a law school, as well as the opportunity cost of leaving one's agricultural or commercial work, meant that relatively few students entered universities. Despite the fact that law was one of the most desired university degrees and attracted a high percentage of university students, the number of law students in relation to the total population of the country remained relatively low.

Development policies altered the scene by promoting urbanisation, industrialisation, and the expansion of primary and secondary education. Table 1 shows the number of law students in the second half, or the last third, of the twentieth century for nine Latin American countries that, as a whole, contained more than 90 per cent of the population of the region.

Notice that it begins with fairly low numbers compared to those at the end of the period, relative to the figures for the total population. The growth in the number of law students can be explained partially by the expansion of primary and secondary education that generally took place in the second third of the twentieth century. Around the middle of the century (or a little earlier or later, depending on the country), the pressure was felt in the universities. The response varied by country: restricting entry, increasing the quota, or creating or permitting the creation of new law schools. Frequently, countries simultaneously tried out more than one policy, or changed them over time. In any case, the growth is related to an appreciable demographic change in the same period with the growth of the cities and the urban population.

There are a few anomalies, such as the substantial decrease in the number of law students in Peru between 1991 and 2000, but this may be related to the different definition of 'law students' depending on the source, since the National Assembly of Rectors (which is the source that we use for 2000) lists 30,396 as the number for 1990.[1] Note that we use UNESCO for 1991, but there are no numbers from this organisation for 2000.

Attributing the increase in law students to the expansion of higher education is obvious in the cases in which the number of university students grew at a higher rate than the number of law students (Brazil, Chile, Ecuador, Venezuela, and, to a lesser degree, Mexico). As opportunities for university study diversified, young people were able to choose from among

---

[1] For example, in some countries law students begin with a basic common cycle where the students can also take some courses from the professional cycle that they have selected. Different sources may include, or exclude, these students. The same thing can occur with postgraduate students: they could be included in one statistical inform, excluded in other. The definition of 'university students' also varies, since one of the important changes in the last third of the 20th century was the growth of institutes of higher education that are not technically universities.

Table 1 Law Students in Latin America

	Number of Law Students	% of University Students	Law Students per 100,000 Inhabitants
Argentina 1970	29,045	13.2	124
Argentina 1997	131,152	14.4	392
Brazil 1961	23,519	23.7	25
Brazil 1965 (a)	33,402	21.5	41
Brazil 1994 (a)	190,712	11.5	122
Brazil 1998	292,728	Not available	183
Colombia 1950 (b)	1,985	20.5	18
Colombia 1965 (a)	5,274	11.9	29
Colombia 1996 (a)	66,778	14	187
Costa Rica 1950 (b)	205	13.3	24
Costa Rica 1965 (a)	328	4.5	22
Costa Rica 1994 (a)	4,262	5.4	125
Chile 1950 (b)	2,284	Not available	19
Chile 1965 (a)	3,431	7.9	39
Chile 1996 (a)	17,462	6.4	122
Chile 2000	24,478	5.4	163
Ecuador 1965 (a)	1,706	12.1	34
Ecuador 1991 (a)	16,903	8.1	170
Mexico 1965 (a)	16,808	12.6	42
Mexico 1995 (a)	137,357	11.3	151
Mexico 2000	188,422	11.9	193
Peru 1950 (b)	1,392	8.7	18
Peru 1965 (a)	4,624	5.8	40
Peru 1991 (a)	43,715	9.2	198
Peru 2000	36,986	Not available	142
Venezuela 1950	1,000	13.5	53
Venezuela 1966 (a)	6,766	12.6	78
Venezuela 1995	33,000	9.0	150

Sources: (a) UNESCO, Statistical Yearbook 1973 and 1997. (b) JH Merryman *et al*, 1979. ARGENTINA: Sistema de Estadísticas Universitaria, Secretaría de Políticas Universitarias, Ministerio de Educación, Buenos Aires (unpublished data collected by MI Bergoglio). BRAZIL 1961: Falcão, 1984. BRAZIL 1998: Junqueira, 2001. CHILE 2000: Persico, 2001: 43. MEXICO 2000: Anuario Estadístico de ANUIES cit por Fix-Fierro, trabajo en curso. PERU 2000: Asamblea Nacional de Rectores. VENEZUELA 1950: R Pérez Perdomo, 1981. VENEZUELA 1995: Estimate of Pérez Perdomo based on partial data from the Oficina de Planificación del Sector Universitario (Unpublished).

a larger number of majors. Thus, the trend is an increase in the number of law students per 100,000 inhabitants but a decrease as a percentage of university students.

This is not a general trend. In Argentina, Colombia, and Costa Rica, there has been an increase in law students both in absolute numbers and as a percentage of university students. This indicates that the demographic change and the change in university offerings do not explain everything, since other studies that are as traditional as law (medicine, theology, and philosophy) did not grow to the same extent and sometimes decreased in absolute numbers. Other studies, nonexistent until the mid-century, such as computer science or business, attract a significant number of students. Without a doubt, the perception of job opportunities after graduation is a powerful incentive in choosing a university career.

The growth in the number of students is a manifestation of a much deeper change: the democratisation of education—that is, access by groups and social classes that were excluded from university education in the past. Thus, women began to have greater access to legal education. The national figures vary considerably, but women went from a third or less of all law students in the 1960s to approximately one half around the end of the century. We will provide some examples. In Mexico, women made up 15 per cent of law students in 1965 (UNESCO Statistical Yearbook, 1973) and 47 per cent in 1997 (López-Ayllón and Fix-Fierro 2001). In Chile, women constituted 23 per cent of the 9,308 lawyers in 1992, while of the total of 2,791 graduates between 1995 and 1999, women made up 39 per cent (Santelices Ariztía 2002; also see Persico 2001:33). In the University of Buenos Aires in 1964, 34 per cent of law students were female; in 1980, 53 per cent (Mackinson de Sorokin 1984). In the Central University of Venezuela, women made up 23 per cent of law graduates in 1959, while they are 57 per cent in 2000 (Roche 2001).

Those gaining access to law schools were people from the lower-income social strata. The racial distribution in Latin America is generally not reported, in part because the ideology of equality and integration means that statistics are not categorised by race or ethnic background. The fact that we have located an article that refers to black students and points to their increase in Brazil, reveals not only a trend in the student population, but also a disposition to study issues barely considered until now (Junqueira and Veras 2001).

In short, in relation to earlier periods, not only are there many more students, but these people have other social and job expectations. This will have repercussions in the changing social function of law schools. As the demand for legal studies has changed in the second half, or last third, of the twentieth century, there has been a change in the supply of law schools. New law schools, especially private ones, have been created as a product of the policies of educational liberalisation. We will look at this later, but note that supply and demand are not independent in this matter; in other words, the growth in the number of law schools in recent years could have augmented the growth in the demand for legal education. At the same time, the increase in the number of students could cause the strengthening or consolidation of the supply.

The changes in the demography of law students are related to the transformations of Latin American societies, and also to their political and social systems. In this sense, the comparison with Cuba is interesting. As we know, this is the only country that chose a socialist path. In 1965, when the Cuban Revolution was initiated with great ideological fervor, legal studies almost disappeared: there were 343 law students, who represented less than 2 per cent of university students and 5 out of 100,000 inhabitants. In 1995, resulting from an official policy that again valued legal studies, the number grew to 1,848. This did not signify a substantial increase in value with respect to its weight within the university, but it meant an increase to 17 law students per 100,000 inhabitants, a figure at any rate very low in comparison with the rest of the Latin American countries. In 1995, 70 per cent of law students were women, and the proportion appears to have increased (data from UNESCO 1997; see Zatz 1994; Bermúdez 2001).[2]

The increase in the demand for legal studies partially explains the emergence or strengthening of private legal education. The reasons for its creation may be ideological or commercial, but only the sustained increase in young people inclined to study law made possible the increase in the number of private law schools and the proportion of students in private universities in nearly all of the countries in the region.

Changes in the Schools and their Programmes

The traditional function of law schools was the training of the political elite. In the nineteenth and early twentieth century, it was an express function. Legal studies were often called 'political science', and parliamentarians, ministers, and high public officials were trained there (Dantas 1955; Falcão 1984; Camp 1996; Pérez Perdomo, 1981; de la Maza 2001). Not only did the law curriculum include subjects like political economy and sociology, but also many of the students, displaced from their home towns, met to discuss politics or literature. These networks were later reflected in the political activity and the administration of the state. Legal training as such was complemented by work in tribunals or in lawyers' offices.

Around the middle of the twentieth century, legal studies turned more to the law (de la Maza 2001; Pérez Perdomo 1981), but its function of training the political elite was preserved, in a latent or implicit way. The presence of lawyers in the distinct fields of politics and state administration as well as the informal networks that were formed in the law schools explain this latent function, which was concentrated in certain universities such as

---

[2] The very low number of law students and lawyers was a characteristic of the socialist countries (Cf. Clark, 1999).

the Autonomous National University of Mexico (Lomnitz and Salazar 1997) or the Central University of Venezuela. The students' political activity, including participation in violent acts, formed part of their political training and the establishment of loyalties.

In the last third of the twentieth century, the political function of these large universities came into conflict with their express function of educating lawyers. The intensification of political agitation damaged education at these universities because of the greater frequency of strikes, class suspensions, and acts of violence. The political activity especially affected the large universities of the capitals, which were the principal educators of the political elite. This contributed to the birth or the growth of private universities, since students who wanted a more continuous course of studies with the possibility of pay, migrated to these private schools.

The first private schools, generally around the end of the nineteenth or the first half of the twentieth century, were in Catholic universities[3] or occasionally, as in the case of the Escuela Libre de Derecho in Mexico City, were developed with the aim of professionalisation as an alternative to a politicised official education. However, through the first half of the century, private universities were few in number and their education had a largely ideological purpose. Nevertheless, the curriculum was very similar to the more traditional schools. In the last 30 years, the number of schools and law programmes has increased substantially.[4] There were very diverse aims behind the foundation of schools and these aims are now reflected in the law curriculum. As a result, someone who wants to study law in any Latin American country generally finds a range of possibilities.

Two types of private universities can be distinguished: those that consider education in terms of business and aspire to provide education to huge numbers, and those that have decided to maintain low numbers and try to offer high-quality education. The latter have attracted the offspring of the economic elite and have begun to stress the training of business lawyers. As a consequence, the law schools of the large, traditional universities have lost their standing as the educators of the political elite and saw their prestige in the training of business lawyers reduced. Likewise, they lost their position as a centre of upward social mobility. They were quickly

---

[3] For example, the Universidad Católica de Chile was created in 1889. The Pontificia Universidad Católica del Perú (Lima) in 1917. The Universidad Católica Andrés Bello, of Caracas, in the 1950s. In almost all the Latin American capitals, there exists a Catholic university with a law school.

[4] For example, of the 40 law schools that exist in Chile, 6 were created before 1979, 13 between 1980 and 1990, and 21 between 1991 and 2000 (de la Maza, 2001). In Venezuela, there were 7 law schools until 1980, and in 2001 there are 16, of which 12 are private (Information of the Oficina de Planificación del Sector Universitario). In Colombia there were few law schools in the 50s; in 1994, there were 38. In 2002, there are 74 with a total of 130 programs (Fuentes Hernandez, work in progress).

replaced by a few private schools in the task of training business lawyers and, more recently, as business lawyers have gained political power, they have also been replaced in the training of the political elite.[5] In short, there has been a shift in the training of the elite from the large public universities to a number of private universities.

At first, there was no difference between private and public education in terms of their content and teaching methods. The curricula were fundamentally the same. Around the middle of the twentieth century, legal education concentrated more on the law, not only increasing the number of classes in civil, criminal, and procedural law, but also including new branches of law to be studied: labour and administrative law, among others. The initial change in the law curriculum therefore saw an increase in the subjects or fields of study, highly concentrated in the law. As a result, general education courses lost relative influence and importance. At the same time, universities created departments in economics, sociology, political science, and other social sciences. Society thus had a variety of specialisations and disciplinary knowledge at its disposal, and lawyers were more confined to the legal field. We should not, then, be surprised that law graduates could no longer claim universal knowledge in the political and social fields, and that their pre-eminence declined (Rosenn, 1969; Steiner 1971; Urzúa 1978; De la Maza 2001).

The accelerated increase in the number of students and the weak social relations of many of the new students meant that the parallel informal education that students traditionally obtained by working in established lawyers' offices or in the courts became more difficult. The increase in subjects of study also reduced the time that students dedicated to these activities, which were extra-curricular but important for socialisation in politics. Most law professors only dedicated the necessary class hours to the university, which caused them to limit themselves to repeating what they had learned or reiterating the most important manuals that existed on the subject. Thus, in the 1960s and 1970s, there was a perception among the intellectual leaders of the main law schools that legal studies were irrelevant,[6]

---

[5] Among these schools are the Catholic universities in Santiago, Rio, Lima, Caracas; Universidad de los Andes y la Javeriana in Bogota; Libre, ITAM, and Iberoamericana in Mexico City; Diego Portales in Santiago; Belgrano, Torcuato di Tella, and Palermo in Buenos Aires; Monte Avila in Caracas. The characteristic feature of these schools is that they are private, they recruit the majority of their students from the social elite, and they have made diverse reform efforts in the teaching of law. A new school in Mexico City has been founded with the intent of innovating legal education and educating the elite, but it has two distinguishing characteristics: it is financed by the federal government and it strives to recruit its students (who must pass very rigorous tests) among people of modest income who live in cities in the interior of the country.

[6] At the time, the perception was not necessarily shared by the majority of legal professionals. A study among Colombian lawyers showed that 64% were 'very satisfied' with their legal education, 24% were 'satisfied', and only 9% were 'unsatisfied' (Lynch, 1981, p 113).

and they began various innovation movements.

One of the first reformist voices was Dantas (1955), who called for a quite radical reform of the law curriculum and a re-examination of the methods of legal education. He proposed a flexible curriculum, the incorporation of cases into teaching, interdisciplinary analysis, and an active or participatory method on the part of the students. All of the later reformist agenda was formulated in that formal discourse. Dantas caused an immediate sensation in Brazil (Bastos 2000:250; Rosenn 1969:273; Steiner 1971). As we will later observe, his ideas can be seen in the conception of legal studies in the Federal University of Brasilia.

Between 1959 and 1964, there were four conferences of Latin American law schools, which produced an abundant literature and called for substantial reforms, including the introduction of class discussion, seminars, and an interdisciplinary focus (Wilson 1989:393; Brown 1961). These conferences were preceded and accompanied by a reaction against the formalism that has been present in Latin American legal studies since the end of the 19th century (Pérez Perdomo 1984).

In 1961, the University of Brasilia began to function. Its legal studies were conceived with a distinct curricular organisation, and innovations in teaching methodology were also planned (Bastos 2000). The military coup of 1964, which resulted in the arrest of several professors and the resignation of a sizable part of the others, halted this first experiment (Rosenn 1969: 258).

In the 1970s, the movement was known as law and development. The angle that generated most attention was the effort of professors from the United States who, conscious of the important political role of law studies and of the backwardness and poor state of the law schools, travelled to Latin America as missionaries of the case method and the interdisciplinary study of law. A much greater number of young Latin American professors (especially in Brazil, Chile, Colombia, and Peru) obtained master's degrees and doctorates in law, or in some other way familiarised themselves with the teaching of law in the United States (Lynch 1981:111; Steiner 1971). A good number of professors began to prepare non-traditional instructive materials and made use of the 'active class', as it was called at that time. A small number were interested in interdisciplinary research. Several of the professors from the United States who participated in the experience considered it a failure, since it did not succeed in changing the Latin American legal culture within a few years, with an investment of approximately five million dollars (Trubek and Galanter 1974).

The view from Latin America is somewhat different. The restlessness for change in legal education predated the presence of scholars from the United States. There was a parallel discussion of the topics considered relevant at the time,[7] and the changes in Latin America continued long after the withdrawal of the American organisations that financed projects and the formal declaration of the cessation of the American programmes that Trubek and Galanter's article signified.

The case of Venezuela is significant, since it never formed part of the law and development movement sponsored by the United States, yet it nevertheless saw considerable reformist activity both at that time and later. A good number of Venezuelan law graduates received postgraduate education, both in civil law countries and in common law ones, with national government and private funds. A significant number of these graduates are now professors in the law schools and a certain number have been innovators in their pedagogy or in their research (Pérez Perdomo 1984, 1985). This case should call attention to the important number of law graduates in Latin America who have done postgraduate studies in Europe or, increasingly, in the United States in the last few decades.

The changes in legal education have been as much in the teaching of law as in legal academic research. In the 1970s, the changes in teaching were very controversial and met with open resistance from part-time lawyer-professors. In Peru, the innovators were sarcastically called the 'Wisconsin boys' and they experienced more than a few conflict situations. In Colombia, there were important political conflicts within the schools that attempted reform, and some deans and professors lost their jobs in these struggles (Lynch 1981). In Chile, the Pinochet government expelled the reformists from the universities, including the Catholic University. Several professors who were part of the political heterodoxy had to go into exile (Fuenzalida, 2002). We have already noted the Brasilia case.

Later, changes in teaching came about largely because the private schools that focused on training business lawyers needed to diversify. The innovative schools introduced activities like legal clinics and negotiation, and courses such as law and economics, sociology of law, and human rights (Meili 1999). They also placed importance on an education in ethics, which the positivist formalists had banished from law schools. Some professors improved their teaching methodologies, although there was not a gener-

---

[7] For a look at subjects in legal education that interested Latin American academics, see Witker, 1976. It is important to point out that the type of teaching that uses the class or the professor's lecture as the main instrument has been consistently criticized from different perspectives. Pérez Perdomo, 1974, for example, places it at the root of the practical skepticism and the lack of compromise with the normative order in lawyers. More recently, Torres Arends 1997, 2001, has emphasized that teaching trains abstract reason but does not develop the capacity to tackle problems, and that it produces an inconsistent construction of the concept of law.

alised change in this area.[8] The emphasis on which matters underwent change and which remained the same varied from one school to another. In the postgraduate programmes, which were not regulated by tradition, the range of subjects and activities was much greater, although we do not know of any evaluation of what happened in this area. Curiously, the large public universities have created the most developed postgraduate programmes, while changes to law curricula have occurred more in a few private schools.[9] The characteristic aspect of these reforms is that they have not formed part of a general movement and have tended to be low profile.

On the other hand, young law graduates have begun to turn to master's programmes in American universities. There, in one year, they familiarise themselves with the language and the problem-solving approach characteristic of legal teaching in the United States. These are abilities that are appreciated in business lawyers today.

The evaluation of law schools by external organisations is a new phenomenon. There is the need, due to the proliferation of law schools and the diversification of programmes, but only few experiences are known. In Colombia, the Ministry of Justice published an evaluation in 1995. In Brazil, the Ministry of Education and the *Ordem dos Advogados* or national bar association (Junqueira 1999, and personal communication) have separately carried out an evaluation. In Chile, the magazine *Qué Pasa?* (11 December 2001) published an evaluation that followed the model of *US News and World Report*. This is the second year that such evaluation has taken place.

During the entire period that we are examining, the perception existed in certain universities that the law schools had lost step with social changes and that legal studies had been left behind. This perception may have come from the perceived speed of the social change as opposed to the much slower and more difficult changes in the curriculum and teaching methods in the law schools. Latin American societies faced severe problems of poverty, marginality, criminality and police brutality, at the same time as

---

[8] Some examples from different times: In Brazil 1980, there were 20 programs with more than 2000 students (Falcão, 1984, p 115). In 1975, the Central University of Venezuela renovated its postgraduate program in law and created one in political science. A good number of courses and seminars were interdisciplinary and could be taken equally by people in either of the postgraduate programs. At present day there is a dozen of postgraduate programs with more than 1000 students. In recent years, the Legal Research Institute of Universidad Nacional Autónoma de México, and the Universidad Nacional de Chile in Santiago created doctorates in law with an interdisciplinary focus.

[9] Mexico seems to be a different case. The law school with the greatest weight in the training of business lawyers (the Escuela Libre) is private and considerably traditional. ITAM and Iberoamericana, two private universities, are also devoted to the training of business lawyers and have made innovations with different degrees of success. The most radical innovation effort is being made in a public school (CIDE) that has barely gotten underway. The characteristic thing about CIDE is its attention to admitting very promising students with scarce resources and providing them with scholarships (AL Magaloni: personal communication).

quite rapid political transformations were taking place: a communications revolution, and greater integration into the global economy—yet these problems and changes did not seem to affect the majority of law schools, which appeared secluded in a culture of codes and old books (Fuentes-Hernández 2002). Without denying these problems, the argument that we have developed does not correspond with this perception, in the sense that we have shown that legal education has been affected by social change and that the dynamic of reform, driven out through the door, has timidly returned through the window. The perception of stasis probably derives from the desire for law schools to be more proactive and dynamic, and from the restrictions on change affecting a few schools and a very small fraction of the students. No doubt it also derives from the perception that lawyers have lost the role of social and political leadership that they had in the past. This is a theme that we will analyse later.

The Lawyers

Demographics

The definition of lawyer or legal professional within the boundaries of Latin America does not present the difficulties that it has when broader comparisons are made, for example with China and Japan (Clark 1999; Abel 1988). In the Latin America of the second half of the twentieth century, all lawyers had a university degree in law. However, the reverse is not always the case: in some countries, like Brazil, there are substantial additional requirements, meaning that not all law graduates can practice law as lawyers. This explains why some countries have a high number of law students, but a relatively lower number of lawyers. In the mid-1990s, Venezuela and Brazil had the same number of law students, but Brazil had a little more than half the number of lawyers (naturally, all of this is in relative terms). In Peru, Zolezzi's study about the graduates of the Catholic University distinguishes between those who received a bachelor's degree in law and those who are lawyers. Only 72 per cent of graduates in the former category also fall into the latter one (Zolezzi Ibárcena 1982:35).

The second difficulty is that we depend on national sources to discover the number of lawyers. In some countries, careful registries are kept in which the names of lawyers are erased when they retire from professional service, are designated as judges or public officials, or die.[10] In other coun-

---

[10] The differences can be substantial. Spain, for instance, keeps separate lists of practicing and

tries, much less attention is payed to keeping the lists. Thus, in these countries, the number of lawyers does not reflect the number of people who actually support themselves as lawyers. For some years we have census figures, for other year we have had to estimate a figure. With all of these qualifications, we present the data in Table 2, knowing that the figures are rough measurements and that one should not necessarily draw hasty conclusions from them.

The figures allow a comparison over time that includes at least one figure from the 1990s in the cases of Brazil, Chile, Costa Rica, Mexico and Venezuela. Brazil more than tripled the number of lawyers per 100,000 inhabitants between 1950 and 1991. The more demanding regulation of admission to the legal profession explains the decrease in the relative number of lawyers in the 1960s. Starting in 1970, the growth of the lawyer population speeds up again. The growth in the relative number of law students quintupled in the same period. This allows us to calculate that approximately half of the law graduates in Brazil are not lawyers. The situation is similar in Peru, although we lack data for recent years.

Chile, Costa Rica, Mexico and Venezuela, —in complete contrast to the case of Brazil—have not established any restrictions on law graduates becoming lawyers. In Venezuela, the degree that the university grants is that of *abogado* (lawyer), and the only other thing required to enable one to practice professionally is formal enrollment in the respective bar association of one's locality and in a collective insurance called *inpreabogados*.[11]

The restriction that the Venezuelan government imposed was in its refusal to authorise the creation of new law schools between 1960 and 1990. The public universities and the Catholic University had a relatively rigorous selection process, which restricted the number of students, but one private university continued the policy of accepting all students choosing to enter into legal studies. The restriction, however, was economic and geographic, since this giant school is situated in Caracas and its tuition fees were often too high for people with low incomes. Despite this modest restriction, the number of lawyers multiplied by a factor of seven between

non-practicing lawyers. In 1999, there were 97,826 practicing lawyers (249 per 100,000 inhabitants) and 34,661 non-practicing lawyers. The sum of both would raise the number of lawyers in the population to 337 per 100,000. The way in which the registry is set up and maintained is clearly important.

[11] Venezuelan figures of 1961 and 1981 come from general population censuses and they include non practicing lawyers. The figure of 1971 come from IMPREABOGADOS' registry. It was relatively new for 1970 and we can trust the figure. As this registry does not exclude dead or retired lawyers, the figures for 1990 and 2000 are estimates that use this registry. The number of lawyers registered in 2001 in INPREABOGADOS is 87,190. We have deduced an estimate from these figures. Our estimate is too rough and cannot be taken as the number of active lawyers, but rather as potentially active.

Table 2 Number of Lawyers in some Latin American Countries

Country and year inhabitants	Number of lawyers	Lawyers per 100,000
Argentina 1996	66,500	179
Brazil 1950	15,666	30
Brazil 1960	30,066	42
Brazil 1970	37,710	41
Brazil 1980	85,716	72
Brazil 1991	148,871	101
Chile 1950 (b)	1,475	24
Chile 1960 (b)	2,602	34
Chile 1970 (b)	4,306	44
Chile 1982	6,546	58
Chile 1992	9,308	70
Chile 2000	11,400	75
Colombia 2000	112,000	254
Costa Rica 1950 (b)	467	54
Costa Rica 1960 (b)	682	55
Costa Rica 1970 (b)	968	57
Costa Rica 1980	1,700	75
Costa Rica 1990	4,400	157
Costa Rica 2000	10,800	309
Ecuador 1991	9,350	85
Mexico 1960	8,426	24
Mexico 1970	14,669	30
Mexico 1990	141,539	174
Mexico 1998	200,000	208
Peru 1950 (b)	1,970	23
Peru 1960 (b)	2,960	30
Peru 1970 (b)	4,080	32
Venezuela 1950	2,087	41
Venezuela 1961	4,256	57
Venezuela 1971	8,102	76
Venezuela 1981	16,045	111
Venezuela 1990	31,350	159
Venezuela 2000	70,000	290

Sources: (b) Merryman *et al* (1979). ARGENTINA: Garavano, 2001. BRAZIL 1950, 1960, 1970, 1980: Falcão, 1984. BRAZIL 1991: Junqueira, 2001. CHILE 19,882, 1992, 2000: De la Maza, 2001. COLOMBIA 2000: A Fuentes Hernández, work in progress. COSTA RICA 1980, 1990 and 2000, information by Alfredo Chirinos, Escuela de la Judicatura. ECUADOR 1991, Chinchilla and Schodt, 1993. MEXICO 1960, 1970: Estimates from Lorey's data (1992). MEXICO 1990: López-Ayllón and Fix-Fierro, 2002. MEXICO 1998: Estimate from Lomnitz' data (1997). VENEZUELA, Pérez Perdomo, 1981, 1996, 2002.

1950 and 2000, with a strong acceleration after 1970. After 1990, the pro-hibition of new schools disappeared, permitting the creation of law schools in a large number of cities, from which one would expect a greater growth in the number of lawyers.

The number of lawyers in Mexico grew very moderately until the 1970s. Figures for 1980s and 1990s show an accelerated growth. The take-off happened in the 1960s. In this decade 8,100 lawyers graduated, while the figure for the previous decade was 3,659.[12] The pattern of growth in Costa Rica is similar to that in Venezuela, although the growth is slightly less explosive. The large jump took place in the 1980s and 1990s, and in each decade the relative number of lawyers doubled.[13]

Between 1950 and 2000, Chile quadrupled the number of lawyers per 100,000 inhabitants. The figure is closer to that of Brazil than that of Venezuela. Compared to the number of law students, this figure remained low until 1980. This was part of an express policy of not allowing an increase in law schools and of restricting the number of students. The pol-icy changes in this period have produced an explosion in the student pop-ulation, but the effect in the number of graduates has still not been felt. It is foreseeable that it will be felt in the near future (De la Maza 2001). In any case, it seems clear that the restriction on the number of students admitted into law schools was responsible for the relatively slow growth of the legal profession until approximately 1990.

If we now compare countries, the number of lawyers seems to vary sub-stantially from one country to another. We have figures from the 1990s for eight countries. Costa Rica and Venezuela have the highest relative number of lawyers (approximately 300 per 100,000), followed at a considerable distance by Colombia (250), Mexico (200), and Argentina (179) and Brazil (101). Ecuador (85) and Chile (75) have the smallest populations. Chile will probably catch up soon. In our judgement, it would be absolutely inappropriate to try to draw conclusions about topics like lawyers and development. We know too little about what the people who hold the title of lawyer effectively do, and we also ignore how many people have some legal training and fulfill functions in the legal system. Without a doubt, information about notary and registry activity, and about lawsuits, could give us a better overview, but the studies and data we have at our disposal

[12] The figures for 1960 and 1970 are estimates from the number of law graduates (Lorey, 1992, 91–92). We have added the graduated for the last 30 years, without adding previous fig-ures or subtracting an estimated of dead or retired lawyers. The 1990 figure (taken from López Ayllón & Fix-Fierro, 2002) comes from the National Institute of Statistics. For the 1997 fig-ure we have add the number of lawyers registered in 1990–1997 (Lomnitz & Salazar, 1997), with a subtraction for dead or retired and for possible double count of 1990.

[13] The source of these figures is the registry of the *Colegio de Abogados de Costa Rica*, but we do not know their quality.

are full of gaps. As a result, we will not attempt to take our quantitative analysis any further. Likewise, our analysis will not support generalisations about the classification of legal cultures based on the control of the number of lawyers or supply of services (which is characteristic of Europe) and expansion of demand (the United States) (Mattei 1997).[14] From our point of view, this type of theorisation would have to include a greater number of national experiences and more information about the formal regulation of the legal profession.

Activity and Social Position

Traditionally, lawyers had a high social status and were eminent members of the political elite. The law was considered the pre-eminent form of political knowledge, and the political legitimacy of lawyers came from this knowledge. They were members of the elite, since in countries with high rates of illiteracy, rural populations, and difficulties in communication, only relatively well-off members of the urban sectors had access to a legal education. As we have seen, this situation changed at different times in the twentieth century, depending on the country. In the last third of the century, the situation is completely different from the scenario at the beginning of the century.

The social change and the change in the organisation of education meant that other disciplines competed with law as technical forms of knowledge about political action. These disciplines varied according to the time and country. In the 1960s and 1970s, economics, sociology, and planning were considered the pre-eminent forms of political knowledge. More recently, economics (although a different version from that which was dominant in 1960) and public policy have attained pre-eminence. Lawyers have maintained a presence in politics not only due to the weight of tradition, but also because certain sectors (which have to do with justice) are considered reserved for jurists, and because some lawyers individually have concerned themselves with learning the new disciplines. But for the majority of lawyers, they no longer seem to have an initial advantage in the field of politics. The influence of lawyers has been decreasing in the high political positions in several countries (López-Ayllón and Fix-Fierro 2001; De la Maza 2001).

In the 1960s and 1970s, one of the incentives in the effort to transform law schools was the perception of the diminished political importance of

---

[14] The generalization ignores the case of Spain, which does not control entry nor does it have policies of expansion of demand. Venezuela and, since 1980, Chile belong to this heterodox model, apparently without economic rationality, if we accept the premises of Mattei, 1997.

lawyers. Steiner (1971:59) takes up the complaint that lawyers were rarely consulted in governmental tasks, including legislation. Economists, engineers and other technical professionals replaced them. The perception is of a decline of the legal profession. Steiner (1971), to a large extent, blamed the formalist legal education for the decline in the importance of lawyers. This diagnosis was probably accurate, but from today's distance we would consider other elements as well. For example, the proliferation of military governments (including Brazil—the country that Steiner was considering—from 1964 until 1985)[15] removed lawyers from many important positions. Because of the nature of the regime, which did not allow any questioning of its decisions, the participation of lawyers no longer made sense. In the countries that maintained a civil government in that period (Costa Rica, Colombia, Mexico, and Venezuela), the participation of lawyers in governmental duties remained considerable (Arias Sánchez 1976; Pérez Perdomo 1981; Lomnitz and Salazar 1997).

When the picture is analysed in detail, the explanation is somewhat more complex. The increase in the number of students and lawyers, and the greater diversity of their social origins, consequentially meant that going to law school was no longer equivalent to membership of the political elite. In fact, many lawyers found their entry into the professional market difficult. On the other hand, the increase in the number of law schools dispersed the centres of elite education and thus broke its unity. As we have already pointed out, the young people most closely linked to elite groups, especially to those of greater economic power, selected certain private schools that became the educational centres of business lawyers. The large public schools lost their privileged place in the education of the political elite.

The result is a stratified profession. At the top end of incomes today are the business lawyers who are partners in large law firms. Large law firms are a novelty in Latin America, and there are not many. For example, until 1980, the biggest Venezuelan firms did not even have 20 lawyers, and in Peru there was apparently only one that exceeded 12 lawyers (Pérez Perdomo 1981; Zolezzi Ibárcena 1982).[16] In Chile only two firms had more than 10 lawyers in 1970. In 1980, there were four, but none had 20 lawyers (Ashton 2002). As Table 3 shows, even today there are no really large firms, if we compare them with those in the United States. The situation is not very different in continental Europe (Pérez Perdomo and

---

[15] The periods of military governments have stages. Usually there a very harsh stage, followed by an opening in which the discussion and later the election of a civil government is permitted. The harsh stage of the Brazilian dictatorship ended in 1974 (Alcántara, 1999, 91ss).

[16] Zolezzi's work is a social and occupational study of lawyers who graduated from the Catholic University, and in the group interviewed, only one firm shows up with more than 12 lawyers.

Friedman 2001), although there are is a greater number of large firms in France and Germany.

Table 3 Large Law Firms in some Latin American Countries, 1999

	100 or more Lawyers	*50–99 Lawyers*
Argentina	2	7
Brazil	4	4
Chile	0	1
Mexico	1	4
Peru	0	1
Venezuela	0	2

Source: Latin Lawyer. A Who's Who of Latin American Law Firms. London. Law Business Research, 1999.

A structural explanation of the moderate size of law firms is the importance of internal business lawyers (in-house counsels). In some countries, the biggest businesses have actual law firms within the business itself. For example, the Venezuelan oil company (PDVSA) had 143 lawyers in 1999, double that of the largest Venezuelan firm (Pérez Perdomo 2001). In-house lawyers usually manage most of the legal matters and decide which should go to external lawyers. The preference is then to consult individual lawyers or specialised firms. The professional prestige of in-house lawyers depends on the importance of the business, and the personal prestige of the specialised lawyers has a very high market value.

This explanation is not valid for all countries. In Chile, in-house counsel have less prestige and power than in Venezuela. Ashton (2002) offers a cultural explanation: even if lawyers are in a big law firm, the client-lawyer relations tend to be personal and very strong. A disgruntled partner can easily split away and carry with him, or her, 'his' or 'her' clients. This explanation could have an extended validity.

Ways of acquiring professional prestige have also changed. Prestige is determined by one's professional accomplishments. Naturally, recently graduated lawyers have little opportunity to demonstrate their professional quality, in addition to the fact that by definition they are less experienced. The traditional path was that of family or mentor relations: the son of an important lawyer, or a young lawyer accepted as a disciple, had the opportunity to attend to important clients or participate in cases that attracted the attention of the professional melieu and the public. If one performed well, one earned prestige. This path still exists, but relatively few lawyers profit from it. Many learn 'in the street', 'asking the employees', 'crashing and burning', and some are able to excel despite the difficulties (Fucito 1997). The firms, the large legal consultants, and certain public organisations institutionalised the career: they accepted young lawyers, who got the chance to learn and make a name for themselves.

Besides professional practice by itself, university teaching and publications can be instrumental in the acquisition of prestige. Nowadays, only association with the most reputable universities confers prestige. It is a kind of circular argument, since these law schools have prestige because, among other reasons, they hire prestigious lawyers for their teaching staff. In practice, social networks exist that allow particular people to join prestigious firms or businesses or university teaching positions. Of course, personal ability acts as a regulating mechanism in receiving as well as keeping the privileged positions that these networks provide.

The biggest employer of lawyers is the state. The meaning of working for the state can differ greatly depending on the state agency in question. The most specialised or important legal duties, like those of lawyers who advise or represent in high governmental proceedings, are generally professionally prestigious positions that carry with them considerable political power (although not necessarily a high salary). The technical legal positions in the agencies that regulate private economic activity are usually a credential to later proceed to the private sphere in a very advantageous position. The state also takes in a large number of graduates who work in jobs related to the operation of the judicial system (in areas like the police or document registry), or in jobs without any relation to the law. In that case, the job lacks professional prestige.

The lowest level of the professional strata is made up of law graduates who have real difficulties entering the job market. These lawyers have trouble surviving and may resort to very degraded types of activity. For example, there are lawyers associated with the term *gestorías* in Venezuela, or *coyotes* in Mexico, whose duties are the low bureaucratic procedures and who are usually in charge of making the useful illegal payments to accelerate procedures or to avoid the queues in front of public offices. Others visit jails to offer their services, or have connections that give them positions close to public offices where legal procedures are carried out so they can offer their services. The difficulties in entering the job market have incorrectly been called the *proletariatisation* of the profession, and it is a phenomenon that appeared in the second half of the twentieth century, at different times depending on the country.

Social Demands

Many questions arise from this description: What are the social and economic changes that explain the increase in the number of lawyers? Why, despite the enormous expansion of the market for lawyers and the high incomes of successful lawyers, does there exist a perception of crisis? What have the effects of the policies of national development and later of globalisation been on the legal profession?

The policies of national development involved the expansion of the state and required a vast army of officials to operate this machinery, as well as a good number who could help citizens navigate it. Citizens required licenses and permits, or could obtain privileges and favours. For many of the officials and the intermediaries, a university education might be necessary or useful. Lawyers, as traditional university graduates, were prepared to occupy many of the positions in the expanded bureaucracy or to serve as intermediaries with them. The informal networks among lawyers were an advantage in getting the machinery to operate for the benefit of clients and, obviously, the lawyers themselves (Lomnitz and Salazar 1997). This explains why the study of law maintained its appeal, since it provided work and social respectability to a significant number of people, including many who came from the modest social strata of the population and were the first in their families to gain a university degree. It is not surprising that the reform attempts of 1970 did not find an enthusiastic public among the majority of lawyers at the time.

Among the elite lawyers, the situation was very different. The lawyers were not intellectually well equipped to occupy the important posts of the interventionist state. Economists, planners, and sociologists seemed to be better equipped for those tasks and better suited to occupy the high state positions, as had been the lawyers' tradition. Hence, lawyers sensed the need to change legal education and make lawyers closer to the ideal of the social engineer, as preached by the American lawyers trained under the policies of the New Deal.

The reduction in the size of the state, favoured by the policies of privatisation and decentralisation, has been more programmatic than an accomplished fact. In practice, the central state has generally diminished in size, but this decentralisation has increased the importance of the municipal and regional governments, and has established problems of negotiation by competition. The policies of privatisation have led many state enterprises to become private. This has affected very important spheres like the production and distribution of energy, telecommunications, and public services. In those highly important areas, new regulations and regulatory bodies were required, since the political system acting as a hierarchy or as an informal network, could not solve conflicts.

Although we can not call on studies that support the claim, our perception is that the general size of the state continued to be very large, and that perhaps this increased the need for lawyers who could co-ordinate the operation of the decentralised state entities and the new private enterprises that provided public services. In any case, the state seems to have continued to be a substantial employer of lawyers, and businesses also required a growing number of them.

Under the regulatory state, an important section of intermediaries were not necessarily lawyers. In each country, they are called by a different name. In Mexico they are called 'coyotes', in Venezuela 'gestores.' They are used as intermediaries only for the most everyday tasks. One phenomenon that is occurring is that their activities have completely lost legitimacy and are today classified as corruption.[17] This is part of the de-bureaucratisation and the anti-corruption fight in almost every country. In the new situation, these intermediaries still remain, but their status has diminished and their work is no longer legitimate.

There is also a greater need for lawyers because of the cultural change that is taking place. The analysis of this cultural change is complex, and it is sufficient merely to mention it here. The central idea is that the mass media, and especially television, has spread a modern, individualist vision through society and that this has produced a greater tendency to pursue claims through legal channels. If one adds to this the growing exchanges taking place between people who do not form multi-connected groups, like the family or the inhabitants of a small city, the need for contracts and the probability of conflicts increases (Friedman 1995, 2001). Cultural changes that we call globalisation involve an increase in the use of lawyers. Many of the claims against the state that are generally pursued with the help of lawyers eventually involve *amparos* or administrative actions, an area of litigation that has clearly increased. In short, our analysis suggests that the new policies have not reduced the need for lawyers, but rather, on the contrary, increased it.

The second major theme is whether Latin American lawyers are 'globalised.' This refers to whether they are active actors in that process and whether their profession has lost its local or national character. In that sense, the answer has to be mixed. Legal education has tended to preserve a strongly national character and has not responded to the enormous changes in law and society that accompany globalisation (Faria 2000; Fuentes-Hernández 2002). Studies centre on the large national codes, along with the principles of law that are believed to be universal. The result could

---

[17] The coyotes' intermediary activity is the typical transactional bribe ('sobornos de transacción' or 'jeitos'), as described by Reissman, 1979, or Rosenn, 1971. Today these are considered unacceptable, and the pressure is for the simplification of everyday procedures. Lawyers are not involved in this process; they act as intermediaries only when the procedure is more complicated. For that reason, lawyers' work is considered to have a technical element, and the fee that lawyers are paid is not merely a disguised bribe. In fact, much of the lawyers' procedural work does not include bribes in the technical sense, although it involves using informal connections.

not be more lamentable. For example, a young recent graduate of a Venezuelan law school believes he knows Venezuelan law and the universal principles of law, but if he were presented with a case in which he would have to handle the law of Colombia or the state of Florida, he would feel absolutely lost. His belief in the universality of law does not help him in the slightest when trying to approach a foreign law. It is likely that he has never studied comparative law and that he does not even suspect the importance of the different legal traditions. One can hypothesise that this is true for the majority of law graduates and lawyers in Latin America. The exceptions are the young graduates who decide to get their postgraduate degree abroad—with growing frequency in the United States—and in the few law schools that place importance on comparative law or international training.

Naturally, lawyers who have the occasion to work in business firms or in companies in frequent contact with foreign providers or clients soon feel the need to learn foreign languages and the fundamentals of other legal cultures and other bodies of law that permit them to communicate with foreign clients and lawyers. Apprenticeships can be found in a disciple-type relationship with a mentor or, more often, with the help of the aforementioned postgraduate degrees. The number of lawyers who work in such an environment is small compared to the total number of lawyers, but they are at the top in terms of professional prestige: they have the most income, and belong to the most reputable firms or work for the most important businesses. In the professional stratification that has transpired, they are at the top of the ladder. As a result, their importance is much greater than their number and they are valuable role models for ambitious young people.

The importance of stratification can even be seen among lawyers who work for the same company. For instance, the internal lawyers of the Venezuelan oil company (Pérez Perdomo 2001) are divided between those who deal with matters in the oil fields or lawsuits, who only need to know national law and the Spanish language, and those lawyers who deal with the corporate part of the company and have to participate in negotiations with foreign companies. The latter know other legal cultures and other languages, especially English. It is no surprise that they tend to have higher salaries and more recognition in the company. Globalisation can be reflected in one's chequebook.

Foreign training, whether in universities, law firms, or international or multilateral organisations, is generally valued highly. Lawyers with that training not only find better job opportunities in firms and businesses, but also in the state agencies. Interest in working in the official sector, as well as the sector's willingness to receive transnationalised lawyers, can vary from country to country (Dezalay and Garth 1998a, 1998b) depending on the culture and political structures of the state. There is one important difference from the past, however: these lawyers generally serve as technocrats, not in traditional political roles. They could be considered to have a role in legitimising the political system in the international arena and, on the other hand, they have other titles to compete for political power. In other words, globalisation has not eliminated the political role of lawyers; it has transformed it. It has also given pre-eminence to a postgraduate education in the United States, instead of Europe (Dezalay and Garth 2002).

Changes in the Legal Culture and the Lawyers

Changes in the Judicial Function

In the civil law tradition, judges had a relatively less important role in the legal system (where legislators and professors were more important) than in the political system (Merryman 1985). It is a well-known position that, since the nineteenth century, judicial duties were considered less creative and more mechanical: they consisted of applying the law to the facts proven in the proceeding. This gave judges a secondary position in the legal system. The conception that judges were officials linked to the government similarly made them not very important or independent. This perception was still dominant in the 1970s. In that decade, those who proposed that law had or should have a more active role in the promotion or guidance of development considered legislative changes and changes in the attitudes of jurists, including lawyers and judges, in order to make them more sensitive to the needs of development. Thus, the principal task was the modification of legal education, not the transformation of judges. This has changed in the period that we examine, in which judges have gained a greater importance in the definition of public policies, the resolution of conflicts among private individuals, and the regulation of political conflicts (Pérez Perdomo and Friedman 2002). This is a worldwide trend (Toharia 2001; Tate and Vallinder 1995; Pérez Perdomo 2000) and, as we will later show, can be considered part of the transformations associated with globalisation. Certainly, Latin American is included in this change.

In the tradition of most Latin American countries, political conflicts tend to be resolved either by violence or by the will or mediation of powerful men. The *caudillos* and the dictators are very important (*political personalism*, to use Soriano's term, 1996). Military men tended to fill important positions in government and had a significant role in domestic repression. In the periods of military government, and in more than a few periods of civil government with a strong military presence, massive violations of human rights were seen. Judges had a very limited and even shameful role. They made a concerted effort to look in the other direction or put themselves at the service of the government (Galín 1984; Frühling 1984; Pásara 1982, 1984; González 2001; Uprimny 2001).

Between World War II and the 1970s, most of the governments in Latin America were developmentalist. Ideologically, this meant that very important aspects of law were put in the background, particularly the role of judges. Issues like the defence of individual rights and concern with legality appeared almost petty in contrast with national security and national development (or the 'revolution'). Control over the legality of governmental acts and protection of human rights, which theoretically were the duties of the judges, were cast aside in the actual functioning of the political system. With some very honorable exceptions, the typical judge in almost all of the countries in the region did not dare take firm action in these matters. The few that dared to do so met with serious difficulties or ceased to be judges. Pásara has defined the role of the judge as that of accomplice and victim (1982).

Rosenn (1987) catalogues the different forms of interference in the judicial systems of Latin America. In some cases, especially as a result of a coup, like in Uruguay in 1977, judicial independence is formally eliminated. This path has been rather exceptional. A more frequent measure was to grant jurisdiction to military tribunals in cases of repression that could be politically important. This occurred in almost every country in Latin America, especially in the periods in which there was a subversive or guerilla movement. Another frequently used tactic was the large-scale dismissal of high court magistrates, as occurred in Argentina under Perón and the later military governments, in El Salvador in 1979, and in Peru in 1969 and 1973 under military rule, and more recently under Fujimori (González 2001; Unterman 2002). A similar attempt was made in Venezuela in 1999.[18] Likewise, another method was the increase or the reduction in the

[18] Starting in 1992, the Supreme Court of Justice of Venezuela showed signs of considerable independence in its decisions, some of which were very politically important. Among these was one that permitted the convocation of a constituent assembly in order to prepare a new constitution, a procedure that was not provided for in the constitution of 1961. Subsequently, it modified the terms of the summons prepared by President Chávez. The 1999 constitution substantially transformed the court, which proceeded to be called the Supreme Tribunal of Justice. Upon elimination of the Judicial Council, the Supreme Tribunal was given the power to manage the judiciary. Once the new Tribunal was established, provisory justices were appointed, including several lawyers who lacked the degree of doctor of law, a necessary requirement according to the new constitution. One year later, the National Assembly, which had an overwhelming majority of Chávez supporters, appointed permanent justices, ratifying several who lacked the doctorate degree. All of this can be understood as an attempt to politically control the Supreme Tribunal. Some later decisions, such as one that severely limited the

number of magistrates, as occurred successively under the Brazilian military governments. Rico and Salas (1990) identify similar conduct in the Central American countries.

The most common way of controlling judges politically was to make the system a vertical hierarchy, with great power at the top, whether in the Supreme Court or a judicial council (Zaffaroni 1995:119). Control had to be secure at the top, which was not especially difficult, given the political instability and the frequent purging of the high ranks of the judiciary. In the case of Venezuela, administration of the system was in the hands of the Judicial Council, a body that was completely controlled by the main political parties and used for shameless clientelist purposes (Pérez Perdomo 2003). Thus, the frequent call in all of Latin America has been for judicial independence—that is, the liberation of judges from improper pressure from the executive branch or the political parties, and even from the Supreme Court judges themselves.

Beyond the lack of independence, the main characteristic of the judicial system was its marginality. Thus, in business matters, policies of intervention and state protection reduced the number of competitors and tied them to the government. This meant that in any case of conflict with the state or between businesses, the mechanism used was in the hands of figures with political power (Pérez Perdomo 1991). On the other hand, as the government could decisively influence any legal decision, recourse to the judicial system was relatively useless. Thus, it is interesting to point out that the discussion about the subject of law and development in the 1970s did not pay any attention to judges.

Rosenn (1987) presents the lack of independence and marginality of Latin American judges as a feature rooted in the Latin American legal culture, going back to Iberian colonisation and associated with the civil law tradition. On the contrary, this work maintains that such features are associated with political and economic structures that are not permanent. Changes in economic policy and democratisation have not only given rise to new actors, but have diminished the power of governments and political parties in most countries.

In the countries where this has occurred, employers have liberated themselves from government protection and judges have become more independent. What is perceived is a general tendency, not exempt from deviations (Hammergren 1998, 1999). There are countries where democratisation produced a greater concentration of power in a person or group,

jurisdiction of the military tribunals, might cause one to think that this political control is not firm. At the time in which this was written (February 2002), there are several pending cases of great importance. The decision of these cases will reveal the degree of the magistrates' independence, or of the control over them.

like the case of Peru under Fujimori,[19] Argentina under Menem (Garrido 1993), or Venezuela first under the parties and later under Chávez (Quintero 1983, 1988; Pérez Perdomo 2003). In these cases, control over judges was an explicit function that these populist governments assumed. But one cannot deny the praiseworthy performance of the Constitutional Court of Colombia or the Supreme Court of Justice of Venezuela in the 1990s. The federal judiciaries of Mexico and Brazil have also acted with independence and have decided cases of enormous political and economic importance (Uprimny Rodríguez and García-Villegas 2003; Pérez Perdomo 2003; Junqueira 2003; López-Ayllón and Fix-Fierro 2003). That affirmation of the principles of law often took place in situations of enormous political and social turbulence. The invocation of the civil law tradition or the Hispanic character shows its weakness when the cases of Spain and Italy are analysed (Clark 2003; Cassesse 2003; Toharia 2003).

The abandonment of the policies of economic intervention has limited the power of political leaders and has caused the emergence of new economic actors, including foreign investors. Naturally, this increases the possibility of conflict among those economic actors and, simultaneously diminishes the ability of politicians to act as regulators of conflicts. The need for judges was thus perceived, although in practice there has been no explosion of business litigation or anything like it (Pérez Perdomo 1996b).

Massive human rights violations in the past, and the later democratisation during the period that we analyse, have given rise to the need for more independent judges to protect the human rights of the population and to effectively control the legality of government acts (Correa 1993). Expression of this problem is called transitional justice—that is, what to do with those massive violators of human rights. The fact that many countries have decided to use judges to try the leaders of those sinister regimes has revalued the importance of judges and legal proceedings. This has been especially true in the cases of Chile and Argentina, where the worst abuses by military governments took place (Correa 1997; Acuña and Smulovitz 1997; Nino 1996).

Democratisation, accompanied by a more active press and greater political conflict, has meant that more cases of corruption have come to light or, in any case, corruption is used as a powerful political argument. Corruption scandals have seen the use of judges to decide the fate of very important political figures. In this way, presidents, ministers, and other high officials in Brazil, Colombia, Ecuador, Mexico, Peru, and Venezuela

---

[19] The case of Peru is paradigmatic. Fujimori, through his 'security advisor' Montesinos, was able to control the judges and falsify the system of checks and balances established in the constitution. Among the many abuses was the dismemberment of the Constitutional Court when it made a decision that might have impeded Fujimori's third attempt at reelection.

have found themselves implicated in legal cases (Pérez Perdomo 1996a). As a result, several have lost their posts and occasionally have spent time in prison. The most severe punishment is the scandal itself and the ruin of more than a few political careers.

These political and economic changes have produced a true juridification and judicialisation of Latin American societies.[20] The trend is for political and economic conflicts to lead to lawsuits and disputes over legality. This does not necessarily mean that the judicial decisions actually solve the conflicts, but they are important elements that must be taken in consideration (Fix-Fierro and López-Ayllón 2001; Pérez Perdomo 2002).

Legal professionals now have the social and political importance that the jurists of the 1960s and 1970s feared they were losing. There are very significant changes, and problems are raised in a different manner. What is desired now is not that law should serve an instrument of development, but that it should fundamentally provide legal certainty and protection of human rights. Naturally, the protection of property rights and respect for contracts is what interests business people and investors most, while other social actors are more concerned about other rights. The reform projects are no longer called 'law and development', but instead modernisation projects or projects to strengthen the rule of law. They concentrate particularly on judges and the judicial system. Critics of the projects generally complain that not enough importance is given to the emancipating elements in those reforms (Santos 1999). This has produced a greater awareness that respect for human rights and access to justice are important subjects that reform efforts must take into consideration. Therefore, we do not see total continuity between the law and development programmes and the rule of law programmes. It is naturally a topic of debate and there are those who affirm that continuity (Rodríguez 2001).[21]

The dominant perception in this age of globalisation is that judges are important, that as arbitrators they are indispensable to the functioning of a market economy and a democratic society. Simultaneously, there exists the perception that the real judges cannot live up to the high performance expected of them. These figures, forgotten for so long, are perceived as largely unqualified, too obedient to the government, with a tendency toward corruption or forming insidious networks, with little ability to take on justice as an efficient public service (Zaffaroni 1995; Garrido 1993;

---

[20] Juridification refers to a greater importance of the law; judicialization, to the greater importance and use of courts. Both phenomena do not necessarily occur simultaneously.
[21] It is a question of degree. The rereading of articles like those by Rosenn (1969) and Steiner (1971) reveals that they gave surprisingly little importance to the fact that Brazil was under a dictatorship that committed massive human rights violations. From the later works of the same authors, one can assume that their treatment of the same topic today would be very different.

Soberanes Fernández 1993; Zolezzi Ibárcena 1993; Pérez Perdomo 1996b). Hence, a significant pressure has arisen to reform the judiciary, to establish good programmes for training judges, to sensitise them to the problems of human rights and the needs of the population, to turn the courts into efficient organisations, and to make judges more independent and impartial. The evaluation of judges and judicial activity is also a central theme. In short, the topic of judicial reform has moved into the political agendas of all of the Latin American countries. Multilateral organisations such as the World Bank, the Inter-American Development Bank, the United Nations Development Program, and a good number of foundations have understood the importance of the judiciary and have financed reform projects.[22]

The task of reforming judicial systems has turned out to be massive. No country in the region is considered to have found suitable formulas, much less to have a completely desirable judicial system. Even in Costa Rica, the country that has most consistently invested abundant resources in the system for the longest time (Rivera-Cira 1993), the matter is still seen as a continuous process that has barely begun (Mora 2001).

However, in practice, judges have become more important politically. European judges from countries culturally very close to Latin America have been important in this change. The actions of the Italian judges and prosecutors who started the operation *mani pulite* (or the 'robed revolution', as it was called), or the Spanish judges who caused the downfall of the socialist government and the crisis of that party, have been followed very closely by the judges of Latin America. Di Pietro and Garzón, among others, have frequently been invited to speak in Latin American countries about their experiences.

This stage of globalisation marks a new era of attention to the law and reformist fever. The subject raised is not how to make the law an instrument of development, as in the 'law and development' stage. The 'modernisation' that is spoken of today focuses on how to strengthen the power of the judges and at the same time make them more responsible for the operation of a true rule of law; how to make them protectors of human rights and at the same time protectors of the property and business security; how to make justice more accessible and more efficient.

The awareness of the political importance of judges explains why more attention was paid to the education of judges than to legal education in general. There has been a definite neglect of the latter, probably out of confidence in the market forces to differentiate between the good law schools

---

[22] The literature generated about the judicial reform in Latin America and the role of the multilateral banks in the 1990s is enormous. Some examples: Inter-American Development Bank (ed), 1992, 1998; Dakolias, 1996; Rowat *et al* (ed), 1995; Hammergren, 1998; Varela, 1999; Van Puymbroeck (ed), 2001; Rodríguez, 2001.

that will train business lawyers, judges, and academics, and the other schools that will train the rest of the lawyers, including the taxi driver-lawyers or the lawyers who are minor officials.

Globalisation

Social change does not affect all people and institutions equally. One can distinguish between those who become agents of change and those who are affected in a more or less passive way. To use an example, modernisation at the beginning of the twentieth century affected small industrialists, in such a way that the policies of promotion or development led to the growth of larger enterprises, in a different way from the *muleteers*, who were replaced by other methods of transportation.

In the beginning of the period that we examine, the preoccupation of elite lawyers came from the perception that other professionals—like economists, planners, and engineers—were replacing them in the positions of political power that they had traditionally occupied. There was also a perception that businesses employed few lawyers, and that business lawyers were subordinated to the businessmen and professionals more directly involved in the planning and operation of companies. Litigious activity, which was considered the pre-eminent field of lawyers, lacked the capacity to absorb the numerous contingents of graduates. What sort of balance might be achieved, following our analysis of the occupation of lawyers and judges? This is the topic of this final section.

The first element looks at the globalised or globalising portion of the legal actors. The most obvious example is that of large international firms of business lawyers. Most firms originate in the United States, but have branches or partner firms in many countries. 'In the early 1990s, US firms had more that 18,000 "affiliates overseas"; German firms had even more' (Friedman 2001:354). They are true legal transnationals (Armitage 1990; Trubek *et al* 1994; Dezalay 1992; Flood 1996). Lawyers within these firms have a common language, although they often speak more than one language, and even more important, they have common professional and legal cultures. Their communication is not hindered by legal or national cultural differences. That common culture is not restricted to lawyers in international firms; lawyers within multinational companies also share the same fundamental traits (Pérez Perdomo 2001).

It would be wrong to think that it is simply a matter of an Americanisation of legal culture worldwide. Internationalisation also created challenges for American lawyers and established a clear distinction between international and purely domestic lawyers in United States. There exists an association and magazines that pay attention to the interests of these international lawyers. These magazines are not only about legal matters, but also practical aspects of negotiation in different cultures, the use and significance of time in different countries, and the rules of courtesy that should be followed (Sunwolf 1997).

Sometimes that culture adopts the form of a club, as in the matter of international arbitration (Dezalay and Garth 1996). Like every culture, it can undergo changes and its actors can change. The important thing is not the content or the actors, but the existence of that global culture itself. In Latin America, there are rather similar forms like the panels created as a result of the free trade agreement between the United States, Canada, and Mexico (NAFTA) (López-Ayllón and Fix-Fierro 1999). Their purpose is the resolution of commercial disputes. Since their initiation, these panels, composed of jurists of different legal cultures, became institutions that transformed legal cultures. From the perspective of the international organisations themselves such as the World Trade Organisation, the new roles mean a change from a diplomatic ethos to a more legal one (Weiler 2001).

The international tribunals are another example of the creation of globalised spaces. In Latin America, the Inter-American Court of Human Rights has become a supranational body deciding cases involving human rights, and is part of a significant transformation in legal culture giving importance to the issue of human rights.

Several legal occupations have internationalised. Apart from business lawyers, the influential group of top law professors should be included; they are generally familiar with several legal cultures and languages, and have frequent contacts amongst themselves. Human rights lawyers, or at least a part of them, also have frequent international meetings and know each other. It is thus a matter of diverse groups with very different predominant ideologies, and with relatively little contact between the groups. Their common characteristic is that they possess the highest professional prestige and a greater ability to influence public policies using their professional tools.

Our analysis should not be understood as an assertion that all of the conflict resolution or regulatory institutions in the international or global sphere are necessarily related to the law. Gessner (1998) and Appelbaum *et al* (2001) identify various cases in which the institutions of globalisation have chosen to avoid the use of law and lawyers. Opposition between the option of juridification and what is generally called relational capitalism should not be exaggerated (Dezalay and Garth 1997).

A related component to globalisation is the multiplication of legal relations that cross national boundaries. This is not only a matter of contracts involving parties of different nationalities, but also transactions that can produce effects in countries other than those of the parties' nationalities. In personal relations also, national borders seem to mean less in this age. For example, it is not unusual for an Argentine to marry a Brazilian and for the couple to settle in Venezuela, and have children there. Matrimonial conflict can arise in one country and can involve investments in a fourth or fifth country. Private international law, which is the formal way of resolving this type of conflict, can turn out to be completely inappropriate. Parties can be taken by surprise by the application of an unexpected legal rule. Judges and lawyers, finding themselves compelled to work with foreign laws, would not feel comfortable either. Hence, when the situation is foreseeable, lawyers seek to define in advance the applicable law and the way in which conflicts will be resolved. In the same way, electronic commerce can involve parties located in distant countries, with property subject to negotiation located in a third party and delivered in a fourth country. It is not easy to determine who should pay taxes to whom, or, if a conflict arises, what the appropriate court and laws are.

The study of how the parties or the courts handle this type of conflict, or how those who do business look for legal certainty in situations such as that described above, is a challenge for the researchers who study legal activity that crosses national borders. Gessner (1996, 1998) has found that legal institutions and most lawyers are poorly equipped to handle these matters and that the tendency is to apply national law. National laws and states have thus shown themselves to be much more resistant to the onslaught of globalisation than is generally supposed. However, the theory can have two interpretations: the descriptive one is the permanence of the importance of states and state laws; the normative one is the necessity of a stronger international order that can provide legal certainty in times of globalisation. Likewise, a greater sensitivity seems necessary on the part of legal professionals to these relations that cross national borders. One can hypothesise that the creation of globalised institutions and personnel will intensify.

Pérez-Perdomo (2001) found that even in the case of international businesses, the importance of supranational law (*lex mercatoria*) is small; rather, in contracts, a national law is selected, although not necessarily that of the jurisdiction of either one of the parties. Lawyers choose a mutually convenient law, whether this is English maritime law, Delaware corporation regulation, or the financial law of New York. International arbitration bodies may also be selected to decide future cases. This produces a division between the lawyers who know only one legal culture, and those who are familiar with more than one. Globalisation, in short, may not mean the existence of a transnational culture, but a greater interaction of national laws and cultures.

The burgeoning of relations among people with greater geographic mobility, and even of different nationalities and cultures, has another dimension as well. People who do not belong to the same community constantly enter into business relations. The hypothesis regarding ethnically homogeneous communities who come from the same small town (Landa 1994), which can provide the mechanisms for social control and predictable behavior, is becoming less common. The existence of communities sharing the same culture with religious elements, like diamond merchants (according to Bernstein, 1992), also become less likely in a more globalised world. This means that law—and above all, lawyers and contracts— becomes more important (Pérez Perdomo 1993). Without a doubt, the visible increase in the market for legal services is related to that feature of the age in which we live.

This assertion is not a prediction that the law will permeate every sphere. In minor transactions, especially since the rise of electronic commerce, confidence has to be re-established, giving new roles to existing institutions: credit card companies and the charge back mechanism. This avoids juridification that would be excessively complicated and too costly for that type of case (Pichler 2000).[23]

Friedman has emphasised the importance of globalisation's impact on the law. He has examined how our age of intense communication has spread values and attitudes that have caused the vertical mechanisms of social control to lose force. The family and other authorities that used to be perceived as natural already lack their previous strength. We think of ourselves more as individuals who have rights and the liberty to make choices. The legitimacy of authority, including the authority of professionals and experts, is questioned. Hence, there is an increase in legal actions against different state agencies or lawsuits for professional malpractice. This more horizontal society is a society that aspires to total justice (Friedman 1999, 1985). We have, therefore, a culture of the complaint (also cf García de la Cruz Herrero 1999) and therefore a greater use of lawyers and eventually courts. Thus, the enormous increase in lawyers that we have seen in Latin America derives not only from the spread of higher education, but also from a societal transformation that requires more lawyers, more efficient courts, and more willingness to seek remedies for various wrongs.

In this way, globalisation affects not only those who enter into international interactions, but also the person with entirely domestic relations confined to a single national space, yet who received the new values through

---

[23] The example refers to an agreement that converts the credit card company in the arbiter of disputes between the card holder and the affiliated merchant.

the mass media. The increase in the number of lawyers cannot be explained solely by the increase in the number of people who receive a higher education; it also reflects the social desirability for there to be people who help us to demand our rights, to arrange social relations in accordance with the law.

Having analysed the present situation of the legal professions, the main preoccupations of the past (including the recent past) have lost much of their force. The demand for legal services has expanded in such a way that now a huge number of lawyers have sufficient work. Perhaps lawyers no longer run the state, as they did in the past. The dividing up of knowledge means that many different kinds of professionals can aspire to run the areas of state operation that best match their training. But the growing importance of the judicial sphere as a forum for debate about the state's most important political problems means that lawyers and judges have great importance in carrying out their specific functions, and that any person with important responsibilities should be able to rely on a lawyer's good advice if he wants his actions to be able to withstand the challenge of lawsuits and media scandals.

Nevertheless, globalisation is far from having transported the legal professions to a world without problems. In the first place, the image of the lawyer as a liberal professional that offers his services to a wide array of clients no longer reflects professional practice. Most lawyers work in organisations—that is, they work for other lawyers or are employees of businesses or public organisations' managers. In an age of technological advances and accumulation of financial power, these organisations can do enormous damage to the community, or can find themselves implicated in scandals that destroy them. The role of lawyers in these organisations is a subject that should be given the most serious consideration. Legal professionals require today, more than ever, very serious attention issues of ethics and professional responsibility.

Another matter of concern is the stratification of law schools. As Lomnitz and Salazar (1997) have observed, in this new age the role that social mobility had in the past has weakened. Young people from different social groups now go to different law schools, and likewise the graduates have different job opportunities. The coveted market for business lawyers is reserved for the children of the elite (who also control the businesses) and young people from the middle class who have excelled due to their abilities. Mobility now takes place within a much more reduced space. Everyone else has a lower quality legal education and a much less desirable job market. For them, law schools really turn out to be 'dream factories', to use Junqueira's (1999) metaphor. The quality of legal education has an impact that extends beyond the professionals themselves. A system of legal education with a bottom layer of poor schools especially affects people with fewer resources, who will have the worst quality legal services and, as a result, access to justice will be most difficult for them. It could produce an overexploitation of the most destitute. The deepening of the poverty of one sector of the population, which we see associated with globalisation, is not only an economic problem.

As much for those who work in the education of professionals as for the judges and lawyers themselves, we have a changing scene. Without a doubt, it is more demanding with respect to the social and professional responsibility of lawyers, judges, and academics. At least, this is the case if we think that legal professionals have something to do with justice, and with the fairer functioning of society.

(Translation of Katherine Unterman)

References

ABEL, Richard L, 'Lawyers in the Civil Law World' in R Abel and P Lewis (eds) *Lawyers in Society. The Civil Law World* (Berkeley University of California, 1988).

ACUÑA, Carlos and C SMULOVITZ, 'Guarding the Guardians in Argentina: Some Lessons about the Risks and Benefits of Empowering the Courts' AJ McAdams ed *Transitional Justice and the Rule of Law in New Democracies* (Notre Dame, University of Notre Dame Press, 1997).

ADORNO, Sergio, Os aprendizes do poder. O bacharelismo liberal na política brasilera (São Paulo, Paz e terra, 1988).

AGUIRRE, Luppy, 'Justicia military: una mirada en cifras'. J Mera Figueroa ed *Justicia military y estado de derecho* (Santiago, Universidad Diego Portales, 1998).

ALCÁNTARA, Manuel, *Sistemas Políticos de América Latina Volumen 1, América del Sur* (Madrid, Tecnos, 1999).

APPELBAUM, Richard, W FELSTINER and V GESSNER 'Introduction'. R Appelbaum, W Felstiner and V Gessner eds *The Legal Culture of Global Business Transactions*, (Oxford, Hart, 2001).

ARIAS Sánchez, Oscar *'Quién gobierna en Costa Rica'* (San José, Educa.Armitage, 1976).

——, 'From Club to Global Firm: Forging International Links', 1990, *International Financial Law Review*, May.

ASHTON, Scot, 'El Torneo de Abogados: Law Firms in Chile' Final paper 2002. Seminario Law in Latin America, Stanford Law School. (unpublished).

BANCO INTERAMERICANO DE DESARROLLO, ed, *Justicia y desarrollo en América Latina y el Caribe* (Washington, Banco Interamericano de Desarrollo, 1993).

BASTOS, Aurélio Wander, O ensino jurídico no Brasil. 2nd edn (Rio de Janeiro, Lumen Juris, 2000).

BERMÚDEZ, Carlos M, 'Studying Law in Cuba: A Law Student's Perspective',

2001.Paper final en el curso Law in Latin America, Stanford Law School (en depósito con el autor).

BERSTEIN, Lisa, 'Opting Out of the Legal System: Extralegal Contractual Relations in the Diamond Trade', 1992 *Journal of Legal Studies* 21.

BINDER, Alberto, 'Los oficios del jurista: la fragmentación de la profesión jurídica y la uniformidad de la carrera judicial', 2001, *Sistemas Judiciales*, v 1.

BOIGEOL, Anne 'El ascenso de los juristas en Francia' En L Friedman, R Pérez-Perdomo and Héctor Fix-Fierro eds *Culturas jurídicas latinas de Europa y América en tiempos de globalización* (en imprenta), (México, Universidad Nacional Autónoma de México, 2002).

BROWN, Brenda, 'Recent Significant Trends in Legal Education in the Americas', 1961 *Inter-American Law Review*, 3.

CAMP, Roderic, *El reclutamiento político en México*, (México, Siglo XXI, 1996).

CAPELLER, Wanda de Lemos, *L'engrenage de la repression. Stratégies sécuritaires et politiques criminelles*, (Paris, Librairie Géneral de Droit et Jurisprudence, 1995).

CASSESSE, Sabino, 'Italia: el sistema jurídico 1945–1999' En L Friedman, R Pérez-Perdomo and Héctor Fix-Fierro eds *Culturas jurídicas latinas de Europa y América en tiempos de globalización* (en imprenta), (México, Universidad Nacional Autónoma de México, 2002).

CHINCHILLA, Laura and D SCHODT, *The Administration of Justice in Ecuador*, (Miami, Florida International University, 1993).

CLARK, David S, 'Comparing the Work and Organisation of Lawyers Worldwide: The Persistence of Legal Traditions' in John Barceló III and R Cramton (eds) *Lawyers practice and Ideals. A Comparative View*, (The Hague, Kluwer, 1999).

—— Italian styles: the penal justice and the rise of an activist judiciary. L. Friedman and Pérez Perdomo (eds): *Legal cultures in the age of globalization: Latin America and Latin Europe.* Stanford University Press. 2003.

CONCHA-CANTÚ, Hugo and A Caballero-Juárez, Diagnóstico sobre la administración de justicia en las entidades federativas. Un estudio institucional sobre justicia local en México, (México, Instituto de Investigaciones Jurídicas UNAM, 2001).

CORREA Sutil, Jorge CONCHA-CANTÚ, Hugo and A Caballero-Juárez 'The Judiciary and the Political System in Chile: The Dilemmas of Judicial Independence during the Transition to Democracy' in I P Stoltzky (ed) *Transition to Democracy in Latin America. The Role of the Judiciary*, (Boulder, Westview, 1993).

CONCHA-CANTÚ, Hugo and A Caballero-Juárez 'No Victorious Army Has Ever Been Prosecuted … The Unsettled Story of Transitional Justice in Chile' in AJ McAdams (ed) *Transitional Justice and the Rule of Law in New Democracies*, (Notre Dame, University of Notre Dame Press, 1997).

CORREA Sutil, Jorge ed Necesidades de capacitación de los funcionarios del poder judicial. Informe a la Academia Judicial de Chile, (Santiago, Universidad Diego Portales, 1998).

CORREAS, Oscar and F CORREAS VÁZQUEZ, 'La sociología jurídica en México' in V Ferrari ed *Developing sociology of law*, (Milano, Giuffrè, 1990).

DAHRENDORF, Ralf, 'Las facultades de derecho y la clase alta alemana' V Aubert ed *Sociología del derecho*, (Caracas, Tiempo Nuevo, 1971).

DAKOLIAS, Maria, 'The Judicial Sector in Latin America and the Caribbean: Elements of Reform' World Bank paper, 1996.

DANTAS, San Tiago, 'A educação jurídica e a crise brasileira' 1955, *Revista Forense*, 159.

DAVID, René, *Les grands systèmes de droit contemporains*, 9th edn (Paris, Dalloz, 1988).

DE LA MAZA, Iñigo Lawyers: From the State to the Market. Tesis para JSM. Stanford Program for International Legal Studies, 2001.

DE SOTO, Hernando *El otro sendero*, (Lima, El Barranco, 1986).

DEZALAY, Yves Marchands de droit. La restructuration de l'ordre juridique international par le multinationales de droit, (Paris, Fayard, 1992).

DEZALAY, Yves and B Garth, Patterns of foreign investments and State transformation in Latin America. L. Friedman and Pérez Perdomo (eds): *Legal cultures in the age of globalization: Latin America and Latin Europe*. Stanford University Press. 2003.

——— , 'Law, Lawyers and Social Capital: "Rule of Law"versus Relational Capitalism', 1997 *Social and Legal Studies*, 6.

——— , 'Argentina: Law at the Periphery and Law in Dependencies: Political and Economic Crisis and the Instrumentalization and Fragmentation of Law' Working Paper. American Bar Foundation. Chicago, 1998a.

——— , 'Chile: Law and the Legitimation of Transitions: From the Patrimonial State to the Internation Neo-Liberal State. Working Paper. American Bar Foundation. Chicago, 1998b.

——— , 'Patrones de inversión extranjera y transformaciones del estado en América Latina' in L Friedman, R Pérez-Perdomo and Héctor Fix-Fierro eds *Culturas jurídicas latinas de Europa y América en tiempos de globalización* (en imprenta), (México, Universidad Nacional Autónoma de México, 2002).

DUCE, Mauricio and R PÉREZ PERDOMO 'Seguridad ciudadana y reforma de la justicia penal en América Latina', 2001 *Boletin Mexicano de Derecho Comparado*, 102.

FALCÃO, Joaquim 'Os cursos jurídicos e a formação do estado nacional', A W Bastos (coordenador), *Os cursos jurídicos e as elites políticas brasileiras*, (Brasilia, Camara dos Deputados, 1978).

——— , 'Lawyers in Brazil: Ideals and Praxis', 1979 *International Journal of the Sociology of Law*, 7.

——— , *Os advogados. Ensino jurídico e mercado de trabalho*, (Recife, Fundação Joaquim Nabuco y Editora Massangana, 1984).

FARIA, Jose Eduardo 'Globalização, direito e ensino jurídico' , 2000 *Revista da Faculade de Direito da UFF*, v 4.

FIGUEROA, Gonzalo, 'Investigaciones socio-jurídicas emprendidas en Chile' in G Figueroa ed *Derecho y Socieda*, (Santiago, Corporación de Promoción Universitaria, 1978).

FIGUEROA, Gonzalo, 'Investigaciones socio-juri

FLOOD, John, 'Megalawyering in the Global Order: The Cultural, Social and Economic Transformation of Global Legal Practice', 1996 *International Journal of the Legal Profession*, 3.

FRIEDMAN, Lawrence *Total Justice*, (New York, Russell Sage Foundation, 1985).

FIX-FIERRO, Héctor and S LÓPEZ AYLLÓN 'Legitimidad contra legalidad. Los dilemas de la transición (New York, Russell Sage Foundation, 1985)

——— , *The Horizontal Society*, (New Haven, Yale University Press, 1999).

——, 'Erewhon: The Coming Global Legal Order', 2001, *Stanford Journal of International Law*, 37.

FRÜHLING, Hugo, 'Poder Judicial y política en Chile' En J de Belaúnde ed *La administración de justicia en América Latina*, (Lima, Consejo Latinoamericano de Derecho y Desarrollo, 1984).

FUCITO, Felipe, 'La profesión jurídica: un estudio cualitativo' 1997, *Revista de Sociología del Derecho*. # 12. (Buenos Aires).

——, 'El profesor de derecho en Argentina', 2000 *Revista da Facultade de Direito da UFF* v 4.

FUENTES-HERNÁNDEZ, Alfredo, 'Globalisation and Legal Education in Latin America. Issues for Law and Development in the 21st Century'. Paper en la reunión anual la Association of American Law Schools. New Orleans. Enero, 2002.

FUENTES-HERNÁNDEZ, Alfredo and C Amaya-Osorio, 'Demanda y oferta judicial: Dificultades de ajuste' En *Nuevos enfoques para atender la demanda de justicia. Conferencia Regional del Banco Mundial para América Latina y el Caribe.*(México, CIDE.Mayo, 2001).

FUENZALIDA, Edmundo, 'Law and Legal Culture in Chile (1974–1999)' in L Friedman, R Pérez Perdomo (eds) *Legal cultures in the age of globalization: Latin America and Latin Europe*. Stanford University Press. 2003.

GALANTER, Marc, 'Mega-law and Mega-Lawyering in the Contemporary US' in R Dingwall and P Lewis (eds) *The Sociology of the Professions*, (London, Macmillan, 1983).

GALÍN, Pedro, 'La independencia del Poder Judicial argentino en la dictadura 1976–1980' En J de Belaúnde ed *La administración de justicia en América Latina*, (Lima, Consejo Latinoamericano de Derecho y Desarrollo, 1984).

GAMARRA, Eduardo, *'The System of Justice in Bolivia: An Institutional Analysis' Colección Monografías 4.* Centro para la Administración de Justicia, (Florida International University, San José, Costa Rica, 1991).

GARAVANO, Germán C, 'Los usuarios del sistema de justicia en Argentina' En *Nuevos enfoques para atender la demanda de justicia.* Conferencia Regional del Banco Mundial para América Latina y el Caribe, (México, CIDE, Mayo, 2001).

GARCÍA DE LA CRUZ Herrero, Juan José, 'La cultura de la reclamación como indicador de desarrollo democrático: tres perspectivas de análisis', 1999 *Politeia*, 22.

GARRIDO, Carlos Manuel 'Informe sobre Argentina' in J Correa Sutil (ed) *Situación y políticas judiciales en América Latina*, (Santiago, Universidad Diego Portales, 1993).

GESSNER, Volkmar 'The Institutional Framework of Cross–Border Interactions' in V Gessner (ed) *Foreign Courts: Civil Litigation in Foreign Cultures*, (Aldershot, Dartmouth, 1996).

——, 'Globalisation and Legal Certainty' in V Gessner and AC Budak (eds) *Emerging Legal Certainty: Empirical Studies on the Globalisation of Law*, (Aldershot, Dartmouth, 1998).

GIDDENS, Anthony, Runaway World: How Globalisation is Reshaping our Lifes, (New York, Routledge, 2000).

GIRALDO Angel, Jaime, 'Informe sobre Colombia' in J Correa Sutil ed *Situación y políticas judiciales en América Latina*, (Santiago, Escuela de Derecho Universidad Diego Portales, 1993).

GONZÁLEZ, Gorki 'La carrera judicial: estudio analítico y comparativo'2001 *Pensamiento constitucional*, 8 (Lima).

HALLIDAY, Terence and L KARPIK, 'Politics Matter: a Comparative Theory of Lawyers in the Making of Political Liberalism', in T Halliday and L Karpik (eds) *Lawyers and the Rise of Western Political Liberalism*, (Oxford, Clarendon Press, 1997).

HAMMERGREN, Lynn, *The Politics of Justice and Justice Reform in Latin America: The Peruvian Case in Comparative Perspective* (Boulder, Westview Press, 1998).

—— , 'The Judicial Career in Latin America: An Overview of Theory and Experience'. Paper. Washington. World Bank, 1999.

HOLSTON, James and T CALDEIRA, 'Democracy, Law and Violence: Disjunctions of Brazilian Citizenship' in F Agüero and J Stark (eds) *Fault Lines of Democracy in Post-Transition Latin America*, (Miami, North-South Center Press at the University of Miami, 1998).

IMAZ, José Luis de, *Los que Mandan* (Buenos Aires Editorial Universitaria, Instituto de la Judicatura Federal, 1964).

—— , 'La formación de los jueces federales en México. Notas para un análisis de la situación actual y perspectivas'. Paper. Distribuido en la reunión Empowerment, Security and Opportunity Through Law and Justice. Banco Mundial. San Petersburgo, 2001.

JUNQUEIRA, Eliane 'A feminizaçao das carreras jurídicas: uma análise quantitativa'. Paper. Rio de Janeiro. Instituto Direito e Sociedade, 1997.

—— , *Facultades de Direito o Fábrica de Ilusões?*(Rio de Janeiro, IDES and Letra Capital Editora, 1999).

—— , 'Brazil: bumps in the road to total justice' in L Friedman, R Pérez-Perdomo (eds) *Legal cultures in the age of globalization: Latin America and Latin Europe.* Stanford University Press. 2003.

JUNQUEIRA, Eliane and CV Veras 'Estudantes e profissionais negros de direito: perspectivas para o novo milênio? Paper, no publicado. Rio de Janeiro. Instituto de Direito e Sociedade, 2001.

LANDA, Janet, *Tai Trust, Ethnicity and Identity. Beyond the New Institutional Economics of Ethnic Trading Networks, Contract Law, and Gift Exchange* (Ann Arbor, The University of Michigan Press, 1994).

LOMNITZ, Larissa and R SALAZAR 'Cultural elements in the Practice of Law in Mexico. Informal Networks in Formal Systems'. Paper en la conferencia New Challenges for the Rule of Law: Lawyers Internationalisation and the Social Construction of Rules. Santa Barbara. University of California and American Bar Foundation, 1997.

LÓPEZ-AYLLÓN, Sergio and H FIX-FIERRO 'Communications Between Legal Cultures: The Case of NAFTA's chapter 19 binational panels' in L Perret (ed) *Evolution of Free Trade in the Americas*, (Montréal, Wilson and Lafleur, 1999).

—— , 'Farewell and so close! Rule of law and legal change in Mexico 1977–1999' in L Friedman, R Pérez Perdomo and H Fix-Fierro (eds) *Legal cultures in the age of globalization: Latin America and Latin Europe.* Stanford University Press. 2003.

LOREY, David, *The Rise of the Professions in Twentieth-Century Mexico. University Graduates and Occupational Change since 1929* (Los Angeles, University of California, 1992).

LOWENSTEIN, Steven, *Lawyers, Legal Education, and Development. An Examination of the Process of Reform in Chile* (New York, International Legal Center, 1970).

LYNCH, Dennis O, Legal Roles in Colombia. Uppsala, Scandinavian Institute for African Studies, and New York, International Center for Law in Development, 1981.

MACKINSON DE SOROKIN, Gladys 'La mujer y el derecho. Estudio sobre las variaciones de la matrícula femenina en la Facultad de Derecho y Ciencias Sociales de la Universidad de Buenos Aires', 1984, *Revista de Sociología del Derecho* # 2.

MATTEI, Ugo *Comparative Law and Economics*, (Ann Arbor, University of Michigan Press, 1997).

MEILI, Stephan 'Legal Education in Argentina and Chile' in L Trubek and J Cooper (eds) *Educating for Justice Around the World. Legal Education, Legal Practice and the Community* (Aldershot, Darmouth, 1999).

MERA FIGUEROA, Jorge, (ed) *Justicia militar y estado de derecho*, (Santiago, Universidad Diego Portales, 1998).

MERRYMAN, John Henry 'On the Convergence (and Divergence) of the Civil Law and the Common Law', 1981 *Stanford Journal of International Law*, #17.

—— , *The Civil Law Tradition*, 2nd edn (Stanford, Stanford University Press, 1985).

MERRYMAN, John, D Clark and L Friedman, *Law and Social Change in Mediterranean Europe and Latin America: A Handbook of Legal and Social Indicators* (Stanford, Stanford Law School, 1979).

MORA, Luis Paulino, Presentación del caso de Costa Rica. En *Nuevos enfoques para atender la demanda de justicia*. Conferencia Regional del Banco Mundial para América Latina y el Caribe, (México, CIDE, Mayo, 2001).

NINO, Carlos, S *Radical Evil on Trial*, (New Haven, Yale University Press, 1996).

O'DONNELL, Guillermo, 'Introduction to Latin American Cases' in O'Donnell, P Schmitter and L Whitehead (eds) *Transitions from Authoritarian Rule*, (Latin America, Baltimore, John Hopkins University Press, 1986).

PÁSARA, Luis, Jueces, justicia y poder en el Perú, (Lima, CEDYS, 1982).

—— , 'Perú: administración de justicia?' in J de Belaúnde ed *La administración de justicia en América Latina*, (Lima, Consejo Latinoamericano de Derecho y Desarrollo, 1984).

PEÑA, Carlos 'Informe sobre Chile' En J Correa ed *Situación y políticas judiciales en América Latina*, (Santiago, Universidad Diego Portales, 1993).

—— , 'Hacia una caracterización del ethos legal: de nuevo sobre la cultura jurídica'. A Squella ed *Evolución de la cultura jurídica chilena*, (Santiago, Corporación de Promoción Universitaria, 1994).

—— , 'Características y desafíos de la enseñanza legal'. Paper, 2000. No publicado.

PÉREZ PERDOMO, Rogelio *Los abogados en Venezuela*, (Caracas, Monte Avila, 1981).

—— , 'La investigación jurídica en Venezuela contemporánea' H Vessuri ed *Ciencia académica en la Venezuela moderna. Historia reciente y perspectivas de las disciplinas científicas*, (Caracas, Fondo Editorial Acta Científica Venezolana, 1984).

—— , 'Corrupción y ambiente de negocios en Venezuela' in R Pérez Perdomo and R Capriles (compiladores) *Corrupción y control. Una perspectiva comparada*, (Caracas, Ediciones IESA, 1991).

——, 'La justicia en tiempos de globalización. Demadas y perspectivas de cambio de la Administración de Justicia en América Latina' in Banco Interamericano de Desarrollo: Justicia y Desarrollo en América Latina y el Caribe, Washington, 1993.

——, 'Corrupción: la difícil relación entre política y derecho', 1996 *Politeia* 19. (1996a).

——, 'De la justicia y otros demonios'. En ME Boza and R Pérez Perdomo compiladores *Seguridad juridical y competitividad*, (Caracas, Ediciones IESA, 1996). (1996b)

——, 'Jueces y estado hoy' in Fundación Manuel García-Pelayo. *Constitución y constitucionalismo hoy*. (Caracas, 2000)

——, 'Oil Lawyers and the Globalisation of Venezuelan Oil Business'. En R Appelbaum, W Felstiner and V Gessner eds *Rules and Networks: The Legal Culture of Global Business Transactions*, (Oxford, Hart, 2001).

——, 'Venezuela 1958–1999. The Legal System in an Impaired Democracy' in L Friedman, R Pérez Perdomo (eds) *Legal cultures in the age of globalization: Latin America and Latin Europe*. Stanford University Press. 2003.

PÉREZ-PERDOMO, Rogelio and L FRIEDMAN, 'Latin Legal Cultures in the age of Globalization' in L Friedman, R Pérez Perdomo (eds) *Legal cultures in the age of globalization: Latin America and Latin Europe*. Stanford University Press. 2003.

PÉREZ-PERDOMO, Rogelio and CL ROCHE 'Balance de la sociología del derecho en la Venezuela actual' En V Ferrari ed *Developing sociology of law*, (Milano, Giuffrè, 1990).

PERSICO, Pablo, *Informe sobre la educación superior en Chile. Análisis de tendencias de la última década* (Santiago, Corporación de Promoción Universitaria, 2001).

PICHLER, Rufus, 'Trust and Reliance. Enforcement and Compliance: Enhancing Consumer Confidence in the Electronic Marketplace' Tesis para JSM. Stanford Program for International Legal Studies, 2000.

QUINTERO, Maria Olga, 'Independencia del Poder Judicial'. *Libro Homenaje a José Melich Orsini. Vol 2*. (Caracas, Universidad Central de Venezuela, 1983).

——, *Justicia y realida*, (Caracas, Universidad Central de Venezuela, 1988).

REISMAN, W Michael, *Folded Lies. Briberies, Cruzades and Reforms*, (New York, Free Press, 1979).

REY, Juan Carlos, *El futuro de la democracia en Venezuela* (Caracas, IDEA, 1989).

RICO, José María and Luis SALAS, *'Independencia judicial en América Latina: Replanteo de un tema tradicional'*, (San José, Costa Rica, Centro para la Administración de Justicia, 1990).

RIVERA-CIRA, Tirza, 'Informe sobre Costa Rica' En J Correa ed *Situación y políticas judiciales en América Latina* (Santiago, Universidad Diego Portales, 1993).

ROCHE, Carmen Luisa, 'The Feminisation of the Legal Profession in Venezuela: It's Meaning for the Profession and for Women Lawyers'. Budapest. Joint Meeting, Law and Society Association e ISA Research Committee on Sociology of Law, 2001.

RODRÍGUEZ, César, 'Globalisation, Judicial Reform and the Rule of Law in Latin America. The Return of Law and Development', 2001 *Beyond Law*, 23.

ROSENN, Keith S, 'The Reform of Legal Education in Brazil', 1969 *Journal of Legal Education*, 21.

——, 'The Jeito: Brazil's Institutional Bypass of the Formal Legal System in its Development Implications', 1971 *American Journal of Comparative Law*, 19.

——, 'The Protection of Judicial Independence in Latin America', 1987 *The University of Miami Inter-American Law Review*, 19.

ROWAT, M, W Malik and M Dakolias, (eds) Judicial Reform in Latin America and the Caribbean. Washington. The World Bank, 1995.

SANTELICES ARIZTÍA, Fernando'Informe sobre la enseñanza legal en Chile'. Documento no publicado. Santiago. Centro de Estudios de Justicia de las Américas, 2002.

SANTOS, Boaventura de Sousa 'The GATT of Law and Democracy' in J Feest (ed) *Globalisation and Legal Cultures*, (Oñati, Instituto Internacional de Sociología Jurídica, 1999).

SMITH, Peter H, *Labyrinths of Power. Political Recruitment in Twentieth-Century Mexico* (Princeton, Princeton University Press, 1979).

SOBERANES Fernández, José LUIS, 'Informe sobre México' En J Correa ed *Situación y políticas judiciales en América Latina*, (Santiago, Universidad Diego Portales, 1993).

SOUTO, Claudio and S SOUTO, 'Sociology of Law in Brazil: The Recent Years' in V Ferrari (ed) *Developing Sociology of Law* (Milano, Giuffrè, 1990).

SQUELLA, Agustín, 'La cultura jurídica chilena'. A Squella editor *La cultura jurídica chilena*, (Santiago, Corporación de Promoción Universitaria, 1988).

STEINER, Henry, 'Legal Education and Socio-Economic Change: Brazilian Perspectives', 1971 *The American Journal of Comparative Law*, v 19.

SUNWOLF, 'Communication between Legal Cultures: Strategies, Perceptions and Beliefs of American Lawyers who Practice International Litigation'. Paper in Workshop on Changing Legal Cultures. Oñati, 1997.

TATE, C NEAL and T VALLINDER, (eds) *The Global Expansion of Judicial Power*, (New York, New York University Press, 1995).

TOHARIA, José Juan, 'Judges' International Encyclopedia of Social Sciences, (London. Elsevier, 2001).

——, 'The judiciary and the legal culture in Spain 1975–1999' En L Friedman, R Pérez-Perdomo (eds) *Legal cultures in the age of globalization: Latin America and Latin Europe*. Stanford University Press. 2003.

TORRES Arends, Irene *Educación jurídica y razonamiento*, (Caracas, Universidad Central de Venezuela, 1997).

——, 'Cultura jurídica y estudiantes de derecho: una medición de cultura jurídica en Venezuela'. Prepublicación. Facultad de Ciencias Jurídicas y Políticas.Universidad Central de Venezuela, 2001.

TRUBEK, DEZALAY, BUCHANAN and DAVIS, 'Global Restructuring and the Law: The Internationalisation of Legal Fields and the Creation of Transational Arenas', 1994 *Case Western Reserve Law Review*, 44.

TRUBEK, David and M GALANTER, 'Scholars in Self-Estrangement: Some Reflexions on the Crisis in Law and Development Studies in the United States', 1974 *Wisconsin Law Review*, 1062.

UPRIMNY, Rodrigo 'Las transformaciones de la justicia en Colombia' in B Sousa Santos and M García Villegas (eds) *El caleidoscopia de las justicias en Colombia*, (Bogotá, Siglo del Hombre, 2001).

UPRIMNY, Rodrigo, R Rodríguez and M García-Villegas, 'Between the protagonism and the routine. A socio legal analysis of Columbian justice' in L Friedman, R Pérez Perdomo (eds) *Legal cultures in the age of globalization: Latin America and Latin Europe*. Stanford University Press. 2003.

URZÚA, Raúl, 'La profesión de abogado y el desarrollo: Antecedentes para un estudio' in G Figueroa (ed) *Derecho y sociedad* (Santiago, Corporación de Promoción Universitaria, 1978). (El artículo fue publicado originariamente en 1971)

VAN PUYMBROECK, Rudolf, *Comprehensive Legal and Judicial Development* (Washington, The World Bank, 2001).

VARELA, David F, 'El Banco Mundial y la reforma judicial en América Latina'. Paper. Segunda conferencia sobre la efectividad y coste de la justicia. Madrid. Centro de Investigaciones en Derecho y Economía, Universidad Complutense, 1999.

VARGAS, Juan Enrique, C PEÑA and J CORREA *El rol del estado y del mercado en la justicia*, (Santiago, Universidad Diego Portales, 2001).

VES LOSADA, Alfredo, 'Current sociology of law in Argentina' in V Ferrari (ed) *Developing sociology of law* (Milano, Giuffrè, 1990).

WEILER, JHH, 'The Rule of Lawyers and the Ethos of Diplomats: Reflections on WTO Dispute Settlements' in RB Porter *et al* (eds), *Efficiency, Equity, Legitimacy. The Multilateral Trading* System *at the Millenium* (Washington, Brookings Institution Press, 2001).

WILSON, Richard, 'The New Legal Education in North and South America', 1989 *Stanford Journal of International Law*, 25.

WITKER, Jorge, *Antología de estudios sobre la enseñanza del derecho*, (México, Universidad Nacional Autónoma de México, 1978).

ZAFFARONI, Eugenio Raúl, *Poder Judiciário. Crise, Acertos e Desacertos* (Sao Paulo, Editora Revista dos Tribunais, 1995).

ZATZ, Marjorie S, *Producing Legality. Law and Socialism in Cuba* (New York, Routledge, 1994).

ZOLEZZI IBÁRCENA, Lorenzo, *La profesión de abogado en Lima (una aproximación empírica)*. (Lima, Pontificia Universidad Católica del Perú, 1982).

—— , 'Informe sobre Perú' En J Correa ed *Situación y políticas judiciales en América Latina*, (Santiago, Universidad Diego Portales, 1993).

9

Legal Professionals Aplenty, But No Legal Profession? Law and Lawyers in Contemporary Mexico*

HÉCTOR FIX-FIERRO
AND SERGIO LÓPEZ AYLLÓN

Introduction

Lawyers and the legal profession are certainly one of the inexhaustible topics of socio-legal research. From a theoretical point of view, it may well be that sociology of law is more about the structures and operations of the legal system than about the behaviors and attitudes of lawyers, which, strictly speaking, would then belong to the sociology of professions (Luhmann 1972:I, 3–4). But the ambiguous fascination that lawyers seem to exert, coupled with the need to give the law a human face, may help obviate some of the subject's theoretical difficulties. Thus, it has given birth to a genuine branch of socio-legal studies in its own right and produced a very vast and rich literature that continues to grow relentlessly.

Despite the fact that Mexico, as a modern nation, is literally a creature of the law and of lawyers (López Ayllón 1995; 1997, chap V), relatively little is known about them as a professional group, especially in contemporary times. Historical studies abound on the founders of modern Mexico,

*This paper is a product of an ongoing research project on legal change in Mexico. It draws from, and expands on, previous publications (Fix-Fierro & López Ayllón, 2001; López Ayllón & Fix-Fierro, 2003; and Fix-Fierro, 2003). We are indebted to Bill Felstiner for the invitation to contribute to this volume, and especially for his patience. Jacqueline Martinez made useful comments and Susana Coen provided valuable research assistance. Ma. Antonia Mendieta Bello greatly helped with the data shown in Table 12 below. Finally, students in our 2002 course on sociology of law at ITAM helped to design and conduct the survey of law schools in Mexico City we describe below.

but not enough is made of the fact that most were distinguished lawyers and many of them actually made a living as such. We are led to be impressed, and rightly so, by their historical deeds, but not enough attention is paid to their handling of ordinary cases and legal matters in daily life.

By contrast, recent research efforts allow us to know more about names and everyday activities of Mexican lawyers in historical times. Thus, for example, we learn about the reports on 'blood purity' that lawyers who aspired to be admitted to the Ilustre y Real Colegio de Abogados de México had to file during the last decades of Spanish rule (Mayagoitia 1999). Or we may be able to reconstruct the names of practicing lawyers in Mexico City at the beginning of the 20th century (Del Arenal 1998). The impressive history of the Mexican federal judiciary that the Supreme Court has been publishing since the mid-1980s also provides interesting albeit indirect evidence on the role of lawyers in the judicial process (Suprema Corte de Justicia de la Nación, 1985ff). But these efforts, however meritorious they may be, are far from being systematic and rarely go beyond a descriptive approach.

The relevant literature becomes even scarcer the more we approach present times. In particular, empirical studies are almost completely lacking, with a few notable exceptions (Dezalay and Garth 1995; Lomnitz and Salazar 2002; Concha Cantú 2002). We still do not have some of the most basic data on lawyers in contemporary Mexico. Thus, we do not know, for example, how many Mexican lawyers are affiliated with a bar association or, for that matter, how many lawyers there are in the country. We are able to describe the composition and influence of the legal elite, but we ignore almost everything about the trials and tribulations of the bulk of legal professionals.

The purpose of this paper is, therefore, a very modest one: to describe, using easily available sources of information, major developments affecting the Mexican legal profession in the last two or three decades. We use a broad concept of 'lawyers' and 'legal profession' that encompasses all individuals (attorneys, notaries public, judges, government officials, legal scholars) who have undergone legal training and are somehow linked, professionally speaking, to the legal system. A good number of lawyers in this sense work as middle or low-level government employees, either at the federal or state governments. Many others have a private practice in solo or small firms mainly concerned with local civil or criminal cases. A relatively small number occupy different positions as court officials or perform other bureaucratic tasks in the administration of justice. A significant number of lawyers are employed in different service sectors not directly related to legal practice. But as already explained, we know little about all these groups of legal professionals that goes beyond very broad generalisations. Therefore, of necessity we have concentrated on what we call the 'legal elite', ie, the visible but small groups of lawyers occupying the highest and most prestigious positions in government, business and academia. We are including a section on legal education, because one cannot understand the structure and practice of the legal profession without an overview of how lawyers are trained and socialised in the law.

In a previous publication we argued that legal education and the legal profession had become the bottlenecks of recent legal transformations in Mexico (López Ayllón and Fix-Fierro 2003). We showed then that Mexico's legal infrastructure (rules, institutions, procedures) had almost completely changed as a result of economic liberalisation and political democratisation. By contrast, legal education and the legal profession continued to behave according to the values and expectations of a closed, less complex legal system. While this is not true to the same extent for the different sectors of the legal profession, the slow transition process that can be observed in some of them poses particular problems and challenges for the consolidation of the rule of law.

We do not try to develop further the normative implications of this argument here. Instead, in the concluding section of this paper we intend to examine the issue whether the Mexican legal profession can be actually be considered a profession (or many professions) in terms of its social role. We find that this is doubtful and that impulses favoring a new sense of solidarity and a new social role among Mexican lawyers are at present rather weak.

Legal Education: An Overview

Legal training has been traditionally a major option for university students in Mexico. But the study of the law has been much more than just training with the aim of practicing the profession. It has been rather, so to speak, a specialised training in the language of the state and in the basic technology of social organisation, since this was, for a long time, the main function expected from the law. As explained elsewhere, a large number of members of the country's political and bureaucratic elite came from the Faculty of Law of the National University until not very long ago. Moreover, the study of the law is still socially regarded as a privileged path to wealth, social prestige, and political power. Thus, the larger role played by the law in social life has had an impact on the organisation of legal education and the legal profession to this day. In this section we attempt to identify basic changes and continuities in legal education since 1970.

Law Students

Mexican higher education has expanded at an accelerated pace in the last decades. Whereas in 1970 there were a total of 210,111 university students (about 0.45 per cent of the population), this number had increased to 731,291 in 1980 (about 1.1 per cent of the population) and to 1,660,973 in 2001 (about 1.7 per cent of the population) (ANUIES 2001). Enrollment in law school has also grown rapidly, especially in the 1990s. The following table shows the number of law students, graduates, degrees and programs between 1979 and 2001:

Table 1 Law Students, Graduates, Degrees and Programs (1979–2001)

Year	Law Students				Graduates (previous year)		Degrees (previous year)		Programs
	Total	Per 100K	% Women	% Enrollment	Total	% Women	Total	% Women	
1979	57,973	89	28.2	8.3	6,011	na	na	na	87
1991	111,025	132	41.0	10.0	12,781	na	6,077	na	118
1997	155,332	162	46.7	11.9	20,983	45.7	10,960	42.0	309
2001	190,338	192	48.4	11.5	26,844	48.2	14,538	47.3	506

Source: ANUIES. Anuarios estadísticos 1979, 1991, 1997 and 2001. 'Programs' refers to the number of facilities ('planteles') that have independent student enrollment. One school or university may have more than one facility or program in one or more states or the Federal District (Mexico City).

The preceding table clearly shows an accelerated increase in the number of students enrolled in law school in the 1980s and especially the 1990s, both in absolute terms and relative to the total population and to the total number of students in higher education. Between 1979 and 2001, the total number of law students increases by 228.3 per cent. Relative to the population, this increase is 115.7 per cent. In 1997 law was still the second most demanded area in higher education; by 1999 it had already climbed to the first position, well above accounting and business administration.

Law school enrollment also increases (and then slightly decreases) in relation to other disciplines: the number of law students, as a percentage of total enrollment in higher education, increased from 8.3 per cent in 1979 to almost 12 per cent in the year 1997. But this development seems to go against expectations, because the growing diversification of university programs could be expected to lead rather to a relative reduction in the number of students choosing law and other 'traditional' disciplines. To the extent that this is happening at all, it occurs at a very slow pace. In 1997, accounting, law, business administration and medicine still accounted for 38.4 per cent of enrollment in higher education; in 2001, this percentage had slightly decreased to 35 per cent, despite a considerable growth in new career options, like computers and industrial engineering (ANUIES 1997; 2001).

Gender composition also shows important changes. The proportion of women studying law in 1979 was less than ⅓ (28.2 per cent); by 2001 it was almost 50 per cent, although in some law schools (notably the Law Faculty of the National University) the percentage of women is already higher.[1] This stands in sharp contrast with other disciplines that are still regarded as either predominantly 'male' (like engineering) or 'female' (like psychology). In law school, at least, women seem to have reached equality. However, in the practice of the legal profession, as will be shown later, women are far from approaching the level of parity they have achieved in law school.

The table provides also data on the number of law school graduates and degrees ('título profesional') granted in the previous years. Thus, we can easily see that the number of graduates, ie, students that have obtained all their credits, increases almost four times after 1979, while the number of students who also obtain their degree grows almost 150 per cent between 1991 and 2001. However, not all students finish law school after 4 or 5 years and still fewer manage to obtain their diploma afterwards. On the contrary, they frequently abandon law school for good. A disincentive for finishing law school is the fact that many students start to work shortly after enrolling in law school (and sometimes even before that). And the study of the law is held by many students as 'easy', among other reasons because it does not seem to require full-time dedication, but just to attend law school a few hours a day.

Roughly speaking, between ⅕ and ¼ of students in law school should graduate each year. Thus, for example, in 1997 34,470 students started law school. Four years later, the number of graduates was approximately 78 per cent of that figure (and this includes students who began law school well before 1997), but in previous years the proportion was much lower (between 50 per cent and 60 per cent). Of those who finish law school, only about 50 per cent to 60 per cent comply with all requirements to obtain their degree and, therefore, the official certificate ('cédula profesional') that legally entitles them to practice law.

Of course, it is reasonable to assume that some schools will be more 'efficient' in the 'production' of law graduates, especially private schools that charge (relatively) high tuition fees.[2] A cursory glance at the statistical data

---

[1] There were 59% women enrolled in the Faculty of Law of the National University in 2001.
[2] A telephone survey of 30 private law schools in the metropolitan area of Mexico City in the first half of 2003 found out that these schools charge on average $300 a month as tuition fee (in addition, students have to pay a first enrollment fee that ranges from one to three monthly rates, and sometimes also a semester enrollment fee). The schools can be divided up in three groups: those that charge between $100 and $250 a month (13 schools); those that charge between $250 and $400 (12 schools), and the top five schools, which charge between $400 and $750 a month.

corresponding to 2000 (ANUIES 2001), however, does not allow us to make any generalisation, because figures vary considerably. Thus, for example, in 2000, of the law students who should have finished law school in the state university of Guerrero, a southern state, about 75 per cent did so, but only ⅙ of graduates obtained their degree. By contrast, in a very prestigious, private law school in Mexico City (Escuela Libre de Derecho), the percentage of graduates was about 50 per cent, but the number of degrees granted in 2000 was higher than the number of graduates that year!

These are just very rough estimates. By contrast, we do have a careful study on the behavior of three classes of law students in the National University after 1980 (Blanco and Rangel 1996). According to the authors' data, the number of students finishing law school after 10 semesters, ie, the normal duration of legal studies at the National University, did not even reach 30 per cent. Although this percentage increased over the years, such increase proceeded at a very slow pace. And while the number of graduates continued to accumulate, the number of degrees granted did not seem to change much between 15 and 20 semesters after students started law school. This means that students who do not obtain their degree after a certain time, will not do so any more. About 20 per cent of a class will abandon law school before a period of 5 years has elapsed, and after 10 years, between 9 per cent and 13 per cent of the class will be still enrolled in law school. A more recent assessment (Facultad de Derecho de la UNAM, 2002, 16–18) shows that an average of 1,433 students enrolled for the first time in the Faculty of Law of the National University each year from 1997 to 2000. However, the number of students (belonging to different classes) finishing their credits decreased from 1,555 in 1997 to 1,084 in 2001.

It should be noted that law students who do not satisfy all requirements to graduate and obtain their degree and 'cédula profesional', are not necessarily prevented from practicing law.[3] In Mexico, lawyers do not enjoy a monopoly on the provision of legal advice, as they do in other countries, and a law degree is not necessary for representing clients in court for certain types of cases (criminal, employment and agrarian cases). Thus, for example, article 20, section IX of the Mexican Constitution provides that defendants in criminal proceedings have a right to an adequate defence, through themselves, through a lawyer or a person they trust. If they do not do so, the judge will appoint a public defender, who must have obtained a

---

[3] Several state laws on the professions provide for the possibility of granting '*pasantes*', ie, students who have finished from 80% to 100% of their credits, authorization to exercise their profession for a limited period of time (up to three years).

law degree.[4] Unfortunately, the majority of public defenders are not well trained (most are lawyers who have just left law school), their pay is very low and they are incredibly overburdened, so they see themselves forced to deal with their cases in a perfunctory manner (Lawyers Committee for Human Rights 2001 45–7). Nevertheless, as a rule, only legal professionals who have had their degree duly registered with the proper authorities are entitled to represent clients in judicial and administrative proceedings.

The panorama we have just described inevitably prompts the question why so many young people are studying law and why the law has become the most important area of professional study. Does this mean that the law and the legal profession have become more relevant from a social point of view? Do students have altruistic motives that make them opt for a legal career, like the pursuit of justice and the settlement of conflicts? Or are they rather after the quick money and whatever job opportunities they can get, even if they do not involve real legal work? What perceptions do they have about the law and its role in society? We cannot answer these questions with certainty and, in particular, we do not have data that allow for comparisons over time. However, at the end of 2002 we conducted a small, non-representative survey of first and last year law students in five law schools in Mexico City.[5] This survey provides a few points of reference for answering the previous questions.

Asked about the three main reasons why they chose to study law, students provide a balanced combination of altruistic and pragmatic motives: 42.5 per cent mention 'economic benefits', 'diversity of professional opportunities', and 'improvement of the legal system'. 41.6 per cent seek to 'promote justice' and 40.4 per cent to 'settle disputes'. Only 18.3 per cent mention the 'influence of relatives and friends' as a reason to study law; none say they chose the law because of the 'influence of the mass media'. With respect to their intended area of work after law school, around a third (34.5 per cent) expect to go to the private sector, while those seeking to work in the public sector would like to go, almost in equal parts, to the legislative branch (14.7 per cent), the public administration (13.3 per cent), the judiciary (14.4 per cent), and criminal prosecution ('procuración de justicia', 14.4 per cent).

A majority of students (52.2 per cent) give a neutral and formal description of the law's purpose in social life: 'regulation of behavior'. By contrast,

[4] Article 28 of the Law on Professions for the Federal District (1944, as amended) provides: 'In criminal matters, the defendant will be heard through himself or a person he trusts or both if he so desires. When the person or persons appointed as defenders are not lawyers, the defendant will be invited to appoint also a defender with a law degree. If he does not make use of this right, the judge will appoint a public defender'.
[5] We surveyed two public and three private law schools. The sample comprised 339 students. Half of them belong to the private law schools.

around 40 per cent incline themselves to ascribe the law a positive function, like the 'realisation of justice' (18.7 per cent) and the 'settlement of disputes in a peaceful manner' (22.8). Only 2.4 per cent think that the law is there to 'make money' and create 'business opportunities'.

At the same time, students do not seem to harbor many illusions that the general population have a favorable perception of the law and the legal profession: asked what three concepts people associate with the law, almost ⅔ (61.6 per cent) mention 'corruption' (in connection with this question, 49.8 per cent think they themselves are going to be forced to participate in corrupt or illegal practices in the exercise of their profession).[6] More than a third mentions also 'trouble' (37.8 per cent), 'money' (34.8 per cent) and 'politics' (34.2 per cent). Nevertheless, a significant group finds that people can also associate law with 'prestige' (33 per cent), 'justice' (31.6 per cent) and 'knowledge' (23.3 per cent).

Law Schools

Table 1 above also shows an impressive growth in the number of law schools and programs, especially in the 1990s. Most of the new programs belong to small private law schools. Until the 1980s, the great majority of law students attended state (public) universities. In the early 1990s, the two largest law schools were the Faculty of Law of the National University and the school of law of the University of Puebla, which had 10,000 and 12,000 students, respectively (1991). At that time, only a small proportion of law students attended private schools (either independent law schools or law schools within private universities). The majority of the most prestigious or well-known among private law schools had been established from the 1960s onwards. Table 2 shows these developments between 1991 and 2001.

The table documents the spectacular growth in the number of, and enrollment in, private law schools. In 1991, private law schools had fewer than 18,000 students. This number increased by about 68,000 to almost 86,000 students, an increase of almost 400 per cent in ten years! The proportion of law students in private schools went from 16 per cent in 1991 to more than 45 per cent in 2001. By contrast, enrollment in public law schools increased by little more than 10 per cent. The total number of programs/facilities, the majority of which are private, also grew in a spectacular way, from 118 in 1991 to 506 in 2001. As already stated, the overwhelming majority of (new)

---

[6] According to an opinion poll conducted in 1996 in Mexico City, more than $1/_3$ of respondents regarded lawyers and judges (including Supreme Court justices) as dishonest or very dishonest. See Voz y Voto, 1996.

private law programs had a small enrollment and belonged to small universities and other institutions of higher education. Their relative size in terms of student enrollment is shown in Table 3.

Table 2 Law Students and Programs (1991 and 2001)

Year		Law Students				Law Programs		
		Private Law Schools		Public Law Schools				
	Total	Total	Women	Total	Women	Total	Private Programs	Public Programs
1991	110,944	17,282	6,875	93,662	38,528	118	72	46
		(15.58%)	(39.78%)	(84.42%)	(41.13%)		(61.02%)	(38.98%)
2001	189,864	85,911	40,213	104,481	51,943	506	431	75
		(45.25%)	(46.80%)	(54.75%)	(49.71%)		(85.18%)	(14.82%)

Source: ANUIES (1991; 2001).

Table 3 Law Programs by Size of Student Enrollment (1991 and 2001)

Student Enrollment	Public Law Programs				Private Law Programs			
	1991 (N=46)		2001 (N=75)		1991 (N=72)		2001 (N=431)	
Less than 50	1	2.2%	4	5.3%	11	15.3%	94	21.8%
51 to 100	2	3.3%	2	2.7%	10	13.9%	83	19.3%
100 to 250	3	6.5%	12	16.0%	25	34.7%	135	31.3%
251 to 500	4	8.7%	15	20.0%	15	20.8%	63	14.6%
501 to 1000	5	10.9%	7	9.3%	8	11.1%	35	8.1%
1001 to 2500	21	45.6%	24	32.0%	1	1.4%	6	1.4%
2501 to 5000	7	15.2%	7	9.3%	0	0.0%	1	0.2%
More than 5000	3	6.5%	4	5.3%	0	0.0%	0	0.0%

Source: ANUIES (1991; 2001). In 1991, two private schools do not report enrollment. In 2001, 13 private law schools do not report enrollment.

The table shows that a considerable proportion of private law schools (between 63 per cent and 70 per cent) have fewer than 250 students enrolled. The new private law schools tend to be smaller than before. So, for example, in 2001, about 20 per cent of all private facilities had fewer than 50 students, and 40 per cent had up to 100. By contrast, public law schools tend to be relatively large. In 1991, about ½ of all public law schools had between 1000 and 2500 students. Ten years later, and considering that no new public universities have been established since the 1980s, the additional 29 new public programs actually mean that there has been a process of decentralisation within existing state universities. Thus, in 2001, more than 40 per cent of programs had up to 500 students and only ⅓ had between 1000 and 2500 students.

With respect to the increase in the number of law schools, especially private institutions, two issues should be explored. First, we should ask how this increase can be explained. Again, is the establishment of so many new law schools a sign of the growing relevance of law in Mexican society? Or is it an indication that legal education can be good business? Is it driven by supply or by demand?

In general terms, there is still a large, unsatisfied demand for higher education in Mexico. Public universities have generally capped enrollment even though demand is increasing. In the case of the National University, demand for enrollment in law school grew on average 10 per cent annually between 1985 and 1995 from 7,856 to 20,627 candidates, but supply (first year enrollment) did not increase and in fact was reduced about 15 per cent, from 4,143 to 3,533 vacancies (Blanco and Rangel 1996:128,135). This has created an incentive for already existing private institutions of higher education to establish new law programs that absorb at least a part of unsatisfied demand. The state of Puebla is a good case in point. In 1991, there were a total of 13,571 students enrolled in seven law programs (12,272 alone in the state university). By 2001, a drastic reduction in the enrollment of the state university to 2,402 students allowed private law programs to grow four times to a total of 45, achieving a total enrollment of 6,457 students (so, the total number of students had actually decreased in comparison with ten years before). In 1991 only two locations outside the state capital had a law school; in 2001 this number had grown to 15 (ANUIES 1991; 2001).

In addition to this, it can be easily seen why law programs have expanded at an accelerated rate. The establishment of a new law school requires very little investment: at a minimum, it demands a classroom and an instructor. There is no real need to invest in a library (except a very basic one) or in an ambitious research and publications program. Moreover, private universities are subject to little control and regulation by the education authorities.

The second issue concerns the significance of the public/private divide in legal education. It can be shown that there are really no essential differences between public and private law schools when it comes to the curriculum, the teaching methods and even teachers themselves. Differences are to be found rather in extra-educational factors, such as the professional contacts and opportunities that students may obtain in law school. In this respect, it is obvious that students coming from the lower social classes do not find in their immediate family and social environment sufficient support and relevant relationships, except those they may be able to cultivate themselves in law school (Lomnitz and Salazar 2002). Thus, they are at a disadvantage from the very beginning *vis-à-vis* students from the upper classes. And among those that did not attend elite schools, this may happen quite apart from the fact that they have graduated from a private or a public law school.

The stratification and segmentation patterns that, also for historical reasons (cf. Dezalay and Garth 1995), can be observed in the Mexican legal profession, are partly a consequence of the public/private divide in legal education. Accordingly, graduates from public law schools tend rather to occupy positions in the public sector, while graduates from private schools have traditionally dominated elite business law firms. More recently, as a consequence of economic liberalisation and political democratisation in the 1980s and 1990s, the borders between both sectors have started to blur. In this process, graduates from elite private law schools are clearly at an advantage. They have started to enter the public sector and have extended their dominant position in the private sector. In short: they simply seem to have more success in entering the most lucrative, specialised and internationalised legal fields, while the graduates of public law schools seem to lag more and more behind, because presumably they are being offered inadequate legal training.

Quality of Legal Education

Finally, a last important issue that has to be addressed is the quality of legal education. Regarding the orientation and quality of legal training, for a long time the Faculty of Law of the National University (UNAM) played a leading role in legal education. Not only was it the most ancient and prestigious law school in the country. It was also the largest school and the most recognised center for political recruitment (Lomnitz and Salazar 2002). Private law schools adopted the UNAM's law curricula and even chose to have their diplomas recognised by the UNAM. This leading role has diminished in recent times, especially after the Faculty of Law introduced a new curriculum in 1993, so many private universities have gradually started to adopt their own curricula

According to many observers, legal education in public universities (UNAM, but also in some state universities with regional prestige, such as Guanajuato, Veracruz and San Luis Potosí) was acceptably good in the 1950s and 1960s. It began to decay with the 'massification' of public universities in the 1970s.[7] This was an important reason for the growth of pri-

---

[7] Some observers have the impression that although reduced in number, the most capable and bright students (and maybe also the worst) come still from the UNAM, perhaps because training in this university is more 'ecumenical': it transmits a more complete view of the law, and it is less directed to a specific market niche, as many private law schools are.

vate universities. But lately, limits have also been imposed on the growth of public law schools, and this means, as we have already seen, further opportunities for private law schools. These schools have also become attractive because they offer a particular professional orientation (for example, in corporate lawyering) and the opportunity to forge significant personal relationships. On the other hand, other schools offer simpler and shorter curricula (three years instead of the customary five).

When asked about the contents and quality of legal education, the same observers describe it as being still too traditional. It has stagnated, transmitting mostly legal-theoretical models of the 19th century. So, for example, while the number of available law books and titles for students has visibly increased, most of them do little more than reproduce traditional legal ideas and models. In fact, the 'classic' Mexican law books of the 1950s and 1960s are still widely used by law students and teachers (López Ayllón and Fix-Fierro 2003).

The great majority of teachers in law schools are not full-time professors, but practitioners who teach for a few hours a week. So, for example, according to recent data, of about 1,000 instructors at the Faculty of Law of the National University, less than 140 are 'career' professors ('La Facultad de Derecho de la UNAM en cifras' 2002:23). This makes it more likely that they will communicate traditional legal education and values. Moreover, teachers do not always update their knowledge and are hardly familiar with modern teaching techniques. Teaching methods still rely heavily on theoretical presentations and are very rarely problem-oriented. They tend to present an isolated view of the law, from both social reality and other social sciences (López Ayllón and Fix-Fierro 2003).

It should be noted, however, that technical legal skills are not, for the most part, the decisive criterion for evaluating a law graduate. Since the legal profession is still highly permeated by personal and social relationships (Dezalay and Garth 1995), law schools play an important role as recruiting centres and employment agencies. On the other hand, the skills expected from a law graduate are apparently so basic, that the quality of education prior to law school may be much more relevant to recruitment.

The overall impression one may get from legal education in Mexico nowadays is that law graduates do not receive a good or even sufficient legal training.[8] Some of its deficiencies are somewhat compensated by the

---

[8] According to the opinion of a colleague, most graduates from public law schools are not capable of practicing any meaningful legal work, because such schools were mostly created to solve an employment problem of middle-class groups. However, he attributes some 'civilizational value' to such legal training, in so far it transmits the notion that there were other options besides violence for solving social problems. In his eyes, the study of law has been, at best, a higher course in 'civic culture'.

training that legal practice itself provides. Most law students are not full-time students and many of them start working in law firms and public agencies after the first year in law school. Unfortunately, this practical training is completely detached from the formal training provided in law school.

If the quality of legal education is generally poor, and if legal technical skills are not decisive for practice, then how can a more technically demanding legal system be sustained? Indeed, there are some law schools which are attempting to modernise and update their curricula and teaching methods. They have also started to show much more openness towards other disciplines and foreign or international legal systems. They have established consortiums for the exchange of faculty members and students,[9] summer courses and joint doctoral programs with foreign universities. However, their impact on the quality of legal education in general is likely to remain limited in the short term.

It is also quite obvious that certain small sectors of the legal profession are capable of adapting quickly to the gap between legal education and the actual demands of legal practice, simply because their professional success depends on it. The question remains open, however, for the bulk of legal professionals.

On the whole, it is quite difficult to assess the quality of legal education. Objective criteria for evaluating law schools and law graduates, either formal or informal, are rather scarce. In 2000, an organisation called CENEVAL ('*Centro Nacional de Evaluación para la Educación Superior*') jointly established by the universities, other institutions of higher education and the government, started to evaluate law graduates through a standard, multiple-choice test that covers 12 areas (history and philosophy of law, constitutional law, civil and criminal law, procedure, international law, etc). According to its 1994–2001 report,[10] 8160 law graduates from 59 institutions submitted to the test in just two years. 309 (or 3.79 per cent) achieved a 'high performance attest'. Of course, the results of two years can be hardly representative of the performance levels of law schools, but it is interesting to note that graduates from public law schools achieved the highest mean grades.

More recently (2002), the daily newspaper *Reforma* has published, for the second time, a ranking of 72 universities in the metropolitan area of Mexico City with respect to the 16 most demanded areas of study.[11] The ranking derives from a survey conducted among students, internal and

---

[9] So, for example, the North American Consortium for Legal Education (NACLE), established by 3 Mexican, 3 Canadian and 3 American law schools (www.nacle.org.).
[10] Available on the Internet at www.ceneval.edu.mx (visited on 9 June 2003).
[11] See *Reforma*, August 26, 8 A.

external teachers, and employers. In the area of law, the five best law schools are private. The Faculty of Law of the National University occupies the sixth place. The first five places were taken by private law schools, but the distance between them and the public universities was not considerable.

Specialised Legal Training and Graduate Studies

Another important trend in the growth of legal education concerns the establishment of institutions for specialised and graduate legal training. As the degree for practicing law does not generally require specialised training for the different legal roles (judges, public prosecutors, attorneys), this function has been fulfilled by graduate studies ('posgrados') as part-time education.

Graduate legal studies have also experienced considerable growth. The most ancient and important graduate legal studies program belongs to the Faculty of Law of the National University (since 1951). In 2002, this institution offered 15 '*especializaciones*', ie, specialised professional training in the different areas of the law (in constitutional, administrative, procedural, private, criminal law, etc).[12] Other public universities outside Mexico City have also established graduate studies, which are mainly imparted during the weekend (Fridays and Saturdays) by local and non-local teachers.[13] Private universities have also opened graduate programs in Mexico City and elsewhere, with considerable success. Attendance, which includes local judges and other public officials, is growing. Since most of their students are already practicing lawyers, private universities (and to some extent also public universities) may charge considerable fees, and thus they are able to hire prestigious scholars and practitioners, both local and non-local, usually for individual weekend sessions.

In 2000 there were 7325 students in '*posgrado*' law programs, an increase of about 45 per cent with respect to 1998 (ANUIES 1998, 2000). 1862 students were studying an '*especialización*', while 5148 and 315 students were pursuing a 'masters' or doctoral degrees, respectively. However, the relatively low participation of graduate law studies in relation to total enrollment in law school seems to confirm the hypothesis that professional practice requires only an undergraduate degree. This has been

[12] Paradoxically, although the '*especializaciones*' at the Faculty of Law of the National University were created with the aim of solving the problems of specialized training for the legal practice, they are often rejected in favor of more academic degrees for prestige reasons.
[13] The Consejo Nacional de Ciencia y Tecnología (CONACyT) has a specific program for giving support to postgraduate studies outside Mexico City, provided certain requirements are fulfilled.

made possible by the existence of the informal training provided by professional practice, which starts during the students' stay in school.

We should also consider the number of students who study abroad. Traditionally, law graduates prefer to study in Europe (mostly in France, Italy and Spain) because of the proximity of legal traditions and languages. However, since the NAFTA entered into force in 1994, legal exchanges with the United States and Canada have been steadily growing. So, it would not be surprising to find that the number of students wishing to study there—especially those who want to go into private professional practice in the areas of business, trade and finance—has also been growing.

Not only university graduate studies have expanded. There has been also an identifiable trend towards the establishment of various institutes, centres, schools, etc for specialised legal training. Presently, courts and tribunals, both federal and state, have established their own judicial schools. In 1978, the Federal Judiciary created the '*Instituto de Especialización Judicial*', which offers a regular annual course since 1983. It changed its name to '*Instituto de la Judicatura Federal*' in 1995 and has expanded its courses, both in Mexico City and outside the capital (Esquinca Muñoa 1999). In 2000, it started an intensive six-month training program for candidates to a district or circuit judgeship (Báez Silva 2001). The federal Electoral Court has its own training center and a recently established judicial school. Other federal tribunals, like the '*Tribunal Federal de Justicia Fiscal y Administrativa*' and the '*Tribunales Agrarios*', have also established their own specialised training centres. The state judiciaries have followed suit. In 2000, only four state judiciaries did not have their own training institute or center (Concha and Caballero 2001:10). However, this does not mean that they all operate regularly or that they satisfy judicial training needs.

The Legal Profession

Quantitative Overview

As already mentioned, in the last 30 years the number of Mexicans who have attended higher education has increased significantly. In 1970 the total number of professionals[14] was 267,012. This figure had grown to 1,897,377 by 1990. In other words, the percentage of professionals went

---

[14] The General Population Census (1990) defines a 'professional' as a person above 25 years stating to have completed at least four years of higher education.

from 1.6 per cent to 5.9 per cent of the population older than 25 years.[15] In 2000, there were 6,590,348 Mexican citizens, 18 years or older, who had completed at least one year of higher education and 1,828,757 had completed up to five years.

Table 4 shows the composition of the population of professionals in 1970 and 1990:[16]

Table 4 Number and Distribution of Professionals in Mexico by Area and Gender (1970 and 1990)

Area	Professionals				Distribution by Gender (percentage by area)	
	1970	/100K	1990	/100K	1990 M	F
Engineering	86,777 (26.7%)	179.9	312,493 (16.5%)	384.6	236,456 (75.7%)	76,037 (24.3%)
Medicine	42,141 (13.0%)	87.4	165,185 (8.7%)	203.3	118,648 (71.8%)	46,537 (28.2%)
Accounting	39,925 (12.3%)	82.8	201,765 (10.6%)	248.3	135,732 (67.3%)	66,033 (32.7%)
Law	35,333 (10.9%)	73.3	141,539 (7.5%)	174.2	106,557 (75.3%)	34,982 (24.7%)
Architecture	11,191 (3.4%)	23.2	62,482 (3.3%)	76.9	52,537 (84.1%)	9,945 (15.9%)
Economics	10,407 (3.2%)	21.6	35,695 (1.9%)	48.8	27,323 (76.5%)	8372 (23.5%)
Business Administration	7649 (2.4%)	15.9	131,310 (6.9%)	161.6	91,123 (69.4%)	40,187 (30.6%)
Political Science and Public Administration	4303 (1.3%)	8.9	15,166 (0.8%)	18.7	9273 (61.1%)	5893 (38.9%)
Social Sciences	2931 (0.9%)	6.1	29,486 (1.6%)	36.3	8648 (29.3%)	20,838 (70.7%)

Source: Secretaría de Industria y Comercio (1972) and INEGI (1993).

[15] Source: INEGI, 1993.
[16] Data for those two years are not completely comparable. For 1970, we have taken the number of persons having completed four o more years of higher education, regardless of age. For the purposes of the following table, we estimate the total number of professionals for 1970 at 324,671. By many accounts, the 1980 population census is not reliable enough, so we have not used it. The corresponding figures for the 2000 population census have not been released yet.

Table 5 Distribution of Professionals by Occupation Practice Setting (1990)

Profession	Occupied	Professionals	Technicians	Education	Government and Executives	Office Personnel
Accounting	168,480 (83.5%)	64,520 (38.3%)	12,116 (7.2%)	4,126 (2.4%)	39,551 (23.5%)	28,462 (16.9%)
Medicine	135,703 (82.2%)	108,406 (79.9%)	2,467 (1.8%)	3,781 (2.8%)	6,195 (4.6%)	8,516 (6.3%)
Law	118,964 (84.0%)	61,048 (51.3%)	1,880 (1.6%)	7,993 (6.7%)	14,550 (12.2%)	20,335 (17.1%)
Business Administration	109,576 (83.4%)	12,329 (11.3%)	4,384 (4.0%)	4,617 (4.2%)	39,802 (36.3%)	26,529 (24.2%)
Economics	30,390 (85.1%)	4,495 (14.8%)	1,474 (4.9%)	3,230 (10.6%)	7,863 (25.9%)	8,591 (28.3%)
Social Sciences	22,092 (74.9%)	2,866 (13.0%)	3,407 (15.4%)	7,345 (33.2%)	1,824 (8.3%)	4,587 (20.8%)
Political Science/ Public Administration	12,092 (79.7%)	1469 (12.1%)	635 (5.3%)	1089 (9.0%)	2732 (22.6%)	3996 (33.0%)

Source: XI Censo General de Población (1990) and INEGI 1993.
Note: The table includes the four professions with most number of professionals, as well as others areas with affinity to law in Mexico. The percentage of the column 'occupied' refers to the total number of professionals in that area. The percentages of the other columns refer to the total number of professionals occupied in that area. The column of 'professionals' may or may not be related with the practice in that area.

As we can see, law was both in 1970 and 1990 the second most important profession in the area of the social sciences. The number of legal professionals was quadrupled in absolute terms and almost doubled in proportion to the total population. However, its relative size with respect to the total number of professionals decreased from almost 11 per cent to 7.5 per cent during the 20-year period. It is interesting to notice that women represented only 24.7 per cent of legal professionals in 1990. However, as we have seen, the percentage of women studying law was already significantly higher (41 per cent in 1991 and 48.4 per cent in 2001).[17] Some available data indicate that the gap between male and female legal professionals may have been progressively reduced in the last ten years.

Of 141,539 legal professionals identified in the census of 1990, 84 per cent had an occupation, but, according to our estimates, only 63.5 per cent

[17] Source: ANUIES, 1991, and ANUIES, 2000.

were likely to work in activities directly related to the law (professionals and government categories). Available data do not allow us to determine with more detail the real rates of practice setting for legal professionals in Mexico. Table 5 summarises the situation for 1990.

We can compare these data with the number of legal professionals registered with the authorities charged with regulating the professions. According to data provided by the Federal Secretariat of Education, of about 222,000 law degrees registered between 1945 and 2002 (⅔ after 1990 alone!), the overwhelming majority have been granted by public universities. The National University (UNAM) has granted more than 50,000 degrees alone, almost a fourth of the total number. Still, we do not know for certain how many belong to practicing lawyers. According to one estimate, there are about 40,000 practicing attorneys in the country.[18]

The Legal Elite

We have already said that the Mexican legal profession is more or less sharply divided between an elite and the bulk of legal professionals. The elite has been relatively influential—perhaps less for their legal skills than for their capabilities at building social networks—and visible. It has been capable of adapting to recent changes and opening towards foreign legal systems. According to Dezalay and Garth (1995), however, the legal elite itself was divided between the private sector and the public sector elite, as a consequence of the cleavage between the political and economic elites of the country that the Mexican Revolution had brought about. This cleavage has started to mend recently and the sharp separation between private-sector and government lawyers is becoming more fluid.

Lawyers in Government

Between the mid-forties and the eighties, a large number of top-level government officials, including the President of the Republic, had a law degree. Numerous studies used to show the importance of legal training, particularly at the Faculty of Law of the UNAM, as the main road to initiate and succeed in a political carrier. Obviously, technical skills may have been less important for political recruitment than the informal networks created among professors and classmates. To 'know who' could have much more weight and influence than to 'know how' (Dezalay and Garth 1995:9; 1997).

---

[18] Claus von Wobeser, former president of the Barra Mexicana Colegio de Abogados, personal communication.

In 1979, an American scholar would still recommend to a young person with political ambitions to go to the National University (UNAM) as an excellent place for making contacts, alliances and friendships. Once at UNAM, it was important to choose a discipline with care. Law had traditionally offered the optimal prospect for a political career, but economics— he added—had been steadily gaining importance over time (Smith 1979:245–50). In fact, the Mexican government was almost on the eve of a major financial crisis that forced it to launch an economic turnaround after 1982. This certainly contributed further to the displacement of lawyers from many of the top-level positions of the federal government (secretaries and undersecretaries of State). Table 6 shows the university degrees of members of the original cabinet of each presidential term after 1946:

Table 6 University Degrees of Members of the Original Cabinet for each Presidential Term between 1946 and 1994 (in %)

Presidential Term	Law	Economics	Medicine	Engineering	Other
1946–1952	68	4	6	16	6
1952–1958	52	4	7	19	18
1958–1964	46	7	15	10	22
1964–1970	48	13	13	14	12
1970–1976	45	17	8	14	16
1976–1982	42	19	8	11	20
1982–1988	39	26	3	14	18
1988–1994	23	23	6	19	29
1994–2000	32	36	All other 32		
2000–*	25	30	All other 45		

Source: Camp (1996, 137; 1995, 54). Presidencia de la República, Website <www.presidencia.gob.mx>, September 2003.
* Refers to 20 cabinet-level positions only. As of September 2003, law had gained two more positions and economics had lost one.

The table clearly shows the diminishing presence of lawyers in top government positions and the growing presence of economists, but also of other professionals. Of course, it would be legitimate to ask to what extent the presence of lawyers in government could be explained precisely by their abilities as lawyers and to what extent was law a preferred university degree in the absence of other options, particularly for the older generations. Nevertheless, changes in the composition of the governmental elite and the displacement of lawyers from the most important positions may have several effects. The most important is the likelihood that law and lawyers may begin to play a more autonomous and technical role in government. In contrast to the traditional elite, the new political elite is characterised by the use of technical skills, mainly in economics and administration. From their point of view, traditional legal training denied lawyers the technical knowledge to 'solve problems'. At first, the decision-makers that came to government after 1988 disregarded law as an instrument, but they rapidly learned that it was a necessary and decisive tool to implement their new policies (Dezalay and Garth 1995:60).

As already stated, this opens the door for a more 'technical' and less political role for lawyers in government,[19] especially in some areas. However, the number of lawyers trained in such matters is still relatively small and the traditional legal education does not provide this kind of technical skills. It is not surprising, then, that the 'new lawyers' in government are relatively young and come from private law schools rather than public universities.[20] Yves Dezalay and Bryant Garth (1995) have shown precisely how and why lawyers possessing the new legal-technical skills required in government have begun to come from the private and academic sectors, and how the new technical role of lawyers in certain areas, like international trade and investment, human rights and elections, has gone hand in hand with what they call the 'international strategies' of lawyers, ie, the legitimacy that flows from the links they cultivate with the foreign centres of economic, political and academic power.

Lawyers in Congress

Parliaments and legislative assemblies have traditionally belonged to the domains of lawyers. Of course, these lawyers are politicians in the first place, but legal expertise comes in handy when dealing with the technology of government and one of its central instruments, legislation. During the heyday of presidential rule in Mexico, legislation was not really 'made' in Congress. Legislative bills, including proposals for constitutional amendments, were usually prepared by administrative agencies, as well as by the office of the Presidency. Even the bill's evaluation ('dictamen legislativo') by the Congress was also frequently prepared by administration officials. This way of doing things started to slowly change in the 1980s and 1990s, as

---

[19] According to one of our informants, when lawyers dominated the top governmental posts, decisions were made following either legal or political criteria, but in any case, legal forms and procedures were respected.

[20] Dezalay & Garth, 1995, p 58, report that the lawyers' group that participated in the NAFTA (1991–1993) negotiations was on average 25–27 years old. Our data indicate that graduates from the National University represented 26% of the group. From the original group, only three lawyers remained in public service after 1994. The rest works either in major law firms or as counsel for private firms. In 2000, the office of the legal counsel for international trade negotiations in SECOFI was composed of lawyers averaging less than 30 years of age. Only one of them had graduated at the Faculty of Law of the UNAM.

opposition parties increasingly gained presence in the Chamber of Deputies. The ruling party had now to engage in political negotiations, and this led frequently to the introduction of changes in the presidential bills.[21] According to some observers, however, the technical quality of legislation began to decay with democratisation (López-Ayllón and Fix-Fierro 2003).

Table 7 Professionals in the Federal Chamber of Deputies (1982–1985 and 2000–2003)

	LII Congress (1982–1985) (N=375)	LVIII Congress (2000–2003) (N=500)
All professionals	267 (71.2%)	457 (91.4%)
Lawyers	116	162
As percentage of Chamber of Deputies	(30.9%)	(32.4%)
As percentage of professionals	(43.4%)	(35.4%)
Engineering	14 (3.7%) (5.2%)	53 (10.6%) (11.6%)
Accounting	23 (6.1%) (8.6%)	41 (8.2%) (9%)
Education	38 (10.1%) (14.2%)	35 (7%) (7.7%)
Administration	13 (3.5%) (4.9%)	35 (7%) (7.7%)
Economics	23 (6.1%) (8.6%)	27 (5.4%) (5.9%)
Health	12 (3.2%) (4.5%)	27 (5.4%) (5.9%)

Source: Presidencia de la República (1984); Congreso de la Unión (2001)
Notes: the table includes deputies with non-completed degrees. 'Lawyers' include deputies with other studies. They are accounted for only as lawyers. 'Education' includes teachers of different levels. 'Health' includes veterinarians and dentists. 'Engineers' includes all kinds of engineering. 'Administration' includes public and business administration.

[21] For example, Raigosa, 1995, 213 f, provides data on the amendment of federal criminal laws between 1982 and 1988. Thus, out of 82 legislative acts, 76 were legislative bills introduced by the Executive and the rest by members of the legislature. Changes were introduced

In view of the growing political weight of the Federal Congress, a reasonable assumption is to expect political parties to invest more resources in
legal-technical capital by sending more of their members with legal skills to
Congress. A comparison of the composition of the Chamber of Deputies
during two different periods (1982–1985 and 2000–2003) may yield some
evidence with respect to this assumption.

The preceding table shows that lawyers were, and are still, the most
important profession in the Mexican Federal Chamber of Deputies. Their
presence in the Chamber of Deputies as a percentage of the total number
of deputies did not decrease but slightly increased in the 18-year period
between 1982 and 2000. Furthermore, even if we could expect an important decrease in their relative presence vis-à-vis other professionals, it is
remarkable that they lost little terrain, considering that all other professions (with the exception of economics and education) also gained new
spaces. However, the data in the table do not clearly confirm the hypothesis that political parties would invest more political capital in legal
resources. The following table does not provide conclusive evidence either:

Table 8 Lawyers in the Federal Chamber of Deputies by Political Party and
Percentage of Parliamentary Group (1982–1985 and 2000–2003)

	LII Congress (1982–1985)	LVIII Congress (2000–2003)
Partido Revolucionario Institucional (PRI)	85 (29.3%)	80 (38.3%)
Partido Acción Nacional (PAN)	19 (38%)	65 (31.5%)
Leftist Parties/ Partido de la Revolución Democrática (PRD)	11 (47.8%)	12 (23%)

Source: Presidencia de la República (1984); Congreso de la Unión (2001)
Note: the PRD was founded in 1989 and incorporated most of the then existing leftist parties.

The preceding table shows an increase in the percentage of lawyers in the
parliamentary group of the then hegemonic and now opposition party, the
PRI, and a relative decline of the number of lawyers in the parliamentary
groups of the then opposition PAN (now in government) and the leftist parties, including their successor party, the PRD. Rather than being a sign of the

in the chamber of origin to 63 of the 82 bills, mostly by legislative committees. By contrast,
the reviewing chamber introduced changes only on two occasions. There is another interesting study (Díaz Cayeros & Magaloni, 1998) which explores the changes introduced to the
draft budget submitted annually by the President to the Chamber of Deputies in the period
between 1960 and 1994. Not surprisingly, such changes become more frequent after 1982.

relative investment of political parties in legal capital, the data may be more readily explained by the particular evolution of each party. In the case of the PRI, the higher proportion of lawyer may mean the growing influence of middle-class and educated groups at the interior of the party, at the expense of its traditional social bases (peasants, workers, teachers, etc). With respect to the other two parties, the explanation is different. Twenty years ago, the leftist parties and PAN were small, cadre-based parties, with a small, limited presence in Congress and which barely survived under the crushing weight of the hegemonic party, the PRI. Their leadership was constituted of a small group of officials among whom lawyers seemed to enjoy a large presence. As their membership and presence in Congress has grown, they have had to diversify their political and social bases. This may explain why the presence of lawyers within their parliamentary groups has been actually reduced.

As already explained, with democratisation, the technical level of legislation has declined. This may suggest the opposite hypothesis, ie, that representatives, even if they possess a law degree, are rather pursuing a political career and are more concerned with successful political bargaining than with the technical requirements of law-making. The following table gives an overview of lawyers with previous experience in government and Congress:

Table 9 Lawyers with Previous Experience in Government (1982–1985 and 2000–2003)

Previous Experience in Government/ Congress	*LII Congress (1982–1985)*	*LVIII Congress (2000–2003)*
1 post	59	96
	(50.9%)	(59.6%)
2 posts	34	72
	(29.3%)	(44.7%)
3 posts	19	49
	(16.4%)	(30.4%)
4 posts	9	27
	(7.8%)	(16.8%)
Previous legislative experience	48	77
	(41.4%)	(47.8%)

Source: Presidencia de la República (1984); Congreso de la Unión 2001

The table shows that a significant number of lawyers in the Federal Chamber of Deputies have previous legislative experience (almost ½ of them), which may be helpful in legislative activities, especially if we consider that in Mexico there is still no legislative career (immediate reelection is forbidden). The number of those who have previous experience in government is high (between 50 per cent and 60 per cent), and the percentage grows in the 19-year period.

Federal Judges: Change and Continuity in the Judicial Elite

The federal judiciary undoubtedly belongs to the legal elite of the country. In contrast with the state judiciaries, federal judges have always enjoyed considerable authority, prestige, and independence. Even considering the authoritarian nature of the PRI-regime, the federal judiciary enjoyed an effective degree of independence and respect as the ultimate guarantor of constitutional rights. However, its resources and powers were limited. Politically sensitive matters, such as electoral disputes, were either not decided by the courts, or the courts themselves would find a way to avoid them. The federal judiciary was relatively isolated from external social developments. The Supreme Court, in particular, voluntarily cultivated a low public profile.

The relative authority and independence of the federal judiciary can be partly explained by the recruitment system that was used between 1944 and 1994. Such independence was partly made possible by the existence of an informal judicial career that allowed judges to remain in office for long periods. Thus, about ½ the justices appointed to the Supreme Court between 1944 and 1994 had pursued a career at the federal judiciary, and they subsequently stayed on the Court for eleven or more years (the presidential term is six years).[22] Their appointments were in contrast with more transient appointees, who left the Court after a few years, either to retire or to occupy more attractive political positions (Fix-Fierro 1999).

This recruitment system was altered in 1994. With respect to the federal judiciary, the 1994 reform changed the rules regarding the appointment and terms of office of Supreme Court justices.[23] The most fundamental change, however, involved the strengthening of the Court's powers of judicial review, giving it a more clear profile as a constitutional court according to the European model. For this reason, the composition of the Court was altered and the number of justices was reduced from 26 to 11. With the exception of two justices, who were reappointed at the beginning of 1995, the other sitting justices were sent into early retirement. Unlike European-style constitutional courts, however, in which a majority of justices do not usually come from the ordinary courts, the judicial component of the Mexican Supreme Court became more, not less, accentuated after

---

[22] According to an unwritten rule, the President of the Republic made about half the appointments to the Supreme Court among the members of the judicial career.

[23] The new rules are also designed to discourage 'political' appointments and the use of the Supreme Court as a sort of spring board for other offices. The Constitution now requires that candidates to the Supreme Court not have occupied high political positions, such as Secretary of State, Attorney General, member of Congress, etc during the year prior to their appointment (Article 95, section VI Mex Const). Likewise, they may not occupy any of these positions for a period of two years after retiring from the Supreme Court (Article 101 Mex Const).

the 1987 and 1994 reforms (Fix-Fierro 2003). Table 10 presents the personal and professional profiles of Supreme Court justices between 1984 and 2003, a twenty-year period in which the Court's composition almost completely changed twice:

Table 10 Personal and Professional Profiles of Supreme Court Justices (1984, 1993 and 2003)

	1984 *(N=26)*	*1993* *(N=25)*	*2003* *(N=11)*
Place of Birth	10 States	13 States	7 States
Federal District	10	10	3
(38.5%)	(40%)	(27.3%)	
Women	3	5	1
(11.5%)	(20%)	(9.9%)	
Age	61.5 years	58.8 years	67.1 years
At Entrance into the Judiciary*	32.2 years	28 years	30.6 years
At Appointment as SC Justice	53.6 years	51.8 years	59.1 years
Legal Training			
Number of Law Schools	5	6	4
Graduates of Public Schools	24	23	9
	(92.3%)	(92%)	(81.8%)
National University (UNAM)	20	18	8
	(77%)	(72%)	(72.7%)
Seniority			
In the Federal Judiciary*	27 years	27 years	32.4 years
In Office	8 years	7 years	9.9 years
Career at the Federal Judiciary	16	13	8
	(60%)	(52%)	(73%)
Clerk at the Supreme Court	14	12	8
	(54%)	(48%)	(73%)
District Judge	8	8	7
	(31%)	(32%)	(64%)
Circuit Judge	11	19	7
	(42%)	(40%)	(64%)

Source: Diccionario biográfico del Gobierno Mexicano, 1984, and Directorios biográficos del Poder Judicial de la Federación 1993 and 1996.
*'Age at entrance' and 'seniority in the Federal Judiciary' refers only to the eight justices with judicial career.

Until 1995, the Supreme Court of Justice appointed lower federal judges. There were no explicit rules, but an informal judicial career had developed within the federal judiciary after 1944 (Cossío Díaz 1996). This career went normally from the lower posts of the district and circuit courts to the position of a clerk ('secretario') at the Supreme Court. From there, a Supreme Court clerk was likely to be appointed as a district judge at the proposal, by turn, of one of the justices. Clerks remained in the Supreme Court for a period between three and six years, in close contact with one of the justices. During this time they not only were trained in the way things were done. They also had the chance to 'absorb', so to speak, the basic judicial philosophy of the federal judiciary and they were also evaluated as to their personal qualifications for occupying a judicial post.

After 1984, the federal judiciary began to grow rapidly and the appointment of judges accelerated. The need to make ever more frequent appointments also reinforced the tendency towards internal 'clientelism'. According to an implicit informal agreement, justices would normally consent to the appointments proposed by their fellow justices (Cossío Díaz 1996:65–66). This meant, for practical purposes, that lower judges would feel obliged towards the justice who proposed their appointment. This, in turn, contributed to the formation of 'family-like' groups of judicial officials, headed by the Supreme Court justices themselves (Soberanes Fernández 1993:453). The perception that this system did not guarantee the personal and professional qualifications of candidates to a judicial post any more was a major consideration for the 1994 judicial reform (Cossío Díaz 1996:72). This reform established the Council of the Federal Judiciary as a body charged with the administration a formal system for the selection and appointment of district and circuit judges through written and oral examinations (*'concursos de oposición'*).

Excluding the eleven justices sitting on the Supreme Court and the judges on the electoral court, at the end of 1995 there were 472 federal judgeships (176 district judgeships and 296 circuit judgeships). At the end of 2002, this number had grown to 822 (264 district judgeships and 558 circuit judgeships), an increase of 74.1 per cent. Over the same period, however, a total of 490 district judges (185.6 per cent of the total number of district judges at the end of 2002) and 387 circuit judges (84.5 per cent of their total number at the end of the same year) were selected. Table 11 gives an overview of the number of appointments between 1987 and 2002.

The table clearly shows that in the 8-year period between 1995 and 2002, there were nearly twice as many appointments in comparison with the preceding 8 years (1987–1994). High turnover and the new appointment system have introduced some interesting changes in the personal and professional profiles of circuit and district judges. However, it is also true

Table 11 Appointments of Circuit and District Judges (1987–2002)

Year	Appointments	
	District Judges	*Circuit Judges*
1987	43	49
1988	48	26
1989	18	12
1990	31	40
1991	35	24
1992	25	24
1993	21	15
1994	33	17
1995	28	14
1996	62	52
1997	60	32
1998	0	11
1999	97	97
2000	85	70
2001	80	44
2002	78	67
Total 1987–1994	254	207
Total 1995–2002	490	387
Total 1987–2002	744	594

Source: Informes anuales de labores de la Suprema Corte de Justicia de la Nación 1987–2002; Consejo de la Judicatura Federal, Website <www.cjf.gob.mx>.

that the degree of continuity remains quite remarkable. Table 12 provides some interesting data on both counts.

Among the most significant signs of continuity in the almost 20-year period between 1984 and 2002 we may mention the following:

—*Age*. Average age of circuit and district judges is very similar in both years, as is the age at appointment. In any case, age of entrance to the judiciary is slightly reduced.

—*Socio-economic class*. Socio-economic class may be approximately deduced from the father's occupation. Accordingly, federal judges come mainly from the middle and lower-middle classes. Notice that the proportion of judges who are children of lawyers is not very high and seems to remain stable throughout the period.

—*Seniority*. As with age, average seniority of judges is similar in both years; in any case, it increases by more than two years in the case of circuit

Table 12 Personal and Professional Profiles of Circuit and District Judges (1984 and 2002)

	District Judges		Circuit Judges	
	1984	2002	1984	2002
	(N=97)	(N=257)	(N=87)	(N=535)
Place of Birth	20 States	28 States	25 States	31 States
Federal District	16	67	9	123
	(16.5%)	(26.0%)	(10.3%)	(23.0%)
Assignment at Place of Birth	20	46	11	155
	(20.6%)	(17.9%)	(12.6%)	(29.0%)
Women	6	59	5	92
	(6.6%)	(23.00%)	(5.7%)	(17.2%)
Age	44.8 years	42.3 years	50.9 years	50.8 years
At Entrance into Federal Judiciary	29.4 years	26.8 years	29.3 years	27.5 years
At Appointment as District Judge	40.4 years	39.8 years	39.5 years	39.3 years
At Appointment as Circuit Judge			43.7 years	43.7 years
Father's Occupation		(N= 162)		(N= 90)
Jurist	11.3%	13.3%	12.6%	13.3%
Professional (All)	22.3%	26.0%	31.0%	24.4%
Merchant	28.7%	21.8%	21.8%	22.2%
Public Servant/Employee	17.0%	26.0%	23.0%	30.0%
Worker/Artisan	10.6%	15.2%	8.0%	11.1%
Peasant/Farmer	13.8%	9.0%	13.8%	11.1%
Entrepreneur	5.3%	1.2%	1.1%	0.0%
Other	2.1%	0.6%	1.1%	1.1%
Law School				
Number of Schools	21	42	16	41
Graduates of Public Law Schools	90	224	84	497
	(95.7%)	(87.8%)	(97.7%)	(93.1%)
Graduates National University	33	70	33	182
(UNAM)	(34.5%)	(27.5%)	(38.4%)	(34.0%)
Seniority				
At the Federal Judiciary	15.1 years	15.2 years	21.1 years	23.6 years
At Appointment as District Judge	10.7 years	12.2 years	10.3 years	12.2 years
At Appointment as Circuit Judge	14.1 years	16.6 years		
As District Judge	4.4 years	2.4 years	5.0 years	4.3 years
As Circuit Judge			7.1 years	7.0 years
Judicial career				
Employee	14	83	7	122
	(14.4%)	(32.3%)	(8.0%)	(22.8%)
Court Executor	41	152	40	295
	(42.3%)	(59.1%)	(46.0%)	(55.1%)
Clerk at District Court	49	166	48	352
	(50.5%)	(64.6%)	(55.2%)	(65.8%)
Clerk at Circuit Court	58	225	43	432
	(59.8%)	(87.5%)	(49.4%)	(80.7%)
Clerk at Supreme Court	78	63	66	361
	(80.40%)	(24.5%)	(75.9%)	(67.5%)
District Judge			80	524
		(92.0%)	(98.1%)	

Source: own elaboration with data from the Consejo de la Judicatura Federal, Website: <http://www.cjf.gob.mx>, visited on May—June 2002 and February—March 2003; Presidencia de la República (1984); Poder Judicial de la Federación (1989, 1993, 1996) and Suprema Corte de Justicia de la Nación (1970–2002).

judges. Notice that seniority prior to appointment does not diminish, but increases. Thus, despite high internal turnover, judges in 2002 had no less prior experience, as individuals, than their predecessors on the bench had in 1984. Nevertheless, seniority in their current office is visibly reduced, especially in the case of district judges. This has to do with the fact that there are presently more circuit than district judgeships (about twice as many). Since circuit judges are normally selected among the ranks of district judges, the turnover at the level of district courts is higher. Indeed, in 2002 only 9 judges out of 257 (3.5 per cent) had been appointed to the bench *before* 1995. The comparable figure for circuit judges was 199 out of 535 (37.2 per cent).

Among the most significant changes we may identify the following:

—*Place of birth and assignment.* The table reveals a greater geographic diversity with respect to the place of birth of district and circuit judges. At the same time, the number of judges born in the Federal District (Mexico City) increases. A minority of judges are assigned to their place of birth, an evidence of the great geographic mobility that a federal judicial post entails.[24] However, it should be noted that whereas the percentage of district judges assigned to their place of birth diminishes between 1984 and 2002, it increases for the circuit judges, reaching almost 30 per cent.

—*Gender.* Women have clearly gained presence in the judiciary since 1984. However, such increasing presence seems to have stagnated since 1995,[25] which may indicate that they have not benefited from the higher opportu-

---

[24] Unlike federal judges in the United States, who are usually appointed and assigned to a court in their home state, changes in the assignment of federal judges in Mexico have been, and still are, quite frequent. According to the data we have, district and circuit judges in office in 1984 had been assigned, on average, 1.8 times to different geographical locations. Prior to 1995 there were no explicit rules governing the assignment process and judges could not challenge this decision. Thus, such changes could be used either to harass or to favor judges. It is reported that the one of the Supreme Court justices appointed in 1995 is a former judge who had been harassed in this way because he declined to decide a case in the way he was told he should decide. After several changes in assignment, he resigned his post (Dezalay & Garth, 1995, p 31, n 18, 74). The Organic Law of the Federal Judiciary contains now explicit rules regarding the criteria that govern the initial assignment of a judge after his or her appointment as well as regarding any future changes (Articles 118 and following). Any such decision can be appealed to the Supreme Court.

[25] In 1995, women occupied 21.8% and 16.4% of district and circuit judgeships, respectively (López Ayllón & Fix-Fierro, 2003).

nities offered by the introduction of a formal judicial career and the examination system.

—*Law school*. The number of law schools from which federal judges have graduated has doubled since 1984. The overwhelming majority still come from public universities, among which the National University still occupies a very significant position. However, the number of graduates of private law school has increased. Given the extraordinary growth of private institutions in the 1990s, we can expect a significant increase over the next ten to fifteen years in the number of judges who are graduates of those schools.

—*Judicial career*. Changes in the judicial career are also significant. The judicial career has become more strict and inward-looking, in the sense that an increasing number of judges have occupied all the posts that make up the judicial hierarchy. In particular, a majority of newly appointed district judges *have not* been clerks at the Supreme Court. Several explanations are possible. The most obvious one is derived from the judiciary's growth, which makes it almost impossible to assign the majority of vacant posts to Supreme Court clerks. In the second place, it may be also a reflection of the increasing specialisation of the Court's functions in constitutional matters. In any case, it means a loss of influence and control of the Supreme Court over the judicial career and, in the long term, on the attitudes and opinions of district and circuit judges.

In short, the data show that the introduction of a formal judicial career in 1995 did not generate a rupture, but the formalisation of something that already existed. This can be observed also in other processes of change without rupture in the country. They have proceeded through the substitution of formal, public and transparent rules by informal rules. They also show that it has been the accelerated pace of growth in the judiciary which explain the changes observed rather than the introduction of examinations for the selection and appointment of judges. This results in a mixture of change and continuity, of greater diversity and uniformity, ie, a transition whose ultimate consequences cannot be assessed yet.

Attorneys and Business Law Firms

The elite of attorneys is formed by a select number of law firms, most of them established in Mexico City. They have close ties to the business and industrial sector of the economy, and more recently, also to the government.[26]

---

[26] Dezalay & Garth, 1995, p 78: 'At present, Mexico's economic powers are served increasingly by legal intermediaries who can go between business and between business and the state,

The analysis in this section is based on the 39 law firms recommended by Latin Lawyer.[27] Latin Lawyer describes the Mexican legal marketplace as the 'most complex and interesting in Latin America', as a 'never-ending saga of changes and splits'. This is the reason why no truly large firms have emerged, as in Brazil and Argentina, and 'none of the larger firms have shown any significant growth over the last two years'. The oldest law firm in Mexico City is 120 years old, but the average age of business law firms is 29.5 years. The following table gives an overview of the most active periods in the establishment of business law firms in Mexico City:

Table 13 Establishment of Business Law Firms in Mexico City

Establishment	Number (N=39)
10 years or less	12 (30.8%)
11 to 20 years	11 (28.2%)
21 to 30 years	4 (10.2%)
31 to 40 years	2 (5.1%)
More than 40 years	10 (25.6%)

Source: Latin Lawyer,Website (http://www.latinlawyer.com, last visited on 6 September 2003).

According to the preceding table, almost 60 per cent of existing firms are 20 years old or less, ie, there were established after 1983. Many of these new firms were not really new, in the sense that their founding partners were just splitting from another law firm because of the lack of professional opportunity.[28] It may be also true that their establishment was just responding, as some would maliciously say, to their urge to see their names on a brass plaque outside the new firm's offices. However, the

all the time building on their own social capital and a primarily "made in USA" legal expertise'.

[27] www.latinlawyer.com, visited on 6 September 2003.

[28] In fact, according to some observers, the internal organization and operation of many business law firms are still very much dependent on the personal whims of partners, thus constraining the professional opportunities of younger lawyers. For this reason, a few firms are trying to 'institutionalize' their internal operation, ie, clearly defining the expectations coupled to the different categories of legal work.

opening of the Mexican economy towards the world market after 1982 and the entry into force of the North American Free Trade Agreement (NAFTA) with the United States and Canada in 1994 have brought along new business opportunities to which elite lawyers have promptly reacted, by opening new areas of practice in existing law firms or by establishing law firms with an innovative profile (for example, so-called multidisciplinary firms). Law firms north of the Rio Grande, and even European law firms, have also tried to establish a beach-head in the Mexican legal market during the past decade. They have either opened offices in Mexico City, or they have entered close alliances with Mexican law firms and lawyers.

With respect to size, law firms have on average 28.5 lawyers (partners and non-partners), with a maximum of 142 and a minimum of 3 lawyers. The following table provides an overview of business law firm size:

Table 14 Law Firm Size According to Total Number of Lawyers

Number of Lawyers	Number of Law Firms (N=39)
10 or less	9 (23.1%)
11 to 20	11 (28.2%)
21 to 30	7 (17.9%)
31 to 40	3 (7.7%)
More than 40	9 (23.1%)

Source: Latin Lawyer, Website (http://www.latinlawyer.com, last visited on 6 September 2003).

The table shows that over 50 per cent of law firms are relatively small, with no more than 20 lawyers. However, a significant number of law firms have more than 40 lawyers.

Law firms have on average 8.1 partners; the ratio of non-partners to partners is 2.5 to 1. Table 15 presents law firms according to the number of partners. More than 70 per cent of law firms have no more than 10 partners. The average partner/non-partner ratio grows with increasing number of partners. This may be a sign that in firms with more partners, non-partners have less opportunity to become partners and have therefore a stronger incentive to leave the firm and seek better opportunities elsewhere.

Table 15 Law Firm Size According to the Number of Partners and Partner/Non-Partner Ratio

Number of Partners	Number of Law Firms (N=39)	Average Partner/Non-Partner Ratio
5 or less	14 (35.9%)	2.0
6 to 10	14 (35.9%)	2.3
11 to 15	7 (17.9%)	2.5
More than 15	4 (10.3%)	3.1

Source: Latin Lawyer, Website (http://www.latinlawyer.com, last visited on 6 September 2003).

An analysis of the résumés of 227 partners of 26 among the 39 law firms recommended by Latin Lawyer[29] shows that Mexico City business lawyers are young and overwhelmingly male. They have attended mostly a small number of private law schools. A majority of them have pursued graduate studies, with many obtaining master's degrees in law or business administration at prestigious American universities. Some of them have worked, as already mentioned, in American law firms; a small group among them has even taken the bar exam, especially in the state of New York.

Partners are on average 44.6 years old; almost 72 per cent of partners are less than 50 years old.[30] Table 16 provides an overview of age groups of partners.

Only 13 partners (5.7 per cent) are women.[31] Thus, women are very far away from achieving the parity they now enjoy in law school. The percentage will surely increase in coming years: a majority of women partners (61.5 per cent) are less than 40 years old, ie, they belong to the younger generation. Of course, their small presence can be blamed on the traditional 'machista' culture in Mexico. And there is certainly something to this explanation. However, it may have more to do with the central importance of women in family life. Many women cannot, or do not want to, make the sacrifice of family time that becoming a partner means.

135 partners in the sample, or 59.5 per cent, mention having undertaken

[29] Data were obtained from the Websites of the respective law firms, visited between September 2002 and September 2003.
[30] The age of more than half the partners (61.6%) had to be estimated, because the Internet resumés did not mention year of birth. Their age was estimated according to their year of admission to the bar, taking an average age of 25 years as age of admission.
[31] Many more women are associates.

Table 16 Partners of Business Law Firms by Age Group

Age Group	Number of Partners (N=219)
30 to 39 years	91 (41.6%)
40 to 49 years	68 (31.0%)
50 to 59 years	36 (16.4%)
60 years or older	24 (11.0%)

Source: Websites of law firms.

graduate studies ('*posgrado*'). A majority of them (108, or 80 per cent) did so abroad (some of them in addition to graduate studies in Mexico). Of those, again an overwhelming majority (89, or 82.4 per cent) went to the United States.[32] Many managed to combine their stay in the United States with practice at an American law firm (notably so in New York). Their close familiarity with the legal system of the United States and the ways it operates allows these lawyers to move back and forth between both legal cultures with utmost ease; they become, so to speak, 'bi-cultural' lawyers (López-Ayllón and Fix-Fierro 1999).[33]

As already mentioned, an undergraduate law degree is all that takes to become a lawyer in Mexico. However, at some point obtaining a graduate degree began to be also very important and not only for prestige reasons, but because of strictly professional considerations. When did a significant number of lawyers start taking graduate courses before joining a business law firm? Table 17 shows the number of partners who mention having a graduate degree by age group.

The table shows no significant difference between the first two age groups, ie, partners who are less than 50 years old. By comparison, the percentage of partners 50 years or older who mention graduate studies is considerably lower. The trend towards obtaining graduate degrees seemed to have started in the 1980s, if we consider that partners in the two first age groups graduated from law school after 1979, that is, around that time that the opening of the Mexican economy towards the world market became inevitable.[34]

---

[32] The rest went to Europe (France, Spain, England and Italy).

[33] NAFTA opened the door for a liberalization of professional practice across the borders of the three countries. However, the divergent interests of the three countries, and especially the fear of Mexican lawyers of being swallowed by the big law firms from beyond the Rio Grande has prevented any further progress on this front. See Nelson, 1998.

[34] Dezalay & Garth, 1995, mention the Mexican debt crisis of 1982 as an opportunity for Mexican lawyers to acquire international exposure and skills.

Table 17 Partners with Graduate Studies by
Age Group

Age Group	Number of Partners/ Percentage of Age Group
30 to 39 years	58 (63.7%)
40 to 49 years	45 (66.2%)
50 to 59 years	17 (47.2%)
60 years or older	7 (29.2%)

Source: Websites of law firms.

We have seen in a previous section how the number of law schools has exploded in recent years. But even in the 1960s and 1970s there were already an important number of law schools, public and private. This diversity notwithstanding, the law firm partners we are surveying graduated from only 15 different Mexican law schools, five public and ten private.[35] The overwhelming majority attended law school in Mexico City; only six partners graduated from a law school outside the capital. The possible explanation is twofold: on the one hand, the most important business opportunities can be undoubtedly found in Mexico City, so it is only rational to go to law school there; and on the other hand, in many law firms a majority of partners, if not all, tend to come from the same school.

79 partners (35.3 per cent) in total graduated from a public law school and 145 (64.7 per cent) from a private law school. Despite a widespread perception that graduates from the National University (UNAM) go to the public sector and are not well trained for a career as business lawyers, a third of all law firm partners (33.5 per cent) did go to UNAM. However, the trend to graduate from private law schools becomes more visible if we look at the law schools by group age, according to Table 18.

Partners who graduated from law school in the mid-1960s or earlier overwhelmingly went to a public university. The current panorama, however, completely reverses the previous situation: young partners now overwhelmingly graduate from private law schools. Once again, the trend becomes visibly stronger in the 1980s.

[35] A couple of partners graduated from an American law school.

Table 18 *Law School of Law Firm Partners by Group Age*

	Age Group Public	Law School Private
30 to 39 years	18 (20%)	72 (80%)
40 to 49 years	18 (26.5%)	50 (73.5%)
50 to 59 years	22 (61.1%)	14 (38.9%)
60 years or older	19 (79.2%)	5 (20.8%)

Source: Websites of law firms.

The Organised Bar

We have stated elsewhere that in Mexico, to this day, it is sufficient to have a law degree to practice law as an attorney (with the exception of criminal, agrarian and labor law).[36] There are no other requirements, and in particular, there is no need to be affiliated with a bar association (*'barra* or *colegio de abogados'*). Still, lawyers are free to establish professional associations. State laws define the requirements for creating a professional association, as well as its rights and duties. Some states and the Federal District limit the number of associations that may be established within one profession or specialised branch of a profession, but others simply state that no two associations having the same or a very similar name may be registered. Some states require that professional associations have a minimum number of members (for example, 30 or 50), others do not. State authorities are charged with authorising the registration of a professional association and of monitoring its behavior. Professional associations, in turn, should monitor their members' behavior, promote continuing education and, in general, contribute towards the improvement of the profession. In addition to this, they may act as arbitrators should a dispute arise between a professional and her client. In view of the lack of specific evidence, we do have the overall impression that neither state authorities nor the *'barras'* take their monitoring responsibilities very seriously. Many bar associations have their own code of ethics, but they do not enforce it, and even if they tried to enforce it, the fact that affiliation is not mandatory deprives them of the necessary leverage for applying effective sanctions.

[36] In some states, the respective authorities may authorize a *'pasante'*, i.e, a student who has finished at least 80% of credits, to practice law for a limited period of time (up to 3 years).

From the point of view of professional advancement, bar associations are active to various degrees. They organise conferences and seminar on new legislation, sometimes in cooperation with public and private law schools. They occasionally make public statements in the press and other media taking a position with respect to the issues of legal policy of the day. However, even their members have the impression that they are more of a social club than effective organisations of practicing attorneys. At worst, they are political pressure groups. Thus, according to a recent study of the state judiciaries (Concha and Caballero 2001:217), many state chief judges believe that bar associations are largely organisations with political goals and which tend to flourish around election time. They argue that many '*barras*' do not perform any significant role with respect to the administration of justice and the legal system of the states. Thus, their commitment to the advancement of the profession and the strengthening of the rule of law could be seriously questioned.

Mandatory bar affiliation has been proposed as a means of controlling lawyers' behavior and performance. Since the 1930s, the Barra Mexicana Colegio de Abogados, the most prestigious of Mexican bar associations,[37] has debated the issue on several occasions. No conclusion has been reached yet, and even the considerable number of lawyers who favor mandatory affiliation concede that it will not be a panacea for the profession's ills (Barra Mexicana Colegio de Abogados 2002:61,78). For the time being, organisations like the Barra Mexicana bet on a gradual strategy of voluntary affiliation, with the intention of slowly gaining influence within the profession. In the long run, attorneys would come to appreciate the advantages of having strong and prestigious professional organisations.

Legal Scholars

In Mexico, the number of professional legal scholars is quite small. Universities employ only a few full-time law professors and researchers. The Faculty of Law of the National University, for example, has over 900 part-time instructors and only relatively few full-time professors who have also the obligation to do research. However, the system of so-called 'professors-researchers' has not worked well, because teaching duties absorb almost all the time available for research (see panel discussion in Debate, 1999). In addition to this, full-time professors and researchers lead a rather precarious life as professional legal scholars. Material resources, such as

---

[37] The Barra Mexicana Colegio de Abogados claims to have around 2000 members, with several chapters or corresponding associations outside Mexico City. The Barra Mexicana Website (www.bma.org.mx) provides basic data on about 1750 members (September 2003).

libraries and other facilities, are usually less than adequate, and salaries are not very attractive, especially for young aspiring scholars. In fact, many full-time professors and researchers combine their duties as legal scholars with other professional activities, as private practitioners or legal advisers. As cannot be otherwise expected, their commitment to legal science and scholarship takes a visible toll.

To this day, the only institution that seems to have been able to 'professionalise' legal research and scholarship is the '*Instituto de Investigaciones Jurídicas*' of the National University. Similar attempts have been made elsewhere, but they have not succeeded in becoming institutionalised, ie, they declined after their founding fathers or sponsors left or disappeared.[38]

The Instituto was founded in 1940 as an 'appendix' to the then National School of Jurisprudence by a small group of Spanish professors who had gone into exile after the Civil War. For a long time, and although it became independent from the Faculty of Law, the Instituto remained as a very small center of legal scholarship, without much visibility or influence. In 1966, the Instituto had only four full-time researchers, three of whom were Spaniards. A change in the Instituto's leadership combined with a university program for the academic training of young people, helped attract a new generation of legal scholars who had been abroad and generally started to adopt a more open and technical approach in the study of the law than their counterparts in law school. In Dezalay and Garth's words, legal scholars at the Instituto started to invest in 'pure law'. In the 1970s and 1980s the Instituto was able to expand its activities, establishing important links with academic institutions and legal scholars in many countries, especially in the Ibero-American world. When the time came in Mexico for starting a process of legal reform, several of the Instituto's members were well prepared to participate in the design and operation of the new, modern laws and institutions, like the national ombudsman for human rights established in 1990 (Dezalay and Garth 1995:25; 1997:123; Lomnitz and Salazar 2002; see also Instituto de Investigaciones Jurídicas, 2000).

At present, the Instituto has over 70 full-time researchers (which seems not to be much for a country now having more than 100 million inhabitants) and is still the main center for the production and dissemination of new legal knowledge, as well as for the recruitment of aspiring legal scholars. However, in recent years, there have been other notable efforts by both some other private and public law schools[39] at innovating the traditional

---

[38] Some of the most prestigious private law schools do have a tradition of publishing law books and legal journals. However, these efforts are not carried out by full-time scholars and are subject to the ups and downs of personal and institutional changes.

[39] For example, ITAM ('*Instituto Tecnológico Autónomo de México*') in the first case, and CIDE ('*Centro de Investigación y Docencia Económicas*') in the second, both in Mexico City.

curriculum and teaching methods. They have combined this with an attempt at building a small group of full-time scholars who are now quite active in the field of legal research and policy. Despite their growing success, these efforts still have to jump the hurdle of permanent institutionalisation.

The Legal Profession in Mexico: One, Many, or None?

Perhaps exaggerating and simplifying in excess, there are two basic ways to look at professions. On the one hand, they can be considered as a group of persons who attempt to collectively exploit the specialised knowledge they possess. They try to control to the extent possible the market for their expertise and the way it is produced and allocated in society. They act as gatekeepers who decide or participate somehow in the decision on who can and who cannot have access to the profession. This we could call the egotistical theory of professions. Another point of view—one which is not necessarily incompatible with the first approach—conceives of professions as a group of persons who perform a valuable social function. By mediating between citizens and legal and political institutions, they contribute to social integration and governance. This we could call the altruistic theory of professions. Under both perspectives, members of a profession cultivate a special solidarity—in the Durkheimian sense—that impels them to stick together and to continuously try to enhance the authority and prestige of the profession as a whole.

Judged by either one or the other standard, Mexican lawyers do not seem to constitute a profession. As a group, they are divided, segmented, and weak. They neither possess, nor attempt to gain, market control, nor do they seem intent enough on obtaining social prestige and political influence as a group. While they may feel sympathy and a certain degree of identification with their fellow lawyers, the interests and opportunities of the different groups of legal professionals do diverge in significant ways. Indeed, the panorama we have presented above points to a process of increasing polarization between the public and the private sectors of professional exercise, as well as between the legal elite and the bulk of lawyers.

The Mexican legal profession, if there is one, does not play a significant role in the process of institutional legitimacy nor in the overall governance of society. The fact that not too long ago the top positions in government were occupied by politicians with a law degree may have deceived lawyers into thinking that the rule of law(yers) had been effectively established. On the contrary, the rule of *legal form* they came to symbolise did not necessarily mean, and in a certain way precluded, the rule of law.

But perhaps it is wrong to speak of a *single* legal profession. It is a well-known fact that the two main legal traditions of the Western world—the common law and the civil law—show important differences in this respect. Whereas the common law world tends to think of the legal profession as *one*, ie, different legal roles (for example attorneys and judges) are regarded as the continuation or extension of a basic professional model, in the civil world it is easier to conceive of different legal professions (or distinct branches of the legal profession). Specialised training and early career opportunities after law school seem to warrant such a consideration. However, even in this case, there are still many communicating channels between these different professions, thus allowing for a kind of 'organic' or 'complementary' solidarity (again in the Durkheimian sense) between different groups or branches of legal professionals.

In the case of Mexico, and despite of recent changes that have somehow eased the isolation between the existing groups of legal professionals (so, for example, between lawyers in the public and private sectors, or between judges and legal scholars), we still do not perceive yet that an effective sense of 'organic' solidarity is emerging.[40] While there are also groups and institutions that are walking the path of change and innovation, the spillover effect of their activities remains very limited.

And then there is a growing awareness that a transformation of legal education and the legal profession is the other half, so to speak, of judicial reform (Fix-Fierro 2003; Gudiño Pelayo 2003). Recent studies document, for example, the utter ineffectiveness of defence lawyers and prosecutors in the criminal process (Bergman *et al* 2003; Pásara 2003). The federal government's concern with the disastrous state of criminal justice may result, in the end, in the introduction of quality controls for obtaining access to and permanence in the legal profession. This means, in short, that if Mexican lawyers ever attain a fraction of the power, prestige and authority they enjoyed at the end of the 19th and beginning of the 20th century, it will be because society forces them to assume a role and a responsibility that has eluded (or they have avoided) for a long time.

---

[40] According to a colleague who has been working for some years in the judiciary, 'academic' is still a word with bad implications in the closed and inward-looking world of Mexican judges. The fact that many of them teach does not seem to make them into 'academics'.

References

ANUIES Anuario estadístico. Población escolar de licenciatura en universidades e institutos tecnológicos. México, ANUIES, 1979, 1991, 1997, 1998, 2000, 2001.

ARENAL FENOCHIO, Jaime del. 1998. 'Abogados en la Ciudad de México a principios del siglo XX (la lista de Manuel Cruzado)', Anuario Mexicano de Historia del Derecho, vol. X.

BÁEZ SILVA, Carlos 'El entrenamiento práctico en el Instituto de la Judicatura Federal-Escuela Judicial: el caso de las prácticas de elaboración de proyectos y de dación de cuenta', 2001, 9, *Revista del Instituto de la Judicatura Federal*, 27–57.

BERGMAN, Marcelo, Elena AZAOLA, Ana Laura MAGALONI and Layda NEGRETE Delincuencia, marginalidad y desempeño institucional. Resultados de la encuesta a población en reclusión en tres entidades de la República Mexicana: Distrito Federal, Morelos y Estado de México, (México, CIDE (División de Estudios Jurídicos) 2003).

BLANCO, José and José RANGEL Las generaciones cambian. Un estudio sobre el desempeño académico de la UNAM, (México, UNAM, 1996).

CAMP, Roderic Ai 'El gabinete de Zedillo: ¿continuidad, cambio o revolución?', 1995, 51 *Este País*, June 46–54.

CAMP, Roderic Ai *El reclutamiento político en México*, (México, Siglo XXI Editores, 1996).

CONCHA CANTÚ, Hugo 'Construyendo la autonomía legal por la vía de la confrontación jurídica: la abogacia de deudores de la banca en Mexiioc, in Juan Vega and Edgar Corzo (eds) *Tribunales y justicia constituucional.Memoria del VII Congreso Iberoamericano de Derecho Constitucional* (México, UNAM, 2002) 137–163.

CONCHA CANTÚ, Hugo and José Antonio CABALLERO JUÁREZ Diagnóstico sobre la administración de justicia en las entidades federativas. Un estudio institucional sobre la justicia local en México, (México, UNAM-National Center for State Courts, 2001).

COSSÍO DÍAZ, José Ramón *Jurisdicción federal y carrera judicial en México*, (México, UNAM 1996)(Cuadernos para la Reforma de la Justicia, 4)

DEBATE 'La investigación jurídica en México (debate)', 1999, 2(7) *El mundo del abogado*, julio-agosto, 44–52.

DEZALAY, Yves and Bryant G GARTH Building the Law and Putting the State Into Play: International Strategies Among Mexico's Divided Elite, (Chicago, ABF, 1995) (ABF Working Paper 9509).

DEZALAY, Yves and Bryant G GARTH 'Law, Lawyers and Social Capital: "Rule of Law"versus Relational Capitalism', 1997, 6(1) *Social and Legal Studies*, 109–41.

DÍAZ CAYEROS, Alberto and Beatriz MAGALONI 'Autoridad presupuestal del poder legislativo en México: una primera aproximación', 1998, 5(2) *Política y gobierno*, segundo semestre, 503–28.

EL MUNDO DEL ABOGADO 'La Facultad de Derecho de la UNAM en cifras', 2002, 5(40) *El mundo del abogado*, August, 22–25.

ESQUINCA MUÑOA, César 'El Instituto de la Judicatura Federal', 1999, 4 *Revista del Instituto de la Judicatura Federal*, 61–92.

FACULTAD DE DERECHO DE LA UNAM Proyecto de reforma al plan de estudios de la licenciatura en derecho. México, Comisión especial (unpublished document), 2002.

FIX-FIERRO, Héctor 'Poder Judicial', in *Transiciones y diseños institucionales. Ma. del Refugio* GONZÁLEZ and Sergio LÓPEZ AYLLÓN (eds (México, UNAM, 1999).

FIX-FIERRO, Héctor 'Judicial Reform in Mexico: What Next?', in *Beyond Common Knowledge: Empirical Approaches to the Rule of Law*. Erik G Jensen and Thomas C Heller, eds (Stanford, Stanford University Press, 2003).

FIX-FIERRO, Héctor and Sergio LÓPEZ AYLLÓN 'Legalidad contra legitimidad. Los dilemas de la transición jurídica y el Estado de derecho en México', 2001, VIII(2) *Política y Gobierno*, segundo semestre, 347–93.

INEGI *Los profesionistas en México. Aguascalientes*, (Instituto Nacional de Estadística, Geografía e Informática, 1993.

GUDIÑO PELAYO, José de Jesús La calidad en la justicia: corresponsabilidad de jueces, litigantes y partes. Paper presented at the XII World Conference of Procedural Law, Mexico City, September, 2003 21–26 (downloaded from www.scjn.gob.mx/Ministros/jjgp/default.asp, February 2004).

INSTITUTO DE INVESTIGACIONES JURÍDICAS *Instituto de Investigaciones Jurídicas. Sexagésimo aniversario*, (México, UNAM, 2000).

LAWYERS COMMITTEE FOR HUMAN RIGHTS Injusticia legalizada. Procedimiento penal mexicano y derechos humanos. México: Lawyers Comittee for Human Rights-Centro de Derechos Humanos 'Miguel Agustín Pro Juárez' (trans. from Legalised Injustice: Mexican Criminal Procedure and Human Rights. New York: Lawyers Committee for Human Rights, 2001)

LOMNITZ, Larissa and Rodrigo SALAZAR 'Cultural Elements in the Practice of Law in Mexico. Informal Networks in a Formal System'. In *Global Prescriptions: The Production, Exportation and Importation of a New Legal Orthodoxy*. Yves DEZALAY and Bryant GARTH, eds (Ann Arbor, University of Michigan Press, 2002).

LÓPEZ AYLLÓN, Sergio 'Notes on Mexican Legal Culture', 1995, 4(4) *Social and Legal Studies*, 477–92.

LÓPEZ AYLLÓN, Sergio Las transformaciones del sistema jurídico y los significados sociales del derecho en México. La encrucijada entre tradición y modernidad, (México, UNAM, 1997).

LÓPEZ AYLLÓN, Sergio and Héctor FIX-FIERRO 'Communication Between Legal Cultures: The Case of NAFTA's Chapter 19 Binational Panels', in *The Evolution of Free Trade in the Americas/L'évolution du libre échange dans les Amériques*, L PERRET ed(Montréal, Wilson and Lafleur, 1999) 3–48 (Collection Bleue)

LÓPEZ AYLLÓN, Sergio and Héctor FIX-FIERRO '"Faraway, So Close!'Rule of Law and Legal Change in Mexico 1970–2000', in *Legal Culture in the Age of Globalisation: Latin America and Latin Europe*. Lawrence M FRIEDMAN and Rogelio PÉREZ PERDOMO, eds (Stanford, Stanford University Press, 2003).

LUHMANN, Niklas *Rechtssoziologie*, (Reinbek, Rowohlt, 1972) 2 vols.

MAYAGOITIA Y HAGELSTEIN, Alejandro 'Aspirantes al Ilustre y Real Colegio de Abogados de México. Extractos de sus informaciones de limpieza de sangre (1760–1823)', 1999, 21 *Ars Iuris*.

NELSON, Steven C 'Law Practice of US Attorneys in Mexico and Mexican Attorneys in the United States: A Status Report', *United States-Mexico Law Journal* 6, Spring, 71–80.

PÁSARA, Luis Cómo sentencian los jueces del DF en material penal. México, CIDE, June, 2003 (unpublished research report).

PODER JUDICIAL DE LA FEDERACIÓN *Directorios biográficos del Poder Judicial de la Federación*, (México, PJF, 1989, 1993, 1996).

PRESIDENCIA DE LA REPÚBLICA *Diccionario biográfico del gobierno mexicano 1984*, (México, Presidencia de la República-Diana, 1984).

RAIGOSA, Luis 'Algunas consideraciones sobre la creación de las leyes en México', 1995, *Isonomía* 3, octubre, 207–16.

SECRETARÍA DE INDUSTRIA Y COMERCIO *Resultados del IX Censo General de Población 1970*. (México, SIC, 1972).

SMITH, Peter Labyrinth of Power: Political Recruitment in Twentieth-Century Mexico, (Princeton, Princeton University Press, 1979).

SOBERANES FERNÁNDEZ, José Luis 'Informe sobre México', in *Situación y políticas judiciales en América Latina*, Jorge CORREA SUTIL, ed (Santiago de Chile, Universidad Diego Portales, 1993). 425–69 (Cuadernos de análisis jurídico, 2)

SUPREMA CORTE DE JUSTICIA DE LA NACIÓN Informes anuales de labores. México, SCJN, 1970–2000.

SUPREMA CORTE DE JUSTICIA DE LA NACIÓN Historia de la Suprema Corte de Justicia de la Nación. México, SCJN, 1985, several volumes.

10

Social Mobility and Hierarchical Structure in Canadian Law Practice*

FIONA M KAY
AND JOHN HAGAN

Introduction

Although women have already had a tremendous impact on the profession
of law through their rising numbers, their progress through the hierarchy
of the Canadian profession remains uncertain. Women have entered law
during a period of dramatic change to a firmly established and intensely
stratified profession. During the last 20 years, the Canadian bar has undergone impressive transformations in the forms of burgeoning numbers, rapidly expanding law firms with branch and international offices, mergers
between large law firms, the decline of solo practice, rising numbers of
lawyers working as employees in various settings, increasing specialisation
and expanding bureaucratisation, together with declining prestige of the
profession. A considerable body of research testifies to women's disadvantaged position vis-à-vis elite specialisations, senior management, and
enhanced remuneration in law. Yet, few studies have carefully explored
women's access to realms of genuine authority and power in practice.
Research has yet to fully examine the position of men and women lawyers

*An earlier version of this paper was presented in June 2002 at the annual meeting of the Law
and Society Association in Vancouver, British Columbia, Canada. The research reported here
was supported by a grant from the Social Sciences and Humanities Research Council of
Canada (Grant #816–96–003) in partnership with the Law Society of Upper Canada which
we gratefully acknowledge. The views expressed in this paper are those of the authors and do
not necessarily reflect the views of the Law Society of Upper Canada. We thank Karen Hindle
and Ryan Causton for valuable research assistance. Direct correspondence to Fiona M Kay,
Department of Sociology, Queen's University, Kingston, Ontario, Canada K7L 3N6. E-mail:
kayf@post.queensu.ca.

in the division of labor and control over work (Dixon and Seron 1995:405). Our study systematically examines the gender hierarchy in the Canadian legal profession through an innovative longitudinal study of lawyers across a range of practice settings. We argue that while women have made inroads to the elite echelons of law practice, breaking through the proverbial 'glass ceiling', invisible barriers remain that separate women from top levels and genuine authority in law practice.

Power and Hierarchy in Law Practice

Law practice reveals an intensely hierarchical structure, one that is continually reshaping itself in response to fluctuations in the market for legal services. One of the most impressive changes has been the continuing growth among the largest law firms in both Canada (Stager and Arthurs 1990:174) and the United States (Abel 1989:179). Daniels's study of 48 law firms across Canada reveals impressive rates of expansion during the period 1960 to 1990 (1999:807) and considerable geographic dispersion through branch and foreign offices (1993:157). Galanter (1983:153) describes this trend as 'mega-lawyering', characterised by the proliferation of large law firms, frequently with branch and international offices. The emergence of 'mega firms' has segmented private practice into parallel 'hemispheres' (Heinz and Laumann 1982; Nelson 1983) in which corporations and institutional clientele are generally represented by large law firms, while small businesses and individuals are represented by small firms or sole practitioners.

Concurrent with this trend, the relative number of sole practitioners has declined in recent decades while the proportion of private practitioners employed as associates has risen dramatically (Abel 1989; Curran *et al*, 1985; Hagan and Kay 1996). Within law firms, partnership has taken on multiple forms. In some cases, two categories of partners exist, the lower of which enjoy only limited rights to share in profits and management. Some large firms have also created a second tier of associates, known as staff attorneys, who are assigned yearly contracts and informed unequivocally that they will not be considered for partnership (Abel 1989:96). These contractual relations have shifted legal practice, traditionally organised around sole practitioners, to a mode of practice more often organised around law firms with tiered levels of partners and lawyer employees (Giesel 1993; Hagan *et al* 1991:240–41; Nelson 1988:141).

In short, the legal profession exhibits its own class structure (Hagan *et al* 1988; 1991), with a complex system of social relations, including a hierarchy of power, ownership over production of legal work, and trajectories of mobility within and between classes of law practice. While some studies focus on formal status in practice (Erlanger 1990), prestige of fields of specialisation (Carlin 1994; Heinz and Lauman 1982; Kritzer 1999), and distinctions based on clientele (Heinz *et al* 1998), our study focuses on inter-professional *social class* among lawyers (see also Hagan *et al* 1988; 1991). Class is fundamentally an economic phenomenon, referring principally to differences in the ownership of property and labor (Spector 1995:30; Wright 1996:693–94). Classes are defined in terms of social relations of control over investments, decision-making, other people's work and one's own work (Wright and Singelmann 1982:709). The concept of class, as measured in this study, centres on aspects of a lawyer's own job that specify location within a complex system of social relations in law practice (see Wright *et al* 1982: 711). This conceptualisation clearly emphasises relational dimensions of power in practice.

Through the conceptual tool of class we are able to investigate the 'permeability' of class boundaries (Wright 1996:704). Permeability refers to the extent to which lawyers move across different kinds of settings, from employees to business, or from supervisory positions to managerial positions. Numerous questions apply to the permeability of class distinctions. For example, how has the class distribution changed among lawyers in recent years? How are ascribed and achieved characteristics of individuals linked to their levels of power? How much class mobility exists among the younger lawyers with a sizeable representation of women among its ranks?

Shifting Demographics:
The Influx of Women into Law

Perhaps the most dramatic demographic change in the legal profession in the past two decades has been the rising number of women entering practice. As late as 1970, women represented less than 10 per cent of law students. This proportion grew to 34 per cent in 1980 (Abel 1989:285) and by 1990 women represented 43 per cent of American law school enrolments (Nelson 1994:375). In Canada the proportion of women entering law schools increased from 4 per cent in the 1950s to nearly 50 per cent by the early 1990s, with the largest increases starting in the 1970s (Hagan and Kay 1996:541). In 2000, for the first time, female graduates of law schools outnumbered men in some Canadian law schools. Women's rising numbers in law school attendance are gradually changing the overall demography of the profession. In 1971 women represented still just 5 per cent of the Canadian legal profession. In 1981 women made up 15 per cent and in

1991, 29 per cent of Canadian lawyers (Hagan and Kay 1996:536). By 1999 this figure had climbed further to 32 per cent (Kay and Brockman 2000:176). Yet, there is considerable variation across Canada. In Ontario, where 41 per cent of all Canadian lawyers practice, women represent 30 per cent of the profession. The next largest percentage of Canadian lawyers work in Quebec (25 per cent), where an even higher proportion of the profession consists of women: 40 per cent of Quebec lawyers are women.[1]

While women have made substantial gains in law school enrollments and in entry level positions within the legal profession, these numeric increases represent only one form of 'feminisation' of law (Menkel-Meadow 1989). Even feminisation by virtue of women's numeric representation in practice begs several questions. For example, has women's entry to law yielded genuine sex integration within this desegregating profession so that women and men perform the same types of legal work? Has women's integration brought them closer to economic equity with male incumbents in the legal profession as it became more feminised in recent decades (Reskin and Roos 1996:6)? Moreover, a critical issue is whether women are as successful as their male counterparts in attaining partnerships and managerial authority within firms and other settings where lawyers work (Nelson 1994: 377).

On the issues of integration, economic equity, and power in practice, some scholars are optimistic. For example, Galanter and Palay (1991:57) contend that barriers against women 'have been swept away. The social exclusiveness in hiring that was still a feature of the world of elite law practice in 1960 has receded into insignificance. Performance in law school and in the office counts for more and social connections for less.' And recent work suggests there is good cause for optimism. A study of American lawyers by Chiu and Leicht (1999) revealed that during the 1980s women's entry to law coexisted with rising wages, a narrowing gender gap, and decreased segregation in positions and work settings.[2]

Yet considerable research offers a more discouraging picture of the prospects for gender equality within law. Berger and Robinson argue that 'Although women's numbers within the legal profession have increased, this has not translated into powerful positions as state and federal court judges, law professors, law partners, or corporate counsel' (1993: 88). Women continue to be distributed differently than their male counterparts among types of legal employment. Women are less likely to work in private practice and

---

[1] By contrast, women make up closer to 24% of lawyers in Manitoba, 25% in Saskatchewan, and 26% in Alberta and New Brunswick (Kay & Brockman, 2000, p 176).

[2] Chiu and Leicht note that the gender earnings gap and the distribution of earnings are generally more favorable for younger than older lawyers. The declining earnings gap was driven substantially by improvements in the lower half of the earnings distribution for women and among elite women lawyers in the top 1% of the earnings distribution (Chiu & Leicht, 1999, p 585).

more likely to work in government sectors of practice than are men (Kay and Brockman 2000:177; Nelson 1994:376). Women are also distributed distinctively among private law firms of differing sizes. Women tend to be over-represented among the smallest and largest law firms in the United States (Menkel-Meadow 1989:213; Nelson 1994:376). This curvilinear relationship between gender and firm size is paralleled in Canada, where the largest proportions of women work as sole practitioners (30 per cent), and in small firm (38 per cent) and very large law firms (15 per cent) (Kay and Brockman 2000:179). Some research suggests that solo practice offers a setting where lawyers may experience a greater degree of autonomy and control over their work (and hence flexibility in schedules), while larger law firms may offer a degree of procedural protection to women through the formal evaluation processes typical of more bureaucratic work places (Hagan *et al* 1991:259; Menkel-Meadow 1989:213; Nelson 1994:377). Larger firms tend also to employ other women, and possibly more women partners, offering a more congenial context for women (Nelson 1994:377). The growth of larger law firms in Canada, with a rising number of young associates as new recruits, was paralleled by a steady decline in the percentage of self-employed lawyers. For men, this figure dropped from 92 per cent in 1931 to 70 per cent in 1986. For women, the change was even more dramatic—from 76 per cent in 1931 and 1941 to 45 per cent in 1986 (Stager and Arthurs 1990:177).

The issue of employees within firms raises the question: Are women entering the higher echelons of law firm practice, specifically partnership? Evidence suggests a significant proportion of women are making partner, but at a lower rate than men (Kay and Hagan 1995; see also Nelson 1994:377). Kay's studies of lawyers in both civil and common law jurisdictions of Canada demonstrate that regardless of experience, specialisation, billable hours, clientele responsibilities, or size of firm, men possess consistently higher chances of attaining partnership status than women (Kay and Hagan 1994; 1999; Kay 2002). Hagan's studies of Toronto city lawyers reveal that women's prospects for partnership are especially weak in small firms, suggesting that small firms dominated by men are more resistant to modifying the work roles assumed by women and men (Hagan *et al* 1991:260). Perhaps most troubling is recent work that suggests women associates are required to embody an exaggerated standard of the 'ideal partner.' Consideration for partnership requires that women demonstrate extraordinary work commitment by actively recruiting new clients, building an extensive network of corporate clientele, returning quickly from any maternity leaves and continuing to bill at elevated levels following leaves, and expressing a commitment to the firm culture by endorsing traditional values and goals of law firm lawyers (Kay and Hagan 1998:741).

These findings suggest a 'glass ceiling' in law practice. The notion of glass ceiling effects implies that gender disadvantages are stronger at the top of the hierarchy than at lower levels and that these disadvantages become worse later in a person's career (Cotter *et al* 2001:658). Certainly, women's reduced probabilities of entering partnership circles (Brockman 1992; Hagan *et al* 1991; Kay and Hagan 1994, 1998; MacKaay 1991) and a growing gender gap in earnings as careers progress (Kay and Hagan 1995) provide some tangible evidence of a glass ceiling, albeit one with visible cracks emerging, in law. As women push through this glass ceiling, new issues are raised about their access to genuine authority in practice. As Berger and Robinson (1993) observe,

> Even with greater numbers of women entering the legal field, women are systematically excluded from top levels possessing the highest prestige, power, and compensation. Feminisation of the legal profession has begun. As women begin to crack the glass ceiling, less prestigious and new tracks are forming for women: the public judge, the legal writing and clinical law professor, and the mommy track lawyer (Berger and Robinson 1993:89).

Are women attaining the higher positions of power and privilege in practice? Within partnership and senior positions in settings other than law firms, are women gaining entitlement to capacities of authority and decision-making? Or, are parallel career tracks emerging for women lawyers, tracks that are less desirable both financially and in terms of status? While studies have documented gender differences in earnings, partnership rates, sectors, and fields of law practice, few studies have examined women's power and authority across sectors of practice or within partnership circles.

Class, Gender, and Legal Practice

And what of women? Perhaps the most glaring omission in studies of social class is the failure to consider gender differences in the reproduction of classes (Robinson and Garnier 1985:255). Although Marxist theory sometimes (eg, Clement and Myles 1994; Wright *et al* 1982, 1995) has highlighted the combined effects of class and gender on outcomes of earnings and social mobility, MacKinnon (1989) has noted a tendency of Marxist analyses to relegate gender issues to the periphery of theoretical concerns (Hagan *et al* 1991:245). Greater attention needs to be paid to how class positions are created over time and social space, and how as part of this process, they are gendered (Savage *et al* 1992; Wright *et al* 1982).

Gender may characterise the reproduction of power relations. Although women entering law practice may share common cultural, class, and educational backgrounds to their male colleagues in law, women are often situated lower in the authority hierarchy than men with equivalent education and experience (Gellis 1991; Wolf and Fligstein 1979).[3] In her classic study of gender and management, Kanter (1977) suggests that male managers in a male dominated hierarchy, such as law, are likely to act in ways that preserve male privileges and advantages. She identifies a process called 'homosocial reproduction' whereby men in positions of authority as managers tend to hire and promote on the basis of social and gender similarity to themselves. The need for trust in the face of considerable uncertainty encourages selecting on the basis of social similarity, such that even women with class and cultural backgrounds similar to their male managers may face exclusion from advancement opportunities (Kanter 1977; Robinson and Garnier 1985). In private law practice, the failure to promote women to partnership status means women are underrepresented in coveted positions that confer authority and decision-making capacity (Epstein 1993; Reskin and Padavic 1994:92). As such, gender inequality in workplace authority becomes a key institutional element in the reproduction of gender inequality in organisations (Wright, Baxter and Birkelund 1995:408) that employ lawyers.

Yet, even for women who break through the glass ceiling to positions as partners or senior lawyers in organisations, such as government and corporations, that employ lawyers, there may be gaps in authority. Reskin and Padavic (1994) point out that

> [w]omen who achieve jobs that typically involve decision-making power cannot always exercise the same level of authority that men can. Women are often denied the use of this power. Employers often give women less authority that they give men with similar qualifications (Reskin and Padavic 1994:93).

The last 25 years have seen large numbers of women entering the bottom ranks of the legal profession. Are these women gaining in power through advancement in the profession? Are they moving into positions of greater authority and leadership within the legal profession? And, for those who enter the circles of partnership and leadership in other domains of practice, are women receiving and exercising equivalent power and authority as their male counterparts? We respond to such concerns through an empirical exploration of structural shifts and gender hierarchy in contemporary Canadian law practice.

---

[3] Gellis argues that '[w]omen do not seem to differ significantly from men in their reasons for choosing law as a profession or in defining the important attributes of their employment. Limited opportunities to advance and salary differentials, moreover, are not confined to the large law firms or to law firms generally. Subtle differential treatment is pervasive. All this suggests that women are still struggling to be recognized' (1991, p 975).

Studying Power and Class among Canadian Lawyers

Specific kinds of data are required to explore the expectations of women and men's positions in a power stratification model of law practice. We collected these data through a mail-back survey of lawyers in the province of Ontario during the winter months of 1990 and 1996. In 1990 we selected a disproportionately stratified random sample of Ontario lawyers for the survey from the membership records of the Law Society of Upper Canada.[4] The sample was stratified by gender to include equally men and women called to the Ontario Bar between 1975 and 1990. These lawyers represent the first cohort of lawyers in Ontario with a significant number of women among its ranks. We mailed surveys to 2358 respondents, and, with one reminder, received a 68 per cent response rate (N=1597). In 1996 we followed up with this same sample of lawyers to explore their career trajectories, family, and life events. Through a single follow-up reminder, we obtained a response rate of 69 per cent.[5] Ontario is an ideal setting for this study. As mentioned, the province is host to the largest population of lawyers in Canada: 29,722 of Canada's 72,761 lawyers (41 per cent) practice law in the province of Ontario (Kay and Brockman 2000:176).

The current study builds on a prior developed typology of class structure in legal practice (see Hagan *et al* 1988; 1991). This typology is summarised in Table 1, which separates lawyers into managing partners, supervising partners, partners in small firms, sole practitioners, managing/supervising lawyers, semi-autonomous lawyers, and non-autonomous lawyers. Table 1 also outlines the criteria applied to place lawyers into these categories.

Building a Typology of Power

Class is among the most contested concepts in sociology. There is little agreement over its definition and considerable debate over the appropriate criteria for the measurement of class (Ahrne and Wright 1983:212). A range of scholars contend that class is best conceptualised as sets of organisational positions that are structurally equivalent in term of relations of

[4] The Law Society of Upper Canada is the analogue to an American state bar association. Membership is mandatory to practice in the Province of Ontario.
[5] These levels of response are remarkably high given the legal profession's reputation for secrecy (Stewart, 1983, p 16) and markedly lower response rates among other surveys of lawyers (Brockman, 1994; Wallace, 1995).

autonomy and authority (Carroll and Mayer 1986; Hedström and Wallin 1988; Wright 1985). Fundamental to class relations in contemporary legal practice are relations to the means of legal work/production (ownership) and relations of authority or control over lawyer labor power (Robinson and Garnier 1985:252; Hagan *et al* 1988:11). Our relies on a Weberian conceptualization of class, emphasising lawyers' 'life chances', as opposed to a Marxist approach, emphasising 'exploitation' as the core of class analysis (Wright 1996:695–96).

Wright and Perrone (1977) identify four primary class locations that are determined by these relations: (1) capitalists (or employers) who own the means of production and purchase the labor power of others; (2) managers (including supervisors) who do not own the means of production but exercise control over labor power on behalf of the owner(s); (3) petty bourgeoisie, who own the means of production but do not purchase labor power (ie, self employed people without employees); and (4) non-supervisory workers, who neither own the means of production nor control labor power (see also Wright and Singelmann 1982).

Our operationalisation is an elaboration of a model used in the work of Wright (1982; Wright and Perrone 1977). Our work emphasises the 'relational' criterion that Wright proposes for class definition. This perspective divides the occupational category of professional into the class categories of employer, manager, self-employed producer, semi-autonomous worker, and worker, primarily on the basis of distinctions in ownership, authority, and autonomy (Brint 1987:38). Relations of ownership are operationalised using information on whether the lawyer was the proprietor of a business (a partner of a law firm) or self-employed (a sole practitioner) or was employed by others. Purchase of labor power distinguishes between owners who had employees (capitalists) and those who did not (petty bourgeoisie). Control over labor power distinguishes between non-workers who had managerial/supervisory positions and those who did not (see Robinson and Garnier 1985: 259). This operationalisation of power relations is based on self-reported features of work experiences.

This strategy for decoding class structure in law practice is provisional. There are areas of ambiguity, including that of semi-autonomous lawyers, and greater specification in the work of non-private practitioners could enhance this basic schema. Also, it is noteworthy that this typology only decodes the class structure of the economically active lawyer labor force. A variety of locations in the social structure outside of the lawyer labor force are thus ignored: lawyers who have returned to school, retired lawyers, lawyers having taken a temporary absence or sabbatical from the profession, those unemployed and who have allowed their membership with the Law Society to lapse, and those having left the profession entirely.

We identify seven classes, or strata of power, within law practice.[6] There are six essential criteria that enable us to draw these distinctions. As in Wright's work, *ownership* and *number of employees* are key criteria in our typology. Owners include partners of law firms and sole practitioners, who employ staff, sometimes including other lawyers. Following Wright, we employ total *number of employees* rather than firm size, as is often the case in studies of lawyers (see Abel 1989; Epstein *et al* 1995; Galanter 1983; Galanter and Palay 1990; Heinz and Lauman 1982; Nelson 1988; Wholey 1985). We also employ criteria of *authority* (based on two questions that allow us to sanctioning versus task authority and supervisory capacities), *hierarchical position* (two questions tapping levels above and below lawyer), *autonomy* (a single question describing design aspects of work), and *decision-making* responsibilities (a single question that inquires about degree of participation in policy decisions).

Hierarchical position is a four-level variable that categorises lawyers according to (not including secretaries): (1) no level of authority above them and two or more levels below them; (2) two or more levels below them; (3) one level below them; or (4) no level below them. *Authority* is a four-level variable that measures whether a lawyer has, in relation to others: (1) sanctioning authority (ability to impose positive and/or negative sanctions on subordinates); (2) task authority (gives direction and assignments to subordinates); (3) nominal supervision (supervises without sanctioning or task authority); or (4) no supervisory responsibilities (supervises no one other than clerical staff).

Decision-making is a five-level variable that sorts lawyers according to whether they: (1) directly participate in all or most policy decisions; (2) directly participate in some policy decisions; (3) directly participate in at least one area of decision-making; (4) provide advice but do not directly participate in decision-making; and (5) do not directly or indirectly participate in decision-making.

These six criteria are then brought together to develop a typology of class structure in law practice. Table 1 specifies the application of each criterion to produce a separate stratum in the typology. The most privileged class in this typology is that of managing partners in medium to large firms. These lawyers are owners, employ at least 10 employees, hold sanctioning or task authority over others, participate directly in decision-making

---

[6] Wright (1982) ultimately has two classes in his analysis. Hagan and colleagues (1988, p 15) identify five classes: capitalists, managerial bourgeoisie, supervisory bourgeoisie, small employers and petty bourgeoisie. A modified version of this class typology (Hagan *et al*, 1991, p 248–49) delineates seven classes with categories more familiar to the profession: managing partner in a medium to large firm, supervising partner in a medium to large firm, partner in a small firm, solo practitioner, managing/supervising lawyer, semiautonomous lawyer, nonautonomous lawyer. It is this latter classification of power that we employ in this study.

Table 1 Operating Typology of Class Structure in Law Practice

Class Position[a]	Ownership Relationship	Number of Employees	Authority	Decision-making	Autonomy	Hierarchical Position
Managing Partner in Medium to Large Firm	Employer	≥10	1–2	1–3	X[b]	1–2
Supervising Partner in Medium to Large Firm[c]	Employer	≥10	1–2	1–3	X	1–2
Partner in Small Firm	Employer	2–9	X	X	X	X
Sole Practitioner	Employer	0–1	X	X	X	X
Managing/ Supervising Lawyer	Employee	X	1–3	1–5	X	1–3
Semi-Autonomous Lawyer	Employee	X	4[d]	X	1–2	4
Non-Autonomous Lawyer	Employee	X	4	X	3–4	4

[a]Definitions of the operational criteria appear in Table 2.
[b]X: criterion not applicable.
[c]Respondents without task and sanctioning authority or without decision-making responsibility are classified as non-managing partners.

regarding firm policies, have considerable autonomy in the design and implementation of their legal work, and at least two levels of lawyers under them at the firm. At the other extreme or the typology, and the least familiar of these categories, are the semi-autonomous and non-autonomous lawyers. These lawyers are associates in law firms or employees of government or businesses where they have no supervisory responsibilities or levels of employees below them other than secretaries. The distinction between semi-autonomous and non-autonomous lawyers rests on whether the lawyer designs some aspects of his or her legal work, for example, in terms of the types of cases they take on, specialisation within fields of practice, or putting new ideas into practice within their workplace.

Table 2 displays the distribution of lawyers from this fifteen-year cohort (individuals called to the bar during the years 1975 to 1990, inclusive) across the power hierarchy of the profession in 1990 and 1996. A sizeable increase in the percentage of lawyers working as employers (ie, sole practitioners and partners) is apparent. In 1990 only 32 per cent of the cohort of lawyers were employers. By 1996, 42 per cent of the cohort were employers. This increase among employers, likely reflects the rise in many of these lawyers through the ranks of associate to partnership in law firms. The distribution of lawyers employed across different sized firms (and organisations) remained much the same across the six-year time span. There was a slight decline among employer-lawyers with one or fewer employees (24 per cent in 1990 and 21 per cent in 1996). A sizeable proportion of employer lawyers had between 2 and 9 employees in 1990 (41 per cent), and this figure increased slightly to 45 per cent in 1996. There were slight reductions among employer-lawyers with 20–49 employees (6.9 per cent to 5.8 per cent) and among lawyer-employers with over fifty employees over the period 1990 to 1996 (21 per cent to 20 per cent). These subtle changes in the work contexts of lawyers may reflect a number of changes taking place in law practice during the decade of the nineties: lateral movement of lawyers out of large law firms into smaller firm settings and solo practice, dissolution of partnerships, reconfiguring of smaller and mid-size firms following unsuccessful attempts a mergers with different firm cultures (eg, law firms that grew too quickly or whose mergers proved incompatible), as well as downsizing in government and industry sectors of the economy. The figures represent changes among this fifteen-year cohort and number of employees applies only to employers. Therefore, this measure of organisational size excludes lawyers who remained as employees, even while changing contexts (for example, moving to larger law firms or from private practice into the government sector).

The most noteworthy changes in Table 2 are perhaps those of transitions to positions of power. For many of these lawyers, their jobs changed in ways that offer them greater autonomy to design all or most aspects of their work. In 1990, only 29 per cent of lawyers among this relatively young cohort were in positions that allowed them to design most aspects of their work. By 1996, over half (52 per cent) of these lawyers possessed this degree of control over their work. Parallel to the increased autonomy in practice, there have also been significant gains in decision-making authority among this cohort of legal practitioners. In 1990, 18 per cent of these lawyers participated directly in all or most decision-making in their place of work. Six years later, 36 per cent held this sort of decision-making authority. While there is evidence that many lawyers are moving up in levels of authority, a not insignificant number of these lawyers continue to work in positions where they do not participate either directly or indirectly in decisions at their firm or organisation (20 per cent), or at best only provide advice to decision-makers (18 per cent). These figures have only declined by less than 4 per cent over the six years. In terms of general authority (including sanctioning, task and supervisory authority), there has been an increase in lawyers with sanctioning authority (18 per cent in 1990

Table 2 Distribution of Criteria Used in Typology

Dimensions of Power	% 1990 (N=1349)	% 1996 (N=972)
Ownership relation		
Employer=partner/sole practitioner	32.1	42.3
Employee=other	67.9	57.7
Number of employees (for employers only)		
0–1	24.2	21.2
2–9	40.6	45.0
10–19	7.4	7.8
20–49	6.9	5.8
50+	21.0	20.2
Authority		
1=sanctioning authority	17.9	21.5
2=task authority	4.7	3.8
3=nominal supervision	0.1	0.0
4=non-supervisor	77.3	74.7
Decision-making		
1=directly participates in all or most decision-making	17.9	35.5
2=directly participates in some policy decisions	23.6	27.0
3=directly participates in at least one area of decision-making	21.1	4.7
4=does not directly participate but provides advice	18.0	16.5
5=does not directly or indirectly participate in decision-making	19.5	16.4
Hierarchical position		
1=no level above respondent/two or more levels below	12.3	13.4
2=two or more levels below respondent	10.5	3.9
3=one level below respondent	56.7	54.1
4=no level below respondent	20.6	28.6
Autonomy		
1=designs all or most aspects of work	28.8	51.9
2=designs some important aspects of work	51.6	35.1
3=designs a few important aspects of work	14.5	6.5
4=not required to design aspects of work	5.1	6.6

to 22 per cent in 1996), yet the majority of lawyers report working in non-supervisory positions. Similarly, there was only a modest decline in the percentage of lawyers working with one level of personnel beneath their position (54 per cent, down from 57 per cent in 1990). Increases took place among lawyers with one and two or more levels beneath them. A nominal increase occurred at the other end of the spectrum, among those lawyers near the top of the organisational hierarchy with no levels above them and at least two levels below their status (13 per cent, up from 12 per cent in 1990). In sum, these results suggest that considerable change took place among the positions occupied by these lawyers over the six year interval: sizeable percentages of these lawyers moved up the professional ladder in hierarchical position, authority, autonomy, and decision-making, yet there is still a sizeable percentage working in non-supervisory capacities with limited control over the content of their legal work and the policies governing their place of employment.

In Table 3 we move beyond these individual measures of authority and autonomy to examine the distribution of men and women lawyers across the power structure of the profession. Some intriguing patterns emerge among this cohort of lawyers during the decade of the nineties. There was a decline among those working as sole practitioners over these years. In 1990, 28 per cent of these men lawyers reported working as sole practitioners, while 10 per cent were sole practitioners six years later. Similarly, the percentage of women sole practitioners fell over this period, from 14 per cent to 8 per cent of women. This decline of sole practitioners parallels the long term trend observed in the United States (Nelson 1994).

Table 3 Changes in the Power and Authority of Men and Women Lawyers in Ontario, 1990–1996

| | Men Lawyers | | | | Women Lawyers | | | |
| | 1990 | | 1996 | | 1990[a] | | 1996[b] | |
	N	%	N	%	N	%	N	%
Managing Partners	37	5.6	33	8.1	15	2.2	23	4.2
Supervising Partners	43	6.5	47	11.5	26	3.8	35	6.4
Partners in Small Firms	23	3.5	109	26.7	12	1.8	74	13.5
Sole Practitioners	182	27.5	41	10.0	94	13.8	46	8.4
Managing/Supervising Lawyers	66	10.0	8	2.0	72	10.5	19	3.5
Semi-autonomous Lawyers	232	35.0	137	33.6	339	49.6	286	52.1
Non-autonomous Lawyers	80	12.1	33	8.1	125	18.3	66	12.0
Total[c]	663	100.0	408	100.0	683	100.0	549	100.0

Note: See Table 2 for operationalisation of class; percentages may not add up to 100 because of rounding.
[a]Gender differences in 1990 were statistically significant (Chi-square=74.92, 6 cl.f., p<.001).
[b]Gender differences in 1996 were statistically significant (Chi-square=59.00, 6 cl.f., p<.001).
[c]Lawyers working on a part-time basis and those no longer practising law are excluded from the power typology.

Among partners, we see impressive increases, and largely anticipated as the majority of these lawyers working in private practice and would have passed the time of partnership decisions by 1996. In 1990, 4 per cent of men were partners in small firms (under 10 lawyers) and in 1996, 27 per cent had made partners in small firms. Women's share of small firm partnerships also increased, although by less impressive numbers (2 to 14 per cent). In the senior levels of partnerships, men were dominant in 1990 and junior male lawyers made greater gains than women in the six years following. For example, in 1990, 7 per cent of men were supervising partners compared with 4 per cent of women. Six years later, 12 per cent of men compared with 6 per cent of women were supervisory partners. The inroads to managing partnership were slow for both men and women. Six per cent of men in 1990 compared with 8 per cent in 1996 were managing partners. Among women 2 per cent were managing partners in 1990 and by 1996, just 4 per cent of women had attained managing partner status. Thus, partnership pyramids appear to have become more steep during the nineties (see Galanter and Palay 1991; Hagan and Kay 1995; Nelson 1988). Among managing-supervising lawyers, both sexes saw their percentages decline. This likely reflects the gradual climb up the career ladder by many lawyers in this cohort. A fuller picture of the entire profession would likely reveal more recent cohorts climbing into these positions on their ascent to power. Yet, surprisingly a sizeable percentage of lawyers within this cohort (all with at least 6 to 21 years experience) remain in the ranks of semi-autonomous and non-autonomous lawyers. These figures are particularly high among women. Consider that in 1996, 42 per cent of men and 64 per cent of women remained in these lower levels of power within the profession. Taken together, these tables suggest that there are higher rates of promotional mobility for men than women out of working-class positions into managerial-supervisory positions during the early to mid stages of careers. Of course, the patterns observed in Tables 2 and 3 are a complex result of career moves and structural changes in the profession over time. In what follows, we will try to disaggregate these processes through an analysis of individuals' mobility paths in law.

Individual Mobility Routes to Power and Privilege

So far our analysis has examined power through individual measures of autonomy, authority, hierarchical position, decision-making capacities, employer versus employee status, and organisational size (and structural location within these hierarchies). We then used these measures to build a model of hierarchical power and examined gender differences across the hierarchies in 1990 and 1996 for this fifteen year cohort of Canadian lawyers. This typology of law practice hierarchy arrays lawyers along a spectrum from the most powerful (managing partners in large elite law firms) to the least (non-autonomous lawyer-employees with few decision-making powers). Yet, the typology, based on the class schema created by Erik Olin Wright (1985; 1996) is limited by its emphasis on ownership/employer positions in firms. As Hull and Nelson (1998) suggest, a more useful ranking of power might give less emphasis to owner/employer relationships and assign greater weight to other aspects of power, status, and related resources.

In the analysis to follow we move beyond the class/power schema to explore power as a continuous measure with incremental changes in levels of authority, supervision, autonomy, decision-making, and status signifiers. To further explore power and authority in practice, we constructed a measure based on summing 17 items intended to capture different dimensions of power in practice. We included the fundamental measures employed in the class/power hierarchical analysis[7] (eg Wright 1982), but without priority assigned to ownership/employer status. We also incorporated new measures specific to law practice. These measures included questions about lawyers' decision-making authority over what clients and specific cases to take on and about what areas of law in which to work (two questions). We also tapped levels of responsibility for hiring articling students, hiring other lawyers, hiring support staff, assigning files to other lawyers, supervising other lawyers, policy, management and remuneration decisions, and bringing clients to the firm (seven questions). This new measure of power and authority ranged from a value of 0 to 18. Men, on average, held greater amounts of power and authority in practice (mean=11.74 versus 9.70 among women, t-test p<.001).

We explore these variations in levels of power and authority across the profession using ordinary least squares regression techniques (See Table 4). A range of individual attributes and structural characteristics are considered, beginning with gender (men=1), ethnic minority (self-identified minority=1), marital status (married or cohabiting=1), and presence of children (one or more children=1). Among our fifteen year cohort of Ontario lawyers, men were more likely than women to be married (89 per cent compared with 78 per cent of women, t-test p<.001) and to have children

---

[7] The scores from nine questions were summed. Questions tapped degree of involvement in policy-making decisions, supervision, task and sanctioning authority, autonomy, and hierarchical position.

Table 4 Descriptive Statistics for Power and Authority Models (All Lawyers) (N=892)

Concepts and Variables	Women (N=500)		Men (N=392)	
	Mean	(S.D.)	Mean	(S.D.)
Dependent Variable:				
Power-Authority[a]	9.70	4.38	11.74	4.38***
Independent Variables:				
Demographics				
Ethnic Minority	.10	.30	.08	.27
Marital Status	.78	.42	.89	.31 ***
Children	.74	.44	.82	.38**
Human Capital and Social Status				
Years of Experience	11.88	3.81	14.13	4.05***
Elite Law School	.37	.48	.38	.49
Prestige of Field of Law Practised	5.62	.96	5.63	1.10
Hours Worked Per Week	49.86	14.20	51.96	13.83*
Organisational Commitment	3.60	1.07	3.60	1.09
Partner/Sole Practitioner	.43	.50	.60	.49***
Social Capital				
Father Business Owner	.27	.44	.25	.44
Job Networks	.41	.49	.38	.49
Professional Activities	3.84	5.40	5.87	7.44***
Membership in Associations	2.29	1.49	2.25	1.21
Contextual Factors				
Organisational Size				
<10 Lawyers	.56	.50	.57	.50
10–19 Lawyers	.13	.33	.09	.29
20–49 Lawyers	.17	.38	.17	.38
50+ Lawyers	.14	.35	.16	.37
Benefits	7.11	4.81	6.99	4.64
Practice District (Toronto=1)	.49	.50	.49	.50
Sectors of Practice				
Private Practice	.52	.50	.68	.47***
Government	.27	.44	.16	.37***
Private Industry	.21	.41	.16	.36*

[a]Multiple item scale is based on sum of 17 items (alpha reliability=. 76).
*p<.05 **p<.01 ***p<.001 (two-tailed tests of significance)

(82 per cent compared with 74 per cent among women, *t*-test p<.01).

We included several measures of human capital and social status in predicting levels of power and authority. Both human capital and credentialist perspectives argue that diplomas/degrees are necessary for individuals to enjoy greater job opportunities (Rubinson and Ralph 1984). The perspectives differ on reasons, however. Human capital theorists contend that the skills learned in higher education result in increased productivity (hence higher wages and promotions) (Becker 1964), while credentialists argue that employers demand high qualifications from prestigious institutions as a way of screening out an increasing number of qualified applicants (Collins 1979). We measure education as a dummy variable that combines elite education at the University of Toronto or Osgoode Hall law schools. The human capital approach also asserts the importance of experience in explaining women's under-representation in managerial authority (Jacobs 1992). Experience in law practice is an important factor in acquiring both ownership and control. As Robinson and Garnier (1985:255) observe, 'In acquiring control, experience is probably a rough indicator of seniority as well as of training and skills inculcated on the job and thus should be related to one's chance of obtaining a position of control over labor power.' Women in our study had on average two years less experience than their male counterparts (12 compared with 14 years experience in practice, t-test p<.001).

Prestige of field of law was measures on a scale from 3.57 to 7.25 based on lawyers' average ranking of each field of law (see Hagan 1990). These resulting prestige scores were then assigned to the field of law which each respondent practiced the most often. Hours worked each week were calculated for lawyers across all practice settings. A measure of work commitment asks respondents to what degree they feel a real loyalty to the organisation/firm/company (Porter *et al* 1974) (1=strongly disagree, 5=strongly agree). As a measure of status affecting access to power and influence, lawyers were asked to report whether they were partners (1=partner). While there were no significant differences between men and women in their attendance at elite law schools, fields of law practiced, or level of organisational commitment; men worked on average 2 hours more per week (50 versus 52 hours per week, t-test p<.05) and were significantly more likely to be partners (60 per cent of men compared with 45 per cent of women, t-test p<.001).

Social capital has also been shown to be relevant to career potential and movement into positions of authority (Friedman and Krackhardt 1997; Kay and Hagan 1999; Kay and Bernard *in press*; Wegener 1991). Social capital involves the structures of relationships. Relationships of particular import are those among colleagues within a firm, links to managing partners, contacts in business, clientele, friendships with other lawyers and justice personnel. In this sense, the character of social capital is less tangible than economic or human capitals. Some social capital may operate in the form of familial connections (Hofferth, Boisjoly and Duncan 1999) friendship networks and job opportunities (Granovetter 1974), collegial contacts within the profession (Meyerson 1994; Petersen, Saporta and Seidel 2000), and broad social circles to clientele (Kay and Hagan 1999; Seron 1993). We measure each of these forms of social capital through father's employment (father business owner=1), job networks (personal network used to obtain current job=1), involvement in professional activities (number of professional activities attended outside 8 am to 5 pm per month), membership in professional associations (total number) and responsibilities for corporate clientele (1=corporate and institutional clients). We also measured a limitation of social capital through exclusion from important files (1=yes). Men were on average involved in a larger number of professional associations (5.87 versus 3.84, t-test p<.01), while women were more often excluded from interesting and important files (16 per cent compared with 9 per cent of men, t-test p<.001).

In addition, we included in our analysis of power, contextual factors and sectors of practice. Organisational size was measured as 4 dummy variables: less than 10 lawyers, 10 to 19 lawyers, 20 to 49 lawyers, and 50 or more lawyers. We inquired about the availability of 18 different workplace benefits and geographic location (1=Toronto). Hull and Nelson (1998:687) suggest that research on law hierarchies should examine power across corporate, government, and law firm sectors. Therefore, we include sectors of practice measured through three dummy variables: private practice, government, and private industry. Men were more highly represented within private practice (68 per cent compared with 52 per cent of women, t-test p<.001), while women were more highly represented in government (27 per cent compared with 16 per cent of men, t-test p<.001) and in private industry (21 per cent compared with 16 per cent, t-test p<.05).

Results summarised in Table 5 reveal women are disadvantaged in access to positions of power and authority regardless of years of experience, fields of law practiced, partnership status, size of organisation, or sector of practice. Model 1 displays the effect of demographic characteristics, human capital and social status variables on levels of power. Men are significantly more likely to attain high levels of power (β=.07**). Not surprisingly, years of experience in practice (β=.08**) and ownership positions (as partners and sole practitioners) also yield significant returns in power (β=.59***). Organisational commitment offers greater authority and power, however, it is also likely that the reverse takes place: having attained positions as owners in law practice, partners and sole practitioners have greater commitment to the firm or their solo practice than lawyers working as associates or employees. In model 2 we introduce dimensions of social capital. Job networks (β=.05*), participation in professional activities (β=.07**)

Table 5 Reduced and Saturated O.L.S. Regression Models of Power and Authority in Law Practice (N=892)

	Eqn 1		Eqn 2		Eqn 3	
			All Practice Settings[a]			
Demographics						
Gender (male=1)	.07	(.25)**	.07	(.25)**	.06	(.24)**
Ethnic Minority	-.02	(.40)	-.02	(.40)	-.01	(.39)
Marital Status	-.03	(.34)	-.03	(.34)	-.04	(.33)
Children	.01	(.31)	.01	(.31)	.01	(.30)
Human Capital and Social Status						
Years of Experience	.08	(.03)**	.09	(.03)***	.11	(.03)***
Elite Law School	-.03	(.24)	-.02	(.24)	-.01	(.25)
Prestige of Field of Law Practised	.03	(.12)	.02	(.11)	.02	(.12)
Partner/Sole Practitioner	.59	(.24)***	.55	(.25)***	.40	(.37)***
Organisational Commitment	.13	(.11)***	.12	(.11)***	.11	(.11)***
Social Capital						
Father Business Owner			.04	(.26)	.03	(.26)
Job Networks			.05	(.23)*	.04	(.23)
Professional Activities			.07	(.02)**	.07	(.02)**
Membership in Associations			.10	(.09)***	.09	(.09)***
Contextual Factors						
Organisational Size[b]					.06	(.37)
<10 Lawyers					-.00	(.43)
20–49 Lawyers					-.05	(.46)
50+ Lawyers					.09	(.03)**
Benefits					-.02	(.25)
Practice District (Toronto=1)						
Sector of Practice[c]						
Private Practice					-.18	(.42)***
Government					-.08	(.36)*
Intercept	4.46	(.91)***	3.70	(.91)***	2.81	(1.03)**
Adjusted R^2		.42		.44		.46
F-test		72.06***		54.03***		39.14***

[a] Standardised beta coefficients displayed with standard errors in parentheses.

[b] Comparison category is offices or organisations employing 10–19 lawyers.

[c] Comparison category is private industry sectors.

*$p<.05$ **$p<.01$ ***$p<.001$ (two-tailed tests of significance)

and membership in associations (β=.10***) all further enhance prospects for power in practice. Model 3 reveals the gains in power and authority offered through private practice (β=.18***) and organisations rich with diverse benefit packages (β=.09*). Prior research suggests that government lawyers may have more predictable hours of work and enhanced workplace supports (eg, parental leaves, day care facilities, part-time options, medical plan), but reduced remuneration and social status in the profession

Table 6 O.L.S. Regression Models of Power and Authority in Law Practice Men and Women (N=892)

	All lawyers		All Practice Settings[a]			
			Men		Women	
Demographics						
Gender (male=1)	.06	(.24)**	–	–	–	–
Ethnic Minority	-.01	(.39)	-.00	(.62)	-.03	(.51)
Marital Status	-.04	(.33)	-.02	(.58)	-.05	(.40)
Children	.01	(.30)	.03	(.48)	-.01	(.38)
Human Capital and Social Status						
Years of Experience	.11	(.03)***	.12	(.04)**	.08	(.04)*
Elite Law School	-.01	(.25)	-.06	(.36)	.04	(.33)
Prestige of Field of Law Practised	.02	(.12)	-.00	(.16)	.04	(.17)
Partner/Sole Practitioner	.40	(.37)***	.36	(.60)***	.43	(.47)***
Organisational Commitment	.11	(.11)***	.22	(.16)***	.05	(.14)
Social Capital						
Father Business Owner	.03	(.26)	-.00	(.39)	.06	(.35)
Job Networks	.04	(.23)	.02	(.34)	.05	(.31)
Professional Activities	.07	(.02)**	.03	(.02)	.11	(.03)**
Membership in Associations	.09	(.09)***	.01	(.15)	.13	(.11)**
Contextual Factors						
Organisational Size[b]						
<10 Lawyers	.06	(.37)	.14	(.61)*	.02	(.47)
20–49 Lawyers	-.00	(.43)	-.00	(.67)	.01	(.56)
50+ Lawyers	-.05	(.46)	-.03	(.71)	-.06	(.61)
Benefits	.09	(.03)**	.07	(.04)	.10	(.04)*
Practice District (Toronto=1)	-.02	(.25)	-.02	(.38)	-.01	(.34)
Sector of Practice[c]						
Private Practice	.18	(.42)***	.19	(.70)*	.20	(.52)**
Government	-.08	(.36)*	-.11	(.60)*	-.05	(.46)
Intercept	2.81	(1.03)**	2.76	(1.57)	3.04	(1.40)*
Adjusted R^2		.46		.46		.43
F-Test		39.14***		18.71***		20.71***

[a]Standardised beta coefficients displayed with standard errors in parentheses.
[b]Comparison category is offices or organisations employing 10–19 lawyers.
[c]Comparison category is private industry sectors.
*p<.05 **p<.01 ***p<.001 (two-tailed tests of significance)

(Dixon and Seron 1995; England 1979; Epstein 1993; Epstein *et al* 1995). Our model confirms that government lawyers have access to lower levels of power than lawyers employed in either private industry (β=-.08*) or private practice. Taken together, these variables explain 46 per cent of the variance in the distribution of power across law practice.

More subtle variations between men and women are revealed in Table 6. Among both men and women years of experience in practice yields increased opportunities for power, although the gains are greater for men than women with each passing year. Demonstrated organisational commitment offers men significant returns in power and authority (β=.22***), but similar rewards are not forthcoming for women who express strong loyalty to the firms and organisations where they work. Measures of social capital are particularly salient to women's career advancement: participation in professional activities (β=.11**) and membership in associations (β=.13**) significantly advance women's authority and decision-making powers in practice. It may also be the case that with rising seniority and experience in practice, women actively engage in professional involvements through activities outside regular work hours and membership in various professional associations. Male lawyers gained more readily positions of power and authority in small organisations compared with their counterparts practicing law in mid-sized settings of 10 to 19 lawyers. In contrast, women's chances for positions of power and influence were greatest in work settings that could afford to offer superior benefit plans (β=.10*) (eg, flexible hours, part-time work, parental leave options, child care, pension plan, dental plan). Not surprisingly, private practice remains the more lucrative sector for both men and women seeking positions of power and authority. Among male lawyers, employment in government was less profitable in terms of power (β=-11*) than careers in private industry where mobility ladders offer greater access to positions of authority, control, and autonomy.

Conclusions

This chapter is concerned with the changing hierarchy of power in the Canadian legal profession. As C. Wright Mills observed (1966:12), 'The skills of a profession shift, externally, as the function of the profession changes with the nature of its clients' interests, and internally, as the rewards of the profession are given to new kinds of success.' Thus, beyond the profession of law, lawyers are recognised for the roles they frequently play in shaping the legal framework of the new economy. Internal to the profession, lawyers are to be found in highly stratified work settings that mirror the changing economic arrangements they facilitate for their clients. Our longitudinal study of a fifteen-year cohort of lawyers (called to the Bar between 1975 and 1990) offers a unique opportunity to examine structural change in the legal profession together with the emergence of diverse career trajectories among mid-career lawyers. This cohort is unique for at least two reasons. This is the first cohort of lawyers in Canada with a significant number of women among its ranks. It is also a generation of lawyers who have confronted numerous transformations in the legal profession, including: two economic recessions during the decade of the eighties (Arnold and Kay 1995), the rapid growth of large law firms with branch offices and international mergers (Daniels 1992, 1993), increasing litigation (Nelson 1994), rising numbers of lawyers with increased employment and declining partnership shares (Abel 1989; Galanter and Palay 1991; Hagan *et al* 1991) and an influx of women to law since the mid-seventies (Curran 1986; Epstein 1993; Kay 1991; Menkel-Meadow 1986). During the era of rapid change in law practice, the Canadian legal profession has been challenged in its ability to offer new recruits attractive opportunities for advancement in the profession.

Our analysis examines relational dimensions of power in practice through the conceptual language of class hierarchy. Our analysis enables us to explore the permeability of class distinctions, specifically the changing nature of the profession's hierarchy in recent years, lawyers' mobility between strata, and the factors contributing to access through class (and glass) ceilings. Feminisation of the legal profession during the last two decades prompts us to incorporate gender into our analysis of class hierarchy in law practice. Macro- and micro-level analyses of data presented here reveal numerous transformations. At the macro-level, these analyses confirm that the broad contours of structural change that are occurring in the legal profession have involved sizeable increases in the number of lawyers who are business owners (partners and sole practitioners) with accordant autonomy and decision-making authority of prestigious positions. Yet, the majority of this cohort of lawyers reported working in non-supervisory capacities with very limited control over the content of their legal work and the policies that govern their place of employment. Gender differences abound. While the number of men working as sole practitioners rose across the six year period, the percentage of women sole practitioners fell. Women's increased access to partnership ranks and senior positions across different domains of practice is beyond dispute. Women made considerable inroads to partnership during this time, although they lagged behind men in their entry to small firm partnerships and more senior levels of larger firm partnerships. Research suggests women's mere presence among law firm partnerships has not brought them access to esteemed partner titles (Epstein 1993; Kay and Hagan 1995, 1998), commensurate monetary rewards (Chiu and Leicht 1999; Dixon and Seron 1995; Kay and Hagan 1995; Robson and Wallace 2002), nor equivalent responsibilities and status (Gorman 1999; Menkel-Meadow 1989).

Our micro-analysis of individual career mobility confirms these findings. Women remain disadvantaged as they accumulate valuable experience and expertise in law practice. Women incur reduced access to positions of power and authority regardless of years of experience, fields of law practiced, partnership, size of organisation, or sector of practice (eg, government, private practice, private industry). Smaller organisations (under ten lawyers) appear more biased toward the promotion of men, while larger organisations that are better able to offer more diverse benefit packages, appear more welcoming to women. This finding is consistent with a prior study of Toronto lawyers where smaller firms were less likely to grant partnership to women and large firms emerged as destinations of choice, at least as point of entry to practice (Hagan *et al* 1991:259). Interestingly, men, but not women, were likely to be rewarded for their demonstrated organisational commitment with enhanced authority and power. Accumulated social capital, in the form of networks developed through participation in professional activities and membership in associations, were invaluable to women's inroads to power over and beyond their experience and specialisation.

Women lawyers' reduced decision-making authority may fall short of that of men due to their lower presence in managerial hierarchies and truncated supervisory ladders (see Reskin and Ross 1992:356). But there is also something more in terms of the changing structure of private practice. Law firms have embarked on a marked departure from the employment model that was dominant in law firms for much of the 20th century (Galanter and Palay 1991; Nelson 1988; Smigel 1969). The traditional 'up-or-out' arrangement of law firms, with associates invited to partnership following employment on a probationary basis for 6 to 10 years from law school graduation, is being surplanted by a diversity of alternative arrangements (Gorman 1999:638). The middle level of the firm pyramid appears to be expanding, or at least diversifying. A new status of permanent employee has emerged. These permanent employees hold the title of 'associate' and are referred to informally as 'permanent associates.' These lawyers may be former probationary associates of the firm who have been denied partnership or they may have been hired directly into these long term positions. In some cases permanent employees remain eligible for partnership, although such consideration is not guaranteed, nor is a date designated by which it must occur (Gorman 1999:638). Permanent employment arrangements also exist as two-tier partnerships. In a two-tier partnership, the top tier of partners are fully fledged partners with a share in firm profits and voting rights. The second tier partners, or 'nonequity partners', hold the title of partner, but receive a salary and lack equity interests and voting rights with regard to firm governance (Gorman 1999:638; Hagan and Kay 1995). Future research should examine the differentiation of status and authority within partnership ranks. What responsibilities and decision-making authority are accorded to different titles among partners? Are men and women equally successful in their entry to these different status distinctions, and is there variation in authority within title distinctions?

Recent research suggests women are highly represented in these emerging secondary levels of partnerships and permanent employees (Gorman 1999; Hagan *et al* 1991; Kay and Hagan 1999). The implications of women's rising representation in these emerging secondary labor markets are considerable. For example, Elizabeth Gorman's research demonstrates that the work of permanent associates tends to be more routine, less challenging, and more bureaucratic (1999:662). Her findings are consistent with the work of Anthony Kronman (1993) who contends that lawyers' role is shrinking. In his book, *The Lost Lawyer: The Failing Ideals of the Legal Profession*, Kronman argues that lawyers once deliberated with clients about ends, whereas contemporary lawyers merely provide technical expertise regarding means. Gorman goes further to argue that permanent employees are particularly vulnerable to this diminishing scope of legal work, and with it a loss of intrinsic meaning and challenge. This more routinised and less intellectually rewarding work is not compensated for through supportive relationships with colleagues because firms that employ permanent associates tend to be firms where norms of collegiality have all but vanished (Gorman 1999:661). As Gorman writes,

> law firms that place a higher value on collegiality than other firms are more reluctant to make use of permanent employees. Permanent employment arrangements are incompatible with traditional collegial norms, which hold that professional colleagues should have autonomy over their own work, enjoy formally equal status, and participate in organisational governance (Gorman 1999:662).

Even for women who successfully break through the glass ceiling to senior ranks of partnership, there remains the question of power exercised versus title attained. As Reskin and Ross (1992) point out, attaining high levels in managerial hierarchies often assures men, more than women, the right to make decisions. Reskin and Ross's study of managers revealed male managers' more extensive authority in the span of their decision-making authority from advisory input to final decision-making (1992:354). Women's assignment to managerial job titles does not always ensure women of commensurate responsibilities and rewards. Future research needs to develop finer grained distinctions within managerial levels to examine the nature of power differential characterised by gender. As Wright, Baxter and Birkelund observe, 'The under-representation of women in positions of authority, especially high levels of management, is not simply an *instance* of gender inequality; it is probably a significant *cause* of gender inequality' (1995: 407).

Why are women lagging behind men in their attainment of power and authority in law practice? One explanation of why women have less access to authority in law practice than men do is human capital. According to this explanation, women have not yet acquired the years of experience and elite education that will allow them to rise to positions in which they can fully exercise authority. Over time, they will gain authority as their numbers increase and women currently in the 'pipeline', the early stages of their legal careers, advance to senior positions (Reskin and Padavic 1994:95). However, this argument remains unconvincing, given our sample consists of a cohort of lawyers well along in their careers, the majority with at least ten years experience in law practice. Moreover, our multivariate analyses reveal that gender differences persist when taking into account various measures of human capital. Women have not advanced into authority-conferring positions in proportion to their presence and years of experience in lower classes of the profession's hierarchy (Reskin and Padavic 1994:95; Menkel-Meadow 1989).

Another explanation stresses institutionalised barriers and organisational inertia that frustrate efforts to close the authority gap (Baron and Bielby 1986). A third explanation of these power differentials emphasises the effects of employers' perceptions through 'expectations states.' This research examines the effects of standards and interpretation of performance outcomes and suggests that differences in inferred ability persist in spite of equal performances because *different standards for competence* are applied to men and women (Foschi 1996:238). There is some evidence that stricter standards are routinely used to judge women versus men associates in law firms (Kay and Hagan 1998). For example, Kay and Hagan (1998:741) found that women must demonstrate extraordinary work commitment to improve their chances of partnership. Such commitment involved bringing in new clients, establishing large networks of corporate clientele, returning swiftly from maternity leaves and continuing to bill at elevated hours, and expressing a strong commitment to traditional career goals within conventional law firm practice. These judgments may transpire in ways that are sometimes both subtle and unintentional, as Kanter's study of corporate managers reveals (1977). The less tangible factors used to determine career progress (eg, collegiality, 'fit' with law firm culture, team player, commitment, shared values, and so on) may encourage a pattern of promotions based on social similarity between senior management and recruitment to the inner circles of power in practice. One way that organisations, such as law firms and other settings that employ lawyers, can shrink gendered promotion and authority gaps is by replacing informal promotion practices with formal criteria. Power holders' biases are less likely to come into play in personnel decisions where the criteria for evaluation are standardised and clearly documented (Roos and Reskin 1994:98).

More broadly, the results of our study raise troubling issues about the changing nature of law practice in contemporary society. Lawyers have been described as a class in of themselves; as the core of the 'new class' of 'knowledge workers' (Brint 1987; Glazer 1979). Yet, recently writers have begun to question whether law has become deprofessionalised or 'proletarianized' (Rothman 1984). In his recent work on the legal profession, Robert Rosen (1999) argues that legal work is becoming proletarianised: technical expertise is being confined to an ever smaller proportion of the lawyer labor force; routinisation of activity is becoming more pervasive, and responsibilities within legal work are becoming much less meaningful (Wright and Singelmann 1982:S177–8). This perspective on the profession views lawyers as becoming less distinguishable from other wage-workers in society because of a gradual decline in their traditional levels of control, autonomy, and skill-based authority in the production process (Braverman 1974; Brint 1987:37). The question our study raises is: What are the implications for women, whose representation is increasing in these contexts of more routinised and alienating sectors of law practice?

References

ABEL, Richard L. *American Lawyers*, (New York, Oxford University Press, 1989).

AHRNE, Goran and Erik Olin WRIGHT. Classes in the United States and Sweden: A Comparison, 183, 26(3/4)*Acta Sociologica*, 211–35.

ARNOLD, Bruce L. and Fiona M. KAY. Social Capital, Violations of Trust, and the Vulnerability of Isolates: The Social Organisation of Law Practice and Professional Self-Regulation, 1995, 23 *International Journal of the Sociology of Law*, 321–46.

BERGER, Marilyn J., and Kari A. Robinson. Woman's Ghetto Within the Legal Profession, 1993, 8 *Wisconsin Women's Law Journal*, 71–141.

BIELBY, William T. and James N. BARON. Men and Women at Work: Sex Segregation and Statistical Discrimination, 1986, 91 *American Journal of Sociology*, 759–99.

BRAVERMAN, Harry. *Labor and Monopoly Capital: The Degradation of Work in the Twentieth Century*, (New York, Monthly Review Press, 1974).

BRINT, Steven. The Occupational Class Identifications of Professionals: Evidence from Cluster Analysis, 1987, 6 *Research in Social Stratification and Mobility*, 35–57.

BROCKMAN, Joan. Gender Bias in the Legal Profession: A Survey of Members of the Law Society of British Columbia, 1992, 17 *Queen's Law Journal*, 91–146.

BROCKMAN, Joan. Leaving the Practice of Law: The Wherefores and the Whys, 1994, 32(1) *Alberta Law Review*, 116–80.

CARLIN, Jerome E. *Lawyers on Their Own: The Solo Practitioner in an Urban Setting*, (San Francisco, Austin and Winfield Publishers, 1994).

CARROLL, Glenn R, and Karl Ulrich Mayer. Job Shift Patterns in the Federal Republic of Germany: The Effects of Social Class, Industrial Sector, and Organisational Size, 1986, 51(3) *American Sociological Review*, 323–41.

CHIU, Charlotte, and Kevin T Leicht. When Does Feminisation Increase Equality? The Case of Lawyers, 1999, 33(3) *Law and Society Review*, 557–94.

CLEMENT, Wallace, John Myles. *Relations of the Ruling: Class and Gender in Postindustrial Societies,* (Montreal, McGill-Queen's University Press, 1994).

COLLINS, Randall. *The Credential Society: A Historical Sociology of Education and Stratification*, (New York, Academic, 1979).

COTTER, David A., Joan M Hermsen, Seth Ovadia, and Reeve Vanneman. The Glass Ceiling Effect. 2001, 80(2) *Social Forces*, 655–82.

CURRAN, Barbara. American Lawyers in the 1980s: A Profession in Transition, 1980, 20 *Law and Society Review* 19, 19–52,

CURRAN, B., K. Rosich, C. Carson and M. Puccetti. *The Lawyer Statistical Report: A Statistical Profile of the U.S. Legal Profession in the 1980s*, (Chicago, American Bar Foundation, 1985).

DANIELS, Ronald J. The Law Firm as an Efficient Community, 1992, 37 *McGill Law Journal*, 807–41.

DANIELS, Ronald J. Growing Pain: The Why and How of Law Firm Expansion, 1993, 47 *University of Toronto Law Journal*, 147–206.

DIXON, Jo and Carroll Seron. Stratification in the Legal Profession: Sex, Sector, and Salary, 1995, 29(3)*Law and Society Review*, 381–412.

ENGLAND, Paula. Women and Occupational Prestige: A Case of Vacuous Sex Equality, 1979, winter *Signs*, 252–65.

EPSTEIN, Cynthia Fuchs. *Women in Law* 2nd edn. (Urbana, University of Illinois Press, 1993).

EPSTEIN, Cynthia Fuchs, Robert Saute, Bonnie Oglensky, and Martha Gever. Report: Glass Ceilings and Open Doors: Women's Advancement in the Legal Profession, 1995, 64(2) *Fordham Law Review* 291–447.

FOSCHI, Martha. Double Standards in the Evaluation of Men and Women, 1996, 59(3) *Social Psychology Quarterly*, 237–54.

FRIEDMAN, Raymond A., and David Krackhardt. Social Capital and Career Mobility: A Structural Theory of Lower Returns to Education for Asian Employees, 1997, 33(3) *Journal of Applied Behavioural Science*, 316–34.

GALANTER, Marc. Mega-Law and Mega-Lawyering in the Contemporary United States. In *The Sociology of the Professions*, edited by R Dingwall and P Lewis, (London, Macmillan, 1983).

GALANTER, Marc and Thomas Palay. Why the Big get Bigger: The Promotion-to-Partner Tournament and the Growth of Large Law Firms, 1990, 76(4) *Virginia Law Review*, 747–811.

GALANTER, Marc, and Thomas Palay. *Tournament of Lawyers: The Transformation of the Big Law Firm*, (Chicago, University of Chicago Press, 1991).

GELLIS, Ann J. Great Expectations: Women in the Legal Profession, A Commentary on State Studies, 1991, 66 *Indiana Law Journal*, 941–76.

GIESEL, Grace M. The Business Client is a Woman: The Effect of Women as In-House Counsel on Women in Law Firms and the Legal Profession, 1993, 72 *Nebraska Law Review*, 760–802.

GLAZER, Nathan. Lawyers and the New Class. In *The New Class?*, edited by B Bruce-Briggs. (New Brunswick, Transaction Books, 1979).

GORMAN, Elizabeth H. Moving Away from 'Up or Out': Determinants of Permanent Employment in Law Firms, 1999, 33(3) *Law and Society Review*, 637–66.

GRANOVETTER, Mark S. *Getting a Job: A Study of Contacts and Careers*, (Cambridge, Harvard University Press, 1974).

HAGAN, John. The Gender Stratification of Income Inequality Among Lawyers, 1990, 6(3), *Social Forces*, 835–55.

HAGAN, John and F. KAY. *Gender in Practice: A Study of Lawyers' Lives*, (Oxford, Oxford University Press, 1995).

HAGAN, John and F. KAY. 'Hierarchy in Practice: The Significance of Gender in Ontario Law Firms.' In *Inside the Law: Canadian Law Firms in Historical Perspective*, edited by Carol Wilton, (Toronto, University of Toronto Press, 1996).

HAGAN, John, Marcie Huxter, and Patricia Parker. Class Structure and Legal Practice: Inequality and Mobility among Toronto Lawyers, 1988, 22(1) *Law and Society Review*, 9–55.

HAGAN, John, Marjorie ZATZ, Bruce ARNOLD, and Fiona KAY. Cultural Capital, Gender, and the Structural Transformation of Legal Practice, 1991, 25(2) *Law and Society Review*, 239–62.

HEDSTRÖM, Peter M. E., and Eva WALLIN. The Structure of Organisations and the Structure of Class, 1988, 7 *Research in Social Stratification and Mobility*, 225–46.

HEINZ, John P., and Edward O. LAUMANN. *Chicago Lawyers: The Social Structure of the Bar*, (New York, Russell Sage Foundation and American Bar Association, 1982).

HEINZ, John P., Robert L. NELSON, Edward O. LAUMANN, and Ethan MICHELSON. The Changing Character of Lawyers' Work: Chicago in 1975 and 1995. 1998, 3(4) *Law and Society Review*, 751–75.

HOFFERTH, Sandra L., Johanne BOISJOLY, and Greg J. DUNCAN. The Development of Social Capital, 1999, 11(1) *Rationality and Society*, 79–110.

HULL, Kathleen E. and Robert L. NELSON. Gender Inequality in Law: Problems of Structure and Agency in Recent Studies of Gender in Anglo-American Legal Professions, 1998, 23(3) *Law and Social Inquiry*, 681–705.

JACOBS, Jerry A. Women's Entry into Management: Trends in Earnings, Authority and Values among Salaried Managers, 1989, 37 *Administrative Science Quarterly*, 282–301.

KANTER, R. *Men and Women of the Corporation*, (New York, Basic Books, 1977).

KAY, F. M. *Transitions in the Ontario Legal Profession: A Survey of Lawyers Called to the Bar Between 1975–1990*. A Report Law Society of Upper Canada, (Toronto, Osgoode Hall, 1991).

KAY, Fiona M. Crossroads to Innovation and Diversity: The Careers of Quebec Lawyers, 2002, 47(4) *McGill Law Journal* 699–746.

KAY, Fiona M. and John HAGAN. Changing Opportunities for Partnership for Men and Women Lawyers During the Transformation of the Modern Law Firm, 1994, 32(3) *Osgoode Law Journal*, 413–56.

KAY, Fiona M. and John HAGAN. The Persistent Glass Ceiling: Gendered Inequalities in the Earnings if Lawyers, 1995, 46(2) *British Journal of Sociology*, 279–309.

KAY, Fiona M. and John HAGAN. Raising the Bar: The Gender Stratification of Law Firm Capitalization, 1998, 63(5) *American Sciological Review*, 728–43.

KAY, Fiona M. and John HAGAN. Cultivating Clients in the Competition for

Partnership: Gender and the Organisation Restructuring of Law Firms in the 1990s, 1999, 33(3), *Law and Society Review*, 517–56.

KAY, Fiona M. and Joan BROCKMAN. Barriers to Gender Equality in the Canadian Legal Establishment, 2000, 8 *Feminist Legal Studies*, 169–98.

KRITZER, Herbert M. The Professions Are Dead, Long Live the Professions: Legal Practice in a Postprofessional World, 1999, 33(4) *Law and Society Review*, 713–59.

KRONMAN, Anthony T. *The Lost Lawyer: Failing Ideals of the Legal Profession*, (Cambridge, Harvard University Press, 1993).

MACKAAY, E. 'L'Etat de la Profession D'Avocat au Quebec en 1991: Resume des Principales Conclusions du Sondage General des Membres du Barreau.' Un rapport au Barreau du Québec, 1991.

MACKINNON, Catherine. *Toward a Feminist Theory of the State*, (Cambridge, Harvard University Press, 1989).

MENKEL-MEADOW, Carrie. The Comparative Sociology of Women Lawyers: The 'Feminisation' of the Legal Profession, 1986, 24(4) *Osgoode Hall Law Journal*, 897–918.

MENKEL-MEADOW, Carrie. Feminisation of the Legal Profession: The Comparative Sociology of Women Lawyers, in *Lawyers in Society: Comparative Theories*, volume 3, edited by Richard Abel and Philip Lewis, (Berkeley, University of California Press, 1989).

MEYERSON, Eva M. Human Capital, Social Capital and Compensation: The Relative Contribution of Social Contacts to Managers' Incomes, 1994, 37 *Acta Sociologica*, 383–99.

MILLS, C. Wright. *White Collar: The American Middle Class*, (Oxford, Oxford University Press, 1966).

NELSON, Robert L. The Changing Structure of Opportunity: Recruitment and Careers in Large Law Firms, 1983, *American Bar Foundation Research Journal*, 109–42.

NELSON, Robert L. *Partners with Power*, (Berkeley and Los Angeles, University of California Press, 1988).

NELSON, Robert L. The Futures of American Lawyers: A Demographic Profile of a Changing Profession in a Changing Society, 1994, 44 *Case Western Reserve Law Review*, 345–406.

PETERSEN, Trond, Ishak SAPORTA, and Marc-David L. SEIDEL. Offering a Job: Meritocracy and Social Networks, 2000, 106(3) *American Journal of Sociology*, 763–816.

PORTER, L. W, R. M. STEERS, R. T. MOWDAY, and P. V. BOULIAN. Organisational Commitment, Job Satisfaction, and Turnover among Psychiatric Technicians, 1974, 59 *Journal of Applied Psychology*, 603–9.

RESKIN, Barbara F. and P. A. ROOS. *Job Queues, Gender Queues*, (Philadelphia, Temple University Press, 1990).

RESKIN, Barbara F. and Catherine E. ROSS. JOBS, Authority, and Earnings Among Managers: The Continuing Significance of Sex, 1992, 19(4) *Work and Occupations*, 342–365.

RESKIN, Barbara, and Irene PADAVIC. *Women and Men at Work*, (Thousand Oaks, Pine Forge Press, 1994).

ROBINSON, Robert V. and Maurice A. Garnier. Class Reproduction among Men and

Women in France: Reproduction Theory on Its Home Ground, 1985, 91(2) *American Journal of Sociology* 250–80.

ROBSON, Karen and Jean E. WALLACE. Gendered Inequalities in Earnings: A Study of Canada Lawyers, 2002, 38(1) *The Canadian Review of Sociology and Anthropology*, 75–95.

ROSEN, Robert. Proletarianizing Lives: Researching Careers, 1999, 33(3) *Law and Society Review*, 703–12.

ROTHMAN, Robert A. Deprofessionalisation: The Case of Law in America, 1984, 11(2)*Work and Occupations*, 183–206.

RUBINSON, Richard, and John RALPH. Technical Change and the Expansion of Schooling in the United States, 1890–1970, 1984, 57(3) *Sociology of Education*, 134–52.

SAVAGE, Mike, James BARLOW, Peter DICKENS, and Tony FIELDING. *Property, Bureaucracy and Culture Middle Class Formation in Contemporary Britain*, (London, Routledge, 1992).

SERON, Carroll. New Strategies for Getting Clients: Urban and Suburban Lawyers' Views, 1993, 27(2) *Law and Society Review* 399–419.

SMIGEL, Erwin O. The Wall Street Lawyer Reconsidered, 1969, 36 *New York* (August).

SPECTOR, Alan J. Class Structure and Social Change: The Contradictions of Class Relations in Advanced Capitalist Society 1995, 65(3–4) *Sociological Inquiry*, 329–38.

STAGER, David A. A., and Harry W. ARTHURS. *Lawyers in Canada*, (Toronto, University of Toronto Press, 1990).

STEWART, James B. *The Partners: Inside America's Most Powerful Law Firms*, (New York, Simon and Schuster, 1983).

WALLACE, Jean E. Corporatist Control and Organisational Commitment among Professionals: The Case of Lawyers Working in Law Firms, 1995, 73(3) *Social Forces*, 811–40.

WEGENER, Bernd. Job Mobility and Social Ties: Social Resources, Prior Job, and Status Attainment, 1991, 56 *American Sociological Review* February 60–71.

WHOLEY, Douglas R. Determinants of Firm Internal Labor Markets in Large Law Firms, 1985, 30 *Administrative Science Quarterly*, 318–35.

WOLF, Wendy C. and Neil D. FLIGSTEIN. Sex and Authority in the Workplace: The Causes of Sexual Inequality, 1979, 44(2) *American Sociological Review*, 235–52.

WRIGHT, Erik Olin. *Classes*, (London, Verso, 1985).

WRIGHT, Erik Olin. The Continuing Relevance of Class Analysis—Comments, 1996, 25 *Theory and Society*, 693–716.

WRIGHT, Erik Olin, and Luca PERRONE. Marxist Class Categories and income Inequality, 1977, 42 *American Sociological Review*, February 32–55.

WRIGHT, Erik Olin, and Joachim SINGELMANN. Proletarianization in the Changing American Class Structure, 1982, 88 *American Journal of Sociology*, Supp: 176–209.

WRIGHT, Erik Olin, Janeen BAXTER, and Gunn Elisabeth BIRKELUND. The Gender Gap in Workplace Authority: A Cross-National Study 1995, 60(3) *American Sociological Review*, 407–35.

11

From Professional Dominance to Organisational Dominance: Professionalism, Inequality, and Social Change Among Chicago Lawyers, 1975–1995

ROBERT L NELSON AND REBECCA L SANDEFUR
WITH JOHN P HEINZ AND EDWARD O LAUMANN

Many of the most significant changes in urban law practice in the United States in the last quarter of the 20th century relate to the organisational restructuring of law practice. Law practice organisations—large corporate law firms, the internal legal departments of corporations, and government law offices—have come to employ a growing share of lawyers, to dominate the supply of experts in important fields of law, and to command an ever larger proportion of the income generated from law practice. Patterns of inequality among lawyers are closely connected with the character of the organisations in which they work and their rank in organisational hierarchies. Twenty-five years ago women and minorities largely were excluded from law practice altogether; Jewish males still suffered the effects of discrimination by corporate law firms. At the turn of this century, women and minorities have gained entry to the legal profession, but are concentrated in particular organisational precincts—the associate ranks of law firms and jobs in internal corporate counsel and government offices. The effects of anti-semitism seem to have waned.

Organisations not only structure the material circumstances of lawyers' lives, they shape the very meaning of lawyer professionalism. The political values of lawyers vary systematically by the kind of organisation in which they work, and this differentiation by practice setting has become more pronounced in the last two decades. The professional autonomy of lawyers varies significantly by work setting. Lawyers working in larger, more bureaucratic organisations report less individual control in the selection of clients and how they do their work than lawyers in smaller, less bureaucratic law firms. Yet do such organisations encounter alienation and lack of commitment from lawyers as a result of size and bureaucratisation? Apparently not. Contrary to widespread reports about the dissatisfaction of lawyers who work in newly large and newly important organisational settings (see, eg Schiltz 1999), most lawyers working in organisational settings are satisfied with their jobs. Thus we see a clear structural trend toward the growth and bureaucratisation of law practice organisations, which results in decreased professional autonomy by lawyers, that is unopposed in the legal workplace.

In this chapter we develop an explicitly organisational perspective on patterns of structural and ideological change in the American legal profession. Much of our effort here is descriptive: to trace out the many ways in which urban law practice has become structured by law practice organisations. But we also have a theoretical objective. We see the organisational changes we document as part of a larger set of changes in the social structure of the American legal profession. Therefore, we first present a theoretical model of social change. We propose that the American legal profession has shifted from an era of 'professional dominance', in which the strategies and practices of individual professionals were of primary importance for structuring the delivery of legal services and the careers of lawyers, to a system of 'organisational dominance', in which the strategies and practices of organisations have become more significant in shaping the social structure of the bar. Second, we summarise a series of important demographic and economic changes among American lawyers that have taken place at the organisational level. Third, we compare the political and professional values of lawyers across organisational settings. Finally we compare measures of professional autonomy, professional service, and professional satisfaction across organisational settings. We conclude by discussing some practical and theoretical implications of the shift to an organisational legal profession in the United States.

From Professional Dominance to Organisational Dominance

In 1970, Eliot Freidson, the prominent medical sociologist, coined the term 'professional dominance' to refer to the power of the medical profession in controlling the provision of medical services in the United States. Freidson asserted that doctors as an occupation possessed 'a special form of legal "power"' and a 'special position of dominance' in the health care system, and that 'these structural characteristics of the profession have far more influence on the nature of medical care in the United States than either the good intentions and skills of individual members of the profession or the economic and administrative arrangements that are usually the focus of attempts at reform.' (1970:77) Interestingly, Freidson saw the dominant position of doctors as a problem that needed to be curbed by new administrative structures and a new role for clients in decisions regarding their health. Twenty years later, Freidson confronted the revolution in the social structure of medical care brought on by the rise of third-party financing and managed care organisations. In *Professionalism Reborn* (1994), he asserted the need for a revitalised conception of professionalism as a counterweight to market and bureaucratic forces in health care and other professional services. Implicit in Freidson's new line of argument was the realisation that professional occupations were no longer dominant actors in professional services. Organisations had assumed dominance in professional services.

In the last two decades the American legal profession also has confronted the tensions between traditional conceptions of lawyer professionalism, major changes in the market for legal services, and transformations in the organisations that deliver legal services. In response to dramatic changes in the number of lawyers and in the economic conditions of practice, a further decline in the popular image of lawyers, reports of rising levels of alienation and dissatisfaction among lawyers with their work, the organised bar and prominent legal academics voiced concerns about the declining professionalism of lawyers (See ABA 1986; Kronman 1993; Glendon 1994). Indeed, Freidson served as a member of the American Bar Association Commission investigating the problems of lawyer professionalism. Professionalism reform activities now operate as a sizeable cottage industry in the form of professionalism centres, law school curricular innovations, state-level professionalism commissions, and judicial professionalism initiatives (See Rhode 2000). Yet, as some critics have suggested (see, eg Nelson and Trubek 1992), these efforts to revitalise professionalism fail to address fundamental changes taking place in the organisation of law practice and ignore the more explicitly business-oriented models of professionalism embraced by many of the lawyers who are leading these innovations in the organisation of law practice (see, eg Seron 1996; Van Hoy 1997).

We suggest that changes in the social structure of the American legal profession may be usefully described as a shift from an occupational system characterised by professional dominance to an occupational system marked by organisational dominance. The salient features of these two models of social structure are presented in Figure 1. In the system of professional dominance, the market position of practitioners serving personal clients was protected by market closure and control; the economic position of corporate practitioners was set by relatively stable relationships between corporations and law firms (see Larson 1977). The stratification system of the profession mirrored this market structure: different segments of the legal market were divided by ethnoreligious segregation and patronage relationships between lawyers and clients. The professional ideology of most lawyers was connected to a vision of professional obligation, including the notion that lawyers somehow were separate from and above commerce, that they owed duties of loyalty to colleagues (law firm partners and opponents) as well as to clients, and that they had special obligations to improve the system of justice in their public and private roles (see Gordon 1988; Luban 1988). Galanter and Palay (1991) refer to many of these features in their description of the 'golden age' of law firms.

In the system of organisational dominance, the market position of practitioners serving personal clients is less secure than in an era of set fees and restrictions on advertising. (The term 'organisational dominance' was developed by Nelson, 1988, in his study of patterns of growth and bureaucratisation among large law firms in Chicago. Nelson used the term to emphasise the capacity of traditionally prestigious corporate law firms to maintain a position of dominance in the market for corporate legal services. Thus we are using the term somewhat differently to refer to the importance of organisations in structuring law practice, rather than the conditions under which certain firms achieve or lose a position of economic and professional status in the field of corporate practice.) The economic fortunes of corporate practitioners are tied to their positions in law firms.

Figure 1 Theoretical Schema: Two Historical Models of the Social Structure of the American, Legal Profession

	Professional Dominance	*Organizational Dominance*
1) Market Position		
-personal client sector	Market Closure	Weakly Regulated Market
-corporate sector	Stable Firm-Client Relationships	Hybrid Relational/ Transactional Competitive
2) Stratification	Ethnoreligious	Gender and Minority Status
3) Professional Ideology		
-ethic	Service/Obligation	Expertise/Economic Value
-rewards	Status	Money

The leading stratum of corporate firms command higher surpluses through the positioning of their firms in the corporate market and by developing new methods of profit accumulation within the firm. Gender inequality and minority status play a more prominent role in professional stratification than ethnoreligious characteristics, for it is these characteristics, more than ethnicity or religion, that correlate with the kinds of practice organisations lawyers work in and the rank individuals achieve in these organisations. Women make up a large share of recent entrants to the profession and thus are crucial to the system as lower level workers. The new managing elite of firms embrace marketisation and explicit strategic planning. As a result, we see a pluralisation of strategies for growth by law firms. Consistent with the entreprenuerialism of these lawyers, their professional ideology emphasises expertise over obligation. Thus in a profession marked by organisational dominance, we see the restructuring of partnership agreements and expectations about long term employment, new forms of competition for business, and efforts to revamp ethical rules to lift restrictions on firm expansion. Contrary to what one might expect based on the rhetoric of professional decline and alienation, we find that most lawyers appear satisfied with their careers and the managerial policies of the organisations in which they work. Hence, the professional ideologies of lawyers seem to embrace the organisational policies that are transforming the landscape of urban law practice in the United States.

Chicago Lawyers 1975–1995

These two historical models help make sense of the changes we can document that have taken place within the legal profession in Chicago between 1975 and 1995. Our purpose here is not to test these models in a statistical sense. Such a test would require data we do not possess. Rather we present selected findings from two studies of lawyers in Chicago, one conducted in 1975 and one conducted in 1995. Both surveys interviewed large random samples of lawyers practicing in the City of Chicago (n=777 and n=788 respectively) and commanded response rates of 82 per cent.

The 1975 survey led to the landmark book, *Chicago Lawyers*, by Heinz and Laumann (1982). It is an estimable baseline study of what arguably were the waning days of the era of professional dominance. In 1975 the Supreme Court had not yet stricken down rules against lawyer advertising or minimum fee schedules by lawyers. The growth in the number of lawyers and the size of large law firms was just beginning. Women and minorities were only starting to enroll in law schools in large numbers. There was no American Lawyer or National Law Journal. By the time of the 1995 survey, much had changed.

Here we present an overview of results that are developed in greater depth in other writings. We bring together findings on structural changes in the organisation of law practice with findings on the political and professional ideologies of practitioners who work in different organisational contexts.

Before presenting our results, we offer three caveats. First, the legal profession is a complex occupational and institutional system. In the last 20 years law and the law's jurisdiction has expanded in some areas, shrunk in others. These changes have produced great gains for some lawyers, while other lawyers have experienced decline. Moreover, it is a system that has undergone massive demographic shifts. While the magnitude of these changes are part of what we seek to explain in the models we present, it is unrealistic to think that one theoretical model can account for all these changes.

Second, many of the changes that we assert are part of a shift from a system of professional dominance to a system of organisational dominance are matters of degree. Very little is entirely new in the legal profession. One finds quotes from New York lawyers in the 1890's decrying the rise of law factories. Erwin Smigel's study of Wall Street law firms (1969) was subtitled with a question: 'The Professional Organisation Man?' And Rayman Solomon (1992) and Robert Gordon (1988) have documented that there have been numerous cycles of complaints about lawyer professionalism throughout the 20th century. Moreover, when Freidson wrote *Professional Dominance* (1970), he was developing an institutional theory of the power of the medical profession. This is even more apparent in *Professional Powers: A Study of the Institutionalisation of Formal Knowledge* (1986). Hence, the shift from professional dominance to organisational dominance is not simply a move from individualised models of professional power to institutionalised models, but rather a change in the way professional power is institutionalised in organisational forms. Yet we suggest that the last two decades have produced fundamental changes in the social structure of the legal profession that deserve comment and further analysis from an organisational perspective.

Third, some of the patterns we report here may be unique to Chicago. Chicago is one of the four major legal centres in the United States, along with New York, Los Angeles, and Washington, DC. Like these other cities, it has a distinctive demographic make-up and some distinctive local professional traditions. Still, much of what we see in Chicago is reflected in patterns we can see in national census data and from the research findings of scholars on other cities, such as Hagan and Kay's work on Toronto (1995) and Dixon and Seron's work on New York (1995).

Changing Patterns of Organisation and Inequality

From 1975 to 1995 there have been dramatic changes in the social organisation of lawyers, some of which are familiar to casual observers, some of which are not widely known.

A. Overall growth. The number of lawyers in the United States more than doubled over the last 30 years, from some 355,242 in 1971 to 857,931 in 1995 (Sikes, Carson and Gorai 1972; Carson 1999). In the City of Chicago the number of lawyers rose from about 15,000 in 1975 to about 30,000 in 1995.

B. Growing organisational scale. There has been a long term trend toward organisational employment in the American legal profession. Outside the judiciary, from 1950 to 1980, the percentage of lawyers in some kind of law firm or organisation increased from 43 per cent to 62 per cent (Spangler 1986). What is most striking in the Chicago data is the increasing proportion of lawyers working in large private firms. Only 31 per cent of private firm attorneys in 1975 worked in firms over 30 lawyers, and only 15 per cent in firms of 100 lawyers or more. By 1995, a majority of lawyers in firms were in firms of 30 or more; 41 per cent were in firms of 100 or more lawyers; and 22 per cent worked in firms with 300 or more lawyers. In 1975 the average size of the law firms in which respondents worked was 27; by 1995 the average size of a respondent's firm was 141 (see Heinz, Nelson and Laumann 2001).

The size of government law offices and corporate counsel offices also have increased significantly. Prosecutors' offices grew from an average size of 127 lawyers to 543 lawyers, while other government offices grew from 42 to 327 lawyers. The average corporate law staff grew from 21 lawyers to 55 lawyers.

Thus a larger percentage of lawyers work in organisational contexts and average organisational size has increased dramatically.

C. The shift to business representation. The Chicago surveys estimated the percentage of legal effort in fields of law in 1975 and 1995. Because the number of lawyers in Chicago roughly doubled between the two years, the base of absolute time for 1995 is twice that for 1975. Thus, the same percentage of effort in 1975 and 1995 indicates a doubling in the absolute amount of legal work of a particular sort; a twofold increase in percentage represents a fourfold increase in absolute effort; and so on. (See Heinz, Nelson, Laumann, and Michelson 1998 for a methodological discussion and presentation of full results.)

The most fundamental change revealed in this analysis is the rise of legal effort devoted to business compared to personal clients, from a split of 53 per cent business work vs. 40 per cent personal client work in 1975 to a split of 64 per cent business work vs. 29 per cent business work in 1995. The Census of Service Industries data suggests a similar pattern nationally. Receipts from individuals decreased from 52 per cent of total receipts in 1972 to 40 per cent in 1992, while receipts from businesses increased from 42 per cent to 51 per cent. (US Census, 1976, 1996).

It is interesting to note shifts in individual fields as well. Some fields experienced striking growth. Most notable is business litigation, which grew from 4 per cent to 14 per cent, or a sevenfold absolute increase. Personal injury defence grew from 4 per cent to 7 per cent, a three and one-half fold absolute increase, compared to personal injury plaintiffs' work, which stayed at 6 per cent, reflecting a doubling of absolute effort. Several fields, such as divorce, were in a steady state. Some fields exhibited real decline, such as public utilities regulation (from 3 per cent to 1 per cent) and probate (from 8 per cent to 3 per cent).

The very significant growth in corporate legal services that these data reveal appears to be the engine driving many of the other changes we observe in the structure of the profession.

D. Increasing specialisation. An index of specialisation by fields of law based on estimates of the amount of time lawyers spent in fields rose from 0.48 to 0.57 between 1975 and 1995. (If a lawyer spent all her time in one field, her index value would equal 1.) Thus it appears that substantive specialisation has increased some 20 per cent in the bar overall. It increased more so in business fields, than in personal client fields. Law firms display a bimodal distribution of specialisation, with associates reporting much higher levels of field specialisation than partners. (See Heinz, Nelson, Laumann, and Michelson, 1998 for a full discussion.)

E. Greater income inequality. The legal profession historically has displayed more income inequality than many other professions, and in the last 20 years earnings inequality among lawyers has increased significantly. According to self-reports from our samples of Chicago lawyers, there has been modest growth in lawyer's income overall between 1975 and 1995, but very dramatic differences across organisational contexts. Solo practitioners experienced significant declines in real income, from $115,694 in 1975 to $78,583 in 1995, as have government lawyers, from $63,458 to $49,894. In 1975, the average salary of the highest earning category of lawyers (partners in firms of 30 or more lawyers) made about four times the average earnings of the lowest paying category of lawyers, government lawyers. By 1995 this disparity had grown to a sevenfold difference.

Individual level regression analyses (see Sandefur and Laumann 1997) indicate that women, minorities, and the graduates of lower status law schools had significantly lower incomes than other lawyers in 1995, but that much of their disadvantage was attributable to the fact that they were less likely to work in large law firms or to be partners in large law firms. The graduates of elite and prestigious schools (as defined by Heinz and Laumann 1982) gained more from their educational credentials in 1995 than 1975, in significant part because they were more likely to gain a position in a large law firm. Differences across ranks in law firms also grew over the period. In 1975, we estimate that the average partner/associate earnings ratio was 2.2. By 1995 the ratio had grown to 3.5.

Multi-variate analyses of income also suggest that practice organisation has become a more important determinant of lawyer income in 1995 than in 1975. When fields of law were added to regression models in 1975, they explained a significant portion of variance in income over what practice setting explained (an increment of 5 per cent in variance explained). In a similar procedure in 1995, adding field of law contributed nothing to variance explained.

F. Shift from ethnoreligious segregation by field and practice setting to stratification by gender and minority status.

A cardinal finding of Heinz and Laumann's 1975 study was the persistence of ethnoreligious stratification in the Chicago bar. Tables 1 and 2 revisit the issue by looking at the distribution of particular subgroups of lawyers by field of law and practice setting in 1975 and 1995. Here we look at Jewish men and women, women, Type 1 Protestants (the traditionally privileged group in Heinz and Laumann's analysis, it includes Presbyterians, Episcopalians, and Congregationalists), and African-American men and women. We will comment on differences of 10 per cent from the presence of a group in the sample overall and their presence in a particular field or practice setting.

By this standard, Tables 1 and 2 replicate Heinz and Laumann's findings for 1975. Jews depart from what we would expect at random in some 7 fields in 1975: they are underrepresented in corporate civil litigation, patents, and securities law, and overrepresented in corporate tax, divorce, personal injury plaintiffs' work, and criminal defence. By 1995, the percentage of Jews in the sample overall has declined (from 33 per cent to 25 per cent), and they have a less distinct profile. While they continue to be overrepresented in divorce practice and criminal defence, they have moved into corporate litigation and securities work at a level proportionate to their presence in the sample, and are underrepresented only in patents and

Table 1 Social Origins of Practitioners in Selected Fields of Law, by Year of Survey

	% of Total Legal Effort		% Female		% Jewish		% Type I Protestant		% African American	
	1975	1995	1975	1995	1975	1995	1975	1995	1975	1995
Corporate Civil Litigation	3.1%	13.8%	3.2%	19.2%	12.9%	24.7%	9.7%	14.4%	0.0%	4.1%
Banking	2.9%	2.0%	0.0%	25.0%	36.4%	25.0%	27.3%	5.0%	3.0%	4.9%
Patents	4.3%	2.2%	0.0%	4.8%	14.7%	9.5%	26.5%	9.5%	0.0%	4.8%
Securities	2.6%	3).4%	4.5%	41.7%	13.6%	25.0%	36.4%	11.0%	0.0%	0.0%
Tax, CFI/Business	3.4%	23%	0.0%	0.0%	43.3%	30.0%	10.0%	20.0%	0.0%	6.3%
Divorce	5.9%	2.5%	5.3%	37.5%	56.1%	34.8%	0.0%	4.4%	3.5%	0.0%
Personal Injury Plaintiff	6.3%	6.2%	1.6%	13.5%	43.5%	21.6%	1.6%	7.8%	0.0%	0.0%
Personal Civil Litigation	2.2%	4.8%	4.2%	20.0%	33.3%	30.0%	0.0%	12.0%	0.0%	0.4%
General Family Paying	3.0%	0.6%	7.4%	28.6%	37.0%	14.3%	7.4%	0.0%	18.0%	0.0%
Criminal Defense	5.3%	2.9%	4.5%	33.3)%	45.5%	41.7%	4.5%	4.2%	2.2%	12.5%
% of Practicing Lawyers	39.0%	40.7%	4.2%	27.6%	32.5%	24.6%	12.6%	11.9%	2.3%	4.2%

Source: Chicago Lawyers Surveys

Note: The characteristics of practitioners are computed from lawyers who report investing at least 25% of their time in the specified field of law. Estimates of legal effort are based on the time reports of practicing lawyers, under the assumption that each lawyer contributes 20 "timeballs" of effort.

Table 2 Social Origins of Practitioners, by Practice Setting, by Year of Survey

| | Practicing Lawyer | | Solo Practice | | Firms of 2–30 | | Firms of 31–99 | |
	1975	1995	1975	1995	1975	1995	1975	1995
n	698	674	146	104	259	184	60	64
% Jewish	32.5%	24.6%	41.1%	32.0%	42.6%	26.5%	20.0%	21.9%
% Female	4.2%	27.6%	2.7%	18.3%	3.1%	19.1%	6.7%	12.5%
% Type I Prot	12.6%	11.9%	6.8%	8.7%	11.5%	9.0%	6.7%	9.4%
% Af-Am	2.3%	4.2%	4.2%	4.9%	0.8%	1.6%	1.8%	1.6%

| | Firms of 100+ | | House Counsel | | Government & PD/LSLA | |
	1975	1995	1975	1995	1975	1995
n	57	165	99	78	77	75
% Jewish	15.%	24.8%	17.2%	23.1%	24.7%	12.5%
% Female	3.5%	26.7%	3.0%	47.4%	10.4%	56.0%
% Type I Prot	38.6%	17.6%	17.2%	16.7%	6.5%	8.3%
% Af-Am	1.8%	1.8%	2.0%	6.4%	6.5%	14.7%

Source: Chicago Lawyers Surveys

family law. The flipside of the pattern for Jews is the pattern for Type 1 Protestants. In 1975 they were overrepresented in banking, patents, and securities work, and underrepresented (indeed absent) from divorce work. By 1995 none of these differences held and the only field from which they were absent was family law. The pattern for these groups was reflected in their distribution across practice settings. In 1975 Jews were overrepresented among small firms and underrepresented in firms of 30 or more and in corporate counsel positions. By 1995 they were underrepresented only in government positions. Type 1 Protestants were overrepresented in Firms of 100 or more lawyers in 1975, but were distributed evenly across settings in 1995. Thus the ethnoreligious segmentation that characterised Chicago lawyers in 1975 has largely eroded by 1995.

The pattern for women and African-American men and women reveals a different history. Women constituted only 4 per cent of practicing lawyers in 1975; by 1995 they made up 28 per cent of Chicago lawyers. African-Americans constituted 2 per cent of practicing lawyers in 1975 and just doubled their presence twenty years later to a mere 4 per cent of Chicago lawyers. (Minorities as a group, including Latinos and Asian-Americans, as well as African-Americans, grew to 7 per cent by 1995. Because there appear to be important differences among these minority subpopulations, we have focused solely on African-Americans in this analysis.) Given the low numbers of both groups in 1975, there are virtually no disparities of note at that time. It is interesting, however, that women and minorities were largely absent from corporate fields in the mid-seventies. By 1995, there are enough numbers of these groups to begin to map their location in the profession. Women are underrepresented in patents, corporate tax, and personal civil litigation, and overrepresented in securities and divorce. The overrepresentation in divorce is understandable based on what we know about the preferences of some female divorce clients to be represented by female attorneys (see, eg Mather, McEwen and Maiman, 2001). The pattern in other fields is more difficult to explain. The overrepresentation of women in securities work in part reflects the organisational contexts in which women are more likely to work: large law firms and corporate counsel offices. As Table 3 indicates, ¼ of securities work is done by inside counsel; ½ is done by lawyers working in firms of 100 or more lawyers. Women are significantly overrepresented in inside counsel positions: they make up almost ½ of corporate counsel, compared to 28 per cent of the sample. And they constitute more than ¼ of attorneys in large firms, albeit largely at the associate level.

By 1995 African-Americans had gained a presence in all the corporate fields listed here except securities; the only field in which they were overrepresented was criminal defence. Again, an organisational mechanism may explain why. African-Americans are three times as likely to work in government jobs as we would predict based on their presence in the sample. As Table 4 shows, some 32 per cent of criminal defence work is undertaken by government lawyers (public defenders). Thus employment as public defenders may contribute to the relatively high presence of African-Americans in criminal defence work.

Table 2 demonstrates that women and minorities tend to have distinctive profiles in terms of the settings where they work in 1995. Women are slightly underrepresented in solo practice and in firms of less than 100 lawyers. Their presence in firms over 100 lawyers roughly equals their presence in the profession overall. Most striking is their overrepresentation as inside counsel and government lawyers, where they make up 47 per cent and 56 per cent respectively of the lawyers in these settings. While the numbers for African-Americans are small, there is a tendency in both 1975 and 1995 for African-Americans to practice alone or in government, and to be slightly underrepresented in private firms. By 1995 they showed slightly higher numbers in inside counsel positions (6.4 per cent compared to 4.2 per cent in sample overall) and much more of a presence in government employment than in the sample as a whole (15 per cent vs. 4 per cent).

A multivariate analysis of the careers of respondents found that there were some differences in where men and women began their careers: women were more likely to begin in government and corporate counsel offices, but

Table 3 Where Work Is Done, Part 1: Distribution of Legal Effort and Income by Type of Organization for Selected Corporate Client Fields, by Year of Survey

	Firms of 2–30		Proportionate Change	Firms of 31–99		Proportionate Change	Firms of 100+		Proportionate Change	House Counsel		Proportionate Change
	1975	1995		1975	1995		1975	1995		1975	1995	
% of Practicing Lawyers	37.1%	27.9%	-0.25	8.6%	9.5%	0.10	8.2%	24.5%	1.99	14.2%	11.6%	-0.18
Corporate Civil Litigation	25.5%	32.8%	0.29	27.6%	12.4%	-0.55	27.9%	37.8%	0.35	13.6%	6.0%	-0.56
Banking	31.9%	19.6%	-0.39	6.7%	2.8%	0.58	14.8%	26.7%	0.80	'19.2%	41.7%	0.06
Patents	71.0%	32.3%	-0.55	1.8%	43.8%	23.33	2.5%	20.6%	7.24	12.7%	3.3%	-0.74
Securities	10.0%	6.9%	-0.31	37.5%	5.2%	-0.86	33.9%	51.0%	0.50	11.7%	26.6%	1.27
Tax, CFI/Business	19.1%	14.5%	-0.24	23.2%	3.9%	-0.83	9.2%	48.2%	4.24	46.2%	25.2%	-0.45
% of Total Income	42.8%	30.8%	-0.28	12.5%	9.6%	-0.23	8.7%	37.0%	3.25	11.6%	8.8%	-0.24

Source: Chicago Lawyers Surveys

Note: Estimates of legal effort are based on the time reports of practicing lawyers, under the assumption that each lawyer contributes 20 "timeballs" of effort. Entries represent the percent of total effort in the field performed in the specified organizational type.

Table 4 Where Work Is Done, Part 1: Distribution of Legal Effort and Income by Type of Organization for Selected Personal Client Fields, by Year of Survey

	Solo Practice		Proportionate Change	Firms of 2–30		Proportionate Change	Firms of 31–99		Proportionate Change	Firms of 100+		Proportionate Change
	1975	1995		1975	1995		1975	1995		1975	1995	
% of Practicing Lawyers	20.9%	15.4%	-0.26	37.1%	27.9%	-0.25	8.6%	9.5%	0.10	8.2%	24.5%	1.99
Divorce	53.0%	43.8%	-0.17	42.5%	33.7%	-0.21	0.4%	0.0%	-1.00	0.6%	5.6%	8.33
Personal Injury, Plaintiff	35.5%	30.3%	-0.15	57.5%	64.4%	0.12	0.0%	2.3%		0.8%	1.8%	1.25
Personal Civil Litigation	30.6%	32.4%	0.06	52.6%	38.5%	-0.27	13.5%	1.5%	-0.15	3.3%	11.2%	2.39
General Family (paying)	41.2%	77.6%	0.88	33.4%	8.8%	-0.74	1.9%	0.0%	-1.00	0.7%	1.7%	1.43
Criminal Defense	46.5%	37.1%	-0.20	26.1%	15.7%	-0.40	0.6%	5.6%	8.33	4.2%	9.3%	1.21
% of Total Income	18.6%	9.5%	-0.49	42.8%	30.8%	-0.28	12.5%	9.6%	-0.23	8.7%	37.0%	3.25

	Government and PD/LS/LA		Proportionate Change
	1975	1995	1995
% of Practicing Lawyers	11%	11%	0.01
Divorce	2.1%	12.4%	4.90
Personal Injury, Plaintiff	1.2%	0.4%	-0.67
Personal Civil Litigation	0.0%	5.7%	
General Family (paying)	17.9%	11.9%	-0.34
Criminal Defense	22.6%	32.3%	0.43
% of Total Income	5.8%	4. 3 %	-0.26

Source: Chicago Lawyers Surveys

Note: Estimates of legal effort are based on the time reports of practicing lawyers, under the assumption that each lawyer contributes 20 "timeballs" of effort. Entries represent tile percent of total effort in the field performed in the specified organizational type.

were equally likely to start with jobs in large law firms (that is, 100 or more lawyers) (Hull and Nelson 2000). Male and female careers diverge, however, as more women exit large law firms for other contexts than their male counterparts. After controlling for a wide range of cohort, human capital, family context, and preference variables, we found that women were only 30 per cent as likely as men to make partner in firms. Kay (1997) and Kay and Hagan (1998) found similar results for attorneys in Toronto. Women who displayed extraordinarily high levels of cultural capital by bringing clients to their firms and by attaining prominence in professional activities were promoted to partner at the same rates as men; 'average' women fared much worse than 'average' men in making partner. Hagan and Kay (1995) assert that women function as pliable workers at the base of the increasingly steep pyramids of corporate partnerships. While we have some reservations about Hagan and Kay's theoretical model, we think they are right that women function as a critical source of labor in firms, where they are much less likely to gain a position where they can benefit from the leveraging of associate labor. Our results and their's are pessimistic about how rapidly this will change and whether women will ever gain partnership positions in major firms at the same rate as their male counterparts.

A similar pattern seems to hold for African-American lawyers. We do not possess enough cases of African-American lawyers in the random sample of Chicago lawyers to mount as elaborate a multivariate analysis as we have done for women. Our sample contains only three African-American partners in any size law firm, or 1.4 per cent of firm partners. None of these respondents are partners in Chicago megafirms of 300 or more lawyers. In the 1995 Chicago survey, we collected interviews from an oversample of some 36 African-American attorneys. (The oversample was generated through an elaborate system of snowball nominations from African-American respondents in the random sample.) Analyses of the combined sample which controlled for prestige of law school attended and age, found that African-American lawyers were significantly less likely than the sample overall to achieve a partnership in any size firm and in law firms of 100 or more lawyers. (For a rich discussion why this is the case see Wilkins and Gulati 1996). A similar analysis of an oversample of 39 Hispanic lawyers, based on a random sample of Hispanic-surnamed individuals in the attorney registration list, demonstrated that Hispanics lawyers also were less likely than other members of our sample to achieve partnership in law firms. Controls for law school status, however, explained away the under-representation of Hispanic lawyers as partners in large law firms.

G. Increasing economic dominance of large law firms. Table 3 reports the share of lawyers, legal effort, and total income among law firms of different size and house counsel, and how these shares has changed from 1975 to 1995.

Consider first the changes in the first and last rows: the percentage of practicing lawyers in these contexts and the share of total income commanded by the lawyers in these contexts. Firms of 2–30 lawyers declined as a percentage of practicing lawyers from 37 per cent to 28 per cent—a 25 per cent decline—while their share of income also declined from 43 per cent to 31 per cent—a 28 per cent decline. Firms of 31–99 lawyers gained slightly as a percentage of practicing lawyers, but experienced a decline in the percentage of total income. The percentage of lawyers in firms of 100 or more rose by 200 per cent, but their share of total income rose by 325 per cent. House counsel experienced a modest decline both in numbers of lawyers and share of income. These figures suggest a clear winner in the market for corporate legal services: the lawyers working in the largest law firms.

The breakdown on the changing shares of firms and house counsel in selected fields of corporate law suggest why this is the case. Firms of 2–30 gained a larger share of corporate civil litigation, but lost share in the four other fields; firms of 31–99 gained significantly in patents (probably as a result of the increasing size of patent firms, that is, the entry of patent firms into the 31–99 size category over the 20 year period), but lost share in the other four fields; and house counsel saw modest gains in their share of banking and tax and more considerable gains in their share of securities work. Firms over 100 lawyers registered substantial growth in all five of these fields.

The breakdown of the share of personal client fields by practice setting (Table 4) shows that solos and small firm lawyers continue to dominate typically lower status, lower paying work. Solo practitioners do more than ¾ of family work, almost ½ of divorce work, more than ⅓ of personal injury plaintiffs' work and personal litigation. Firms of 2–30 lawyers are especially dominant in personal injury plaintiffs' practice. Larger firms do less than 10 per cent of the work in most of these fields. It is interesting to observe, however, that firms over 100 lawyers now do a small amount of divorce work (5.4 per cent) whereas they did none in 1975. And they have doubled their share of criminal defence work (from 4.2 per cent to 9.3 per cent). No doubt these increments represent the presence of so-called blue chip divorce work and white collar criminal defence work in large firms, practice areas that have become more respectable in corporate law firms over the last twenty years. Government lawyers, public defenders, and legal services lawyers do a significant amount of criminal defence (32.3 per cent) and modest amounts of divorce and family law (12.4 per cent and 11.9 per cent, respectively).

These data drive home a simple but important point about the segmentation in the fields of legal practice. The rise of large law firms and the increase in their share of lawyer income has not come from invading the personal client sector of the profession, but rather by increasing dominance in traditional fields of corporate practice.

These data demonstrate that urban law practice is structured by the organisations in which lawyers practice. A larger proportion of lawyers work in organisational contexts, and these organisations have grown in size dramatically. The rapid increase in the demand for legal services by business clients has fed the process of law firm growth. The clearest beneficiary of this trend have been the largest law firms, those with 100 lawyers or more, who have significantly increased their share of corporate fields and have increased their share of total income from law practice at an even faster rate. As a result, government lawyers and solo practitioners have fallen seriously behind their professional counterparts in terms of economic rewards. Stratification in the profession is increasingly defined by the hierarchies among and within organisations. While ethno-religious characteristics are no longer strongly correlated with these hierarchies, gender and race are now very strongly correlated with organisational stratification. Women (white and minority), African-Americans, and Hispanics are much less likely to gain partnership in large corporate firms, and are much more likely to practice in government or corporate counsel departments.

The personal client sector of the profession, which may depend more on the legal profession's ability to retain control of the market for legal transactions, appears to have suffered the most in economic terms over the last twenty years. The demand for many types of personal legal services has been stagnant or declined, while large numbers of new lawyers have gained the license to practice. The result has been a decline in real earnings for solo practitioners.

While organisational variables are powerful determinants of the material aspects of American lawyers' careers, do they also shape the political values of lawyers and the attitudes and behaviors that we associate with lawyer professionalism? We now turn to those questions.

Lawyer Professionalism from an Organisational Perspective

While discussions of lawyer professionalism consistently bemoan the ambiguity of the term, the Chicago surveys contain measures of three elements of professionalism that are central to most discussions: a) whether lawyers can exercise autonomous professional judgment in their work—free from control by clients and by superordinates; b) whether lawyers provide public service through pro bono representation or professional or community activities; and c) whether they remain committed to their professional identity as a lawyer and are satisfied with their work. A related but distinct set of concerns is raised about the political orientations of lawyers. Where in the broad divide between political identification with government regulation and redistribution and corporate power and market-based distributions of rewards do lawyers reside? We will compare lawyers practicing in different organisational contexts along these dimensions of professionalism.

The Political Orientation of Lawyers

In 1975 and 1995 respondents were presented with a set of agree–disagree items that asked about matters of social welfare and policy in the United States. The items yield a scale of economic liberalism that reliably distinguishes the political orientations of individuals (see, eg Heinz, Laumann, Nelson and Salisbury 1993). Table 5 reports the mean economic liberalism scores of practitioners by practice setting for both years of the survey, along with the percentage reporting they identified with the Democratic Party on national politics. According to this measure, it appears that lawyers have become more politically conservative even as they have become more likely to self-identify as Democrats. The mean scale score in 1975 was 3.28, but dropped to 3.02 in 1995, while the per cent Democrat rose from 36 per cent to 44 per cent. This pattern may reflect actual political trends: as the Democratic Party under Bill Clinton became more centrist, it attracted a larger number of self-identifying Democrats. It may also reflect the complexities of conducting surveys in different historical periods. The lower scale values may result in part from intervening events. One item in the scale concerned the government's obligation to provide health care to those who cannot afford to pay for it. In the mid-seventies this item received broad support. By 1995, in the wake of the Clinton administration's failed health care initiative, the item commanded far less agreement. But party affiliation also may have been shaped by context. In 1975, when the first Mayor Richard Daley ruled Chicago with a Democratic machine, some lawyers reported they were independents rather than Democrats, even though the question attempted to avoid this problem by asking about national political party affiliation.

Putting these worries aside, we find interesting differences across practice settings. By far the most liberal group in both years are government attorneys, followed by solo practitioners. It is quite striking that lawyers in the

Table 5 Political Orientation by Practice Setting, 1975, 1995

| | Economic Liberalism Scale | | % Democrat | |
	1975	1995	1975	1995
Solos	3.31	3.23	35.4%	44.8%
Firms of 2-9	3.19	2.99	36.9%	41.5%
Firms of 10-30	3.35	3.07	34.2%	60.7%
Firms of 31-99	3.18	3.02	31.0%	34.4%
Firms of 100+	3.29	2.82	41.9%	37.2%
House Counsel	3.13	2.86	28.6%	44.6%
Government and PD/LSLA	3.63	3.36	47.3%	56.7%
Overall	3.28	3.02.	36.2%	43.7%
Sig For Chi-square	.000	.000	.082	.008
n	662	625	680	634

Note: The economic liberalism scale can range from 1 to 5, from politically conservative to politically liberal. The scale is based on 7 Likert-scale items.

largest law firms in 1975 scored just above the mean on liberalism. Large firm attorneys show the largest drop in liberalism across the period, so that they are the most conservative segment of the bar in 1995. Thus the two groups of practitioners most closely identified with business clients, large firms and inside counsel, have the most conservative political values.

The shift in the political values of attorneys in large law firms is relevant to the research literature on the social role of corporate attorneys. One formulation of the autonomy of corporate lawyers is that they act as a mediating influence on powerful corporate clients, infusing corporate practices with regard for the broader social consequences of corporate conduct rather than narrow economic interest (Parsons 1962; Horsky 1952; Macaulay 1979; Rosen 1984; Gordon 1988). The findings of research in the 1970's and early 1980's suggested that lawyers representing corporations had political values that were more liberal than corporate management, which made it more likely that lawyers would attempt to serve this mediating role (see, eg Erlanger and Klegon 1978; Nelson 1988). While the research also cast doubt on whether corporate lawyers acted on these values in practice (Nelson 1988), there might at least be some tendency for corporate lawyers to moderate corporate positions.

The Chicago data suggest that corporate attorneys no longer are liberally inclined and are now more closely aligned with the political positions of corporate business. Moreover, a multivariate analysis of the values data suggests that practice setting is more strongly correlated with political values in

1995 than was the case in 1975 (Payne and Nelson 2000). After controlling for individual characteristics that correlate with political values (chiefly age, gender, and race), this analysis found that a larger percentage of the variance in political values was accounted for by practice context in 1995 than in 1975. Thus lawyers working in different organisational settings had become more different in their basic political outlook over the last twenty years.

Professional Autonomy

Heinz and Laumann (1982) made professional autonomy a central theme of the conclusion of their book. They asserted that there was an inverse relationship between the status of lawyers and their autonomy from clients: lawyers in the corporate hemisphere of the profession had more status and resources but were more closely controlled by clients; lawyers in the personal client sector enjoyed less status within the profession but more autonomy from clients. Yet the 1975 version of the instrument asked relatively few questions that actually tried to measure it. Two items they did employ, which were replicated in the 1995 survey, asked the respondent to characterise their work by identifying where it fell between two polar opposite descriptions. One set of polar opposites sought to measure freedom in choosing clients. Another set of polar opposites sought to measure freedom from supervision or guidance by more senior lawyers. In an attempt to better measure professional autonomy, the 1995 survey included a pair of polar opposites asking whether the respondent had control over the strategies they pursue in practice or whether they were designed and executed with others. The 1995 survey also borrowed a question from Nelson's (1988) study of large law firms and asked whether they ever had refused to do an assignment for a client 'because of their personal values.'

Table 6 summarises the results. Solo practitioners consistently report more autonomy than lawyers in other settings. They are the most likely to say they have latitude in choosing clients, in controlling their own work, in designing work strategies, and in refusing clients for personal reasons. Attorneys in private firms, regardless of size, are only slightly less likely than solos to say they choose their clients, but inside counsel and government lawyers in 1995 admit that they have little choice over who they represent. Interestingly, inside counsel report more control over their work than do lawyers in firms of 10 or more. But only a small portion of attorneys in firms, corporate law departments, or government law offices are free to design and pursue their own practice strategies. A similar pattern holds for refusing client assignments. Not surprisingly, perhaps, corporate counsel (who serve one client, even though they often refer to different managers as 'clients') rarely refuse a client assignment. No more than one

Table 6 Measures of Professional Antonorny by Practice Setting and Year of Survey

	Wide Latitude in Selecting Clients (%)		Largely Control My Own Work (%)		Design & Pursue My Own Strategies (%)	Have Refused Clients in Current Job (%)
	1975	1995	1975	1995	1995	1995
Solos	60.2	61.6	84.8	72.3	40.6	38.8
Firms of 2–9	56.3	52.7	53.7	50.9	27.8	36.7
Firms of 10–30	59.4	46.0	39.7	46.1	25.0	18.4
Firms of 31–99	56.2	49.2	40.0	27.0	12.9	14.1
Firms of 100+	59.3	59.9	30.9	30.5	10.9	20.0
House Counsel	41.8	21.4	50.0	48.7	12.8	9.0
Govt/PD/ LS/LA	29.0	20.6	38.4	35.6	13.7	15.1
Overall	55.1	48.0	53.6	44.3	20.5	23.1
Significance (Chi square)	.000	.000	.000	.000	.000	.000
n	585	646	672	663	663	668

in five government lawyers and attorneys in firms of 10 or more lawyers, report refusing an assignment in their current job. Only solos and small firm lawyers report refusals in substantial numbers.

These data indicate that organisational context does shape the nature of professional autonomy. Lawyers employed in organisational contexts report less freedom to choose the clients they work for, to control how they work, to design practice strategies, and fewer instances in which they actually have refused an assignment. These findings tend to support Heinz and Laumann's position, as well as the position of many critics of large law firms, that lawyers working in corporate contexts have less discretion than solo and small firm attorneys. This lack of autonomy is not unique to corporate lawyers, however. Government lawyers also responded to these questions in ways that indicate that their professional judgments are constrained.

While the variation in responses across practice settings can be interpreted meaningfully, there are no striking changes over time in the two measures taken in 1975 and 1995.

Public and Professional Service

One of the main concerns of observers of the bar has been that the intensification of work demands on lawyers by large firms and other organisations will leave them little time and inclination to do pro bono work or to participate in professional associations and community activities. Table 7 suggests that this is only partially true. Chicago lawyers report modest amounts of unpaid pro bono work, an overall average of just under five hours a month. The highest reported hours come from solo practitioners and attorneys in firms of 100 or more lawyers, followed by smaller firms, government lawyers, and inside counsel. If these responses are to be believed, large law firm attorneys supply an above average amount of pro bono work. If lawyers perform 5 hours of pro bono work per month, it represents about 2.7 per cent of their total legal effort (computed as 60 hours from a base of 2,250 hours a year). If we multiplied this estimate by 30,000 lawyers, it is equivalent to some 810 lawyers working 2,250 hours a year. While this is a nontrivial amount, given the unorganised character of this labor, it is unlikely to significantly redress the legal needs of less resourceful members of society.

The majority of the sample does not favor making pro bono work mandatory for members of the bar. Somewhat surprisingly, there are no significant differences across practice settings in these views. Some studies report that solo practitioners and small firm attorneys are especially disposed against such requirements, claiming that they often provide the equivalent of pro bono representation when they discount fees for poor

Table 7 Pro Bono and Bar Association Activity by Practice Setting, 1995

	Pro Bono Hrs Per Month	Mandatory Pro Bono (% Agree)	Bar Assoc Membership (% Yes)	Held Office/ Chaired Com (% Yes)
Solos	7.1	36.0	82.4	32.0
Firms of 2–9	4.4	28.4	95.4	22.2
Firms of 10–30	4.1	32.8	96.1	25.3
Firms of 31-99	3.8	37.1	95.3	17.2
Firms of 100+	6.7	33.5	91.5	18.9
House Counsel	2.1	36.4	89.7	17.9
Govt/PD/LS/LA	2.4	34.1	88.4	22.1
Overall	4.8	34.1	88.4	22.1
Significance (Chi-square)	.000	.944	.000	.178
n	653	634	665	662

clients (see Mather, McEwen and Maiman 2001). Our data do not indicate a divergence in attitudes across practice organisations.

The concern of bar leaders and others that the intensification of practice demands has prevented lawyers from joining and participating in bar associations and other community activities does not appear well founded. Table 7 shows that almost 9 out of 10 practicing lawyers in Chicago in 1995 belonged to at least one bar association. Only solo practitioners report a slightly lower rate of membership. Many fewer lawyers (22 per cent) have participated in bar associations in some significant way. Here solo practitioners show the highest levels of participation, 32 per cent, compared to 19 per cent of attorneys in firms of 100 or more. But here the numbers also seem respectable. Data on the involvements of lawyers in community organisations in 1975 and 1995 (see Heinz and Schnorr with Laumann and Nelson 2001) do not suggest that these involvements have declined. While lawyers are somewhat less likely to hold leadership positions in community organisations in 1995 than in 1975, this may well be attributable to the doubling of the lawyer population, which would reduce the odds that any given lawyer could hold such a position.

Professional Commitment and Job Satisfaction

Finally Table 8 reports two measures of the professional satisfaction of lawyers, whether 'if they had it all to do over again' they would become a lawyer and 'generally how satisfied you are with your job.' The Chicago

Table 8 Measures of Professional Commitment and Job Satisfaction by Practice Setting, 1995

	Would Become Lawyer Again	Very Satisfied/Satisfied with Job
Solos	78.3	84.5
Firms of 2–9	72.1	84.1
Firms of 10–30	80.0	82.4
Firrns of 31–99	73.8	80.9
Firms of 100+	80.5	85.1
House Counsel	77.0	89.7
Govt/PD/LS/LA	74.3	76.0
Overall	77.0	83.7
Significance (Chi-square)	.736	.025
n	625	650

data contradict the suggestions of many commentators that alienation among lawyers is rampant (see, eg Shiltz 1999; for a full discussion and critique see Heinz, Hull and Harter 1999). Some 77 per cent of practicing lawyers in 1995 would choose to become lawyers again and 84 per cent are satisfied or very satisfied with their jobs. There are no significant differences across practice settings on the first of these items. Government lawyers are the least satisfied subgroup on the general job satisfaction variable, a response that Heinz, Hull, and Harter (1999) attribute to the relatively low pay for government jobs. (Lempert, Chambers and Adams (2000) found in their study of Michigan Law School graduates that government attorneys made less than other Michigan graduates, but had higher levels of job satisfaction. For a full discussion of the job satisfaction items and the reasons for the differences between the Chicago findings and the results of other research, see Heinz, Hull, and Harter 1999. See also Hull 1999 for an interesting discussion of the gendered dimensions of job satisfaction among Chicago lawyers.)

These data indicate that the rise of organisational employment in the private sector has not negatively affected the satisfaction of practitioners, despite the fact that lawyers in large firms and inside counsel offices appear to have less professional autonomy than solo practitioners and attorneys in small firms. Indeed, there seems to be an extraordinary disjuncture between some of the academic and elite discourse about professional alienation, and the attitudes of the practicing attorneys we interviewed in Chicago in 1995. While we have not yet fully analysed these data, and in particular have yet to analyse questions about workplace governance and democracy, we can draw some tentative conclusions about the character of lawyer professionalism in 1995. The reorganisation of practice has had an effect on the professional autonomy of lawyers. The professional decisions of practitioners in organisational contexts are more constrained by clients and supervisors than is the case for solo practitioners and attorneys in small firms. As larger numbers of lawyers are encompassed in organisational settings, more of the professional judgments of lawyers will be shaped by organisational constraints. Moreover, it appears that there is now a stronger affinity between the political values of lawyers representing corporations (both in large law firms and corporate counsel's offices) and the political values of their clients than was the case twenty years ago. By these indicators then, there has been a loss of professional autonomy by lawyers. But these trends apparently are not a source of angst for practicing attorneys. They report high levels of identification with their profession and high levels of satisfaction with the jobs they hold. The relative absence of dissonance generated by the organisational restructuring of practice suggests that these trends will not be opposed in the legal workplace. On the contrary, urban lawyers appear to embrace work in large professional organisations and voice dissatisfaction primarily when they see their economic rewards falling below expectation.

Conclusion

This selective tour through data on 20 years of change in the social structure of the Chicago bar suggests the value of an organisational perspective on social change in the legal profession. Significant transformations in the individual careers of lawyers, in the character of gender and racial inequality within the profession, in the professional autonomy of practitioners, and in the ethical orientations of lawyers are deeply connected with trends in the organisational structure of the profession. Although we have not sought to directly test what we presented as a model of organisational dominance, many of the changes we noted here are consistent with the emergence of such a model.

Some may reasonably question whether the various changes we have documented actually hang together and are causally linked to organisation-level changes in law practice. For example, is not the shift from ethnicity to gender and race as primary principles of stratification a reflection of changing attitudes toward Jews and the recent entry of larger numbers of women and minorities in the profession? Such questions warrant more thorough analysis and require additional historical data. Yet we assert that it is interesting to test whether there is a link between organisational changes in the profession and changes in patterns of inequality. Here is why we think there is a link.

It is not be mere coincidence that anti-semitism plays a less prominent role in the labor market for corporate legal services in the current era, in which more premium corporate legal work is transactional in character than was the case when the allocation of premium corporate work was controlled by established relationships between stable groups of partners in law firms and stable management groups in corporations. As Hagan and Kay (1995) have pointed out with respect to Toronto law firms, it is not mere coincidence that law firms began to grow rapidly and limit the odds of making partner, just as large numbers of women were entering the profession. The shift to transactional work allowed the entry of 'new' social groups into elite work. The growth of law firms could not have taken place without a significant increase in the size of the legal profession, most of which was fed by women and minorities. The new larger firms could not sustain the same promotion-to-partner policies. Those organisational changes called for different kinds of inequality within and across law firms.

This is just one example of how mechanisms of organisational change become mechanisms of social inequality. Similar arguments can be constructed about mechanisms of change in political values, in patterns of commitment, in values of professionalism, and so forth.

The rising importance of organisations to the social structure of the bar has significant practical and theoretical implications. Bar associations and law schools risk a loss of relevance if they do not recognise the centrality of the organisational transformations taking place in the profession. The recent controversy on multidisciplinary practices, in which the ABA House of Delegates rejected the recommendations of its own study commission and voted not to allow multidisciplinary firms under the profession's ethical codes, could be interpreted as a clash between a professional dominance and an organisational dominance perspective. It appears that the House of Delegates' position is to insist that lawyers must control the organisations in which they practice, for fear that lawyers cannot preserve their autonomy and ethicality in organisations in which the management is shared with non-lawyers. Thus ethical concerns are cited as a basis for prohibiting within law an organisational form that is growing rapidly in the financial and professional services sector here and abroad. The proponents of multidisciplinary practices, fearing that lawyers would be disadvantaged if they could not compete through such organisational forms, sought an accommodation of professional rules to a new organisational context.

It will be interesting to watch whether the House of Delegates position will endure, particularly in the aftermath of the Enron and Arhur Anderson scandal. That scandal has produced widespread calls for the splitting consulting and auditing services in professional service firms. (New York Times 2002) Similar arguments can be made that legal representation should not be offered by the same firm that is providing other types of professional services to a corporation. If it turns out that there is no strong market imperative for multidisciplinary firms after all, the multidisciplinary debate may turn out to be much ado about nothing. (See the discussion by Dezalay and Garth 2001). But if the organisational advantages of multidisciplinary firms begin to manifest themselves in the market for legal services, we might anticipate that lawyers will begin to circumvent ABA rules until they can get the rules revised. The potential gravity of these ethical strictures was brought home to us in a recent seminar by the managing partner of the Chicago office of a leading New York law firm. He estimated that his firm must turn away between ⅓ and ½ of its potential business due to conflicts of interest problems. (25 October 2000) Large law firms have enormous stakes in trying to limit the impact of such ethical rules on their practice.

The ABA position also suggests that the organised bar assumes that it can regulate lawyer conduct in traditional terms, treating lawyers largely as autonomous professionals. While some states make law firms responsible for the ethical oversight of their members, the recognition that the professional judgments of lawyers are increasingly undertaken in an organisational context underscores the importance of devising organisation-level regimes of ethical control. The same may be said of the bar's efforts at encouraging diversity. The employment policies and practices of corporate law firms will heavily influence the professional prospects of women and minorities.

The recognition that the legal profession is structured by practice organisations also may have implications for legal education. As ethical crises have arisen within the legal profession, bar leaders have asked law schools to remedy the problem by 'innoculating' students with required ethics courses. Something perhaps more fundamental may now be at issue. If law schools begin to conceive of their function as preparing students to enter highly differentiated practice organisations, rather than to train individual producers of legal services, it might lead to significant curricular changes. Recently the leading eight solicitors' firms in the United Kingdom formed a consortium to develop their own university based training program rather than rely on the university training programs now regulated by the Law Society (Sherr 2000). The proposal caused a huge uproar within the Law Society and among the second tier solicitors' firms who complained about the elitism of the plan. Law schools and corporate law firms in the United States have a much different structure and history than does legal education and corporate practice in the UK. Still the UK events are another indication that large legal services organisations are gaining power and resources and are beginning to rethink basic organisational processes, such as recruitment and promotion.

The theoretical significance of our results and of the organisational dominance model is that sociologists of the professions must continue to analyse the organisational roots of changes in the social structures of professions. The brilliant analysis by Scott and his colleagues of the organisational transformation of American medical services (1999) is one example of the analytic payoff to a sustained organisational perspective. While there is a growing body of work on certain kinds of law practice organisations, especially large law firms (Smigel 1969; Nelson 1988; Galanter and Palay 1991; Wilkins and Gulati 1996; also see Van Hoy 1997; Seron 1996), there is more work to be done on the relationship between organisations and the social structure of the legal profession as a whole. Our work suggests that practice organisations in law are engines for increasing inequality, within and across organisations. Moreover, organisations select or train lawyers to develop political values and professional ideologies that are consistent with the organisation's mission. Law practice organisations, perhaps more than any other institutional actor, will shape the future of legal services and careers of lawyers.

Our tentative conclusion is that when Freidson wrote about the medical profession in 1970 he was half right, both with respect to medicine and law. He was right to observe that the 'structural characteristics of the profession have far more influence on the nature of medical care (read legal services) in the United States than ... the good intentions and skills of individual members of the profession.' But he was wrong to think the professional dominance of doctors (or of lawyers) would be more important than 'economic and administrative arrangements ...' (p 77). Just as Freidson was forced to reconsider his position on the professional dominance of doctors by the 1990's, in recognition of the impact of market and organisational forces on medicine, it is necessary for the sociology of the legal profession to recognise the significance of organisational dominance for the changing character of inequality and professionalism in the American legal profession.

References

AMERICAN BAR ASSOCIATION In the Spirit of Public Service: A Blueprint for Rekindling Lawyer Professionalism, (Chicago, American Bar Association, 1986).

CARSON CLARA The Lawyer Statistical Report: The US Legal Profession in 1995, (Chicago, American Bar Foundation, 1999).

DEZALAY, Yves and Bryant GARTH 'The Big Five versus Big Law: Confrontational Rhetoric in the Service of Legitimating Shifting Relationships Between Business and Law', in J Drolshammer and M Pfeifer, *The Internationalisation of the Practice of Law*, (The Hague, Kluwer Law International, 2001).

ERLANGER, Howard S, and Douglas A KLEGON 'Socialisation Effects in Professional School,' 1978, 13 *Law and Society Review*, 11–35.

FREIDSON, Eliot Professional Dominance: The Social Structure of Medical Care, (Chicago, Aldine, 1970).

FREIDSON, Eliot Professional Powers: A Study in the Institutionalisation of Formal Knowledge, (Chicago, IL, University of Chicago Press, 1986).

FREIDSON, Eliot *Professionalism Reborn: Theory, Prophesy, and Policy*, (Chicago, IL, University of Chicago Press, 1994).

GALANTER, Marc and Thomas PALAY *Tournament of Lawyers: The Transformation of the Big Law Firm*, (Chicago, IL, University of Chicago Press, 1991).

GLENDON Mary Ann A Nation Under Lawyers: How the Crisis in the Legal Profession is Transforming American Society, (New York, Farrar, Straus and Giroux, 1994).

GORDON, Robert W 'The Independence of Lawyers,' 1988, 68 *Boston University Law Review* 61–83.

HAGAN, John and Fiona KAY *Gender in Practice: A Study of Lawyers' Lives*, (New York, Oxford University Press, 1995).

HEINZ, John P and Edward O LAUMANN *Chicago Lawyers: The Social Structure of the Bar*, (New York and Chicago, Russell Sage Foundation and American Bar Foundation, 1982).

HEINZ, John P, Edward O LAUMANN, Robert L NELSON, and Robert H SALISBURY *The Hollow Core: Private Interests in National Policymaking*, (Cambridge, MA, Harvard University Press, 1993).

HEINZ, John P and Edward O LAUMANN, with Robert L NELSON and Paul S SCHNORR 'The Constituencies of Elite Urban Lawyers,' 1977, 31 *Law and Society Review*, 441.

HEINZ, John P, Robert L NELSON, Edward O LAUMANN, and Ethan MICHELSON 'The Changing Character of Lawyers' Work: Chicago in 1975 and 1995.' 1998, 32 *Law and Society Review* 751–75.

HEINZ John P, HULL Kathleen E, HARTER Ava A 'Lawyers and their Discontents: Findings from a Survey of the Chicago Bar,' 1999, 74 *Indiana Law Journal*, 735–58.

HEINZ, John P, Robert L NELSON, and Edward O LAUMANN 'The Scale of Justice: Observations on the Transformation of Urban Law Practice.' 2001, 27 *Annual Review of Sociology*, 337–62.

HEINZ, John P, and Paul S SCHNORR with Edward O LAUMANN and Robert L NELSON 'Lawyers' Roles in Voluntary Associations: Declining Social Capital?' 2001, 26 *Law and Social Inquiry*, 597–629.

HORSKY, Charles A *The Washington Lawyer: A Series of Lectures*, (Boston, Little Brown, 1952).

HULL, Kathleen E 'The Paradox of the Contented Female Lawyer,' 1999, 33 *Law and Society Review*, 687–702.

HULL, Kathleen E and Robert L NELSON 'Assimilation, Choice or Constraint? Testing Three Theories of Gender Differences in the Careers of Lawyers,' 2000, 79 *Social Forces*, 1–36.

KAY, Fiona M 'Flight from Law: A Competing Risks Model of Departures from Law Firms,' 1997, 31 *Law and Society Review*, 301–35.

KAY, Fiona M, and John HAGAN 'Raising the Bar: The Gender Stratification of Law Firm Capital,' 1998, 63 *American Sociological Review* 728–43.

KRONMAN, AT *The Lost Lawyer: Failing Ideals of the Legal Profession*, (Cambridge, Belknap press of Harvard University Press, 1993).

LARSON, Margali Sarfatti *The Rise of Professionalism:A Sociological Analysis*, (Berkeley, University of California Press, 1977).

LEMPERT, Richard O, David L CHAMBERS, and Terry K ADAMS 'Michigan's Minority Graduates in Practice: The River Runs Through Law School,' 2000, 25 *Law and Social Inquiry*, 395–505.

LUBAN, David *Lawyers and Justice*, (Princeton, Princeton University Press, 1988).

MATHER, Lynn, Craig A MCEWEN, and Richard J MAIMAN *Divorce Lawyers at Work:Varieties of Professionalism in Practice*, (New York, Oxford University Press, 2001).

MACAULAY, Stewart 'Lawyers and Consumer Protection Laws,' 1979, 14 *Law and Society Review*, 115–71.

NELSON, Robert L *Partners with Power: The Social Transformation of the Large*

Law Firm, (Berkeley and Los Angeles, CA, University of California Press, 1988).

NELSON, Robert L and David M TRUBEK 'Arenas of Professionalism: The Professional Ideologies of Lawyers in Context, 'in *Lawyers Ideas/Lawyers Practices: Transformations in the American Legal Profession*, edited by Robert L Nelson, David M Trubek and Rayman L Soloman, (Ithaca, NY, Cornell University Press, 1992).

OPPEL, Richard A Jr 'Senate Committee Approves Measure on Audit Industry, 'New York Times 2002 p.1, col. 2, p.c9, cols. 1–4. June 19, 2002.

PARSONS, Talcott 'The Law and Social Control, 'in *Law and Sociology: Exploratory Essays*, edited by William M Evan, (Glencoe, IL, The Free Press of Glencoe, 1962).

PAYNE, Monique R and Robert L NELSON 'Divided Opinions: The Political and Economic Values of Chicago Lawyers, 1975 and 1995.' Paper presented at the Annual Meetings of the Law and Society Association, May, Miami, 2000.

RHODE, Deborah L Opening Remarks: Professionalism.' Symposium on Improving the Professionalism of Lawyers: Can Commissions, Committees, and Centres Make a Difference? 2001, 52 *South Carolina Law Review* 458–71.

ROSEN, Robert. 1984. Lawyers in Corporate Decision Making. PhD dissertion University of California, Berkeley.

SANDEFUR Rebecca L, LAUMANN Edward O Changing Patterns of Income Stratification in the Chicago Bar. Unpublished paper presented at Law and Society Association annual meeting. St. Louis, 1997.

SCHILTZ, Patrick J 'On Being a Happy, Healthy, and Ethical Member of an Unhappy, Unhealthy and Unethical Profession,' 1999, 52 *Vanderbilt Law Review*, 871–952.

SERON, Carroll The Business of Practicing Law: The Work Lives of Solo and Small-Firm Attorneys, (Philadelphia, Temple University Press, 1996).

SHERR, Avrom 'The Big Five and the Legal Practice Course.' Paper presented 17 July 2000 to the Working Group on the Comparative Study of Legal Professions, Peyresq, France.

SIKES Bette H, CARSON Clara N, GORAI Patricia *The 1971 Lawyer Statistical Report*, (Chicago, American Bar Foundation, 1972).

SMIGEL Erwin *The Wall Street Lawyer: Professional Organisation Man?*(Bloomington, Indiana University Press, 1969).

SOLOMON, Rayman L 'Five Crises or One: The Concept of Legal Professionalism, 1925–1960.' in *Lawyers Ideas/Lawyers Practices: Transformations in the American Legal Profession*, edited by Robert L Nelson, David M Trubek and Rayman L Soloman(Ithaca, NY, Cornell University Press, 1992).

SPANGLER, Eve *Lawyers for Hire: Salaried Professionals at Work*, (New Haven, Yale University Press, 1986).

US BUREAU OF THE CENSUS, 1976. 1972 Census of Selected Service Industries, vol. 1. Washington, DC: US Department of Commerce.

US BUREAU OF THE CENSUS, 1996. 1992 Census of Service Industries. Washington, US Department of Commerce.

VAN HOY, Jerry Franchise Law Firms and the Transformation of Personal Legal Services, (Westport, CT, Quorum Books, 1997).

WILKINS, David B and G Mitu GULATI 'Why Are There So Few Black Lawyers in Corporate Law Firms? An Institutional Analysis,' 1996, 84 *California Law Review*, 493–625.

Index